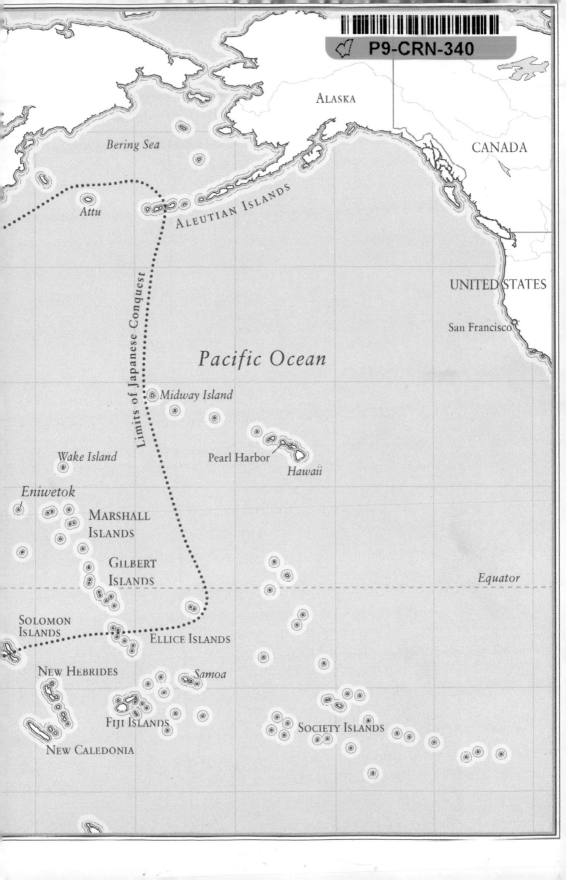

ALASKA

CANADA

Bering Sea

Attu

ALEUTIAN ISLANDS

UNITED STATES

San Francisco

Pacific Ocean

Limits of Japanese Conquest

Midway Island

Wake Island

Pearl Harbor

Hawaii

Eniwetok

MARSHALL
ISLANDS

GILBERT
ISLANDS

Equator

SOLOMON
ISLANDS

ELLICE ISLANDS

NEW HEBRIDES

Samoa

Fiji Islands

SOCIETY ISLANDS

NEW CALEDONIA

# The COLOR of War

## ALSO BY JAMES CAMPBELL

*The Final Frontiersman*

*The Ghost Mountain Boys*

# The COLOR of War

## HOW ONE BATTLE BROKE JAPAN AND ANOTHER CHANGED AMERICA

## James Campbell

CROWN PUBLISHERS, NEW YORK

Library of Congress Cataloging-in-Publication Data
Campbell, James.
    The color of war: how one battle broke Japan and another
changed America / James Campbell. —1st ed.
        p.   cm.
    Includes bibliographical references and index.
    1. Port Chicago Mutiny, Port Chicago, Calif., 1944. 2. Port
Chicago Mutiny Trial, San Francisco, Calif., 1944. 3. World War,
1939–1945—Participation, African American. 4. United States.
Navy—African Americans—History—20th century. 5. World War,
1939–1945—Campaigns—New Guinea. I. Title.
    D810.N4C36    2012
    940.54'5308896073079463—dc23          2011023913

ISBN 978-0-307-46121-6
eISBN 978-0-307-46123-0

Printed in the United States of America

*Maps by Joe LeMonnier*
*Jacket design by Gabriele Wilson*
*Jacket photographs: (top) W. Eugene Smith/Time & Life Pictures/Getty*
*Images; (bottom) Schomburg Center, NYPL/Art Resource, NY*

10 9 8 7 6 5 4 3 2 1

First Edition

*In memory of my mother-in-law,*

*Elaine DeGaetano Harvey*

Show me the two so closely bound
As we, by the wet bond of blood.

—Robert Graves


I believe as long as we allow conditions to exist that make for second-class citizens, we are making of ourselves less than first-class citizens.

—Dwight D. Eisenhower

# CONTENTS

# A GUIDE TO THE BOOK'S MAJOR CHARACTERS

## U.S. COMMAND STRUCTURE

**Admiral Ernest King:** commander in chief, United States Fleet and Chief of Naval Operations

**Admiral Chester Nimitz:** commander of the Pacific Fleet

**Admiral Raymond Spruance:** commander of the United States 5th Fleet (originally the Central Pacific Force)

**Admiral Richmond Kelly Turner:** commander of the Joint Expeditionary Force and Northern Attack Force and commander of the amphibious landing

**General Holland "Howlin' Mad" Smith:** commander V Amphibious Corps and commander of all expeditionary troops

**General Douglas MacArthur:** commander in chief Southwest Pacific Area

**General George Marshall:** U.S. Army chief of staff

**Frank Knox:** secretary of the Navy

**James Forrestal:** secretary of the Navy following Knox's death

**Vice Admiral Randall Jacobs:** chief of naval personnel

## SAIPAN

**Second Lieutenant Carl Roth:** E Company, 23rd Regiment, 4th Marine Division

**Gunnery Sergeant Emberg Townsley:** E Company

**Robert Graf:** E Company, from Ballston Spa, New York

**Dick Crerar:** E Company, Graf's buddy

**Bill More:** E Company, Graf's buddy

**Lieutenant James Stanley Leary Jr:** G Company, 23rd Regiment, 4th Marine Division, from Ashokie, North Carolina

**Sergeant Jack Campbell:** G Company, platoon sergeant

**Carl Matthews:** G Company, Gold Dust Twin, from Hubbard, Texas

**Richard Freeby:** G Company, Gold Dust Twin, from Quanah, Texas

**Wendell Nightingale:** G Company, from Skowhegan, Maine

**Sergeant John Rachitsky:** "Bastard" Battalion, 29th Marines

**Frank "Chick" Borta:** "Bastard" Battalion, 29th Marines, from Chicago

**Glen "Pluto" Brem:** "Bastard" Battalion, 29th Marines, from Gilroy, California

**Richard Carney:** "Bastard" Battalion, 29th Marines, from Bronx, New York

**Milt Lemon:** "Bastard" Battalion, 29th Marines, from Texas Panhandle

## MONTFORD POINT

**Edgar Lee Huff:** One of Montford Point's first black recruits, from Gadsden, Alabama

**Colonel Samuel Woods:** commanding officer of Montford Point

## PORT CHICAGO

### Black Seamen

**George Booth:** carpenter striker, Division #4, from Detroit

**Sammie Lee Boykin:** carpenter striker, ammunition handler and winch operator, Division #1, from Bessemer, Alabama

**Percy Robinson, Jr.:** hold boss and winch operator, Division #4, from Chicago

**Spencer Sikes:** boxcar inspector and shore patrol, from West Palm Beach, Florida

**Joe Small:** cadence caller and winch operator, Division #4, from Middlesex County, New Jersey

### White Officers

**Lieutenant Ernest Delucchi:** head of Division #4

**Captain Nelson Goss:** commanding officer at Mare Island and Port Chicago

**Lieutenant Commander Alexander Holman:** head loading officer and officer in charge of training

**Captain Merrill Kinne:** officer-in-charge of the Port Chicago Naval Magazine

**Lieutenant Commander Glen Ringquist:** assistant loading officer

**Lieutenant Richard Terstenson:** assistant loading officer

**Lieutenant James Tobin:** head of Division #2

**Lieutenant Raymond Robert "Bob" White:** junior officer in charge of Division #3

## KEY FIGURES OF ALLEGED MUTINY AND TRIAL

### Black Seamen

**Ollie Green:** witness for the defense

**Joseph Gray:** witness for the prosecution

**Edward Longmire:** witness for the defense

**Alphonso McPherson:** witness for the defense

**Edward Stubblefield:** witness for the prosecution

**Joe Small:** witness for the defense

**Thurgood Marshall:** chief counsel of the NAACP's Legal and Educational Defense Fund

### White Officers

**Lieutenant Commander Charles Bridges:** executive Officer Mare Island Naval Barracks

**Lieutenant Commander James Coakley:** head of the prosecution team

**Lieutenant Commander Jefferson Flowers:** chaplain, Mare Island

**Rear Admiral Hugo Osterhaus:** head of the seven-member general court martial

**Lieutenant Gerald Veltmann:** head of the defense team

**Rear Admiral Carleton Wright:** commandant of the Twelfth Naval District

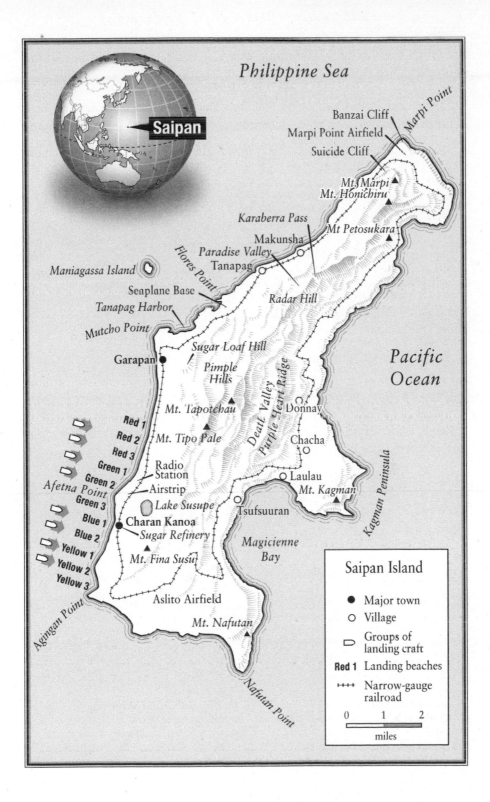

Philippine Sea

Banzai Cliff
Marpi Point Airfield
Suicide Cliff

Marpi Point

Saipan

Mt. Marpi
Mt. Honichiru

Mt Petosukara

Karaberra Pass
Makunsha
Paradise Valley
Tanapag

Flores Point

Radar Hill

Maniagassa Island

Seaplane Base
Tanapag Harbor
Mutcho Point

Garapan

Sugar Loaf Hill
Pimple
Hills

Mt. Tapotchau

Death Valley
Purple Heart Ridge

Donnay

Pacific
Ocean

Red 1
Red 2
Red 3
Green 1
Green 2
Afetna Point
Green 3
Blue 1
Blue 2
Yellow 1
Yellow 2
Yellow 3

Mt. Tipo Pale

Radio
Station
Airstrip
Lake Susupe

Charan Kanoa
Sugar Refinery
Mt. Fina Susu

Chacha

Laulau
Mt. Kagman

Kagman Peninsula

Tsufsuuran

Magicienne
Bay

Aslito Airfield

Agingan Point

Mt. Nafutan

Nafutan Point

### Saipan Island

● Major town
○ Village
▭ Groups of landing craft
**Red 1** Landing beaches
┼┼┼ Narrow-gauge railroad

0        1        2
miles

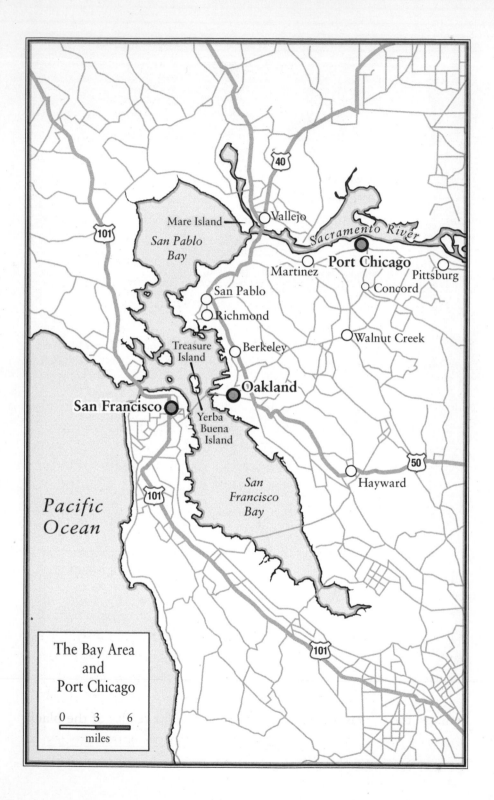

Mare Island
Vallejo
*San Pablo Bay*
*Sacramento River*
Port Chicago
Martinez
Pittsburg
Concord
San Pablo
Richmond
Treasure Island
Berkeley
Walnut Creek
Oakland
San Francisco
Yerba Buena Island
Hayward
*San Francisco Bay*
*Pacific Ocean*

The Bay Area
and
Port Chicago

0   3   6
miles

# FOREWORD

The inspiration for the African American portion of this story dates back to 2005 when I began writing *The Ghost Mountain Boys*. While researching that book, I first found out about the 96th Engineers, a group of black laborers that braved snakes, malaria, endless rain, and some of the roughest terrain on the planet to build roads, airfields, and piers throughout New Guinea. En route to the island, their ship docked in Brisbane and Townsville, Australia. In both places they were refused entrance to the city. The story of the 96th is told by one of its white officers, Captain Hyman Samuelson.

If not for Captain Samuelson, the travails and accomplishments of the 96th might have gone unmentioned. Black narratives about the war, and historical accounts of the contributions of black servicemen to it, are hard to find. According to historian Ulysses Lee, who conducted a study titled "The Employment of Negro Troops" for the U.S. Center of Military History, Negro units in the Pacific were primarily "quartermaster, port, and engineer types, attached to divisions, engineer special brigades, construction groups, or boat and shore battalions." In light of General Douglas MacArthur's comment that the war in the Pacific was an "engineer's war," one in which military support groups played a critical role, the lack of black history struck me as conspicuous. Certainly the extraordinary victories could not have happened without the support of a great war machine and the forgotten sacrifices of the men behind the scenes.

African American servicemen performed their jobs ably. Then why was there not a larger record of their achievements, I wondered. Certainly a pervasive racism accounted for the military establishment's historic reluctance to use black troops in battle. Perhaps much of that same racism prevailed when chronicling the history of the Good War. Perhaps, too, it was a function of mythology. The reality of the black experience does not conform nicely with the celebrated stories of white heroism and sacrifice.

Black servicemen were often treated as nuisances and trouble-makers. Soldiers were court-martialed, hanged, beaten, mugged, belittled, and forced to endure the indignities and humiliations of Jim Crow wherever they went. If, as William Manchester writes, the war provided a "tremendous impetus to egalitarianism," that egalitarianism was resisted by both the military and the country at large. The *Baltimore Afro-American* published an editorial saying that the war would help blacks to "breathe the air of freedom." The truth was that African Americans had to fight fiercely for the advances they made. Perhaps nothing captures the reality of that ordeal like the story of the Port Chicago Naval Ammunition Depot.

# PROLOGUE

From deep in the hold, the black sailors looked up and saw the six-foot-long, one-ton projectile looming above them momentarily blotting out the light of the sun. The white lieutenant who was supervising the loading had told them that these were the weapons that were going to save America's boys in the Central Pacific.

Although the dock's crew had replaced the old, overworked cable and had attached steadying wires to the shell's nose and tail to keep it from bucking, the sweating men, dozens of feet down in the gut of the ship, knew that a sudden strain could snap the cable like a dead branch. The ugly green monster would come hurtling toward them. Fortunately their best man was on the winches. Slow and steady, they thought as they craned their necks. Set it down like a newborn baby.

The winch driver put the projectile on the floor of the deck and the crew unhooked the harnesses. Now came the hard part. Using five-foot steel pinch bars, four sailors maneuvered the shell toward the bulkhead. The idea was to do it as gently as possible without banging it. Once they had positioned the shell just right, someone would take a pinch bar and wedge it in just behind the nose while the three men spun the tail.

The plan was to put down the first layer before their shift was over. If they succeeded, the loading officer might reward them with a twelve-hour pass. Most of them, though, would barely make it to the showers. After manhandling shark-sized shells all day, few would have the energy to hit the town.

Once the sailors got the shell moving, the hold's crew chief yelled up to the signalman. Up above, the sailors had wrestled another projectile off the boxcar and put it on the pier. The goal was to keep the process moving: while one was being stored, another was being lowered. Days later, filled with nearly 9,000 deadweight tons of cargo, the liberty ship would steam downriver, past the city of San Francisco and out into the Pacific Ocean.

The white lieutenant boasted that the Navy would use the two-thousand-pounders to plaster godforsaken South Seas islands, paving the way for the Marines to come in and kill every Jap soldier they could. High-capacity projectiles would scatter shrapnel that could slaughter or maim everything in its path. The armor-piercing shells would put gashes in the hulls of enemy ships or shatter their bunkers like a bunch of boys blowing up woodchuck holes. This was the kind of patriotic talk that the lieutenant thought would motivate the men. They were not allowed to carry rifles and fight. They were not permitted to do anything more than serve as stewards or cooks aboard ship. But they could load ammunition. They could do their part.

As the shell neared the ship's hull, the men realized that it was rolling too fast. When the aluminum nose hit the steel ladder with a loud clang, they jumped back and everyone tensed. The projectile hissed like a boiler spitting steam, and red dye leaked from a puncture hole. The black sailors ran for the ladders, fleeing to escape the hold before the flying metal tore everything apart. In the mad scramble, two men tumbled from the ladder. Later both would be taken to sick bay, one with a broken arm and another with a fractured leg. Up on the deck of the ship, the men ran to the gangway. Before they could dash across to the pier, the white lieutenant shouted for them to stop.

"There're no fuzes* in them damn projectiles," he cried. "They're harmless."

Then one of the black sailors told him that it was hissing like a snake.

"That's spotting dye," he said. "You're lucky it wasn't filled with Torpex. Then it won't matter how fast you run."

---

* The official Navy spelling, which will be used throughout.

# The COLOR of War

# CHAPTER 1

# "Another Sunday, Another Pearl Harbor Attack"

On May 20, 1944, Robert Graf's landing ship, tank (LST) 43 ar rived in Pearl Harbor. Although the LST was capable of twelve knots on the open water, the captain had powered down the big General Motors diesel engines. As it made its way past Battleship Row, young Robert Graf and his fellow Marines assembled at the ship's rails. For many, it was the first time they would see the destruction caused by the December 7, 1941, Japanese military strike. Graf looked out and saw a battleship lying on her side like an injured fish gasping for air. Beside him, a sailor spoke: "The *Arizona*—sunk." The sailor paused long enough for the men to absorb the reality of the disaster: the hulking, 600-foot ship and nearly 1,200 men aboard, lost. Then he continued: "The *California*—sunk; the *Maryland*—damaged; the *Nevada*—beached; the *Oklahoma*—sunk; the *Pennsylvania*—damaged; the *Tennessee*—damaged; the *Utah*—sunk; the *West Virginia*—sunk." Graf felt his stomach knot up. Two and a half years had passed since he'd first heard the words he had vowed not to forget: "The Japanese are attacking Pearl Harbor." He clenched his fists as tears welled in his eyes. Then, lowering his head, he mumbled a prayer.

The convoy then separated and the various vessels went to anchorages throughout the harbor's West Loch channel. One and a half miles from shore, LST 43 tied off to two other LSTs anchored in the middle of a group of eight. The Navy called this gathering of ships a "tare." A sailor dropped the hook to prevent drifting. Graf looked around West Loch, the staging area for the first two waves of the upcoming invasion of Saipan. It was full of 330-foot LSTs, all grouped in tares, and all packed with Marines, many of whom would be going into battle for their first time.

Originally designed to deliver troops during island assaults, LSTs had been replaced by 1944. Encouraged by huge shipbuilding budgets, American engineers experimented with designs ideally suited to the island campaign of the Central Pacific and developed smaller, more versatile amphibious vehicles. Amtracs capable of transporting a platoon of men through the surf and onto an invasion beach took the place of the durable LSTs, which, with their 2,100-ton capacity, were increasingly used to transport troops, wounded soldiers, and cargo across the Pacific Ocean.

Although the Honolulu hotspots beckoned, the men from the 4th Marine Division had orders to stay aboard their LSTs. No liberty passes would be issued until the following day. Graf and his best buddy, Dick Crerar, stripped down to their skivvies and claimed two of the three dozen folding cots placed under an amtrac landing vehicle that had been fastened to the deck of the LST. Mounted over the length of the amtrac was a 130-foot canvas cover. Graf and Crerar enjoyed the breeze that drifted through the harbor, but avoided the blazing sun.

Comfortable as he was, Graf was concerned about the drums of high-octane gasoline lashed to the deck of the landing ship. Someone—maybe Crerar—said what everyone else was thinking: "This is one heck of a way to run a war. Suppose we get strafed or a shell from the shore hits us? We'd be on our way to hell in no time."

The next day, May 21, broke blissfully, but neither Robert Graf nor any of the other men had time to enjoy it. The vessels had to be provisioned for the upcoming invasion. Because of a shortage of

ammunition ships, a number of the LSTs would be used as floating ammo dumps—"suicide ships," the Marines called them. They
would carry rifle ammunition, rockets, drums of diesel fuel, torpedoes, and TNT.

On two nearby landing ships, civilian Navy Yard workers were
doing some last-minute welding. Graf could hear the spitting of the
gas flame. Two vessels down, one hundred black laborers from the
U.S. Army's 29th Chemical Decontamination Company were unloading mortars from LST 353. The 29th had arrived at Schofield Barracks, Hawaii, in the summer of 1942.

Theoretically, a chemical decontamination company's mission was
to decontaminate men and equipment after an enemy chemical attack,
but its soldiers also offered a ready source of manual labor. Because
of a shortage of 4.2-inch mortars, the batteries had been dropped
from the upcoming invasion plans. The workers had backed a succession of heavy trucks onto LST 353, and raised them on an elevator to
the main deck. Although handling ordnance was sensitive work, since
early morning the untrained members of the 29th had been removing
mortars and passing boxes of ammunition from one man to the next.
At the end of the chain, a man would slide a box or a mortar down a
chute to men below, who loaded them onto truck beds.

Aboard LST 43, after noon chow, some guys were playing cards,
using a stack of ammunition as their table. Graf and Crerar, too, had
retired to the deck. Although there would be no liberty, at least they
had the afternoon off. Standing at the rail, Graf could see boats filled
with Marines bound for shore, where they would rush off to Waikiki
for one last night of carousing before sailing for Saipan. If Graf or
Crerar envied them, neither showed it. They would spend their day
napping, reading, and writing letters before the mail went ashore for
the last time.

Although Carl Matthews and Wendell Nightingale had liberty
passes, Nightingale did not drink. So instead of accompanying
a group of friends who would be drowning in booze at the Royal
Hawaiian Hotel, Matthews joined Nightingale at a ball game. As a

staging area for the war in the Pacific, Honolulu hosted two baseball leagues, the all-service Pearl Harbor League and the Hawaii League. Both leagues played their games at the 25,000-seat Honolulu Stadium. Servicemen knew they could see great baseball here. Catching a game with minor leaguers was guaranteed; seeing a major-league player was also a good bet. For the heads of the armed services, the games were about bragging rights, and by 1944 they were transferring the best talent in the armed forces to Hawaii.

Just three weeks before going into battle, Matthews was watching the best baseball of his life. Nobody back home would have believed it. Nor could he tell them. If he even mentioned Pearl Harbor in a letter, the censors would cut it up like a kid snipping a paper snowflake.

At 3:08, Matthews, Nightingale, and everyone else at the ballpark heard an explosion. It sounded as if one of Oahu's volcanoes had blown. The baseball game stopped in mid-inning and the crowd rushed out of its seats.

Private Raymond Smith of the 29th Chemical Company saw balls of fire shoot from the deck of LST 353 as if propelled by a giant anti-aircraft gun, and boil through the sky. Realizing that soon the mortars and the drums of gasoline outside the elevator would blow, he ran to the rear of the ship and dove into the water. Tech 5 James Caldwell of the 29th crouched to pick up a box of mortars when he saw a "bright yellow flame" and heard "a deafening noise" coming from the elevator. Nearby, Private James Cleveland was carrying a box when he was hurled through the air. When he hit the deck of the vessel, his head spun and fire encircled him. *I'm a dead man,* he thought. He got to his knees, wobbled, and balanced himself. Then he dashed through the flames, struggling through thick black smoke to reach the back of the LST. Like Smith he jumped into the harbor just before the fuel drums and ammunition aboard the landing ship detonated with a thunderous roar, sending flames, body parts, and red-hot fragments flying in every direction. Almost everyone from the 29th who had been lucky enough to survive the first blast perished in the second.

Robert Graf and Dick Crerar were dozing when they felt an

explosion rock their LST. The blast was so intense that the air itself felt as if it was on fire. The canvas tarp was burning and pieces of it were falling down on the deck. One terrified Marine, wakened from his afternoon slumber, yelled, "A bombing. Jap planes are hitting us. . . . Corpsman, Corpsman!" For a moment, everything stood still. *Another Sunday,* Graf thought. *Another Pearl Harbor attack.* Then he realized that if he and Crerar did not move fast, they would be burned alive in their cots. They ran thirty feet to the starboard rail as sizzling shards of shrapnel ripped across the LST, and were planning to jump when they saw that even the water was on fire.

At 3:11 there was a blinding flash, and another explosion rocked the harbor. Everything on LST 43 was burning now—cots, blankets, seabags, even the halyards and the paint on the bulkhead. Then it hit Graf: *The oil drums!* Seconds later, they erupted. The blast threw men high into the air. They landed on the deck in the middle of the swirling flames. Graf and Crerar had already jumped onto an adjoining ship, but the LSTs were berthed so close together that the fire moved from one vessel to the next, igniting the ammunition caches as it spread. Graf could hear the detonations: .30-caliber ammunition from Marine ammo belts, boxes of 20-mm rounds piled haphazardly on the decks, and heavier blasts from what might have been howitzer shells stored in the cargo holds. At the far rail of the neighboring LST, he and Crerar stopped long enough to see that Navy corpsmen were already tending to the injured men.

At 3:17, Captain Craven, Navy duty officer, got a radio message from an unknown ship in the harbor: "Violent explosion in LST next to us. Send all available help." The Navy Air Signal reported that it was already too late. The vessel blew up just seconds after sending the message. At 3:19, another LST radioed, "Two on fire here. The whole nest will soon be." Graf and Crerar were caught in the conflagration. Every nearby LST was now engulfed in flames. LST 353 had sunk, and a number of the others were dragging their anchor chains, drifting in the direction of a collection of seven more LSTs in Tare No. 9. In Tare No. 9, men were trying to cut the hawsers that tied the vessels to the dock, knowing that it might be their only chance of escape.

At 3:20, as ammunition burst en masse, a flame shot a thousand feet into the sky. Graf and Crerar ran, jumping from one landing ship to the next. Wading through the choking smoke, they reached the last one in the nest. Graf felt as if a siren were ringing in his ears. His feet were bleeding, cut by shards of glass and razor-sharp steel, and his shoulder felt as if someone had sucker-punched him. At the rail, a crowd of men was gathered, waiting for rescue boats. Others were tearing around, looking for life jackets. If they jumped, maybe the fire tugs would rescue them.

"Let's swim for it!" Graf yelled to Crerar. "I can't swim!" Crerar shouted back. Graf looked at him in disbelief. A Marine could not make it through boot camp without knowing how to swim.

*I'll carry him on my back,* Graf thought. Then he did a rough calculation. They were at least a mile from shore. Shrapnel was falling like hail, and the harbor was on fire. *One of us, or both of us, will die.* Then Graf turned to his friend. "I'll send a rescue boat back to get you."

"It's a hell of a long way," an officer cautioned Graf. Seconds later Graf dove into the waters of West Loch.

By 3:34, Captain Craven realized that he had a disaster of major proportions on his hands. Tare Nos. 6 and 10 were on fire now, too, and aboard the LSTs, many of the water pumps were disabled. At 3:35 he notified the commandant of the Fourteenth Naval District and the commandant of the Pearl Harbor Navy Yard. Ten minutes later, Craven instructed all able LSTs in Tare Nos. 6 and 10 to proceed to sea. At 4:00 p.m., he ordered LSTs in Tare 5 to leave the harbor. Just minutes later, officers radioed to report that their vessels were not seaworthy. Aboard them, small crews were trying to put out fires, but flying debris was cutting their hose lines. At 4:17, Craven witnessed another "tremendous explosion," and a large but lesser detonation seven minutes later. At 4:30, hoping to stem the spread of the fire, he ordered three PT boats to torpedo the drifting LSTs.

Graf had not been swimming for long when he found himself swallowing oily water and fighting to breathe. His shoulder throbbed, and in the salt water the cuts on the bottoms of his feet made him feel as if he had stepped on a hornet's nest. The water ahead of him was on fire. He filled his lungs and dove as deep as he could. His lungs, however, failed him and he came up in the middle of the blaze, wheezing and thrashing his arms. Then he dove again. This time when he rose, the fire was behind him. He looked in the direction of shore; it seemed so far away. Then he rolled onto his back and gulped at the air.

Graf looked for other swimmers. He knew they were out there—perhaps hundreds of them—because he had seen them jumping from the rails of the LSTs. But he could not spot a single person. Perhaps they had all drowned. An overwhelming sense of loneliness came over him, as if he were the last man left on a doomed earth. He rolled onto his back again to regain his strength, but saw nothing except smoke and fire. It was as if the whole of West Loch were burning.

When his feet touched bottom, he was too tired to feel relief or elation. He staggered to shore, wearing nothing more than his underwear, a belt, and his throwing knife tucked into a sheath, and collapsed. Then he realized that someone was pulling at his feet and yelling at him. Standing, Graf looked around and saw that the ground was covered with burned and exhausted men. He stumbled down a dirt road flanked by a large cane field. Glancing back at the harbor, he saw a search boat trailing a lifeline, and managed to summon the strength to call out. Motioning for the boat to come closer, he yelled to the officer that there were still men stranded on the LSTs.

"I'll get them," the officer shouted, pointing the bow of his craft into the wall of smoke.

Graf did not go far before trucks, ambulances, and jeeps arrived. Someone helped him aboard a vehicle, and minutes later he was in line at a field station waiting to see a Navy doctor. The scuttlebutt was that a Jap sub had slipped through the nets that guarded the entrance to Pearl Harbor and had torpedoed an LST, setting off a chain reaction. Some disagreed, saying that it was welders or ammunition loaders who set off the first blast. One man claimed he had seen oil-stained water catch fire as dozens of men swam for shore. He doubted that any of them had survived. Those who had stayed aboard ship and fled to the rope lockers to escape the fire suffocated to death. Another told a story about swimmers getting caught in an LST's propeller. Still others saw rescue workers pulling headless and shrapnel-shredded bodies from the water. All Graf could think about was Dick Crerar.

After the doctor checked his ears and took care of his cuts and burns, Graf was issued new dungarees, shoes, a blanket, and a cot. That night, surrounded by other injured survivors, he tried to sleep, but was plagued by nightmares.

On Monday morning, May 22, Captain Craven was getting a more complete picture of the disaster. Six LSTs and three amtracs had been lost. Coast Guard boats were still fighting isolated fires. Worse yet was the human toll. Aiea Heights Naval Hospital was full of wounded troops, hundreds of them, and corpses in coolers, waiting to be identified.

That morning the *Honolulu Star Bulletin* reported on the incident: "There was a small explosion, yesterday, at Pearl Harbor." Perhaps someone from Admiral Chester Nimitz's headquarters had advised the paper to downplay the incident in order not to tip off the Japanese to the upcoming invasion. Also, it would be bad publicity for the Navy—nearly four hundred men wounded and almost two hundred killed, over one third of them from the Army's all-black 29th Chemical Decontamination Company. If the African American press got hold of the information, there would be a great hue and cry in the civil rights community.

By the afternoon, a naval board of inquiry was questioning its first witness, the executive officer of LST 353, which was berthed in Tare No. 8. Hours later it interviewed Lieutenant Commander Joseph Hoyt, who was in charge of a flotilla of LSTs. Hoyt testified that the kind of load they were putting on the decks of the LSTs violated every safety precaution of the Navy, adding, however, that, "When you have to do it, you do it."

On Monday morning, Robert Graf woke sore and tired and with his ears still ringing. A field kitchen had been set up near the tent where he had spent the night. He was standing in line, filling his tray with food, when he heard a loud bang. Without thinking, he dove to the ground. Lying on his belly, he realized that the sound had been nothing more than a jeep backfiring. He felt foolish until he saw that a handful of other jittery Marines had responded to the noise in the same way.

Later that day he was reunited with E Company and was overjoyed to find out that his platoon leader, Second Lieutenant Carl Roth, had survived. When he inquired about Crerar, however, Roth just shook his head; he had not been found among the survivors, and no one had heard anything about him. Lieutenant Roth then informed the company that it would be quartered at the Marine Corps transient center, where the men would draw new 782 equipment—rifles, packs, knives, canteens, and other field gear they would need to go into battle.

For the next two days, Company E reloaded ammo belts and generally prepared for combat. Graf's mind, however, was elsewhere. He kept hoping that Dick Crerar would walk into the tent, smiling his smart-alecky grin, and asking where the hell he had been.

On May 25, trucks picked up the company and drove it to West Loch beach. There, for the first time since the explosion, Graf saw the destruction: ships burned beyond repair; large pieces of LSTs that had been torn apart by the explosions; debris scattered everywhere; and boats and their crews using giant hooks to comb the harbor for bodies. The only man from Company E who he knew had definitely died was Corporal Weber, a gentle giant of a man, liked by everyone. Where was Crerar, he wondered. Was his one of the bodies that was never recovered?

Lieutenant Roth pointed to one of a number of LSTs lying on the beach, its bow doors open and ramp down. Graf could see that the LST was empty. Near it lay a large pile of equipment. For the next few days he and his fellow Marines brought the gear aboard. The hard physical labor cleared his head and calmed his nerves, and each night after saying a prayer for Dick Crerar, he fell quickly asleep.

Meanwhile the board of inquiry investigating the cause of the explosion came up with little. It emphasized the "necessity for more careful ammunition handling," but placed the onus on the U.S. Army. According to the U.S. Navy Bureau of Ordnance, "The ammunition was of Army design, supplied by the Army, and at the time of the accident being handled by Army personnel." Because it was not "material under" its "cognizance," the bureau recommended that no more action be taken. One month later it was still dodging responsibility. In a letter to Admiral Ernest King, Commander in Chief, United States Fleet, and Chief of Naval Operations, the chief of the bureau wrote that "no revision" of the Bureau of Ordnance Manual, which detailed ammunition storage on cargo vessels and combatant ships, "seems necessary as a result of [the] lessons of this accident."

On May 29, three days after the *New York Times* reported the West Loch explosion, burying the news on page 44 (minus any details), LST 84 sailed for "parts unknown." Under a hanging life raft, Graf found a comfortable spot on deck, just forward of the ship's bridge, near the starboard rail.

# CHAPTER 2

# Big Dreams

In Ballston Spa, New York, the city once famous for its healing mineral water springs and the elegant Sans Soucie Hotel, Robert Graf grew up dreaming of becoming a Navy man like his father. When he was four, his father told him that the Navy would never take anyone who did not know how to lace up and tie his own shoes. Day in and day out, Graf worked until he had mastered the skill, and then announced to his father that he was ready to go to sea.

Years later, though still a boy, Graf spent the summer with his grandmother in New York City. There he met his uncles, Joe and Harold Finneran, who worked on tugboats in New York's bustling harbor. On Sundays his uncles would allow young Robert to join them. Uncle Harold was the captain. He wore civilian clothes and spent most of his time reading the newspaper. Joe was the pilot, steering the tug through the harbor and river traffic, and shouting commands to the engine room. Wearing an officer's cap and a blue turtleneck sweater, Uncle Joe looked the part of an old salt. He acted it, too, shaking his fist at other pilots and shouting imprecations that left young Graf in awe. Often he ordered Graf to take the tug's wheel and

steer a straight course, while he opened the pilothouse door and uri-
nated into the harbor.

In his senior year of high school, after earning his Eagle Scout
badge, Graf signed up with the Sea Scouts and decided that he would
try to land an appointment as a Merchant Marine cadet. Pearl Harbor changed that. On December 8, 1941, *The Saratogian* blared,
"Tokyo Declares War on U.S.! Hawaii Bombed." While the elder Graf
contemplated what the attack meant, young Graf and two buddies
hitched a ride to Saratoga Springs to watch a basketball game. On the
way home, the three young men talked of revenge. The moment Graf
walked through the door, he informed his parents that the Japanese
had become his personal enemy and he wanted to sign up. He needed
their signature. It was hard for them to hide their disappointment,
but they agreed to give it if he promised that first he would finish high
school.

Robert Graf was a gifted student. He wrote poetry, acted, loved
literature and history, and was an accomplished public speaker. But
the attack altered everyone's plans. Young men who might once have
thought of going off to college now talked only of war and battlefield
glory and making Japan pay.

One month after graduating from high school, Graf went to the
recruiting station in Schenectady. First he went into the Navy recruiting office. The chief petty officer was busy and did not notice him, so
Graf went to the Marine recruiting office down the hall.

Graf returned home feeling like a hero and handed his parents the
enlistment papers. "Why the Marines?" they asked. What happened
to the Navy or the Merchant Marine? And what about college? He
was a smart boy who should be going to a good university and holding hands with a pretty girl rather than clutching a rifle. That night,
after Graf had gone to bed, his parents agonized over their decision.
Did they dare give him permission to join the Marines?

Over breakfast the following morning, his father, pen in hand and
tears in his eyes, looked at his young son: "I'm signing your death
warrant."

# CHAPTER 3

# Leaving Texas

On the afternoon West Loch blew, just minutes before Robert Graf dove from the LST into the harbor, Carl Matthews was enjoying a baseball game at Honolulu Stadium. He had grown up playing sandlot baseball and like his father he loved America's national pastime.

Not yet seventeen, and still months short of his first shave, Matthews had signed on with the Marines on August 12, 1941. Like much of America, his hometown of Hubbard, Texas, had suffered through hard economic times during the previous decade. But unlike lots of towns that by 1941 were climbing out of the Great Depression, Hubbard was still down on its luck. If the Depression was over, or almost over, no one had taken the time to inform the good folks south of Dallas. While things could have been worse, simply trying to survive was not enough for Carl. He wanted more out of life. To make matters worse, the summer of 1941 had been a "dud." In high school he had played fiddle in a string band that was a hit at country dances and Lions Club events. Matthews loved making music. But Royce Reeves, the band's leader and promoter, was busy working on his father's farm. Matthews's other sidekick, Gene Suddeth, had joined the

Civilian Conservation Corps (CCC) in Waxahachie, Texas. Without Reeves and Suddeth, Matthews was left to bake in the hot Texas sun, feeling the absence of his best buddies.

One morning during the dog days of August, Matthews strolled uptown, along Main Street, where some of the local merchants were sweeping the sidewalks in front of their stores. South of the railroad depot, Matthews spotted a flashy blue 1940 Chevrolet convertible parked in front of Creamland, the local sandwich and ice cream shop. It stuck out in Hubbard, where folks, if they owned a car at all, drove something practical. He could not take his eyes off the car until a handsome man stepped out and walked confidently toward the front door of the shop. The man wore a uniform every bit as impressive as the car, a white barracks hat, a crisply starched khaki shirt, a Sunday tie with a gleaming gold tie clip, perfectly creased blue trousers with red stripes running down the length of each pant leg, and spit-shined shoes brighter than Matthews's mother's silver platter. People stopped on the sidewalk to gawk, and the man acknowledged each of them with a nod and a smile.

It was clear to Matthews that he was military. Young men from the area had joined the service and had come home to visit, parading through town in their uniforms, nodding to the admiring girls. But none of them sparkled like this fella. Compared to him, the Hubbard boys looked like dusty, dried-up streambeds.

Barely over 120 pounds, Matthews might have been too small to play on the high school team, but what he lacked in size, he made up for in spirit. Unlike many young men who would have been too timid to approach the man, Matthews strode into Creamland and introduced himself.

"Corporal Earl S. Wade," the man replied. "United States Marine Corps."

Matthews had heard of the Army and the Navy; he even knew about the Coast Guard. But the United States Marine Corps? The name sounded exotic, as if Corporal Wade had just told him that he had arrived in Hubbard from the Amazon.

Matthews slid into the booth next to Corporal Wade, who seemed eager to talk, explaining that he was in town to "hire" good men. Matthews was on the puny side, but Wade knew that the Texas boys were tough. Besides, the Marines could always put some meat on him.

Wade opened his briefcase, revealing photographs, pins, emblems, and striking brochures, all of which depicted the proud history of the United States Marines. The Marine Corps, Wade said, took only the finest young men in the country. Matthews wondered if he was Marine material, if he would ever amble down the sidewalks of Hubbard and be the envy of every young man and woman in town. Not long after, he got his answer. Corporal Wade asked him to take a ride with him. Cruising down Main Street, he told the starry-eyed Matthews that the Marines would be honored to have a man of his caliber join their ranks. Then he told him that he would like to meet his parents and personally congratulate them on raising such a fine son.

Feeling good and enjoying his brief celebrity, Matthews waved to everyone they passed—whether he knew them well or not—and Pecan Street came too quickly.

Matthews introduced Corporal Wade to his mother and father. The corporal wasted no time telling the couple that the Marines only chose the best and that, in his opinion, their son was an extraordinary young man. To Matthews's embarrassment, his parents seemed skeptical.

When Corporal Wade left the Matthewses' house on Pecan Street to make another appointment, he made it clear that he would return to Creamland at twelve-thirty and hoped to find the boy waiting there for him. Then he informed Mr. and Mrs. Matthews that he had filled out all the necessary paperwork, which simply awaited their signatures.

Mr. Matthews sat down on the couch. Carl could see the concern on his father's face. But why? Didn't his father understand that the Marines wanted him? Mrs. Matthews left no question about how she felt; she sat crying softly into a white handkerchief.

Young Matthews felt as if he had been swept up by a Texas tornado. Just days after his parents reluctantly signed the papers, he met

Corporal Wade and a number of other recruits at the Waco Marine office. Matthews studied the other young men and was not impressed. To him they hardly looked like blue-ribbon recruits. One young man, he learned, had just been released from a juvenile reform school with the understanding that he would join the service. In Dallas the following morning they joined other prospects and went through processing. Then a doctor administered physicals, poking and prodding them, checking their teeth, feet, and legs like a rancher contemplating the purchase of a cow at a county fair. Next came the swearing-in ceremony. Barely an hour later, Matthews boarded a train bound for San Diego, California, or "Dago" as the Marines called it. The Pullman car reinforced his belief that the Marines did everything first class—convertibles and sleeping cars with fresh sheets and pillowcases and Negro porters to attend to one's every need. He played "penny ante" poker for much of the journey. In El Paso, cabdrivers tried to entice the young men across the Rio Grande to the red-light district in Ciudad Juarez. Some of the men were sorely tempted, but decided not to risk it. What if the train left them behind? All of them, however, made a pact that if they should ever again find themselves in El Paso, they would cross the river and discover the charms of the exotic Mexican whores. When they arrived in San Diego, the bus they had boarded came to a stop at some dreary-looking buildings with dull yellow wood siding and asphalt shingles. Matthews sensed that the fun was over.

Boot camp was not easy for him. The drill instructor—Matthews referred to him as "Sergeant Mean and Ugly"—knew every foul-mouthed expression ever invented, and quickly singled him out. At five-six and 123 pounds, Matthews was the runt, the platoon's feather merchant, and the DI never let him forget it. Struggling to keep up, Matthews cursed the sergeant and reminded himself that he would get a chance to prove his worth on the rifle range.

Shooting was one thing Matthews knew he could do well. He had grown up hunting squirrels along the rich river bottoms of Navarro County, Texas. His father gave him a .22 for his ninth birthday and spent time showing him how to use it. Days later Matthews shot a crow and brought it home feeling as proud as if he had killed a charging lion on the plains of East Africa.

During week nine of the twelve-week program, Matthews's platoon visited the rifle range at La Jolla, California, where he was introduced to his coach, a good-looking American Indian by the name of Corporal Bonchu, who was a star marksman on the Marine Rifle Team. Corporal Bonchu competed in shooting competitions all over the country. The corporal was the polar opposite of Matthews's drill instructor. Quietly he taught the men the basics: firing positions—standing (offhand), sitting, kneeling, prone—safety, breathing techniques, trigger squeeze. Once they had mastered those fundamental skills, they moved on to the finer points of windage and elevation. At the rifle range, they began shooting with .22s. When they graduated to their 1903A3 Springfield rifles with iron sights, Corporal Bonchu walked up and down the lines, coaching them in a calm and patient voice.

On the final day on the range, Matthews and the other members of his platoon were firing for record. Matthews adjusted the rifle sights based on the speed and direction of the wind. Then the range officer gave orders over the loudspeaker: "Lock and load. All ready on the firing line. Fire at will." Undersized and unable to hold the rifle steady, Matthews did poorly standing and kneeling. But shooting prone, he excelled. At five hundred yards, he pressed his cheekbone against the sleek wooden stock, spread his legs and dug his boondockers into the dirt, and put ten .306-caliber cartridges dead on through the bull's-eye, a perfect score.

One week later, Matthews and Platoon 110 assembled for the final parade and inspection. The band played the marches that he had come to love. When the platoon passed the review stand and executed a precise turn, Matthews, sixteen pounds heavier than when he'd left Hubbard in August, knew that he would soon be able to return home on his ten-day boot camp furlough a proud member of the United States Marine Corps.

After visiting Texas, Matthews was assigned to Camp Elliott and

B Company in the Eighth Marine Regiment. At Elliott, Matthews's Marine Corps career got off to a less than auspicious start. He was given thirty days of mess duty, but still he had to admit that the Marines at Camp Elliott were well looked after. There were free movies and popcorn, five-cent beers at the "slop chute," and weekend boxing "smokers."

On Sunday, December 7, Matthews was relaxing in his bunk. Someone in the barracks was listening to a radio station. Matthews was not paying attention until he heard a special announcement: "We interrupt this program to bring the news that the Japanese are bombing Pearl Harbor." Matthews thought it was part of an on-air radio drama. When he saw his buddies huddling around the radio, he knew that he was mistaken: the Japanese really were bombing Pearl Harbor.

Matthews and his platoon were fully outfitted and assigned to loading and unloading at the San Diego docks. In just a few days, by his assessment, they had unloaded enough artillery and mortar shells, .30-caliber ammunition, hand grenades, and wooden boxes containing five-gallon cans of gasoline to take out the entire city of San Diego.

For Christmas 1941, Matthews was staying put at Camp Elliott. What he wanted more than anything was to be home with his family, sitting in front of the fireplace that the family used for special occasions, while the aromas of his mother's cooking wafted into the living room from the kitchen. Instead he was lying on his bunk on Christmas Eve, listening to a group of sergeants with nearly thirty years in the Marine Corps play a spirited game of cribbage. Outside, a rainy, lifeless day was turning to night. Later he wrote that he was so depressed, he would have had to "reach up to touch bottom."

Though Matthews did not feel like laughing, he chuckled as Sergeants Frenchy LaPoint and Dave Wasserman traded insults. They were crusty, old, tough-as-nails China Marines. Both had served in France during World War I, where Sergeant Wasserman had won the French Medal of Honor for bravery for saving LaPoint's life. When the subject had come up in the past, Wasserman was quick to dismiss his heroism. He had saved his buddy's "ass," because LaPoint owed him money.

After the war, the sergeants had served together in Central America for the "banana wars," sweating it out aboard battleships and in jungle outposts from Nicaragua to Haiti. They had drunk hard together. By the looks of it, their drinking excursions had often led them to the tattoo parlor. Both had Oriental dragon designs that wound around their arms from their wrists to their shoulders.

Over the din of the cribbage game, Matthews listened to the sound of Christmas carols over the radio. Then Gabriel Heatter, the beloved radio commentator, came on the air. Instead of greeting his audience with his usual cheery catchphrase, "Good evening, everyone—there is good news tonight," he said, "Good evening, America. Tonight is Christmas Eve. Many of our young men are not home with their families tonight. Some of them will never go home again."

# CHAPTER 4

# Mosquitoes, Mud, and Mayhem

Just days after Christmas, Matthews found himself part of a depot platoon assigned to the 2nd Marine Brigade, working round the clock, loading onto two transport ships the many tons of ammunition, food, medical supplies, trucks, and tanks that had been stockpiled at the San Diego docks.

On January 6, 1942, the 2nd Brigade boarded the *Lurline,* a former Matson luxury liner that had been semi-converted to a troopship. The men were proud of the fact that they were part of the first expeditionary force to go overseas following the Pearl Harbor disaster. The Marines, they bragged, were the only ones brave enough to sail into hostile waters. The convoy consisted of two other Matson Line ships, two freighters, USS *Jupiter* and *Lassen,* a tanker, and a Navy escort that included the carriers *Yorktown* and *Enterprise,* Admiral "Bull" Halsey's flagship, which met the convoy along the way.

Although Matthews carried the lucky rifle with which he had shot for record, he was grateful for the naval escort. Although the Matson ships had been outfitted with .30- and .50-caliber machine guns, without the Navy carriers the ships and the five thousand enlisted men and 245 officers would have been sitting ducks in the event of a Japanese attack.

On January 11, a ship's announcer informed the Marines that an enemy submarine had just shelled the naval station on Pago Pago in American Samoa. Military analysts predicted follow-up strikes. The announcement confirmed the general scuttlebutt regarding their destination. But the men still wondered: just where in the hell was Samoa? Some had heard the beautiful Dorothy Lamour, playing the daughter of a South Seas island chief, sing about Samoa in John Ford's 1937 movie *The Hurricane*. But that was their only association.

One thing the men did know was that wherever Samoa was, it was an important piece of real estate. General Thomas Holcomb, the commandant of the Marine Corps, who had agreed to participate in a Navy public relations program, went on NBC radio on November 22, 1941, to reassure the American public that his men would fiercely defend the country's interests abroad. He had 61,000 men in uniform, and they would perform their "duty as the frontiersmen of the nation's huge new defense network."

What that meant in early 1942 was a matter for debate. The Allies' strategic situation in the Pacific was a fragile one. If, as the Combined Chiefs of Staff had directed, Australia was to be held at all costs, Admiral Ernest King insisted that air, ground, and naval forces be used to ensure the safety of the sea routes and lines of communication to the Southwest Pacific. Although King grew bolder as the war progressed, in early 1942 he could not even consider the possibility of staging an offensive. His only strategic alternative was to defend the island bases between Hawaii and Australia, which meant fortifying New Caledonia, Fiji, and especially American Samoa. If one of the island bases fell, King envisioned convoys having to detour far to the south in order to supply Australia. Worse yet, he feared that Japan would try to take Hawaii, the Aleutians, even mainland Alaska.

By the time the 2nd Brigade arrived in Pago Pago on Tutuila, American Samoa's largest island, 2,300 miles southwest of Hawaii, it was clear that the Japanese were headed eastward down the Solomon

Islands in an effort to isolate Australia. Perhaps they also had designs on Samoa.

After two weeks at sea, the 2nd Brigade arrived in Samoa. Now it had an enormous task ahead of it: first to unload, then to fortify the island. Had the men known what lay in store for them, some might have jumped ship somewhere along their blue water route.

When the *Lurline* made its way through the narrow channel into the oil-slick calm of Pago Pago Harbor, the heat, which had turned from torrid to unbearable, nearly brought Matthews to his knees. Like the others aboard ship, Matthews was still wearing the cold-weather gear he was issued before leaving San Diego. Someone made a wisecrack about half-naked savages being a lot smarter than the Marine Corps.

The heat was like nothing he had ever experienced before. Summers in Hubbard, Texas, were hell-hot. But in Samoa the heat was obscene; it permeated everything. The leaves on the trees gleamed and dripped with it. It hung over the land like a disease. Only the daily rain provided a respite. Sounding like a West Texas tornado, it came down in great sheets. Trees hung uncertainly on steep mountain slopes, looking as if they might rush down on rivers of mud. The parched Marines loved it. They held their palms up and bent back their heads like tent preachers barnstorming through the Bible Belt. The downpours, though, subsided as quickly as they came and all that remained was a light mist that lay over the hillside forests. Metal roofs steamed in the sun, and pools pockmarked the harbor road.

As the *Lurline* neared the dock, Matthews smelled the stink of the place: diesel fuel, rotting bananas, dead fish. It assaulted his nose and stuck in the back of his throat. He would have retched had it not been for the timely humor of one of his fellow Marines. Perhaps it was Wasserman or LaPoint who broke out in a parody of Dorothy Lamour's song "I'd Like to See Samoa of Samoa." Whoever it was sang the new lyrics to what could have been the 2nd Brigade's theme song, "I'd Like to See Nomoa of Samoa."

Pago Pago was certainly not the idyllic South Seas spot of the men's imaginations—many had expected that they would be listening to Glenn Miller's "Moonlight Serenade" while marveling at the rainbow colors of a tropical twilight—or an exciting port with bars, tattoo parlors, and a busy red-light district. In fact, Pago Pago had few if any temptations. It was a tiny, abject speck of a town, consisting of boarded-up shops, the dingy houses of the island's administrators, and a grassy oval three hundred yards long. Dressed in white T-shirts and khaki lavalavas (sarongs), and shoeless, the men of the 1st Samoan Marine Corps Reserve Battalion used the green for close-order drill.

Just days after reaching Pago Pago, Matthews did not care if he never saw another hatch cover or boom again. At the crumbling harbor dock, amid the stink and the cloying humidity, he and the rest of his platoon fell into a mind-numbing routine. Stripped to the waist, and clutching the slippery rails, they climbed into the *Jupiter*'s suffocating hold, where even the harbor's dismal breeze could not find them. Looking up, they watched as the crane operators lowered cargo nets or wood pallets. Then they went to work, lugging mortar and artillery shells, machine guns in packing grease, and 116-pound crates of .30-caliber ammunition. Matthews learned to stay away from the hatch when the nets and pallets were being raised. A free-falling load could crush a man like a cockroach. If a shell blew, everyone would be blown to bits. Matthews tried to put the possibility out of his mind, consoling himself with the thought that it would be over fast and his G.I. insurance would pay his family $10,000.

Working at a whirlwind pace, the Marines unloaded the *Jupiter* and the *Lassen*, and the two transports left Pago Pago Harbor for a return trip to the United States. They had no sooner left than American Samoa came under alert: on January 23, 1942, the Japanese Imperial Army took the Australian-held port of Rabaul on the island of New Britain, off the east coast of New Guinea. The loss of Rabaul caused great consternation in Washington. Admiral King knew that Japanese carriers, battleships, cruisers, and troopships could use Rabaul as a jumping-off point for strikes against Australia and the Allied supply line. The most likely scenario was that Japan would disable the supply route first and then turn its attention to Australia. King called for a show of force, and ordered Admiral Halsey's *Enterprise* to sail from Samoa and exercise retaliatory strikes in the Marshalls, and Admiral Fletcher's *Yorktown* to do the same in the Gilberts. If the Japanese were worried about protecting their possessions in the north, they would be less likely to make military forays into the south.

When the *Enterprise* and the *Yorktown* left, Matthews wondered about his ability to defend an essential military outpost. In reality he had had very little training. His tentmates did not inspire confidence, either. They were hardly the valiant men depicted on the Marine recruiting posters. One was a likable, clean-cut fella out of Indianapolis; another a Jewish kid from Wisconsin named Schlessinger who was more poet than warrior; the third, Corporal Walter Ernest George Godinius, Matthews's squad leader, was a friendly guy from Duluth, Minnesota, who gave Matthews his first introduction to what everyone called "jungle juice," an island concoction that the men made from fermented coconut juice, sugar, and yeast; the fourth was a tow-headed ranch hand from Montana who had an affection for dirty songs and liked to sleep in the buff. His favorite tune, to which he could sing eight verses, was one about a randy Indian maid. In the heat of the night, he would lie naked under his mosquito netting and croon, "There was an Indian maid, who said she wasn't afraid, she lay on her back in a tumbledown shack . . ."

Throughout the first half of 1942, American Samoa braced itself for an attack. Meanwhile the day-to-day life of the Marines remained unchanged. For Matthews, mail from his mother was all he had to remind him that a world still existed beyond the mud and heat of Samoa. Otherwise, movies and a few cupfuls of jungle hooch were his only diversions from the strenuous work of fortifying the islands. His platoon became part of a team whose job it was to lug ammunition, mostly boxes of .30-caliber shells, and food to the mountain storage shelters. It was an undertaking that often left him and his fellow platoon members lying by the side of the trail in the oil-colored mud, gulping at the air and grunting like pack animals, while tiny leeches slithered up their pant legs, and clouds of mosquitoes searched for any bare skin they could find.

The men cursed their fate. What had brought them to this miserable place where nature ran rampant, and at dusk fruit bats floated like ghosts among the banyan trees, where everything from canvas tents to food supplies rotted, and ticks and mosquitoes carried diseases that could swell a man's scrotum to the size of a medicine ball, make his body temperature soar, and haunt his sleep? Late at night, Matthews would lie in his cot exhausted, staring up at the dim canopy of the tent, listening to the moths and the flicker of their soft, powdery wings, and dream of home.

That spring, Matthews received news that he had been passed over for promotion. He was devastated. Returning to his tent, he lay on his bunk and imitated Schlessinger. Schlessinger was always composing poems or reciting stanzas from those he loved.

Matthews began:

> *You have read of the boy who didn't pass,*
> *And went to his room and cried,*
> *I just failed to make PFC*
> *And I had tried and tried.*

He thought some more, and miraculously the lines seemed to flow:

> *I have gone on hikes and made patrols*
> *And read all through the book,*
> *I have braved the dangers of the South Seas Isle,*
> *And still I'm just a rook.*

> *I guess I'll be a Buck Ass Boot*
> *When I get back to the States,*
> *But I know I'll be as good as the rest,*
> *Even though not in the rates.*

> *So I'll hit the line and go over the top*
> *And then . . . back across the sea.*

*I'll go marching home at last,*
*As a "Hashmark PFC."*

When Corporal Godinius heard the poem, he posted a copy of it on the company bulletin board. Word circulated quickly, and soon everyone had read it and was now referring to Private Matthews as "Hashmark." When the poem came to Lieutenant Levitt's attention, he sent it on to Hubbard, Texas, and penned a letter to Matthews's mother.

> *Dear Mrs. Matthews,*
> *I desire to congratulate you on having such a*
> *fine son. I thought his poem was so entertaining (if*
> *somewhat heartbreaking) that I have sent it to the papers.*
> *Incidentally, the only reason that "Tubby" did not make*
> *the PFC (Private First Class) was that several others*
> *had more time in the service than he. His intelligence,*
> *industry, and spirit are admirable.*

# CHAPTER 5

# Semper Fi

Robert Graf boarded a bus from Parris Island, South Carolina, to New River, North Carolina, for his final three weeks of boot camp. Still just a recruit, Graf could never have imagined that just nine months later he would be swimming through a sea of fire while his best buddy waited aboard a burning ship for a rescue boat.

When Graf arrived at Camp New River, the base was nearly deserted. The 1st Marine Division, which had trained at this same camp, had been sent overseas. It was now defending the ground it had taken in the southern Solomons.

Graf took a measure of pride in the camp's roughness, surrounded as it was by dreary Carolina swamp country of sluggish brown streams, broad estuaries, and primitive woods of scrub oak, tupelo, palmetto, cypress, and longleaf pine. The training further convinced the "boots" that rumors of deployment were true. Most of their day consisted of maneuvers in the fierce, steamy heat. When they were not in the field, they spent hours on the rifle range. Graf was not a natural with a rifle. Unlike many of the country boys, especially the Southern ones, he had not grown up hunting squirrels or rabbits in the woods.

The various positions felt uncomfortable and awkward and left his cramped muscles trembling. He wasn't squeezing his shots so much as jerking them. But unlike the guys who had grown up shooting, he was raw material and did not have to unlearn a host of bad habits in order to learn the Marine Corps way.

"Squeeze it like your girl back home," his instructor advised. "Slow and soft."

On the day he fired for record, Graf shot well enough at 100, 300, and 500 yards to get by. He was certainly not a marksman, but he had achieved his dream and now he had three bronze Marine Corps globe-and-anchor emblems to prove it. He was then transferred from Recruit Training Command to a heavy-weapons group—H Company, 2nd Battalion, 23rd Marines, 3rd Marine Division.

His new status must have filled him with a keen sense of accomplishment and expectation, but also uncertainty. Graf, like everyone else, was curious—what was next? Barely out of boot camp, would he and the others be sent to Guadalcanal? They had all heard the reports of the savage battles in the island's tangled jungles.

Soon enough, Graf and the ex-boots got their answer. They were going nowhere fast. New River would be their home for many months to come. They continued their training, learning basic judo moves, hand-to-hand combat skills, how to use dynamite, and how to stab and slash with knives and bayonets. They studied concealment and practiced digging camouflaged spider holes that a tank could roll over. When they were not learning specific skills, they spent their time in the field on maneuvers amid the mosquitoes, ticks, chiggers, and poisonous water moccasins, or at the beach learning the art of shore landings.

Finally, furlough came. When his train reached the depot in Ballston Spa, Graf exited and began his slow, self-conscious walk home, enjoying the feel of the two dogtags hanging from a blackened string around his neck. Secretly he hoped that people would be out, braving the cold, doing their shopping and errands. Attired in dress blues, he wanted to be noticed.

To cover the few blocks from the train depot to his parents' house,

Graf did not so much walk as parade. He stopped at the park to admire his name on the billboard, and at Allen's Restaurant to make sure that his photo in full combat gear from boot camp was on the wall. Walking with a swagger, he passed by his high school as young men and women with whom he had gone to school looked on.

Graf's week-long leave went quickly, and before he knew it he was making his way back to the train station. Again he passed the park, and this time he noticed the gold stars that had been added to the billboard. Each star meant that a local man had died defending his country. Had they been there the week before? Graf lingered in front of the board and noticed a star next to the name of a childhood friend. He had been in the Scouts with Kenny Le Barron and had worked at the county fair with him.

Back at New River, the rumor mill was churning again. Graf learned that he and the rest of the 23rd Marine Regiment would be shipping out. "Shipping out"—the phrase held such promise. Days later, however, the old China Marine, the company's gunnery sergeant, clarified the gossip and doused Graf's notions of heading for the "canal." They would be shipping out, but they were not going overseas. They were going north to Norfolk, Virginia, for sea maneuvers.

Graf knew better than to doubt Sergeant Townsley. Emberg Townsley was a rugged, no-nonsense Marine who, along with Colonel Louis R. Jones, the 23rd's commanding officer, had served in China, beginning in the late 1920s. By the time Graf came to the regiment, Townsley had already put in eighteen years in the Marines, a record of which he was proud. It was not the kind of swollen, presumptuous pride of someone who was eager to climb the ranks. Like a host of other regular Marines, Townsley had no desire to become a commissioned officer. The younger Marines revered him. They might have been tough, but Townsley could lick any one of them. Although barely half the size of some of the men in the regiment, he was made of forged steel and was known for his fierce will and athletic ability. He was widely regarded as the greatest track-and-field man the Marines ever had, winning numerous cups in international competition with the Russian, Japanese, and Italian military units.

At the Norfolk Navy Yard, the USS *Monrovia* waited to take the 23rd out into the waters of the Chesapeake Bay. Graf was disappointed that Walt "Jimmy" Haskell, a wisecracking buddy from Ballston Spa, would not be making the trip. While on leave, Haskell had been led astray by a woman who was determined to show a Marine a good time. When he got word that the regiment was headed for maneuvers, he jumped a train and tried to get to Norfolk in time. He failed and was declared AOL—absent over leave—and was tossed in the brig.

Except for a flock of swooping gulls, the skies over the bay were a blank, icy blue. As the January winds thrashed across the water and cut through his overcoat, Graf realized that this was to be no pleasure cruise.

Combined with its training at New River, the regiment experienced some of the most rigorous training Marines had ever undergone. Day in and day out, the men of the 23rd climbed up and down rope nets and in and out of Higgins boats until their shoulders ached and they could hardly lift their legs. Soaked and chilled, Graf and the others swore that they would jump ship before they joined their fellow Marines in Iceland. The tropical jungles of the South Pacific might have been teeming with Japanese and disease, but sweating out a malarial fever was preferable to dying of hypothermia in a place that did not even have trees.

For two weeks the regiment practiced its landings, and then it was back to New River where Graf and his fellow Marines learned that the 23rd regiment was being detached from the 3rd Division to become the nucleus of the recently formed 4th Marine Division.

To bring the 23rd Marines up to strength, the regiment for the first time took on draftees who had just finished boot camp. To this group it added men who had fought on Guadalcanal who were returning from thirty-day leaves. The final change came in late spring when the regiment received word that in early July the entire 4th Division was leaving New River and shipping out for Camp Pendleton in California.

For Graf, the journey west was a grand adventure. The division went first class aboard a civilian train with sleepers. Graf drew a lower berth, and unlike most of the men, who played high-stakes card and dice games, he studied the countryside as the train traveled south and then west. Graf was not above gambling, but who wanted to gamble when there was so much to see?

At night he watched the lights flicker in the misty hills and then fell asleep to the comforting rhythms of the train. During the day, people gathered along the route to cheer and wave. On the outside of the train, someone had scrawled WE ARE THE UNITED STATES MA-RINES. At the whistle-stops, Negro vendors sold coffee in paper cups while black-skinned boys danced on the platforms and scrambled for the pennies and nickels that the Marines tossed to them. The young women who gathered to pay their respects were especially enthusiastic. Graf and the men of Company H cursed their bad luck: "All these girls and no liberty."

In New Orleans, the men left the train for exercises. They all wanted to stretch their legs in the historic French Quarter with its jazz and booze and women, but their officers herded them back onto the train before any of them tried to slip away.

The trip through Texas was a long one. The troops grumbled about the heat until someone reminded them that July in New River or Parris Island, when the air was thick enough to slice, had been no picnic. Graf did not like the heat any more than the others, but he was too taken with Texas to complain. He loved the small-town names—Apple Springs, Pecan Gap, Crow, Comfort, Cottonwood, Comanche.

In Albuquerque, New Mexico, the train stopped again. The men were treated to a delicious meal at the local Fred Harvey Restaurant, which had been feeding travelers since the 1870s and serving men aboard troop trains since the war began.

It was not until the train reached Los Angeles that the serious gamblers looked out the windows. Now everyone talked of getting drunk and strolling along the beach at night with a beautiful Hollywood woman. With the alcohol loosening their tongues, they would tell tales of Guadalcanal that they had overhead from veterans who had recently joined the regiment, and claim the stories as their own.

# CHAPTER 6

# Eleanor Roosevelt's Niggers

The first time Sammie Lee Boykin ever saw a black man in a uniform was in the late summer of 1941. J. C. Clark paraded through the Old Camp neighborhood of Bessemer, Alabama, looking so handsome and important. The girls swooned, mothers hugged him, and the old men shook his hand. Although he might have been a romantic figure to Boykin, J. C. Clark was nothing more than a glorified waiter, a Navy messman destined to wait on the officer corps for his entire career, to clean and press their uniforms, iron linens, and set their tables with silverware. To Boykin and his friend Elester Cunningham, however, Clark was someone who commanded attention, and they promptly made a pact. When they graduated from school, they would take the bus to Birmingham and sign up for the Navy. Then they, too, would return home to soak up the admiration.

In a Japanese best-seller of the 1920s, *If Japan and America Fight,* Lieutenant General Kojiro Sato predicted that America's "colored people" would not be willing to take up arms to defend the United States if a war broke out. The author could not have been more incorrect. Before the war, the editors of the *Baltimore Afro-American* promised President Roosevelt that, should the country need them, black people would put aside their historic grievances and do their part. "Mr. President, you can count on us," they promised. However, the editors added that they could not be expected to defend their country "with a whiskbroom and a wide grin."

The truth was that although every branch of service desperately needed men, neither the Army nor the Marines nor the Navy wanted black men. In 1940 a group of fifteen black mess attendants aboard the cruiser *Philadelphia* risked their careers by signing a letter to the black-owned *Pittsburgh Courier,* which the paper promptly published. "Our main reason for writing," the signers explained, "is to let all our colored mothers and fathers know how their sons are treated after taking an oath pledging allegiance and loyalty to their flag and country. . . . We sincerely hope to discourage any other colored boys who might have planned to join the Navy and make the same mistake as we did. All they would become is seagoing bellhops, chambermaids and dishwashers."

The Navy threw all fifteen into jail, and the men were eventually discharged as undesirables. Following its ruling against the men, the Navy attempted to explain its rationale for using blacks only as messmen. "After many years of experience, the policy of not enlisting men of the colored race for any branch of the naval service except the messman's branch was adopted to meet the best interests of the general ship efficiency."

The severity of the Navy's punishment, intended to intimidate other so-called malcontents, backfired. Men aboard other ships, inspired by the courage of the fifteen rebels, began to vent their anger. They, too, wrote the *Courier* and described the demoralizing conditions under which they served. The *Pittsburgh Courier* launched a vigorous national advertising campaign to push for minority participation in every aspect of the armed services. Meanwhile, the National Association for the Advancement of Colored People committed itself to eliminating Jim Crow in all branches of the military. Discrimination had become a powerful symbol of injustice for blacks. Restrictions on their service were painful reminders of their status as second-class citizens.

By late summer 1940, under the threat of impending war, black resentment swelled across the country, and President Roosevelt fretted about what the racial disturbances meant for his reelection bid. With good cause, he worried about a black boycott of the election or, worse yet, support for his opponent, Wendell Willkie. Roosevelt knew that the election would be close enough that he would need to depend on the black vote. Blacks voted as a bloc, and that bloc had clearly gained political power.

In late September, in a meeting arranged by his wife, Eleanor, the president, along with Secretary of the Navy Frank Knox, U.S. Army Chief of Staff General George Marshall, and Robert Patterson, the assistant secretary of war, met with three black civil rights leaders. Much to the chagrin of Knox, Marshall, and Patterson, Roosevelt seemed ready to make changes in the military's racial policies. That evening, Secretary of War Stimson, who was briefed on the details of the meeting by his undersecretary, confided in his diary that the president had "acted rambunctiously." Later he would write, "We must not place too much responsibility on a race which is not showing initiative. The foolish leaders of the colored race are seeking, at bottom, social equality." He considered the racial issue an annoying intrusion that distracted him from his primary job, which was to get the Army ready for war. Patterson, Marshall, and Knox were more direct. Patterson advised Roosevelt to "wait until V-E day to reform the world." Marshall told the president that this was no time "for critical experiments which would have a highly destructive effect on morale." Not mincing words either, Knox told the president that he would have to resign his position if the president forced him to desegregate the Navy at the same time he was gearing up for the monumental task of fielding a two-ocean force.

A. Philip Randolph, president of the Brotherhood of Sleeping Car Porters, Walter White, executive director of the NAACP, and Arnold Hill, former secretary of the Urban League, left the president's office with high expectations. After a week passed, they tried to reach the president by telephone. They sent telegrams, too. When it became apparent that the president was avoiding them, White contacted Eleanor Roosevelt. What he wanted was for the president to approve a draft of a statement highlighting their discussion of the prior week regarding incremental integration. White, Randolph, and Hill all hoped that they could issue the statement in conjunction with the White House. Roosevelt's War Department, however, had very different ideas.

Eleanor Roosevelt intervened once again, pushing the War Department for a statement of its position regarding the use of black troops. Angered by Mrs. Roosevelt's advocacy, Secretary Stimson issued an announcement that deeply disappointed Randolph and his associates. At their meeting with the president, the civil rights leaders had broached the idea of integrated Northern regiments and Negro officers leading white troops. Their understanding was that the president was willing to consider both proposals. The reality, though, was that from the moment they left the White House, the president's military advisers dismissed those notions as reckless.

The War Department's announcement was little more than a reiteration of General Marshall's earlier statement to the president. "The policy of the War Department," it said, "is not to intermingle colored and white enlisted personnel. . . . This policy has been proven satisfactory over a long period of years and to make changes would produce situations destructive to morale and detrimental to the preparation of national defense."

When Roosevelt's press secretary, Steve Early, suggested to newspaper and magazine reporters that the three civil rights leaders had approved the War Department's proposal, White, Randolph, and Hill were incensed. Accused of having sold out minorities, they lashed out and issued a hard-hitting statement titled "White House Charged with Trickery in Announcing Jim Crow Policy of Army," suggesting that the White House had misled them, had gutted the nation's democracy, and had struck a "blow at the patriotism of twelve million Negro citizens."

The president promptly and publicly apologized for his press secretary's misstep, and further admitted that he believed that desegregating the military was a worthwhile goal. "Further developments of policy," he explained to White, "will be forthcoming to ensure fair treatment on a non-discriminatory basis."

In mid-September 1940, President Roosevelt made good on his promise, signing the Selective Training and Service Act, which established the first peacetime draft in American history. The legislation was extremely popular in the black community. Black leaders considered it a milestone because of two important antidiscrimination clauses. The first provided that all men between the ages of eighteen and thirty-six could volunteer for service in the land and naval forces of the United States. The second clause prohibited discrimination (based on race) in the selection and training of men. The addition of the antidiscrimination clause was a major achievement for the civil rights movement and influential black coalitions across the country. It was this clause that so worried members of the president's own administration, especially Secretary of War Henry Stimson. Stimson wrote in his diary, "Colored men do very well under white officers but every time we try to lift them a little beyond where they can go, disaster and confusion follows. . . . I hope for heaven sakes they don't mix the white and colored troops together in the same units for then we shall certainly have trouble."

In the spring of 1941, Roosevelt was three months into an unprecedented third term. Although he had supported major legislative breakthroughs, progress had come slowly for blacks. Frustrated by continuing roadblocks to integration in the military and defense industries, A. Philip Randolph hit upon a solution: he would stage a massive protest march on Washington.

Randolph traveled the country raising money and rallying support for the march. The response, though tepid at first, became overwhelmingly positive. "Never before in the history of the nation," wrote the *Chicago Defender,* had blacks "ever been so united in an objective and so insistent upon action being taken." Randolph established a March on Washington Committee with branches in major cities across the country. Although the prospect of the rally worried the Roosevelt administration, the president repeatedly declined Walter

White's requests to meet. Not until mid-June did the president make time for Randolph and the NAACP's executive director, finally agreeing to meet with Stimson, Knox, and a number of civilian affairs officials. Early on, Randolph pushed the conversation toward the matter at hand.

"Well, Phil," the president asked, "what do you want me to do?"

Randolph did not demur. "Mr. President," he said, "we want you to issue an executive order making it mandatory that Negroes be permitted to work in these plants."

When the president replied that he would be unable to meet Randolph's request, Randolph answered, "I'm sorry, Mr. President, then the march cannot be called off."

"How many people do you plan to bring?" inquired Roosevelt.

"One hundred thousand," Randolph countered.

Randolph may have exaggerated its size, but Roosevelt could not risk the possibility of 100,000, or even tens of thousands, of blacks gathering on the streets of Washington. It spelled trouble, perhaps disaster. If signing an executive order was the only way to stop the march and the potential unrest and bloodshed, then he would do it.

A lawyer drafted the language and sent it to Randolph for his approval. The activist refused to let this final step fall short of his expectations, and sent the draft back numerous times for revisions. On June 25, 1941, after Randolph had endorsed the language, Roosevelt signed Executive Order 8802, which called upon employers and labor unions "to provide for the full and equitable participation of all workers in defense industries, without discrimination because of race, creed, color or national origin . . . all departments of the government, including the Armed Forces, shall lead the way in erasing discrimination over color or race." To ensure compliance, the order established a five-member Fair Employment Practices Commission (FEPC).

Black newspapers heralded the decision as "epochal." The *Chicago Defender* wrote that the order renewed Negroes' faith in a democracy that had gone astray. The National Negro Congress lauded the move as a "bold, patriotic action in smashing age-old color restrictions."

While the news thrilled the black community, generals and admirals across the country deeply resented the order. They felt that Roosevelt, by giving in to the black community, had opened Pandora's box. Now they were being told to accept blacks as the nation geared up for the possibility of war. During a meeting of the General Board of the Navy, the commandant of the Marine Corps, Major General Thomas Holcomb, argued that blacks had no place in the Marines. "If it were a question of having a Marine Corps of 5,000 whites or 250,000 Negroes, I would rather have the whites." Later the obdurate commandant added, "The Negro race has every opportunity now to satisfy its aspirations for combat in the Army—a very much larger organization than the Navy or Marine Corps—and their desire to enter the naval service is largely, I think, to break into a club that doesn't want them."

In the wake of Roosevelt's order, realizing that the admission of blacks into the Marine Corps was an inevitability, General Holcomb issued an urgent memorandum: "The mixing of white and colored enlisted personnel within the same unit," it said, "will be avoided."

# CHAPTER 7

# The Right to Fight

Hoping to stave off the entrance of blacks, every branch of service seized upon an Army War College Report on "The Use of Negro Manpower in War." "In the process of evolution," the report stipulated, "the American Negro has not progressed as far as other sub species of the human family. . . . The cranial cavity of the Negro is smaller than whites. . . . The psychology of the Negro, based on heredity derived from mediocre African ancestors, cultivated by generations of slavery, is one from which we cannot expect to draw leadership material. . . . In general the Negro is jolly, docile, tractable, and lively but with harsh or unkind treatment can become stubborn, sullen and unruly. In physical courage, [he] falls well back of whites. . . . He is most susceptible to 'Crowd Psychology.' He cannot control himself in fear of danger. . . . He is a rank coward in the dark."

Outraged, William Hastie, the man chosen by the president to advise Secretary of War Henry Stimson on racial affairs, disputed the logic of the report. "The evidence of field commanders," he wrote, "indicates that a high percentage of the men with little education or acquired skill at the time of their induction, can be used effectively in combat units. Many such men have basic intelligence and are eager to learn for the very reason that opportunity has been denied them in civilian life."

On December 1, 1941, General George Marshall addressed himself to Hastie's reponse. In a memorandum to Henry Stimson, he wrote that Hastie's suggestions "would be tantamount to solving a social problem which has perplexed the American people throughout the history of this nation. The Army cannot accomplish such a solution, and should not be charged with the undertaking."

Within twenty-four hours of the Japanese attack on Pearl Harbor, the NAACP, believing the demands of war would force the military to reconsider its racist policies, issued a public statement to the president offering its unwavering support. That statement read, "Though thirteen million Negroes have more often than not been denied democracy, they are American citizens and will as in every war give unqualified support to the protection of their country." Two days later the NAACP wired Secretary Knox, asking whether the Navy planned to accept colored recruits for service other than the messman's branch. "We will fight," the NAACP added, "but we demand the right to fight as equals in every branch of military, naval and aviation service." The Bureau of the Navy Personnel replied that no policy change was being discussed. Furious, the NAACP took its case to the president on December 17, 1941.

Roosevelt now had a war brewing on three fronts: Europe, the Pacific, and at home, too. While he deliberated on how to reply to the NAACP, the committee that Knox had appointed to look into the Navy's racial policies issued an uninspired report that did little more than uphold the status quo. It concluded that "the enlistment of Negroes (other than as mess attendants) leads to disruptive and undermining conditions."

On January 9, 1942, the president sent the NAACP's letter of December 17 to Secretary Knox. "I think that with all the Navy activities," Roosevelt wrote, "BuNav [Bureau of Navy Personnel] might invent something that colored enlistees could do in addition to the rating of messman."

Just one week later, responding to the commander-in-chief's memo, Secretary Knox instructed the Navy's General Board to describe what assignments would "permit the Navy to best utilize the services of these [Negro] men." In early February the board responded. The mixing of races aboard ship, it said, would lead to "race friction and lowered efficiency." It added further that if restricting Negroes to the messman's branch was discrimination, "it is but part and parcel of similar discrimination throughout the United States."

President Roosevelt reviewed the board's report and again wrote Secretary Knox encouraging him to find a middle ground between confining Negroes to messman duties and opening up all duties to them. But "to go the whole way," Roosevelt cautioned, "at one fell swoop would seriously impair the general average efficiency of the Navy." Wartime mobilization had already proved chaotic enough.

Days later, Admiral King weighed in on the issue. His recommendation was that if Negroes were going to be enlisted in the Navy in ratings other than the messman's branch, they should be assigned to "Construction Battalions under the Bureau of Yards and Docks; and Shore Stations . . . in places like Naval Supply Depots, Navy Yards, Ordnance Stations, Training Stations, Experimental Stations. Section Bases, Air Stations, etc.,—in general—the Naval Shore Establishment." What this meant for blacks in the Navy was that they would not be allowed to serve at sea. Rather, they would be confined to a support role, to behind-the-scenes jobs where they would have little opportunity for promotion or the kind of service they had envisioned when they signed up.

Almost one month later, the Navy's General Board again reported to Secretary Knox. The "organization of colored units," it said, "could be effected with the least amount of turmoil, if they were assigned to service units, construction battalions, and composite Marine battalions."

By early spring, after nearly a year, the executive order to end discrimination in the armed forces and repay the black community for its election support was still sitting on Secretary Knox's desk. On April 7, realizing that he now had a solution to the problem of how to utilize large numbers of blacks in the Navy, Knox announced that beginning on June 1, 1942, Negroes could enlist in general service. The plan established a weekly quota of 277 men. By year's end, Knox hoped to have seven thousand blacks enlisted for general service.

# CHAPTER 8

# The First

In the summer of 1942, with high school behind them, and still inspired by the image of J. C. Clark in his dashing uniform, Sammie Boykin and Elester Cunningham made their way to the recruiting station in Birmingham, Alabama. They walked through the front door and saw only one recruiter, a tall, serious-looking man with close-cropped brown hair. He spoke cordially, even solicitously, telling Boykin and Cunningham that the Navy was looking for the best Negroes in all of Alabama. What he did not say was that having resisted the enlistment of Negroes for general service for its entire history, the Navy was trying to kick-start its "Negro" program and was desperate to find "qualified" black men willing to commit themselves to a branch of service that had never wanted them.

The following day, Boykin and Cunningham returned to the Birmingham recruiting station. A doctor examined them and declared them fit. After scoring their Navy General Classification Tests, the recruiter told them to get home and start packing. Five days later Boykin and Cunningham were bound for the Great Lakes Naval

Training Center, outside of Waukegan, Illinois, which had just opened its doors to blacks.

After traveling seven hundred miles north from Birmingham, Alabama, Sammie Lee Boykin arrived at Chicago's Union Station. Aboard the segregated Louisville & Nashville line, Boykin and Cunningham had sat in a crowded, dirty car that smelled of stale sweat. Both young men were nervous, especially Cunningham, who was large but clumsy, and sensitive. Based on what he knew of boot camp, he might have had a premonition that he would never make it in the Navy.

When the train arrived in Evansville, Indiana, after groaning and lurching its way through a series of whistle-stops, both young men looked as if they had been farming in the Alabama bottoms. Because the Negro car was right behind the engine and the coal car, every time they opened a window to relieve the stifling heat, they would be covered in soot. In Evansville, when they transferred to the Chicago & Eastern Illinois, both were surprised to find that the cars were no longer segregated.

When the train arrived in Chicago, Boykin was awestruck. Never before had he even crossed the Alabama state line. Now he found himself in one of the country's largest cities. Although it was early morning and shadows still darkened the station, there were people everywhere, hustling to and fro with a sense of purpose. Boykin, however, heeded his mother's warnings about the vices and temptations of the big city. He stayed put and did not stray from Union Station until a Navy lieutenant led him and the other flustered and frightened eighteen-year-olds onto a bus that would take them north to the Great Lakes Naval Training Station.

Just three months before Boykin and Cunningham walked through the door of the Birmingham recruiting office, the Great Lakes Naval Station *Bulletin* proclaimed that "Great Lakes has been singularly honored by being chosen as the training station for the first Negro recruits to come to the service under the new program." Despite the auspicious-sounding proclamation, the truth was very different. Many in the Navy were deeply uneasy about training black recruits for anything other than messman's (steward's) duties.

Heading up the new program was Lieutenant Commander D. W. Armstrong, son of General Samuel Armstrong, an officer in the Union Army and the founder and first principal of what would eventually be called Hampton University, the famous black college, where Booker T. Washington was educated. The young commander had been a trustee there, and was said to be someone who had the ear of Eleanor Roosevelt. Armstrong's official title was "Assistant Recruit Training Officer in Charge of Negroes." Eventually Armstrong would gain admirers who considered his policies enlightened and his advocacy work essential. He encouraged the recruits to recite a daily creed dealing with the advancement of the "Negro race." It was clear that blacks were great drillers and marched with a "rhythm that whites did not possess." However, their skill in parading served to underscore a stereotype that they were musical but simple-minded.

Armstrong believed that if the Great Lakes experiment had any chance of success, the recruits needed to overcome the perception in the black community that the Navy was a place "where men are men and colored men are cooks." Quotas needed to be set up in the various service schools (Gunner's Mate, Yeoman, Radioman, Machinist's Mate, Shore Patrol, Cooks and Bakers, etc.)—which the Bureau of Personnel had opened to blacks in July 1942—and a specified number of spots held just for blacks who aspired to more than cooking and drilling.

Upon arriving, the hungry recruits were taken to the chow hall at Camp Robert Smalls, the segregated training center named in honor of a black Civil War hero. Then, after a quick meal in the basement of the chow hall, Boykin, Cunningham, and the rest of the men marched out to the drill field, where they were introduced to the Recruit Training Commander. The lieutenant welcomed them. They were the beginning, the first black seamen trainees ever to be part of the United States Navy. "Your performance will determine the fate of future black enlistees," he said. "All eyes are on you." He encouraged the men to aspire to the highest code of conduct and to come down hard on those among them who were a threat to what he called the "experiment." "You are the first," he continued. "You do not want to be the

last. It will not be easy. Work hard and keep your eyes on the ball."
It was a message that the lieutenant would deliver often through
Boykin's twelve weeks of boot camp. In those three months Boykin
would come to admire the white officer's commitment and honesty.
He told the men the truth: that change would not come easy. They
would be taunted, mocked, belittled, and intimidated. It was their
job, he said, always to maintain their cool and to keep their dignity. If
they ever made it aboard ship, that composure would be tested. They
would be vastly outnumbered. Many of the sailors would resent their
presence, and some of the officers would deliberately make their lives
miserable.

The Navy's approach was to supply Camp Smalls with everything
that the white training center had so that there was "no necessity for
Negro recruits to mingle with whites." In reality, despite the Navy's
attempts to achieve separate but equal status for its blacks, and despite Armstrong's best efforts to bring parity to the camp, discrepancies were marked. On the firing range, the black units used .22s while
the white sailors shot with Springfield rifles; white trainees fired three-
inch antiaircraft guns and machine guns while the black recruits' instruction was theoretical; white sailors trained on ships while blacks
were confined to rowboats with oars.

Boykin had never expected to be treated like a white man. At the
age of thirteen, he got a stark lesson in inequality. When a fight between black and white children erupted one Sunday afternoon, the
police moved the entire black population to the other side of a string
of high hills so that it was separated from the white neighborhood.
No one dared to object.

At Great Lakes, if Boykin felt any bitterness, no one would have
known it. He flew through basic training. He knew how to work
hard, he could read and write—one out of five of the recruits was
illiterate or nearly illiterate and was sent to Great Lakes' "Remedial
School"—he did not drink, smoke, or gamble, and he took pride in
getting high grades during inspection. He was the ideal recruit and
proved himself on the drill field, the firing range, the pool—he was
one of the few who knew how to swim—and the commando course.

As he excelled and drew the attention of the drill instructors, he allowed himself to dream. Perhaps he would be assigned to a destroyer or submarine in the South Pacific, or one of the service schools. There he could learn a trade that he could put to good use in the Navy and after he got out. That way he would never have to leave his family to scrounge for a job. He could be a provider and husband and father.

Sammie Lee Boykin was born in Camden, a small farming town in south central Alabama. When his father heard about the mining jobs in the north of the state, he packed up the family and moved it 120 miles to the steel center of Bessemer, just outside of Birmingham, one of the surging cities of the new South, where he went to work in the iron-ore mines, surrounded by slag heaps and pools of toxic effluent. For him, anything was better than life in the fields. In Bessemer, he and other black men extracted ore with picks and drills in dark, deep-shaft mines where the air was so bad that longtime workers had coughing fits every time they tried to take a deep breath. Some never even saw daylight. A supervisor escorted them to and from the mines in the pitch-black hours of early morning and in the evening after the sun had set.

Mine work was a backbreaking, dispiriting job that just barely allowed the elder Boykin to support his family. When cheaper imports from Brazil caused the mines of northern Alabama to shut down, Willie Boykin left home to work in the steel mills of the North. His intention might have been to send for his family, but that never happened. No one ever really knew what became of Willie Boykin. Perhaps, like lots of other men, he was led astray by the nightlife, by the drinking, illegal gambling, and prostitution. Maybe he got lost in the squalor of a big-city slum. One thing was clear: at some point he decided to close the book on the Alabama chapter of his life.

When Willie Boykin left Alabama, Johnny Hicks, Boykin's maternal grandfather, assumed an even larger role in young Sammie's life. Outside the Boykins' old hometown of Camden, Alabama, just eighty miles southwest of the once-sprawling slave market at Montgomery, the city that served briefly as the national capital of the Confederacy,

Hicks sharecropped, and at various times raised hogs, goats, laying hens, and dairy cows, and put in a small cash crop of cotton and a garden of peas, beans, sweet corn, tomatoes, and cucumbers, which he kept exclusively for the family's use. It was a hard life, but other area sharecroppers, most of whom lived in drafty, unpainted shotgun shacks with dirt yards, and often did not own a mule, had it even worse. Hicks at least had stock, which meant that he was technically a "share tenant" rather than a "sharecropper," and depending upon the deal he struck with the landowner, he might get to keep and sell half of his cotton crop. Those who did not own a mule were entitled only to a quarter, which was not near enough for a family to live on. Mule or no, sharecropping was not much of a life; it left tenant farmers like Hicks barely better off than their parents or grandparents who had grown up in the grip of slavery.

The land that Hicks worked had once been covered from horizon to horizon in snakes, malaria-carrying mosquitoes, and virgin timber. After winning government land grants, white farmers often used slaves to cut the teeming stands of oak, hickory, and pine, to dig up and burn the byzantine root systems, and then to drain and level the land for planting. It was a huge undertaking that literally transformed the landscape of the South from a place of vast, antediluvian forests and swamplands to one of neat row crops—especially cotton—cultivated by sometimes driven and pitiless planters.

From the day he got out of school for summer vacation, Boykin lived and worked on his grandfather's farm, performing an assortment of jobs, the most important of which was tending the cotton field that represented his grandfather's only means of income.

Johnny Hicks knew that he was destined for a life of poverty, prescribed for him by a system set up for the explicit purpose of keeping him poor and landless. Yet Sammie Boykin never saw his grandfather defeated or heard him utter a word of objection or regret. He swallowed the pain. Johnny Hicks would grow old, working from what sharecroppers called "Can't see to can't see," waking at 3:45 a.m. to begin his day, finishing up well after supper, never quite extinguishing his debts to the white planter who owned the land he worked. At harvesttime, even if the rain and the boll weevils stayed away, and he brought in a good crop, he could be certain that he would get paid less than a white farmer bringing cotton to the same gin.

There was nothing easy about picking cotton, either. When referring to other unpleasant jobs, sharecroppers had an expression, "It ain't easy, but it sure 'nuf beats pickin' cotton." The work, as the heat pressed down on the land, numbed the mind, blistered the hands, and exhausted the body, and would one day leave Hicks and other farmers stooped with arthritis, looking like old, bent-over fruit trees.

At harvesttime, as the cotton plants leaned over with the weight of the fat, erupting bolls that had ripened in the summer heat, Hicks moved down the clean rows with a canvas or burlap sack strapped over his shoulders, ignoring the cuts and slashes from the barbs of thousands of bolls, picking them as clean as he could so he would not get downgraded at the gin. If the weather was dry and the air did not smell of rain, Hicks drove himself each day, not stopping until he had picked an entire bale, 480 pounds of cotton. Afterward, more often than not, he fell asleep at the kitchen table before his wife could serve him supper. The following morning he woke early, as the fog lifted slowly from the fields and the crickets clamored and the nighthawks hunted. Then, after milking, and a breakfast of leftovers—butter beans and cornbread or boiled grits and a pot of chicory—he would be at it again, praying away the clouds, and lugging one heaving sack after another to the waiting wagon.

At the end of the year, when settling up accounts, he could virtually count on the white landowner to withhold additional money for any number of reasons. The man who ran the gin would keep his seed and he would be forced to buy it back the following year. So, in the end, if he was lucky, and bad weather and misfortune did not strike, he would take home a bale or two of profit, enough to make it through the year.

The only break in the summer schedule was during lay-by, the time just before harvest when the farm was idle, and Boykin and his younger brother and occasionally one or two of the other sharecroppers' kids or grandkids headed for the spring-fed creek that ran into the Alabama River. With cane poles they fished for catfish in the deep, cool holes along the bank and lolled in the shallows to escape the rank August heat. Johnny Hicks's only demand was that Boykin and his brother get home by the time the lightning bugs started to flit and flicker across the fields.

After three months of hard work, Boykin returned home in time for the start of school. He loved the farm, but there life was slow and backward and poorer than poor. Some of the kids he knew wore flour-sack clothes, slept on dirt floors, and had pellagra scales on their hands, wrists, and ankles, and hookworm rashes on their feet. By comparison, Bessemer was a modern city, where Boykin could do something they could only imagine—he could go to the picture show.

Boykin loved the movies and sometimes, ignoring his mother's warnings about getting home while it was still light, he would sit, oblivious of time, through two showings of the same film. One day the sun was setting when he left the theater, via the separate black exit door, to make the eight-mile trip back home. Leaving this late meant that he would have to walk home in the dark, and in Bessemer in the 1930s, black boys were not allowed to be out at night, especially if they were walking in white neighborhoods. Boykin heard his mother's warning dozens of times: "The only place colored folks go walking after dark is to and from the outhouse." He had also heard stories about boys, barely older than he, whose only infraction was to be found in the white section of town after sunset. If a sheriff wanted to, he could pick them up and put them on chain gangs or lease them out to mining, timber, and turpentine camps throughout the South.

His plan was to dive behind a building or into the woods if he saw or sensed trouble. By the light of the rising moon, he walked, careful not to slip in the gravel or stumble on a timber tie. The sound might wake the area dogs and their barking would attract attention. The image that haunted young Boykin was that of a black man who had been lynched. He had not witnessed the hanging or watched as they cut the hanged man down, but he did see the corpse being dragged behind a truck, bouncing over the dirt road, his clothes and skin shredded, his mouth open as if screaming, his hand dangling, held to his wrist by a frayed tendon. Back and forth the truck went through "nigger town," the driver gunning the engine for effect. Every man knew what the warning meant. The next time he could be the one strung up and bouncing behind the truck.

When he reached a white neighborhood, Boykin had a choice: to slip in and out as fast as he could and risk getting picked up by the sheriff, or make a beeline for the steep hills and go overland. He hated walking through the hills at night, trudging through the shadowed ravines and the twisted ridges. He knew that mining pits and gaping, abandoned shafts scarred the sides of the rises, and he feared falling in and never being found again. Still, he chose the latter. A black boy rambling through the woods at night had a chance. A black boy running through a white neighborhood after dark would immediately be suspected of doing no good.

He was deep in the mountains, wading through the forest, when he heard a screech. The sound took his breath away and made his muscles seize up. Locals who hunted possum, rabbits, and squirrels claimed that big cats, living in limestone caves, still roamed the deep hollows and forested peaks. Boykin stood as still as he could and waited for the sound. He never heard it again, and ten minutes later he summoned the courage to continue, forcing his reluctant legs to carry him across the mountains. By the time he made it home, he doubted whether he had even heard the cry of the big cat.

When Boykin walked through the door, he got a tongue-lashing from his mother. On that day he resolved that when the time came he would leave the South behind and follow his father's path north. He could not know that, despite all his hopes, the United States Navy would lead him to a place not much different from the Alabama he had left behind.

# CHAPTER 9

# Port Chicago

After twelve weeks of boot camp, Sammie Boykin waited for his next assignment. After pulling a long day of guard duty at Camp Robert Smalls, he was resting back at the barracks when a messenger entered and announced that he should get ready to ship out. Into his seabag Boykin stuffed his Bible, his books and letters, and his *Blue-jackets' Manual,* which contained everything a seaman needed to know about the Navy, including its rules and regulations, and how to tie knots and use a compass, and assembled with a group of others outside the hall. It was a cold late-November night. Icy raindrops fell as if the skies could not decide whether or not to snow.

After boarding the train, Boykin allowed himself to hope, as he had on the day he left Alabama. He could hardly wait to see what the future had in store for him. His only regret was that he was forced to leave in such a hurry that he did not even have a chance to say good-bye to his childhood friend, Elester Cunningham.

Unlike many of the white servicemen who had been transported cross-country by train, the Great Lakes men did not travel in a special sleeper car. It was a troop train, grimy, slow-moving, and crowded with men and cargo. Nevertheless, once Boykin heard via the grape-vine that they would be going to California, he was giddy at the pros-pect of traveling across the West. Back in Alabama, he had been an avid reader of Zane Grey's Western novels, and soon he would see a world that previously he could only imagine. He would search the wide-open plains for cowboys on cattle drives, buffaloes, ranches, sagebrush, and lone horsemen riding the fences.

In Raton, New Mexico, the train stopped and the men debarked, looking forward to Coca-Colas and a good meal at the Fred Harvey Restaurant. A small contingent of Marine guards also left the train. The waitstaff welcomed the white Marine guards with smiles. When Boykin and his fellow black sailors tried to enter, however, the head steward informed them that the restaurant did not serve Negroes.

The men were hot and hungry, and as their grumbling grew louder, a white officer stepped forward. He informed the manager that his men were members of the United States Navy, its first black sailors. He also told him that these men had traveled for thousands of miles, and now they were hoping to get a good meal. Persuaded, the manager let the black sailors in to eat.

Despite their experience in Raton, as the train rolled across the mountains of northern New Mexico, the black seamen were filled with dreams. The troop train arrived at the town of Port Chicago at mid-night. Trains were always going to and from Port Chicago. Sounding their horns and clanking slowly over the steel rails, they were as com-mon as the briny wind off Suisun Bay. The sleeping townspeople paid no attention. Later, when they realized that the depot was bringing in hundreds of black stevedores, their indifference turned to displeasure.

Boykin looked out his window, straining his eyes. A fog had settled over the area. Hard as he tried, he could see nothing more than the outline of buildings. When an officer yelled, "Fall out, fall out!" he struggled out of his seat and tumbled out of the train with the rest of the men. Soon the officer screamed, "Fall in, goddammit, I said fall in!"

*Fall in! Fall out!* Boykin thought. *That's the military.* Always someone roaring at the top of his lungs and using God's name in vain. The men were tired, stiff, and slow to respond, and the officer worked himself into a lather. He boomed again, "I said fall in!" When the men finally lined up in formation a junior officer shouted roll call. The next thing Boykin knew, he was marching through the gray night, unaware of where he was or where he was going. In the distance, lights flickered faintly. The pungent scent of the sea filled his nose and lungs. It smelled almost like home, like rich Alabama bottomland.

After a mile or so, Boykin and the others stood outside the Port Chicago Naval Ammunition Depot. Marine guards with dogs were posted at the gates. Once they entered the base, the officers showed the hundred or so men to their barracks. Some slept while others, too unsettled to sleep, talked until the dawn light brightened the room. That morning, white sailors, billeted on the barracks' second floor, discovered the black men below them. Angered that they were boarding in the same building, some of the white sailors shouted racial epithets. When they spotted a few fair-skinned black men, they taunted them, "What are you white sailors doing with those niggers?" Tempers flared and men challenged one another.

Fights would have broken out had officers not intervened. Later the base commander would move the whites into separate barracks. But for the moment, the officers marched the black men, still in their skivvies, to the parade ground. There they stood at attention while the base commander welcomed them and explained to them why they were there. They would be loading ships, a job that was critical to the war effort. The forces overseas needed bombs and ammunition. Without them, Americans would be eating rice and drinking sake and bowing to the Emperor of Japan.

Claude Ellington knew immediately that he had gotten a raw deal. When he decided to sign up, he'd left a good job as a fireman with the Georgia Railroad Company in Augusta. In downtown Augusta an enthusiastic recruiter had told him that the Navy was changing. Blacks could be seamen; they could do more than shine shoes, polish silver, and serve officers. To top it off, he told Ellington that because of his experience he could enter as a fireman first class and might end up working in the engine room of one of the big transpacific ships. The recruiter might have believed what he was saying, but more than likely he was aware that he had either exaggerated or deliberately lied about Ellington's opportunities. This was not unusual. Early on, recruiters were urged by the Navy to help it meet its numbers, especially among Southern blacks who the Navy thought might be more accepting of second-class status.

At Great Lakes, Ellington quickly discovered the reality of his situation. Although a Port Chicago seaman could make the jump from seaman second class to seaman first class, real promotional opportunities were nonexistent. The pay, too, was paltry—just twenty-one dollars a month. Even black women who had migrated to California in the wake of the Fair Employment Act were making more money in the Bay Area defense industries.

A few days later, a personnel officer told Ellington that he would have to take a demotion to fireman third class. If initially he had high hopes of doing something meaningful in the Navy, Ellington's prospects now looked grim. Instead of firing boilers aboard a destroyer, he would be hardly better off than a Georgia sharecropper.

# CHAPTER 10

# Bombs for the Black Boys

In 1847, Army and Navy engineers, searching for a location for a military base, reported favorably on a point they called "Seal Bluff" on the south shore of Suisin Bay, just upriver from Richmond, California. The military base, however, was never built.

Following World War I, the Navy conducted a thorough assessment of its West Coast loading docks. Would it be able to meet the awesome needs of a Pacific fleet? The answer was no, and in 1927 the Navy began a search for a site for a modern facility on the West Coast, preferably in the San Francisco Bay area. That same year the Bureau of Yards and Docks recommended to the Board for the Development of Navy Yard Plans the building of a Bay Area depot capable of storing high explosives.

Just prior to Pearl Harbor, the Navy recognized the urgency of the situation: its West Coast facilities could handle a portion of the ammunition manufactured at the Hawthorne Army Ammunition Depot in western Nevada, but not all of it. Shipping through commercial ports was too dangerous. So the Navy began a hurried acquisition and building program in the four-state region (Colorado, Utah,

Nevada, and northern California) that made up its Twelfth Naval District. That effort led to a confidential report titled "Terminal Facilities for Shipment of Explosives—San Francisco Bay Area," which, in turn, led to Port Chicago, California. After it was deemed by the commandant of the Twelfth District to be the ideal location for an ammunition depot, on December 10, 1941, the Navy reached a decision and, under the War Powers Act, took control of 640 acres of waterfront, just one mile north of the town of Port Chicago.

Port Chicago had everything the Navy was looking for: calm, protected waters; a wide river channel that could accommodate deep-draft oceangoing ships; highways; and transcontinental rail lines (Southern Pacific and the Atchison, Topeka & Santa Fe) to facilitate the transport of munitions. Unlike Mare Island, which was the Navy's largest shipping facility on the West Coast, the Port Chicago location was isolated from major population centers. Using his new authority to green-light construction projects financed by the 300-million-dollar public works fund of the Third Supplemental National Defense Appropriation Act, Frank Knox approved the undertaking. In early February 1942, the Navy began construction. Its plan was to make Port Chicago the only war-scale shipping point on the West Coast deliberately located and designed to minimize the dangers of an accidental explosion. Because it would operate under the auspices of the over-burdened ammunition depot at Mare Island, Captain Nelson Goss, Mare Island's commanding officer, supervised the construction with the help of the Public Works Officer of the Twelfth Naval District.

Building proceeded at an urgent pace. The channel and an approach basin were dredged as a precaution. Bulldozers dug at the camel-colored hills south of the town. Fleets of trucks, working around the clock, hauled dirt by the tons to the river to backfill the salt marsh and to construct huge pier side bunkers that would one day protect ammo-laden boxcars. When the marsh was filled in, the Navy built a single pier with one dock out into the river channel. The pier, which would be used exclusively to ship ordnance, was five hundred feet long by seven feet wide with an inboard and outboard berth, each of which could accommodate the largest ammunition carriers in the Navy and three railroad tracks. By the time it opened in the late fall of 1942, the new facility had nine storage buildings, an administration building, a dispensary and ship's service store, a machine shop, a combined fire pump house and electric shop, a boiler house, a commissary, a Marine barracks, a building that held the naval barracks, four more barracks with enough beds to accommodate more than nine hundred men, magazines for ordnance storage, and twenty-seven barricaded sidings capable of holding over two hundred railroad cars. The barricades were essential. With all the high explosives and projectiles that the Navy expected to ship through Port Chicago, the depot would be a powder keg. In the event of a blast, it was hoped that the barricades would protect against a chain-reaction detonation of hundreds of boxcars loaded with tens of thousands of tons of ordnance capable of doing the kind of damage that would make the Halifax, Nova Scotia, explosion of 1917 seem small. On December 6 of that year, a French cargo ship, filled with wartime explosives, collided with another vessel in the Halifax Harbor and detonated with the force of three kilotons of TNT, killing two thousand people and injuring another nine thousand.

If being assigned to the Port Chicago Naval Ammunition Depot disappointed Boykin, Ellington, and the rest of the men from Great Lakes, they were equally disappointed with the town of Port Chicago itself. San Diego it was not. In 1940, one thousand people called it home. By the time the depot opened, it had grown, but still it was a speck of a town. In Port Chicago, people lived in modest houses, tended orderly gardens and lawns, kept their fences painted, and took pride in the fact they did not have to lock or latch their doors. Kids wandered freely from the candy store to the hills outside of town and to the fishing sloughs along the river. Although Contra Costa County was the epicenter for the sprawling Bay Area defense with its naval contracts and production facilities, for entertainment Port Chicago had little to offer the men at the depot. There were a few bars and small restaurants, a movie theater, a Legion Hall where people could go for drinks and dancing, Lichti's Fountain for ice cream sundaes, and Peterson's Pool Hall, which sold cigarettes and booze. But in the way of adult fun, especially for black men, Port Chicago might as well have been a ghost town. Though it was settled by successive waves of immigrants—first the Irish and English, then Scandinavians from the Midwest, then the Portuguese, and finally Italians—Port Chicago was not especially friendly to blacks. The men who did occasionally venture there never felt the threat of violence, but they never felt welcome either.

To go elsewhere was anything but easy. To cover the forty miles between Port Chicago and San Francisco, the men could use passenger bus service. Public buses also went to Vallejo, Pittsburg, Antioch, Oakland, Sacramento, and other cities in the San Joaquin and Sacramento valleys. But the depot, at least early on, offered no liberty buses (the only base on the West Coast not to do so) to and from these places. It did provide what the black seamen called "horse cars" or "cattle trucks" because of their resemblance to trailers used to haul farm animals, but the seamen found these demeaning and uncomfortable and refused to use them. Instead, many hitchhiked. Often they traveled in groups for protection, which made getting rides difficult.

Just eight miles from Port Chicago, Pittsburg was the closest liberty town. It was also home to a sizable black population. However, the town had one large drawback in the eyes of the Port Chicago men. It served as a major staging area for the U.S. Army. Pittsburg's Camp Stoneman was the principal jumping-off point for American soldiers bound for the Pacific Theater. In other words, Pittsburg's streets were often teeming with white American soldiers trying to get in a few last drinking bouts before being sent overseas, and sometimes that spelled trouble for the black sailors from Port Chicago. Although the line separating Pittsburg's black and white neighborhoods could not have been more clear, young, inebriated white soldiers, spoiling for a fight, often wandered into the black section of town. The black sailors did their part to sow the seeds of conflict. Some openly courted the white wives of soldiers en route to the Pacific or soldiers assigned to Camp Stoneman.

Sammie Boykin knew the town's reputation, so he avoided it like the plague. He learned his lesson about San Francisco, too. Like many of his fellow sailors, he had high hopes for "Frisco." But his experiences there disabused him of any quixotic notions about how Bay Area people might treat his kind. Usually when he entered a white establishment, the staff saw a black man rather than a sailor in a United States Navy uniform, and refused to serve him. Fortunately for Boykin, he had never cultivated a taste for liquor or women or confrontation. More often than not, he stayed behind, reading Westerns. Some of the other men at the base, however, were not gifted with Boykin's prudence or temperament.

No one, it seems, was happy to have the Port Chicago men in their midst—and no one less so than Captain Nelson Goss. Goss was a high-profile career naval officer, a Naval Academy graduate and a commander of two destroyers, the USS *O'Brien* and USS *Wadsworth,* during World War I, for which he won the coveted Navy Cross for courageous service in patrol and convoy escort duty. Between the wars he commanded a number of ships, performed shore duty assignments on both coasts, distinguished himself, and was promoted to captain. In 1938 he began his second tour as an inspector of ordnance, this time at Mare Island. In 1917 he had served in a similar position at the Watervliet Arsenal in West Troy, New York. Though he officially retired from the Navy in 1940, he stayed on active duty as commanding officer at Mare Island through the war.

In his nearly five years at Mare Island, Goss had numerous run-ins with contract stevedores—largely white—and was determined not to use them at Port Chicago. They were too expensive, governed by union regulations regarding working conditions and overtime, too influenced by unscrupulous union leaders, socialistic in their sympathies, and untrustworthy. So, instead of using professional stevedores, as was the practice at most other Bay Area facilities, he explicitly requested white enlisted personnel to man the new Port Chicago installation. What Goss got was black seamen from Great Lakes.

Though racism was prevalent among naval officers, Goss may have been more than a garden-variety bigot, and he made his displeasure clear. In his opinion, blacks were unmotivated, intellectually inferior workers, worse even than the contract stevedores. The Port

Chicago crew, in his estimation, stood out in its inability. The seamen were of the "sullen, stupid type . . . taken from the lower strata of Negro recruits after the more intelligent ones had been shipped off to trade schools." In his opinion, they would be lucky to do sixty percent of what a white worker could.

Goss was aware of their scores on the Naval General Classification Test (NGCT) and he often referred to the tests to object to the quality of men he was receiving. According to him, they were clearly of "lower mental caliber."

Worse yet, Goss protested, was that the few blacks he considered intelligent were also the "worst trouble makers," "subversives," and easy prey for agitators and radicals. Black civil rights leaders, the newspapers that aired their allegedly militant racial views, and socialist union "agitators" were his bogeymen, smuggling in inflammatory propaganda and stirring up strife among the Port Chicago enlisted men and civilian workers alike. Nevertheless, he was convinced that the depot played an important role in a "desperate war" and would perform its duties despite the shortcomings of its men. According to Goss, it was Port Chicago's responsibility to "get the job done with the tools with which we are provided," adding that the depot was "part of the Navy" and no one "should sit down and complain."

But complain he did. In a confidential letter to the Chief of Naval Personnel, dated 30 December 1942, Goss provided an assessment of those "tools" with which he had been provided. "These recruits," he wrote, "arrive with what may be described as at least an attitude of alertness for any indication of discrimination against them, which I have never previously observed in long contact with members of the colored race in the Navy. They appear particularly impressed with the idea that they are enlisted in general service and not for any work which might be regarded or classed as menial (messman branch). Some of them also manifest an attitude of asserting equality (a sort of chip on their shoulder) which is not customarily observed among colored people except in regular Negro sections of some large northern cities. . . . They, of course, have the natural characteristics of Negroes. They will loaf or straggle if permitted. They are prone to act like sheep and they are easily excitable. They require considerably more care . . . than any enlisted man I have been associated with. They are quick to resent. . . . It is not always possible to avoid some discrimination against them, despite earnest efforts. . . . They really do not take kindly to an assignment of industrial work. They reiterate that they enlisted for combat service and many of them insist that they were led to believe they would receive general service assignments when they enlisted. They frequently inquire why they can't have guns like the marines [depot guards]."

At noon on December 8, 1942, the Port Chicago's first ship, the SS *Brewer,* moored at the depot's Pier No. 1, which reached out into the Sacramento River's swirling tidal current. The following day, Sammie Boykin and the rest of the black seamen reported for their first assignment: loading the *Brewer* with ordnance. A biting wind blew in off the bay, and gray clouds, spitting rain, crawled up the river. Clad only in cotton jumpsuits, the men could feel the cold creep into their bones. It was not as chilly as November on the shores of Lake Michigan, but at least at Great Lakes the men had been issued proper gear. Here they had neither rain gear nor gloves.

Boykin had been looking forward to seeing sunny California skies and a big oceangoing ship, but the *Brewer,* like the weather, was a disappointment. It was a Liberty ship, plain and unimpressive looking. The *Brewer*'s captain was equally astonished to see an all-black work crew. Standing on the pier, Boykin could tell what he was thinking: *Hell if I'm gonna let these niggers onto my ship.* When informed by an officer that they would not be allowed to board the ship, Boykin and the rest of the men returned to the barracks.

Had Boykin, Ellington, and the others known the first thing about ordnance, they might never have left the barracks again. The Navy considered antiaircraft ammunition to be especially hazardous. Ballistite, which antiaircraft ammunition contained, was a smokeless propellant made from two high explosives—nitrocellulose and nitroglycerine. Both were known to deteriorate over time, sometimes igniting spontaneously. The men would be handling sensitive fuzes too. A manual that the Navy published late in the war declared that fuzes not only needed to be stored separately, far from high explosives, but they were never to be handled by unskilled personnel. Detonators, which formed another part of the *Brewer*'s load, were not to be treated lightly, either. This same manual advised that they be shipped and loaded in protective boxes, "carried aboard by hand and placed in their assigned stowage space prior to removal of the balance of the ammunition," and surrounded by bags of sand. Never were they to be "placed in a cargo net or sling." What's more, detonators and high-explosive material were never to be moved on the same ship.

The day after the *Brewer* pulled up to the Port Chicago pier, its captain relented and allowed the black seamen aboard his ship. Despite a small contingent of officers and civilian ordnancemen and the presence of a handful of Great Lakes graduates who had some loading experience, pandemonium reigned.

Spencer Sikes worked in the hold with the new arrivals, sharing with them what little he knew about loading ordnance. Sikes was part of the first contingent of black seamen from Great Lakes and arrived in Vallejo, California, twenty miles north of San Francisco, in the late fall of 1942. A sixteen-wheeler showed up to meet the train, and an officer loaded the Great Lakes men into the back of a trailer. Minutes later the main gate at Mare Island opened to allow the truck to enter. On the island's far end, the men peered out of the trailer, admiring the large ships and submarines that sat in various stages of construction. Many still harbored the hope of going to sea. At the very least they hoped that they might be trained as welders, plumbers, and electricians, and used right there in the bustling yard to help with the building and repair of submarines and ships.

Reality set in when Captain Goss separated the Great Lakes men from the rest of the base, banishing them to an old, rusty ferryboat that they soon learned would be tied permanently to the dock. Aware of the irony of sailors being confined to a ship that would never go anywhere, the men dubbed it the "USS Never Sail."

As soon as DeWhitt Jamison laid his eyes on the USS Never Sail, he knew that his dream was fantasy. Jamison started working at a Civilian Conservation Corps camp in South Carolina at the age of fourteen. After Pearl Harbor, when the government discharged the CCC men needed for the war effort, he joined the Navy, hoping to see the world and to get an education. At Great Lakes he discovered that the Navy was as segregated as South Carolina.

It did not take long, either, for Spencer Sikes to realize that all the high ideals and inspiring speeches at Great Lakes were empty words. At Mare Island, blacks were not even allowed to use the heads aboard the ships. In case there was any doubt in the minds of the Great Lakes men about how they would be treated, they only had to read the signs: NO BLACKS ALLOWED. To go to the bathroom they had to walk a half-mile and use the restroom set aside for "their kind." One day, while loading a ship, and disgusted with the situation, they simply stopped working. Befuddled, the officers did not know how to respond. Eventually, Captain Goss intervened. His solution was to divide the ship's head, roping off a small section for the black loaders, and a larger section for the ship's white crew members and the white loading officers. Sikes laughed at the absurdity of it. The head was nothing more than a long, unwalled trough with water running through it. On one side of the rope, the black loaders were allowed to relieve themselves within whispering distance of the whites assigned to the other side.

The first time Sikes saw a net of bombs hanging above his hold, it scared him half to death. "I'll never make it back home," he thought. "I'll never see my mom again, or my brother and sisters." The winch driver, working with loud, grinding steam winches that puffed and coughed, tried to steady the load, lowering it as slowly as he could. When it picked up speed, he rode the foot brake, struggling to keep the net from tumbling two stories into the hold of the ship. Sikes looked up and saw the net pitch back and forth. He said a prayer that the winchman knew what he was doing and that the boom could stand up to the weight of the bombs. When the load hit the deck with a thud, he was sure he was a dead man.

The sight of torpedoes and bombs still scared him, but on the *Brewer* he tried to stay calm and put on a brave face for the new seamen. The key, he told them, was to handle the weapons as gently as possible.

Despite the inexperience of the Port Chicago men, five days after arriving, the Brewer had her entire load, and at three in the afternoon on December 13, 1942, she sailed for Noumea, New Caledonia, which was 6,200 miles away. Boykin, for one, was relieved to see her go. If good fortune smiled on her and she could avoid prowling Japanese submarines and the high-seas storms that could break her in half, she would arrive in Noumea twenty days later with 3,800 tons of munitions bound for Admiral "Bull" Halsey's forces in the Solomon Islands.

By the summer of 1943, Naval Ammunition Depots (NADs) were becoming hotbeds of discontent. The single biggest reason stemmed from the Navy's policy of concentrating large populations of blacks at depots, where the ability to strike for new ratings (even openings in the unpopular cooks' and bakers' positions were severely restricted) and black leadership opportunities were almost nonexistent. The Navy's rationale for confining blacks to NADs was to maintain harmony. At the depots, it said, "the issue of social mixture would not be acute."

No place was more troubled than Port Chicago. Lieutenant Raymond Robert "Bob" White, who was one of the few officers at the depot who had managed to establish a rapport with the black seamen, was alarmed by the developments. In a letter to her in-laws, dated July 14, 1943, Bob White's wife, Inez, tells of a recent disaster. "I don't know how much of this I'm supposed to be telling," she writes, uncertain of whether or not her husband would approve of her sharing what he had told her in confidence, "but I know it won't go any farther than your house—it certainly wouldn't make good publicity for the U.S. Navy. . . . They've been having a lot of excitement over at the base in the last week. The first thing that happened was that a colored boy drowned while they were loading a ship." The depot's War Diary for July 5 confirms the details of Inez's story, stating, "At 2150, Spriggs, John Walter (Negro), S2c, 644 79 77, V6, USNR, accidentally fell from the dock into Suisun Bay, while on duty and was drowned," and adding that the USS *Sangay* was "loaded and discharged" on the same day.

Inez White continues, "That night, the colored boys mutinied—they wouldn't work because they said one of the officers could have saved the boy." Then she adds, "You know, that the extreme punishment for mutiny is death—and that according to Navy Law they should have been court martialed." Although "mutiny" might have been an exaggeration, this was not the first time Port Chicago's black seamen refused to work. They often grumbled about conditions, racist officers, a lack of promotional opportunity, and inedible food, and most often their complaints fell on deaf ears. So occasionally, as a group, they staged slowdowns or work stoppages. Individuals could and did go AWOL, but as a group they resorted to what Mrs. White refers to as "mutiny" as their only real form of protest. Whether her thoughts reflect her husband's feelings, Inez White does not say. What she does write about is what happened the next morning.

According to her, Lieutenant Lee Cordiner apparently decided that he was going to teach the "colored boys" a lesson. Cordiner had been at the depot longer than any of the other lieutenants. He was a Naval Reserve officer who in civilian life had been a newspaper accountant. When the black loaders made their way to the mess hall the following morning, Cordiner yelled, "Halt!" and then told them that if they were not going to work, they sure as hell were not going to eat. Unintimidated by his ultimatum, the men pushed past him and entered the mess hall anyway. Later, according to Inez White, "some of the colored fellows threatened his life."

When Captain Goss got wind of the turmoil, he called for an investigation. Although Inez White uses the loaded word "mutiny," it is likely that Captain Goss wanted to spare the Navy an onerous court case and also wanted to avoid the notoriety that a mutiny charge would have brought him and Port Chicago. Perhaps, too, he understood the seriousness of the accusation. According to Colonel William Winthrop, who in 1886 wrote an authoritative treatise on military law that the Navy still used as its legal standard, mutiny was "the gravest and most criminal of the offenses known to the military code." Goss would be obliged to show that the black seamen had "a deliberate purpose to usurp, subvert or override superior military authority."

What Goss did instead was to order a deck court. According to the Navy's *Bluejackets' Manual,* a deck court could be ordered for the trial of enlisted men by the commandant of a navy yard, and should be initiated "for offenses not warranting punishment" severe enough to be handled by a summary court-martial. Goss sentenced eighteen of the men to an unprecedented twenty days in the brig on a bread-and-water diet, informing them that if they refused they would be subject to summary courts-martial. (Mrs. White adds in her letter that Goss should have been tougher.)

Perhaps after sentencing them, the captain returned to his quarters and read Article 24 of the Articles for the Government of the U.S. Navy (Rocks and Shoals) and realized that legally he was allowed to give them "solitary confinement, on bread and water, not exceeding five days." So, after only a few days, he released them. His alleged leniency angered Port Chicago's white enlisted men and officers, who may not have understood Goss's legal restrictions. "The whole place," Inez informs her in-laws, "is an awful mess with the black enlisted men accusing the officers of discrimination and the officers carrying side arms for protection."

And things got worse. Just one week later a white officer locked the door to his room and shot himself in the head. His suicide rattled everyone, but no one more than Lieutenant Cordiner. According to Inez White, the agitated lieutenant kept saying, "That's what this place does to you."

# Like a Dog on a Bone

When the train pulled into Jacksonville, North Carolina, Edgar Lee Huff, along with four other black recruits he had been traveling with, got off. At the Jacksonville station, a white corporal waited in an idling truck with his arm resting on the window. When Huff walked up and gave his name, the corporal flicked his cigarette onto the ground. "All right," he said, "Let's go, then."

Huff and the other four walked around to the back of the truck, stepped on the bumper, and climbed under the canvas flap. The corporal stuck his head out the window and looked back. "What the hell do you think you're doing? Get out." When Huff and the others jumped out, he gunned the engine, spattering dirt and stones in their direction. "Follow me!" he yelled.

Choking on the dust stirred up by the truck, Huff tried to keep pace. Eventually tall pine trees flanked a narrow road. After a mile, the road ended at a large clearing—what would eventually be called the intersection of Montford Landing Road and Harlem Drive—that looked as if it had been hacked out of the jungle. Soaked in sweat, with the sun beating down on him, Huff shaded his eyes. *So this is home,* he thought.

Home was Montford Point (originally Mumford Point), located on the western end of Marine Barracks, New River. Montford Point was the Marines' lone boot-camp training facility for African Americans, the equivalent of Great Lakes' Camp Robert Smalls. Not long after it opened in late August 1942, Edgar Huff was the only black recruit from the state of Alabama, the product of Marine Corps Commandant Thomas Holcomb's reluctant decision to accept "colored male citizens of the United States between the ages of 17 and 29." Holcomb had his orders straight from the president of the United States and the secretary of the navy, and by fall 1942, he was expected to have the 1,200 recruits needed to man a black defense battalion, which would be in charge of protecting the bases that made up America's supply line in the Pacific.

Late that afternoon, a heavily muscled corporal started to yell. "All right, you black maggots. Fall out here on the road. Now move, move, move." When he screamed "Tenshun," Huff knew enough to stand ramrod straight. The corporal checked the muster roll and then walked up to Huff, the cords of his bull neck straining against his khaki shirt, the blood rushing to his eyes in anger. At six feet four inches, and well over two hundred pounds, Huff was hard to intimidate. But the corporal had worked himself into a state. Just inches from Huff's face—Huff had never been that close to a white man before—he spat, "Boy, I just know you know how to say 'yes, sir.' You been saying it all your life. Can you teach the rest of these assholes how y'all say it back down in Alabama?" Then the corporal marched the recruits to the edge of a nearby woods. There he told them they could stand and shout "yes, sir," until hell froze over.

The big trees hid it, but the recruits knew it was there, just a few feet into the woods, a bug- and snake-infested bayou. As near as Huff could tell, the camp was nothing but dark sloughs and thick woods. In fact, it was little more than five and a half acres of swamp and flooded timber, bound by Scales Creek on the east and the New River on the west. Most of the white Marines, on the other side of the river, did not even know that Montford Point existed. The two worlds could not have been more different. On one side of the river, young white Marines worshiped Betty Grable and participated in a tradition that was almost two centuries old. On the other, young men dreamed of Lena Horne and of becoming the first black Marines ever.

As the sun fell, and the sticky day turned into night, the air hummed and buzzed with the sounds of millions of insects. The air was so wet that Huff felt as though he needed gills to breathe. While mosquitoes preyed on them, and frogs piped incessantly, he and his fellow black recruits yelled "yes, sir" until they were hoarse, until their voiceboxes ached and their legs grew wobbly. Hours later the corporal returned. "You turds ain't gonna make it. I'll see to it personally." Then he added, "I will see to it there will never be a black-ass Marine."

On his second night of boot camp, the white drill instructors rousted Huff and the other black recruits from their beds at 1:00 a.m., and ushered them outside. The men stood, arms stiff, chests thrown out, legs spread slightly, stomachs in. "You may as well go over the hill," one of the DIs snickered. Another drill instructor chimed in, "The best thing *you people* can do is sneak out of here after the lights go out. Nobody'll miss you. Hell, no one even knows you're here. Why try to play ball on a team that doesn't want you? Just leave quietly and shove the hell off for home. You may as well pack up your shit and git. You shitbirds ain't gonna make it."

The NCOs sent the recruits back to their huts. Scared and disillusioned, many of them started packing. The college boys and the Army Reserve officers who had resigned commissions to become Marines were really pissed off. They didn't have to take this shit! Who in the hell did these uneducated, rednecked, moonshine-drinkin' motherfuckers think they were?

Huff had always relied on his size and physical strength to prove his worth. He had never been an outspoken man, but now he cleared his throat and searched for the courage to say what he felt.

The day he entered camp, the DI had tried to intimidate him and chase him back to Alabama, but Huff was not going anywhere. He had arrived at Montford Point with holes in his shoes, nothing more than a quarter in pocket change, and in clothes he had worn for five days straight. In Gadsden he had grown up without running water, using an outhouse with seed books as toilet paper. And now the DI was telling him that things were going to get worse? How much worse could they get?

So Huff spoke up. "They want us to fail. Don't let anybody push you out of the Marines. I've found a chance to be a man and I am going to hold to it like a dog on a bone." Two other men joined Huff. Then Huff added, "You want to leave, you'll have to go through us."

The next morning, when the drill sergeant blew his whistle and screamed, "Hit the deck, you black bastards," men came pouring out of the green, prefab huts. He had them line up and counted them in formation. All the black recruits were present. Not a single one—not the college boys or the reserve officers—had left in the middle of the night.

Angered by their impudence, the sergeant stared coldly. "I'm going to make sure you wish you had never joined the Marine Corps."

Raised in northern Alabama, in the heart of the Jim Crow South, Edgar Huff could count on poverty and racism the way white folks counted on the sun to rise every day. Blacks joked that the Great Depression was a white misfortune. In or out of the Depression, blacks in the South lived the same—poor—and the Huffs were no exception. A pall of coal dust often hung over the area hills and trees. The Huffs' house rested at the foot of one of those steep hills. When it rained hard the water came pouring down, pooling around the foundation and in the yard like thick gumbo, nearly sweeping the structure away. Emily Lee Huff, Edgar's mother, would say to her young boy, "God never gives us a task or a burden without giving us the means to see it through. It's gonna change some day, Edgar. Don't you worry. It's gonna change." Only it never did.

It was especially bad in winter, when the Huffs had no coal for their stove. Edgar would tote a sack and go around to the white houses in Gadsden, the ones with coal furnaces, and ask if he could go to their bin, though he made it clear he would be grateful for anything, cinders or clinkers.

Edgar hated asking for coal. "Mr. Reed," he'd say, "could I please go out ta you ash pile and see if I ken find 'nough coke for a fire tonight?" Mr. Reed was no "nigger lover," but he was a kindhearted man and often said yes, but some of the others, even the Jenkinses, for whom his mother worked as a domestic, would almost always turn him away, no matter how cold it was. It was the Depression, and few families were in a position to be giving away coal. On those nights when he would return home empty-handed, Edgar would build a small wood fire that gave off little heat, and he and his mother would drag their chairs across the cold plank floor as close to the stove as they could. They would eat their dinner quickly, before the heat disappeared, and go to bed not long after sunset. On nights when he managed to bring home a small sack of coal, Edgar would sit by the fire with his mother while she told stories about the daddy he barely remembered.

When President Woodrow Wilson asked for a declaration of war against Germany, W. E. B. Du Bois urged young black men to take up arms, saying, "Our country is at war . . . if this is OUR country, then this is OUR war." Edgar Huff Sr. heeded Du Bois's call. Raised among Creek Indians—in fact, Edgar senior was part Creek—in the rough ridges of Attalla, Alabama, Edgar senior became fluent in the language. Much like the Navajo "code talkers" of World War II, Huff put that knowledge to use during World War I, serving as a corporal in intelligence and transmitting secret messages for the Army's Signal Corps. It was a war that he had been determined to fight, though it was one he could have avoided. Before the American Indian Citizenship Act of 1924, Native Americans were not considered citizens and were not obligated to serve.

Edgar junior could never understand why his father went to fight in a faraway place like Germany. Not knowing whether to be mad at his father or proud, Edgar junior once asked his mother as they sat near the stove, "Why couldn't Daddy just stay home and fight some white folks uptown?"

When Edgar senior returned home after the war, he hoped that his service would entitle him to pursue the kind of life he wanted. His postwar life, however, was both disappointing and short. He felt that he had earned from white America some measure of appreciation and acceptance, but he, like thousands of other black soldiers, instead encountered full-blown animosity. Rage boiled, erupting in race riots from Texas to South Carolina to Illinois. James Weldon Johnson, the civil rights activist, dubbed the summer of 1919 the "Red Summer" because of the blood spilled on the streets of cities across the country.

Not long after the birth of his son, the elder Huff died from mustard-gas wounds sustained in France. With no one to support her, Emily Huff took a job as a domestic with a prominent local family. She pumped water, scoured, scraped, swept, cooked, and cooked some more, snapping beans and twisting the necks of chickens, digging the eyes out of potatoes, shucking corn, and kneading dough for what amounted to a pittance. The Jenkins family, who employed her, had a reputation for being wealthy but stingy. People in town laughed that the family still had fifty-five cents of the first dollar they ever made.

One day, Edgar woke up to find his mother too weak to get out of bed. Edgar begged her to let him get the doctor. She objected, saying they did not have the money. Edgar sat at the side of her bed, holding her hand, until she fell asleep. When a cousin stopped by, Edgar had him watch over his mother while he ran to town and brought the doctor back with him.

When the doctor finished examining Emily Huff, he took the sixteen-year-old Huff aside. "Son," he said, "your mama is mighty sick. She needs attention," then he paused, "or you're going to lose her."

This time it was Edgar's turn to comfort his mother. "Don't you worry, Mama," he said. "Don't you worry none."

Edgar went to the Republic Steel Company in Alabama City, two and a half miles from Gadsden. A long line greeted him. It seemed to

Edgar that nearly the whole state of Alabama was looking for work, white and black alike. The odds of his finding a job did not look good. Edgar took a chance and walked to the front of the line.

"Didn't you see the men in line, boy?" the chief timekeeper asked.

"I did, sir," Edgar responded. "But my mother is ill and I need a good job bad."

"Times is tough," the man responded. "I don't need another nigger when so many white men are out of work."

Huff felt the desperation rising in him. "I'm eighteen years old, sir," he lied. "And I need the job bad or my momma's gonna die." Huff had not expected the emotion, but when he said those words, tears trickled down his cheeks.

The man gave Huff a "black boys need to know their place" look. What he did not need was an uppity nigger. What he did need, however, was a worker, and Huff looked as though he could do the work of two men. Whatever the case, Edgar left Alabama City with a job. The following day he was processed into the company's health insurance plan. Later that week, Mrs. Emily Lee Huff got the medical attention that quite probably saved her life.

Edgar had dropped out of school, and at sixteen he was working eleven hours a day, six days a week, for $1.25 a day. A bus ran regularly from Gadsden to the steel mill, but the fare was five cents each way. Rather than spend the dime on the round-trip, Edgar walked. It didn't take him long to wear out the soles of his cheap shoes; the October rains and the deep gullies of red mud were especially hard on them. Slipping cardboard into the bottoms, Edgar covered five miles a day, over three hundred days a year, returning home shortly before midnight. Edgar was no stranger to hard work, but the walk to and from the mill, in sleet, rain, and heat, hardened him.

On June 25, 1942, a foreman at Republic Steel approached Edgar, waving a paper. He poked his finger at a headline that said the Marine Corps was accepting blacks. "What do you think about that, Mr. Tough Man?" Edgar knew he was being baited. What the foreman didn't say was, "Nigger, you ain't tough enough for the Marines." But that was the implication.

The next morning Edgar sat with his mother at the kitchen table. He could hardly contain his enthusiasm. He told her the news, and said that he intended to sign up. She shook her head. "I forbid you to join." Mrs. Emily Lee Huff was a presence. More than once she said to her grown son, "You mind your tongue. You ain't too big for me to take the ironing cord after you."

Edgar did not argue. He had anticipated her reaction, and had already resolved to disobey her. Four months later, on October 10, 1942, an envelope containing a meal pass and a train ticket to New River, North Carolina, arrived in the mail.

# CHAPTER 12

# A War of Their Own

When Edgar Huff left for Montford Point, his mother took one of his large, callused hands in hers. Holding it gently, and stroking it as if he were not her six-foot four-inch son, but still a kid, she looked into his eyes and said, "Edgar, you don't need to die to be your daddy's boy."

Edgar would never forget that. Eventually some of the black recruits crapped out. But not Huff. Determined to prove that a black man could take anything the DIs could dish out, he pushed himself through boot camp. At night, after lights out, he went to the dimly lit bathroom and sat on the toilet and read books that he had borrowed from the college boys in his platoon.

Huff was in the 9th Platoon, which was run by the meanest, toughest man Huff had ever encountered. The other DIs were hard on the recruits, but no one could compare with the man they called Chuck, an "old line" Marine for whom discipline was gospel. The thing Chuck liked to do more than anything else was run. He ran for enjoyment; he ran to punish. Gifted with the endurance of a marathoner, he could go forever, and he would push the men till they were ready to drop. "Run, run, run," he would taunt them. "Run, you niggers, run."

In December 1942, after eight weeks of training, Huff finished boot camp. The entire group of 198 graduates had something to be proud of. After two weeks of marksmanship training and a week of live firing at the rifle range near Stone Bay at the former Marine barracks, New River, now called Camp Lejeune, the men got a chance to fire for record. Many of them qualified either as marksmen or sharpshooters and displayed their badges on their uniforms. Sixteen of the men, including Huff, received promotions to private first class and sewed rank stripes on those same uniforms. Huff had definitely earned the stripe. For the last few weeks of boot camp, he acted as assistant DI, what was called an "acting jack," to the NCO of the Special Enlisted Staff (SES), a group of handpicked white senior non-commissioned officers that oversaw boot training. In the final week, Huff took over command of the platoon.

Huff and the other graduates decided to go to Jacksonville, or as they called it, "J-ville," to catch a bus to one of North Carolina's larger towns, where they could celebrate their accomplishment and blow off steam in style. Just a few days after boot camp ended, they left the camp's main gate. Jacksonville was not one of the politely segregated Southern towns where whites and blacks accepted a kind of genteel separation. It had a reputation as a mean, small-minded place.

When the townspeople saw hundreds of black Marines walking boldly down the middle of the street on the white side of the tracks, they trembled. All their long-standing fears about being overrun by black men had finally come true. It was not as if J-ville had not seen its share of Marines. White Marines kept the town's stores, whore-houses, bars, restaurants, and theaters afloat. But black Marines were another matter.

Terrified merchants bolted their doors. To hell with J-ville, Huff thought. Let's get out of here. He led the men in the direction of the bus station. When the ticket agent saw them coming, he, too, closed his office.

Now the group was angry. They were United States Marines, and they could not even buy a bus ticket. Some threatened to tear down the building with their bare hands.

It was 2:00 p.m. when Huff called the commanding officer of Montford Point, Colonel Samuel Woods. When Huff reached the colonel's office, he was transferred to Woods himself. "Sir," he said, "this is PFC Huff, and I feel that I need to apprise the colonel that we have a bit of a situation down here at the bus station. We are not being allowed to ride."

"Just hold tight. I'll be there," Woods replied.

Minutes later, the colonel appeared and calmed the men. Shortly after, trucks showed up to take them to the liberty destinations of their choice. About half chose to go to the Negro USO in Wilmington. Others went to New Bern and Kinston. Under strict orders from Colonel Woods, the drivers waited in their trucks until the men were ready to return to camp.

By mid-December, Huff was excited as he prepared for his first furlough as a full-fledged Marine. Emily Lee Huff was eager, too. She would have her boy home for a week. She could not wait to make his favorite meals and to hear his stories and to show him the scrapbook she was putting together. She had already pasted in the two postcards that he had sent her from boot camp, addressed to the "Dearest Mother in the World, Mrs. Emily Huff."

When Huff boarded the bus in J-ville, he felt proud. He had been pushed and challenged and taunted. Now he was going home a member of the United States Marines.

In Atlanta, a place that many considered to be the South's most progressive city, Huff got off the bus to stretch his legs and noticed two white Marine Corps military policemen watching him. Walking in his direction, one of them called out, "Boy, where'd you get that uniform? You musta stole it. There ain't no niggers in our Marine Corps!" When Huff showed them his leave papers, they accused him of impersonating a Marine, claiming the documents were forged. It was Christmas Day, Huff told them, and he was returning home to see his mother. He pleaded with them, "I'm going to Gadsen, Alabama."

"You ain't going nowhere but jail," one of them said.

While Huff was trying to reason with them, one got behind him and cracked his patrol stick over the back of his neck. Too dazed to resist, Huff fell, and they dragged him out of the station.

The MPs took the money he had in his pocket, his watch, and his papers. When Huff regained his senses he realized that he was in the drunk tank. When the jailers came by, he pleaded with them to let him out. He would make a phone call and prove to them that he was a Marine. "The Marine Corps don't take niggers," they yelled. "Now, keep that black mouth of yours shut till you get before the judge."

For three days the two policemen kept Huff locked up. Then, on December 28, a representative of the 6th Marine Corps District came down, verified that Huff was indeed a Marine, and insisted that the jail release him. Now that Huff was out, he realized that the police had not returned his watch or his money, and without money it would be impossible for him to make it home. Wandering down the street, Huff passed a pawnshop. The only things he had of value were the shoes on his feet. So he sold them for three dollars.

Walking barefoot in the gravel at the edge of the southwest highway, Huff hoped for a ride, but was determined to walk all the way to Alabama if he had to. After all, he was a United States Marine. And he had not just made it through boot camp; he had distinguished himself. The saying was that if a black man could make it through recruit training, enduring the daily indignities on top of being pushed to his physical limits, he was tough enough to "march through hell singing a song." So if he had to walk home, he would.

At a truck stop, he took a break to warm his feet and tend to the cut on his head, which had broken open and was bleeding. There he struck up a conversation with a man who was driving a cotton truck to Alabama. *What the heck,* Huff thought, *I got nothin' to lose.* So he asked the man for a ride. The man looked him up and down. "Yeah," he replied. "Only I can't let you ride inside. You gotta ride in back." It was December, and Huff knew it would be a long, cold trip. But it might be the only chance he had to get home, so he took it. Huff sat on top of the bales of cotton, trying to hide from the wind. By the time he made it to Gadsden, his feet were so cold he could barely feel them.

Huff returned to Montford Point on January 2. Colonel Woods called him into his office the following day. The black Marines referred to the commander as "the great white father of everybody." They joked that if the sun were shining and the colonel said it was raining, their job was to put on raincoats. If everyone knew it was 8:00 a.m., but the colonel said it was 2200, they damn well better get sleepy fast. Woods explained to Huff that white Marines were getting ready to be sent overseas and that he and some of the others would have to take over the training of the black troops. In other words, the colonel continued, congratulations were in order. Woods was making Huff a legitimate DI in the Recruit Depot in charge of the 16th Platoon. The plan was for him to spend a few weeks in school learning to be a drill instructor, and then to head up the platoon.

Huff had hoped to stay with the 51st Composite Defense Battalion and go overseas to man the big guns, but now he had a new home and a demanding job ahead of him. As a result of President Roosevelt's December 1, 1942, decision to make Selective Service the routine source of recruits for all branches of the military, one thousand African American draftees would walk through the gates at Montford Point every month. All would have to go through eight weeks of boot camp, and Huff was one of the men charged with training them.

As if driven by the devil himself, Huff pushed his men unrelentingly. Together with some of the other DIs, he put together a program that was as good as any the white Marines across the New River got. Huff took them through armed and unarmed training that included hip-level quick firing, bayonet, knife, and club fighting, judo, camouflage, and conditioning exercises, and demanded nothing less than perfection, ignoring the reality that the Marine Corps never intended for them to be fully qualified infantrymen. They would be limited to noncombatant roles in radar, gunnery, carpentry, mechanics, transport, cooking and baking, and supply.

By April 1943 the Montford Point DIs were churning out men. The problem was that because blacks could not serve in a combat role once recruit training was over, there was almost nowhere for them to go. Among Huff and the other DIs, the running joke was that they (blacks) needed a war all to themselves.

Seeing the potential for a crisis, Secretary of the Navy Frank Knox intervened, authorizing the creation of a second defense battalion, the 52nd, as well as a Messman Branch to be commanded by a veteran of World War I and a restaurateur from Albany, New York.

Recognizing that a surplus of black Marines still posed problems, the Corps sought something more than a stopgap solution. By early March 1943, it had found its answer: Marine depot and ammunition companies. The Marine Corps, like the Navy, had been using white combat troops in a supply role. By opening new supply units to blacks, as the Navy was doing, the Corps could simultaneously send white Marines overseas and alleviate the problem of too many black Marines with nowhere to go.

The 1st Marine Depot Company was activated on March 8, 1943. Between March and December 1943, the Corps created ten more depot companies. The companies were labor outfits charged with loading and unloading ships and hauling ammunition and supplies to frontline troops. They would be involved at every point along the supply line, moving cargo from the United States through rear area and forward support bases, over the beaches, and to frontline Marines.

The ammunition companies were intended to be a step up from the depot companies. Although they, too, performed supply jobs, their members were better trained, receiving two months' education in ammunition handling and limited infantry instruction.

For Huff, the new companies represented a source of frustration. Why did the Marines refuse to send them into battle? Annoyed, Huff told his buddy Gilbert Johnson, "All they do is just take the new men, no matter what their qualifications, and send them to 'tote dat bale' and load that ammo." Hashmark, whom the men affectionately called "the Preacher" because of his predilection for inspirational speeches and his positive outlook, emphasized the need for patience. Their job, he said, was to turn out the best men they could until the Marine Corps recognized its mistake.

As Montford Point expanded and talented black NCOs were being groomed for positions of responsibility, Huff hit the fast track. On April 17, 1943, he made sergeant, and Colonel Woods called him in to his office to congratulate him.

"Go wet down your stripes," the colonel encouraged Huff. "You deserve it."

Huff could not have been prouder. Here he was, a poor kid from the sticks of Alabama who had never even heard of the Marines before he joined up, and now he was a respected sergeant with a future.

Deciding that he would follow the colonel's advice, Huff went into Jacksonville, planning to catch a bus to Wilmington. When he got there, a carnival was going on, and he bought himself a bag of popcorn. Eating his popcorn and enjoying the day, he saw six white Marines approaching him. Usually MPs walked the town. After some early scuffles, Colonel Woods had taken the precaution of sending them into Jacksonville on a regular basis. There they patrolled the bars and the restaurants where white and black Marines were likely to clash. On this day, however, there were no MPs in sight. *Damn*, Huff thought. *This ain't gonna be good.*

The Marines circled him. Their leader was a first lieutenant. The others were sergeants or PFCs. All wore the Guadalcanal patch. Huff had never seen the patch before and was fascinated by it. *These men are heroes*, Huff thought, and for a moment he harbored the hope that they were not looking for trouble.

The lieutenant motioned to Huff's stripes. "Nigger, who gave you them?"

*What's this guy doing?* Huff thought. He had been taught to revere Guadalcanal veterans. And lieutenants were like Lord God Almighty.

Had the man not used the word "nigger," Huff might have answered. Instead he did not say a word. The lieutenant asked again, goading Huff. "Nigger, I'm talking to you. Who gave you them stripes?"

Now Huff was mad. There would be no more pickin' the white folks cotton and beggin' their pardon. "Your mama," he replied.

At that, the lieutenant reached out to pull the stripes off Huff's sleeve. Huff seized his wrist and shoulder and broke the lieutenant's arm across his leg. Then the sergeants rushed him. Huff pounded them with uppercuts and both fell to the ground. When one of the PFCs tried to tackle him, Huff crushed his ribs with a punch and stomped him while he lay in the street. The other two ran off to find a military policeman.

As Huff smoothed his clothes and wiped his sweaty forehead, Montford Point's white provost sergeant ran up to him. "God-dammit," he said. "All this trouble. I gotta take you back to camp." The sergeant knew Huff, knew him to be a good man and a dedicated Marine. But he had gone too far.

"I ain't goin' no damn where," Huff exclaimed. The adrenaline surged. No white man was going to tell him what to do.

"You've gotta come back to camp," the provost sergeant persisted.

Huff stood his ground. "I'll be back in camp on Monday," he replied. "You can put me in jail then, but you aren't going to put me in jail today."

On Monday morning, Huff was training his platoon when a warrant officer walked up to him. Huff snapped him a salute and then turned the platoon over to his assistant DI.

The officer looked at him. "Nothing wrong with you?" he asked.

"No, sir," Huff answered.

"Well, good God Almighty. The colonel wants to see you now. He says he's got people lined up there that you been fighting. I knew it couldn't be you."

"It was me," Huff corrected him.

"But there are six of them," the warrant officer said. "And there's nothing wrong with you?"

When Huff entered Colonel Woods's office, he saluted. "Sergeant Huff reporting as ordered, sir."

The colonel got up from his desk and looked Huff up and down. "Did you have some trouble on Friday?"

"Yes, sir," Huff answered.

"Just what were you using?"

"What?" Huff asked. "I didn't use nothing but my hands. That's all I had, just my hands."

"They say you must have been using brass knuckles," Woods replied. Huff had never even seen a pair of brass knuckles.

"No, sir," he answered.

"What happened, then?" the colonel inquired. When Huff finished telling him his version of the story, Colonel Woods fastened his eyes on him. "I don't want you starting fights." Then he walked out into the hall where the other Marines were now standing. "When you get back," he said, "make sure to tell the rest of them damn men over there that they better let my boys alone. Now get off this post."

Later Woods assembled all the Montford Point men in the theater. He told them about the incident, and urged them to be careful in town. Then he said that he did not want them looking for trouble, but if a fight did break out, the last thing he wanted was for them to come back to base like a bunch of whipped dogs. If Huff and the others did not know it before, they did now: "The great white father of everybody" had their backs.

By the summer of 1943, Huff was growing restless. Sometimes it felt as if he were taking on not only white cracker Marines and the racist Corps, but the whole goddamn country. He wanted to be overseas fighting. With one thousand African Americans coming through the Montford Point gates every month via Selective Service, however, the training facility was teeming with recruits. Colonel Woods could not spare him.

Huff and the other drill instructors pushed themselves to the brink of exhaustion. They did not take any shortcuts, either. White Marines were doing all the fighting, and black Marines were providing the labor, but Huff was committed to putting his black "boots" through an intense eight-week training program, making certain that they measured up in every way to Marine Corps standards.

To the recruits it seemed sometimes as if the sergeant were possessed. They all knew his reputation. He was the giant of a man who had single-handedly whipped a handful of combat-hardened white Marines. Not only had Colonel Woods not disciplined him for fighting, he assembled all of Montford Point at the theater, stood on the stage, and then praised him in front of everyone. After that incident, Huff achieved godlike status. Not every black Marine believed the story. But whether or not they believed it, they all loved telling it. Now they had a myth of their own.

By late 1943 there was a palpable sense of enthusiasm as all of Montford Point geared up for Secretary Knox's visit. Even Huff felt it. The secretary of the Navy had never been to the facility. On the morning Knox arrived, Huff and his fellow drill instructors had nearly two thousand men standing in formation by 4:00 a.m. When the secretary did his inspection, the men did Huff proud, standing as tall and straight as rows of corn. Later that morning, Knox went out to Onslow Point. Accompanied by General Holcomb, he watched as a crew from the 51st Defense Battalion went through firing exercises. Using a 90-mm gun, the crew fired on a sleeve target being towed overhead by a plane, and to everyone's astonishment hit it within a minute. Commandant Holcomb was nearly speechless. Turning to the secretary, he said, "I think they're ready now."

Later that afternoon, Knox returned to the drilling field to observe some of Montford Point's more seasoned recruits demonstrate advanced training, unarmed combat, and bayonet skills. Huff swelled with pride when he saw Knox talking with the officer in charge of training, Lieutenant Colonel Holdahl. The men had performed well, and he imagined what the secretary might be saying. Later one of the Marine sergeants who overheard the exchange filled him in on Knox's remarks.

"Now, all that's fine," the secretary had said to Lieutenant Colonel Holdahl. "But these people don't need all that stuff. They don't need all this learning. . . . Teach these people how to move at an orderly pace and courtesy and discipline, because what they are going to do is unload and load ships and supplies for the fighting troops. You're wasting your time with that other stuff." Huff burned inside when he heard what the secretary had said. It was hard not to curse the very men he was serving.

# CHAPTER 13

# A Desolate Place

Percy Robinson Jr. was inducted into active service in the Navy on July 10, 1943. The day after being inducted, Robinson left for Great Lakes, but not before his mother gave him a piece of advice. "Take care of yourself," she said to him. "Keep God in your prayers." Then she added, "And don't let the white man lynch you."

Percy Robinson was born in the heart of Chicago's Black Belt just five years after the Chicago race riots. The Black Belt (later it acquired the spiffed-up name Bronzeville), which ran down State Street from 22nd to 55th Street, and was bordered on the east by Cottage Grove and on the west by the Rock Island Railroad, was where the vast majority of Chicago's blacks lived. Here, like most people, Percy Robinson Sr. scrambled to make ends meet. After serving in World War I and coming north to Chicago, he cobbled together a life in the stockyards, painted houses, and made moonshine. It was Prohibition and bootlegging was illegal, but the neighborhood's white policemen looked the other way as long as he paid his tribute.

Ruth Robinson chipped in, too, throwing the best "rent parties" around with good cheap soul food—fried chicken, buttered corn, chitlins, red beans and rice, gumbo, collard greens, banana pudding, and sweet potato pone—bootleg whiskey, and a room in the back that could be rented by the hour. On the morning of the party, Ruth Robinson removed much of the furniture from the apartment, rolled up the rugs, and put folding chairs in the rooms. For the price of some corn liquor, she hired family friends as bouncers. At night, dozens of people packed into the apartment to flirt, drink, dance, gamble, eat, play the Robinsons' piano, and listen to the jukebox until the wee hours of the morning. By Sunday afternoon, after they collected their jukebox coins, the Robinsons had enough to pay the rent.

Like his parents, Percy junior was a "born hustler." Over summer vacation, he sold vegetables and fruit on the street. Waking at 3:00 a.m., he would help his cousin hitch the horse to the wagon and bargain with the Jewish vendors in what was called "Jewtown" on Halsted Street. He would haggle until the wagon was full, and then he and his cousin would ride down the streets and alleys of the Black Belt, peddling whatever they had bought that morning. At night he would turn over most of his money to his mother.

Young Percy was a scrapper in the ring, too. Although he was not big, he was a plucky kid, boxing flyweight on the Catholic Youth Organization team that combined fighting with Bible study. Some of the boxers were Golden Gloves hopefuls, but Percy never had that kind of ability. He did not move his feet fast enough, his jab was less than lightning quick, and he never developed the kind of ease in the ring that a good fighter had to have. But he was all work. He devoted himself to the speed bag to quicken his reflexes, and hit the heavy bag like a demon.

In the summer of 1937 the Robinson home, like much of Chicago, was abuzz with excitement. Jimmy Braddock, the "Cinderella Man" who had won the heavyweight championship from Max Baer at Madison Square Garden, was scheduled to defend his title for the first time against Joe Louis, the "Brown Bomber," at Chicago's Comiskey Park. Promoters pitched the ring in the middle of the ballpark's outfield. Braddock was a gentleman and refused to play the obvious race card. Nevertheless, he was Irish and wore a green robe with a shamrock. Joe Louis was black America's fighter. Louis was a man whose roots resembled theirs. Born in a sagging sharecropper's shack in rural Alabama to illiterate parents, he moved north to Detroit with his family at the age of twelve.

Forty-five thousand people attended the fight, nearly half of them black ticket holders who bought cheap seats in the bleachers. At the Robinson home everyone was crowded around the radio—aunts, cousins, neighbors too poor to own a radio, and Eugene, Percy's younger brother. Percy had never heard it before—utter quiet. Not a person gathered around the radio made a sound. Even the streets were still.

Percy and Eugene were two of Louis's biggest fans. Louis, who had moved to Chicago in 1934, liked to go horseback riding in Washington Park, in the heart of Chicago's South Side ghetto. Percy knew this, and when he and Eugene could get away, they would go there to catch a glimpse of their favorite fighter, with his bodyguards in tow, riding his white horse across the grounds.

For Louis the fight began inauspiciously when Braddock caught him with a right uppercut in the first couple of minutes. With the beloved challenger down on the canvas, all of black America held its breath. Was this to be a repeat of Louis's devastating loss to the German fighter Max Schmeling? Percy and Eugene refused to breathe until Louis was back on his feet.

From the fourth round on, Louis pummeled Braddock with fierce body blows and quick jabs to the face. When, in the eighth round, Louis knocked the champ off his feet with a punch, according to Braddock, that "about blowed half my head off," Percy looked around the living room at the frozen faces. Eugene looked as if he had just been visited by the Angel Gabriel. No one, not even the children, had dared to utter a word or laugh or scream until the final punch that sent Braddock crashing to the floor. There was a moment of euphoric silence, and then, after everyone had absorbed the impact of that punch, the Robinson house blew. The streets of Chicago erupted, too, in a collective roar the likes of which Percy had never heard before.

That night Ruth Robinson broke her own rule and let Percy out after dark to join the celebration. Revelers donned costumes and hugged and danced in the middle of the avenues. Drivers laid on their horns in jubilation. Though it was June, people built bonfires, grabbing whatever they could to feed the flames. Newsboys hawked fight extras. On 47th Street revelers staged an impromptu parade. In "the Stroll," the Black Belt's version of Harlem, ecstatic fans jammed the gambling houses and sporting dens, dance halls, clubs, and cabarets. They drank whiskey and smoked one-dollar joints until the sun rose over Lake Michigan. For all of black America, painfully aware of its second-class status, and hungry for a hero, it was a day to be celebrated and remembered. The Brown Bomber was the Heavyweight Champion of the World.

By the time Percy entered high school, these gambling houses and sporting dens were familiar to him. By day he was a diligent student, making the honor society despite DuSable High School's rigorous curriculum of English, chemistry, physics, algebra, geometry, trigonometry, civics, and history. On Sundays he studied his catechism so he could be baptized. But after the sun went down, he cultivated a double life, running with a gang from which he had to hide his other identity. Had the members known of it, they would have roughed him up and run him out. No one wanted to be associated with an ass-kissin' goody-two-shoes.

At night the rival gangs warred with each other, using knives, razors, bats, clubs, and crowbars where they once fought with their fists and feet. Women, booze, fashionable clothes, and running numbers were also part of the scene. In order to maintain his street credentials, Percy played the part. He shot dice, learned to walk with a malicious swagger, and committed petty acts of thievery.

When Percy Robinson entered the gates of the Great Lakes Naval Training Center, with his mother's words echoing in his head, he witnessed a Navy undergoing tremendous change as it struggled to meet quotas prescribed by the Selective Service headquarters. To handle the influx, the Navy created two new camps, Lawrence and Moffett, and cut recruit training from twelve to eight weeks.

Because the Navy still discouraged any "mingling with the whites" at Great Lakes, Lieutenant Commander Armstrong initiated other changes to bring the black training camps up to par with the white ones. He oversaw the construction of a new school building with state-of-the-art classrooms and laboratories, promoting "Negro pride," and assembled three Great Lakes bands that were on a par with the best bands in the country.

Despite Armstrong's efforts to make the three camps the kinds of places where black men could thrive, recruits like Percy Robinson quickly discovered that the Navy had sold them a bill of goods. Nothing, not even a world-class band, could make up for the fact that the Navy was steeped in segregation and unlikely to change. Service School openings for anything other than musicians or cooks and bakers were few and far between. What's more, there was little rhyme or reason to the selection process. Well-educated blacks were often passed over for appointments. Talk among the recruits was that the Navy divided blacks into two classes—"good niggers" and "bad niggers"—and, fearing that intelligence made them ripe for radicalism, put the smart ones into the latter category.

Percy Robinson witnessed the inequity of the selection process firsthand. He had done well on his aptitude test, and based on his high school grades, his pre-engineering classes, and four years of high school "shop" at one of Chicago's top city schools, he should have been a shoo-in for a service school. He could have been a machinist's mate or a metalsmith's mate and stayed right there at Great Lakes. By the time he made it through training, however, he had come to the bitter realization that he was not going to be staying at Great Lakes and was never going to get the chance to go to Hampton University or the Air Training Command in Memphis, Tennessee.

Every day Robinson checked the bulletin board where they posted assignments. One day he saw "Port Chicago Naval Ammunition Depot" next to his name. He had never heard of it before. He had always tried to project a worldly image, to exude cool and experience, but the truth was that before going to Great Lakes, the farthest he had ever strayed from home was for a high school sporting event in Gary, Indiana. Now he was headed for Port Chicago, California.

Robinson packed his seabag and waited for orders. A few days later he was on the parade ground drilling when an officer came up and said to the unit, "Follow me!" Robinson ran back to the barracks to get his bag. Minutes later he was aboard a truck bound for Union Station and the train that would carry him west.

On October 3, 1943, Lieutenant Ernest Delucchi met Robinson's train at the station in Port Chicago, California. Delucchi had not been at Port Chicago Naval Ammunition Depot for more than a few months, but already he had cultivated an air of authority. He swaggered, chest out, like a prize rooster at a cockfight. After a number of years as a noncommissioned officer, he took the Port Chicago job, was sent to Annapolis for officers' training, and was promptly promoted to lieutenant.

Percy Robinson did not pay much attention to Delucchi. He was too dumbfounded by the sight of Port Chicago. To him it looked like an Old West town out of the movies.

Suddenly Delucchi's voice boomed. "Which one of you boys wants to unload the duffels?" he asked, emphasizing the word "boys."

When no one else volunteered, Percy Robinson saw a dark-skinned black man volunteer. *What the hell,* George Booth thought. *I'd better put my best foot forward.* Booth was hoping for a new start. According to Detroit police, he had been one of the instigators of the Belle Isle riots, and had it not been for the Navy, he might still be in a jail.

The night he ended up in the riot wagon, he had been partying with his buddies and their girlfriends on Belle Isle, a Frederick Law Olmsted–designed island park in the Detroit River. It had been less a celebration than a chance to say good-bye. Booth would soon be leaving for Great Lakes.

At 982 acres, Belle Isle had always been a place where blacks and whites tolerated each other. But on the evening of June 20, not long after 10:00 p.m., Booth and his friends were leaving the island when they saw a large group of whites fighting a smaller group of blacks. They jumped out of their cars and dove in. Minutes later, dozens more joined in.

When the police showed up, Booth realized that they were in trouble. Booth was an unlikely agitator. He had grown up singing opera, was the president of the camera club in high school, and had decided not to play football because the game was too rough. All his life he had gotten along with whites. He fished with them and played sports with them on the sandlots and vacant fields.

The police began swinging their nightclubs, and Booth got cracked over the head. He felt a sudden wave of nausea and then blacked out. Regaining his senses, he found himself curled up in the back of one of the wagons. By early morning he and his buddies and dozens of other bruised and bloody young black men were sitting in a jail cell.

Meanwhile riots broke out across the city, fueled by rumors that whites had thrown a black woman and her baby off the Belle Isle Bridge. Enraged blacks stormed through a neighborhood, breaking windows and looting stores, while white rioters approached from the opposite direction, burning cars and plundering businesses. City police and state troopers were soon overwhelmed—six were shot and another seventy-five injured—and began firing indiscriminately into the rebellious black crowds. A white doctor, entering a black neighborhood on a house call, was pulled from his car and beaten to death.

When the Detroit mayor and Michigan's governor begged the president to help, Roosevelt sent in federal troops. The troops restored peace two days later, but the NAACP, whom many accused of having instigated the violence, pointed out that three quarters of the people killed or injured or arrested were black. In his report on the riot, Thurgood Marshall claimed that an aggressive police force had set off the violence. "The trouble," he wrote, "reached riot proportions because the police of Detroit once again enforced the law under an unequal hand. They used 'persuasion' rather than firm action with white rioters while against Negroes they used the ultimate in force."

When two officers pulled George Booth out of the jail, cuffed him, and took him to court, Booth told the judge, "I'm in the Navy."

"Like heck you are," the judge responded.

At that, a Navy officer—Booth's sister Violet had gone down to the recruitment office to explain what had happened to her brother—stood up and asked to speak. When the judge granted him the right, the lieutenant said, "He's government property, sir." Although Booth did not especially like the lieutenant's choice of words, he did not relish the idea of going back to jail or having a criminal record.

When he arrived at Great Lakes' Camp Moffett, Booth wrote his sister Violet informing her that it was his intention to be "the *best* damn midshipman in the whole Navy." He sang with the all-black Blue Jackets choir, minded his p's and q's, and tried to make good on a promise that he would never have the chance to keep.

When Booth finished throwing the seabags off the train and the men had them draped over their shoulders, Delucchi led the procession to the gates of the Port Chicago Naval Ammunition Depot. It was a far cry from the United States Naval Academy, where white midshipmen trained to be commissioned officers. All Booth saw was a chain-link fence, a parade ground, and a few buildings. Not even an outdoor basketball court, and not a destroyer, cruiser, or battleship in sight.

For the second time in less than an hour, Percy Robinson could not believe his eyes. If at some point he believed that he was destined for something important in the Navy, the sight of the depot relieved him of any illusions. The Port Chicago Naval Ammunition Depot looked like a prisoner-of-war camp.

The following morning, Lieutenant Delucchi assembled the men on the parade grounds. He told them that if they had any questions about what the U.S. Navy expected of them, to refer to their *Bluejackets' Manual,* and told them, too, that they were at Port Chicago for only one reason—to load bombs onto ships. Then he said that they were the men behind the men who were doing the fighting. Without their work at Port Chicago, there would be no victory over the Japs.

After the brief pep talk, he announced the names of the petty officers and section leaders. Then he gave the men their assignments. The entire group would be assigned to Division 4, Barracks B. The men would be allowed to choose their bunks and footlockers. At this, some of the men shook their heads. This was the Navy's version of freedom?

Delucchi then explained the depot's setup. Division No. 4 and its 105 men would be divided into sections, and the sections would be further divided into five crews. All the crews would be split into a ship's crew, which would work in the hold, and a dock crew, which would unload ammunition from the boxcars onto the dock. Before they began working he would choose the hatch tenders and the winchmen based on their military and civilian records. Experienced operators, he added, would train the winchmen, but with ordnance demands on the increase and more ships loading at Port Chicago, they would be expected to be up to speed as soon as possible.

At 6:00 a.m. on October 5, Division No. 4 fell out for roll call. Robinson noticed a vehicle pull up to the barracks. It was a large, gray sixteen-wheeler with a trailer, the kind they used for hauling cattle. Delucchi ordered the division to board. The men settled onto the benches inside, nearly sitting on each other's laps in the cramped quarters. Others, who could not find enough bench space to squeeze into, leaned against the wall of the truck. Then someone closed the doors and locked them from the outside.

*Ah, hell, man,* Carl Tuggle thought, *why you gotta do that? Even if we wanted, where in the hell we gonna run to?* Tuggle kicked himself for not having joined the Army. Growing up in Cincinnati he had been a good student. He had done well, too, at Great Lakes, passing all the skill tests. He wanted to go to Aviation Mechanics School, but had been denied a service school appointment. After making it through the recruit training program at Great Lakes, the Navy had him wandering the grounds of the camp, picking up cigarette butts. Now he was at Port Chicago, locked up like a Civil War–era slave.

The trailer was a claustrophobic's nightmare, and George Booth found himself hyperventilating. For a moment he felt as if he was back again in the riot wagon. His head spun. That's when the driver of the truck popped the clutch. The benches toppled over and the men were thrown to the floor and against the rear doors.

"Bastards," someone seethed.

A few minutes later the truck wound its way through the ammunition bunkers and stopped, and Lieutenant Delucchi opened the doors.

"You boys okay?" he asked. Percy Robinson wondered if the lieutenant was mocking them, as he jumped out of the truck. Then, for the first time, he got a look at what the Navy had in store for him. A hulking Liberty ship was tied to the pier. Men in denim work suits were unloading crates of ammunition from boxcars onto a thump mat on the pier. A black crew leader explained what the men were doing. When he finished, Delucchi announced that it was time to move on into the hold of the ship. As Robinson walked up the gangplank, he realized that he did not even know what a hold was. After reaching the main deck, the men followed Delucchi down the steel hand ladder to the bottom deck. There they watched as a winchman lowered a bomb in a net. When the winchman brought the net all the way down, the section leader explained how to move and stack the bombs safely.

After the demonstration, the men climbed the hand ladder back to the ship's main deck. Many of them breathed a sigh of relief. Dock work was definitely better than being stuck in the hold. At least on the dock a guy could feel the sun on his face and fill his lungs with good, clean air, even if it did smell of fish and brine.

Carl Tuggle could not shake the feeling that he had made a mistake. As he gazed back in the direction of the barracks, Port Chicago Naval Ammunition Depot looked to him like the most desolate place he had ever laid his eyes on.

# CHAPTER 14

# Whom Are We Fighting This Time?

As General Douglas MacArthur's forces pushed up the coast of New Guinea, and Admiral Chester Nimitz, commander of the Pacific Fleet, made plans for the invasion of Tarawa, the Port Chicago Naval Ammunition Depot was becoming the principal loading port and storage point for ammunition and high explosives on the Pacific Coast. As Port Chicago assumed its new role, Captain Nelson Goss recognized that he was short of qualified officers. In response to a letter he had written the commandant of the Twelfth Naval District, he had received a number of Naval Reserve officers earlier in the year. Few of them, however, had any training in ordnance.

On September 29, 1943, Captain Goss acquired the one man who had the experience and know-how to run the fast growing Port Chicago loading operation. Lieutenant Commander Alexander Holman had devoted three decades of his life to service in the Navy. Prior to coming to Port Chicago, he was stationed at the naval installation at Coco Solo, Panama, and before that he served as the executive officer of the USS *Nitro*, an ammunition ship. Before that, he worked on a number of naval vessels in connection with fire control.

Realizing that Port Chicago officers had to be "negro psychologists, ship riggers, safety engineers, professional stevedores, carpenters, and ordnancemen," Lieutenant Commander Holman soon became discouraged by the situation. What's more, he had little patience for, or interest in, training black seamen who did not want to be there in the first place for the critical work of "selective discharge." Selective discharge or "combat loading" was a sophisticated procedure that required the kind of familiarity with ordnance that few of the black loaders or, for that matter, their white officer bosses possessed. It demanded a thorough cataloging of ammunition. Once loading began, the cargo had to be arranged aboard ship so that in battle whatever was needed could be accessed without having to unload what was not needed. In Holman's opinion, Port Chicago's black enlisted men lacked the intelligence to perform the job.

Perhaps Captain Goss recognized that no one man, regardless of his qualifications, could oversee Port Chicago's round-the-clock loading demands, because not long after Lieutenant Commander Holman arrived, the captain was again appealing to the commandant. The depot, he complained, was still "desperately short of officers of any previous experience in ship loading," especially as it geared up for significant expansion. Weeks later, Goss fired off another urgent memo. "Not enough officers on hand to identify and segregate ammunition," he wrote. "Present deficiencies must be supplied at once."

The captain was not overstating his case. As of early October, Port Chicago had 591 black enlisted men and thirty officers. Lieutenant Lee Cordiner, who had been at the depot longer than any of the other lieutenants, was certainly not a man he could rely on to build good relations with the black loaders. Cordiner had lost all standing in July after the death of the black seaman when he tried to prevent the men from entering the mess hall. Nor was he an experienced ordnance man. Prior to being attached to the magazine in late 1942, he had never worked with explosives.

Lieutenant James Tobin was not a man he could depend on, either. Tobin, who arrived at Port Chicago in January 1943, was put in charge of the 2nd Division. He had been an auditor in civilian life and had never handled projectiles or TNT, was unfamiliar with the regulations regarding the handling of dangerous ordnance, and had never worked with blacks. He judged them to be a very "emotional race" not given to "self-control and discipline." In his estimation the Port Chicago men fell into two categories: the first group was unreliable; sometimes they "worked very hard" and sometimes they "shirked duty." The second group was a thoroughly unhappy bunch. These were the men who had come to Port Chicago in late 1942, the ones whom recruiters had lured into the Navy with false promises of sea duty.

Lieutenant Ernest Delucchi had many of Tobin's limitations. The black seamen disliked him. In their eyes he was a demagogue who, like Moses, believed that he had been chosen by God himself to pass down Port Chicago's version of the Ten Commandments. He ran Division 4 like his own private domain, dispensing privileges and punishments as he saw fit. Most of the seamen thought he was a power-hungry prick.

There were other officers, of course, but Captain Goss seemed to lack faith in them, too. Writing again to the commandant of the Twelfth Naval District, he explained, "Many principal difficulties at Port Chicago have stemmed directly from inability to obtain an adequate nucleus of experienced and trained officer personnel. . . . It is decidedly dangerous to entrust the administration and control of large numbers of green (colored) enlisted men to inexperienced officers. The good name of the Navy, as well as the efficiency of these stations, is involved."

By mid-October 1943, the depot was midway through loading the SS *Otto Mears,* which had moored into the starboard side of Pier No. 1 soon after the SS *Anthony Revalle* left the depot. The *Anthony Revalle* was bound for Hawaii, Samoa, and then the coast of Australia, from Sydney to Port Stephens and north to Brisbane. She carried bombs, ammunition, explosives, parachute flares, warheads, and torpedoes delivered by train from the Naval Ammunition Depot at Hawthorne, Nevada, and from a variety of other depots across the country.

The SS *Otto Mears* would carry a similar load, but in far larger quantities that included over eighty cars of ammunition, over forty cars of explosives, and ten cars of bombs, all destined for depots in Hawaii and Samoa. In the lead-up to the invasion of Tarawa, Port Chicago was being asked to do what prior to October would have been considered impossible. Loading the *Otto Mears* was easily the biggest challenge it had ever undertaken. On October 17, shortly after noon, and seven days after mooring, the vessel steamed down the Sacramento River, loaded to the gills, her gunwales barely out of the water.

The following day, the USS *Rainier*, another one of the Navy's hardworking ammunition ships, moored at Pier No. 1 at Port Chicago. The *Rainier* had made her inaugural trip in March 1941, delivering supplies and ammunition to Pearl Harbor. A year later she provided ammunition for the Dolittle Raid on Japan and the Battle of Midway. In late July 1942 she sailed to Fiji, where she supplied ships taking part in the assault on the Solomons. Barely a week later she set off for Noumea, New Caledonia, and stayed put during the early stages of the Guadalcanal campaign. Just over six months later she loaded for the first time at Port Chicago, and then set sail for Espiritu Santo and Efate Island in the New Hebrides, where she discharged a cargo of ammunition and torpedoes. In late August 1943 she returned to Port Chicago to pick up a large load of warheads, ammunition, and explosives bound for Oahu, Pearl Harbor, and Midway.

Sammie Boykin recognized the *Rainier* right off, knowing that her arrival spelled a week of hard work. The pace would be frenetic, and the division officers would lean on the men harder than ever.

Boykin worked the boxcars, a job he had come to dislike, but not because of the heavy lifting or because he had grown lazy. The truth was that he was scared, and not just because he was handling explosives. That summer he discovered racial slurs scrawled on the walls of the boxcars. Once he found a drawing of a bomb and underneath it the words "This is what's going to happen to you." Not long after, more boxcars arrived with images of exploding bombs and the message, "This is the niggers." Sometimes he encountered Nazi insignia or notes signed allegedly by the KKK. What disturbed him

most was that the boxcars were coming from naval and army ammunition depots. In other words, men with whom he was presumably
helping to fight a war were making the threats. It shook him so badly
that he began having nightmares. When the Port Chicago men retaliated, trading insults and challenges, he worried that the war of words
would escalate to violence.

He took some consolation from the fact that it was Spencer Sikes's
job to inspect the railroad cars in their bunkers to see if they had been
tampered with. Sikes was as conscientious as they came, and if he noticed anything suspicious he would certainly bring it to the attention
of one of the lieutenants. If everything checked out, he would pull
the serial number tags so that the officers knew which shipments had
come in and which had not. But Boykin was also aware that when
things got busy and there were dozens upon dozens of cars bringing
in thousands of tons of ordnance for both transshipment and storage,
the officers would push Sikes, and he might miss something. What
if some bigoted ammunition depot employee wanted to do the Port
Chicago men harm?

No one was less excited to see the *Rainier* than George Booth.
In the two weeks since he had arrived at Port Chicago, he had been
working nonstop. He had only had one twelve-hour liberty pass, and
on that outing he only made it as far as Pittsburg. What he wanted
more than anything else was to see "Frisco."

Like Boykin, George Booth worked the boxcars as a carpenter
striker. Lieutenant Delucchi told him that being assigned to a car crew
was his reward for volunteering to take the seabags off the train.
Booth never figured out if Delucchi had given him a job that no one
else wanted, or if the lieutenant had done right by him. Whatever the
case, Booth never paid much attention to the racial slurs.

Besides, being a carpenter striker was dangerous enough without
worrying about some racist asshole at one of the ammunition depots.
Using an eight-pound sledgehammer and a pinch bar, his job was
to break out the wood braces, or dunnage, holding the ordnance in
place. Swinging a sledgehammer around bombs was a scary thing. Regardless of how careful he was, sometimes he and the other carpenter

strikers missed the wood braces and hit something that could blow them to kingdom come.

Perhaps Delucchi had suckered him into the job, but that was okay as far as Booth was concerned, because the lieutenant also granted him access to the library. Booth took full advantage of the privilege, using it to study first aid, and referring to the library's dictionary when writing his female friends. Letters at Port Chicago were status symbols. The "big man" of the barracks was always the guy who received the most letters at mail call. The competition allowed Percy Robinson to use his DuSable High School education and establish an energetic business helping other Port Chicago men write to women from whom they hoped to receive letters back.

But with the *Rainier* in the harbor, and the USS *Shasta* and the SS *Alcoa Planter* expected in a few days, no one would have time for writing letters, especially Percy Robinson. As crew boss of Hold No. 1, he worked the graveyard shift on the *Rainier* from eleven at night until nine the next morning.

On the evening of October 18, a petty officer assembled the division for roll call and then turned it over to Lieutenant Delucchi, who announced that on the *Rainier* he wanted no fighting, no slacking, and no sleeping. The *Rainier* was going directly to the front. When Delucchi dismissed them, Robinson thought, *He may be short and pudgy, but that man thinks he's God.*

Some of the guys had not even bothered to assemble for roll call. They were the ones already angling for a Section Eight discharge for being mentally unfit. One fella from Detroit walked around saying, "I gotta have pussy. I can't live without pussy." Robinson may not have liked Port Chicago, but he was too proud to grovel for a Section Eight.

Down at the dock, the *Rainier* was tied off and its holds were lit up like movie stages. As Hold No. 1's boss, Robinson knew that his group—"the Hawks"—which was made up of two guys from Youngstown, Ohio, another from Cleveland, and one from Philadelphia, could be relied upon to work hard. It was the others that worried him. A few of the guys would slough off any chance they got.

One thing he was grateful for was the consistently dry weather. It got chilly at night, but nothing was worse than rain. It made the projectiles wet and slippery and almost impossible to handle.

After all his men had climbed down into the hold, Robinson motioned to the signalman. Minutes later the winchmen lowered a metal box of armor-piercing projectiles onto the floor. Each projectile was painted black with white markings, weighed nearly 130 pounds, was packed with a burster charge of Dunnite (ammonium picrate), and was slathered in grease to prevent rusting. The Navy used the armor-piercing shells to bring down planes and bombard enemy bunkers. The shell would penetrate the structure and a fuze would trigger the Dunnite.

Robinson's men knew the drill. They formed a line from the metal box to the bulkhead. The strongest among them—a heavily muscled member of Robinson's "Hawks"—squatted like a deadlifter and pulled the projectile from the box. Still crouching, he let it roll back into his arms. Then he rose slowly until he was standing and handed it to the next guy, who cradled it and carefully passed it on to the next. Robinson was at the end of the line. When the projectile reached him, he straightened his back as he had learned to do on the *Mears*. His boxing training had taught him balance, and he did not waver as he bent his knees and lowered his buttocks to the floor. When he was down as low as he could get, he uncradled his arms and opened his hands and the projectile rolled forward. For a second or two it rested on his knees. When he leaned forward, the projectile fell almost silently to the floor of the hold. That was the key, Robinson thought, discipline. If a guy kept his form, he could lower the projectile without banging it all to hell. Once the projectile was on the deck, he pushed it into position and a carpenter's mate inserted pegs to keep it from rolling.

At 4:00 a.m., the men were allowed to return to the chow hall for coffee and a sandwich. Their jumpsuits were covered in sweat and grease. "How many more days of this?" they thought. "How long can we keep this up?"

Seven more days was the answer. On October 25, one week after she had arrived, the USS *Rainier* unmoored and left Pier No. 1 at 1:20 in the afternoon. If that evening any of the ammunition handlers thought that a happy Lieutenant Delucchi would hand out twenty-four-hour liberty passes, they were mistaken. Delucchi did not want any of his men coming back too hungover to work. Perhaps when the *Alcoa Planter* and the *Shasta* left the depot, the men would get a break.

War demands being what they were, the amounts of cargo coming into and going out of Port Chicago had reached "astronomical figures" and the depot was firing on all cylinders twenty-four hours a day. When Coast Guard observers assigned to Port Chicago to enforce safety regulations objected to a number of common Port Chicago practices, including the rolling, skidding, and dropping of bombs, and suggested alternatives that Goss deemed impractical, the irritated captain pressed to have the observers removed.

In late October, Goss met with the Port of San Francisco's director, Coast Guard Captain Milton Davis, under whose jurisdiction Port Chicago fell. Concerned about safety lapses, Davis urged Goss to bring on experienced contract stevedores. "Conditions are bad up there [referring to Port Chicago]," he warned Goss. "You've got to do something about it. . . . Something's going to happen, and you'll be responsible for it."

# CHAPTER 15

# Waiting for War

"Well, bite my ass!" After its 3,000-mile train trip, when the 23rd Marine Regiment arrived at Camp Pendleton, outside of Oceanside, California, no one in the regiment could believe his good fortune. Compared to New River, North Carolina, Camp Pendleton's digs were impressive: a brand-new barracks with large heads, a king-size PX, a slop chute, a soda fountain, and even an indoor movie theater. They were going to enjoy being pampered West Coast Marines.

As H Company's newest clerk, Robert Graf, the upstate New York honor student, took care of his buddies. Because the drinking age in many of the Los Angeles hotspots was twenty-one, Graf falsified the birthdates on their liberty cards, making sure they could enter any big city drinking establishment they wanted to. No one appreciated his efforts more than his good buddy Bill More. The company's Huck Finn, More had a way of sniffing out fun and adventure, like Graf's old Ballston Spa buddy, Jimmy Haskell. "Damn the torpedoes," he would say when he left the base. "Full steam ahead!"

After a time, though, Graf grew sick and tired of being a clerk. Although his buddies encouraged him to stay put—they worried that the new clerk might be an officious stickler—Graf decided he wanted to be a runner like Bill More and his other good friend Dick Crerar. According to Crerar, it had its benefits: since a runner carried important messages from one field headquarters to another, a guy could enjoy being outdoors and still always have access to the inside news.

Just weeks after leaving the comfort of the office, Graf was already questioning his decision. He had been assigned to Second Lieutenant Carl Roth, who was always on the move, darting up and down the sun-baked hills and tramping through the tangled ravines. Graf's job was to move with him, to act as scout, sounding board, and messenger. By day they covered dozens of miles, and at night, as the temperature plunged, they slept under shelter halves and rough woven blankets.

In November 1943, after weeks in the field, machine-gun and mortar classes, and a November 10 celebration honoring the 168th birthday of the Marine Corps, the 23rd Marine's 2nd Battalion was loaded onto trucks and shipped forty miles south to the Navy base in San Diego for two weeks of sea maneuvers. Just weeks later they were at it again, descending nets on the sides of the troopships into new amphibious tractors. As the coxswains circled and the amtracs made a beeline for shore, destroyers fired their five-inch guns. When the time came for a real invasion, the hope was that none of the Marines would flinch at the sound. Once on dry land, the men rolled out of the amphibious boats and ran like maniacs in their shin-high boondockers, slipping and stumbling in the soft sand. Riflemen moved forward as artillery units set up behind them. As the teamwork got better, tanks joined them and planes screamed overhead, searching for the colored oilcloth panels that the riflemen had laid out to highlight their positions.

Christmas 1943 arrived, and Lieutenant Roth informed the company that it would be doing guard duty. The men groaned, but Bill More somehow managed to finagle seventy-two-hour passes for both himself and Graf. While the others were stuck behind on base, they were going to Tinseltown!

On their first night in Los Angeles, More and Graf ran into three others from Company H who had also received liberty passes. Sergeant Gordon Duff, Corporal Charlie Hill, and Corporal Steve Jabo were veterans of Guadalcanal and had the campaign ribbons to prove it. In a bar just off Pershing Square, More and Graf drank scotch and sodas and peppered the three survivors with questions. Unlike a lot of their buddies from the 'Canal, the three veterans had been spared the carnage of Tarawa, where a portion of the first wave of Marines came in on deep-draft Higgins boats that slammed into the coral and stopped. Men were forced to wade five hundred yards through chest-deep water into withering Japanese fire. Soon blood stained the surf red. Now, however, as Duff, Hill, and Jabo talked of another tour, their stories grew grim.

After leaving the Guadalcanal veterans, Graf and More proceeded to drink themselves silly. The following morning they made their way to downtown Hollywood for more alcohol and perhaps a weekend fling. Two days later they returned to Camp Pendleton spilling over with stories of voluptuous women, and with crippling hangovers.

By fall 1943, having just finished Combat Training School at Camp Elliott, just outside of San Diego, Carl Matthews, the small but spirited Texan, was assigned to Company G, 23rd Regiment, 4th Marine Division, at Camp Pendleton. There he met the fellow Marine who would become his inseparable sidekick, Richard Freeby, a free spirit from Quannah, Texas. Named for Quannah Parker, the last Comanche chief, the town was situated in the Texas Panhandle on the Oklahoma border, north of where Matthews grew up. Freeby was raised by an uncle and aunt after his parents died and, eager for a life of adventure, joined the Marines not long after graduating from high school. The Texans realized that they had a lot in common and immediately took to each other. It was a rare occasion when they were not together.

It did not take long for platoon leader Sergeant Jack Campbell to dub the two friends the "Gold Dust Twins" after the popular early-1900s vaudeville act. The name stuck.

For the Gold Dust Twins, liberty came infrequently. Instead the

23rd Marines trained hard. In places like Aliso Beach and Las Pulgas, Windmill Canyons and Chappo Flats, Matthews and Freeby were undergoing the same training as Graf, rigorous combat instruction that intensified once the rifle companies began coordinated training with artillery battalions and tank groups. By the end of the year, all that was left for the Gold Dust Twins was to pass their high-dive test.

Designed to teach them how to abandon a sinking ship in case of an at-sea emergency, the high-dive test was an essential part of Marine Corps training. A company of men would assemble at the swimming pool, and there each one learned how to jump from a twenty-foot platform feet first into the water, with one hand covering his crotch and the other protecting his chin and face. Upon hitting the water and coming to the surface, each man would take off his trousers, tie knots in the bottom of each leg, and fill the pants with air, fashioning a kind of crude flotation device.

The jump filled Matthews with dread. He was a boy from the flatlands of Texas and had never jumped off anything higher than a riverbank. Meanwhile, Freeby loved heights. He loved to dive, but if the Marine instructors just wanted him to jump, he could do that, too.

Freeby's group went first, while Matthews looked on, trying to summon the courage he would need when his turn came. When Freeby exited the pool, he looked at Matthews. "Hell, it was fun," he said.

"All right," Matthews responded. "Then you can have my turn, too."

So while Matthews left the pool area, Freeby jumped for his new friend. The instructor had no idea that the Gold Dust Twins had put one over on him.

Late that autumn, the Gold Dust Twins met their new platoon leader, Lieutenant James Stanley Leary Jr. Leary was a kid, barely older than Matthews. At first the new lieutenant kept his distance. Not until night maneuvers, sitting in front of a fire, did the men get a sense of who Lieutenant Leary really was. What eventually endeared him to his men was that he was not a show-off. He, too, was learning and he was willing to admit it. If he had a question, he would go to Sergeant Jack Campbell, who knew more about the Marine Corps than just about anyone alive. As Stanley Leary's runner, Matthews would grow closer to him than anyone in the platoon. He would come to love and trust the lieutenant from Ashokie, North Carolina, with the deep Piedmont drawl.

# CHAPTER 16

# Broken Promises

In late 1943 the Marines prepared to invade Bougainville in the northern Solomon Islands and geared up for the assault on Tarawa, while Allied forces prepared to bomb Japan's main South Pacific base at Rabaul, on the island of New Britain, off the coast of New Guinea. Meanwhile, the tonnage moving in and out of Port Chicago reached heights never dreamed of. In just six months the depot had tripled its output. In October the seamen loaded 22,000 tons of ordnance, and 26,500 tons in November. The question on everyone's mind was how long Port Chicago could keep up such a brutal pace before something happened. The black seamen were handling warheads, projectiles, and bombs, which they knew little about, and risking their lives. It was as if the Navy, which had forbidden them to fight, refused to acknowledge just how dangerous their job was.

Finally a group of seamen decided to act, drafting a letter and sending it to the black Berkeley attorney Walter Gordon (Gordon, in turn, passed it on to the NAACP in New York). The gist of the letter was this: the patriotic black seamen of Port Chicago were happy to serve their country, but they wanted a chance to prove themselves capable of fighting. They wanted the Navy to reconsider its policy against integrating fleet vessels. The letter ended with a heartfelt appeal. "We the Negro sailors," it said, "of the Naval Enlisted Barracks of Port Chicago, California, are waiting for a new deal. Will we wait in vain?"

While they hoped for a reply, a tragedy rocked Port Chicago. One night a number of off-duty loaders were shooting craps in the barracks. The games were rarely for high stakes; the men simply did not make enough money. However, the gambling was always lively and sometimes, if someone managed to smuggle alcohol onto the base (only three-two beer was sold on base), it would be fueled by cheap booze. On this occasion one of the players, who had just lost, refused to pay up. Shots were fired. Those who had gathered to watch the game scattered. The man who had objected to paying his debt lay in a pool of blood, with three bullets in his abdomen.

An alarmed Inez White, who, four months earlier, had written about the drowning of the black seaman, related the details of the event to her husband's parents in a letter dated November 23, 1943. "I don't know yet what they're going to do with the fellow [the gunman]," she wrote. "There'll be a Court Martial of course and Bob said maybe a firing squad."

The killing hung like a pall over the depot. Most of the seamen, understanding that the division officers would use the incident to clamp down and deny them liberty, were sullen and contrary. More and more, Port Chicago had the feel of a prison work camp. Even the tenacious Percy Robinson was contemplating requesting a transfer.

To make matters worse, the sailors who had written the letter had heard nothing from either the NAACP or the Navy, despite the fact that in 1943 the Navy was once again considering the wisdom of assigning blacks to the fleet in proportion to their distribution in the general population—one black sailor to every ten white sailors. A "situation memorandum," circulating throughout the Bureau of Naval Personnel, suggested including "Negroes in small numbers in the crews of larger combatant ships." According to the authors of the memo, this small concession to integration offered the best solution to the "problem of absorbing such large numbers of Negroes" and was "the only means by which any appreciable reduction can be made in the high percentage of Negroes that will be concentrated in all shore activities." As it was, black base companies, waiting to be assigned to duty in the Pacific, were sitting idle on the West Coast. White servicemen being sent into battle could not help but notice. Why were blacks not spilling their blood in the service of their country?

Although the reasons for integrating the Navy were compelling, by mid-December 1943, Secretary Knox had made his decision: the Navy would make no significant changes to its policies. The seamen of Port Chicago knew nothing of the Navy's deliberations. What they did know was that they were being asked to handle more tonnage with a shorter turnaround time. To cope with the new schedule, Great Lakes delivered another 183 men, bringing Port Chicago's number of black enlisted men to 706 by late December.

The Navy Bureau of Ordnance expected that these men would be trained. "Stevedoring," it said, "requires special technical knowledge . . . owing to the hazards involved." However, because Captain Goss was under the impression that loading depended "principally on common sense," he put them into the holds and into boxcars, handling torpedoes and fragmentation bombs after nothing more than a lecture.

For the civil rights community, 1944 began with a bang. Secretary Knox, who had originally dismissed the idea of having black naval officers, bent to pressure from the NAACP, Eleanor Roosevelt, and Adlai Stevenson, then one of his assistants, and decided to allow sixteen men to become the first black American naval officers. In January the candidates entered Great Lakes for segregated training. But for the ammunition handlers of Port Chicago, Knox's decision was more of a slap in the face than anything else. It was a symbolic gesture. Sixteen out of 100,000 black enlisted men would get a chance to do something meaningful in the Navy.

In January 1944, Captain Goss announced a new depot-wide goal of ten tons per hold per hour. In a Liberty ship with five cargo holds (three in the forward section of the ship and two in the aft), Goss's target meant that the seamen were expected to load fifty tons per hour, or four hundred tons per eight-hour shift. Lieutenant James Tobin was alarmed by the demand. With basic cargo, fifty tons per hour was doable. Given the hazardous nature of the ammunition passing through the depot, however, Tobin was convinced that the mark was unobtainable. Lieutenant Herbert Woodland, head officer of the 3rd Division, and later also assistant educational officer, believed, too, that the new mark was risky. In his opinion, most of Port Chicago's officers—many of them reserve officers unfamiliar with dangerous ordnance—were too inexperienced to teach what he considered incompetent work crews how to handle ammunition. As far as he was concerned, the Navy Bureau of Personnel had created a bad situation, which Captain Goss had made worse. From the perspective of the longshoremen's union, Port Chicago was a catastrophe waiting to happen. Allegedly the union warned the Navy Bureau of Ordnance that none of the divisions at Port Chicago were up to the challenges of handling ammunition, and offered to send in experienced advisers. The bureau, however, chose to ignore the union's offer.

That month Port Chicago received 403 railroad cars of freight and handled in excess of 23,000 tons of ordnance. Among the ships that docked at Port Chicago was the Navy's workhorse, the USS *Lassen,* which was scheduled to return to the Central Pacific to replenish the 2,655 tons of shells American battleships had fired on Roi and Namur in the lead-up to the invasion of the Marshall Islands.

By February 1944, ordnance demands from the Southwest and Central Pacific had outstripped the capabilities of the country's supply line. Shipments of ammunition from depots were seldom accomplished within a three-day margin of their projected arrival times. Delays complicated loading operations, tying up ships that were scheduled to take part in invasions. Last-minute deletions, substitutions, and additions to orders based on the needs of the fleet and ground troops also caused significant holdups. From a standpoint of safety, the biggest problem for Port Chicago was the buildup of un-protected ordnance. The depot was forced to keep more boxcars of explosives than it was set up to handle, a situation that flew in the face of critical Navy Ordnance and Coast Guard regulations designed to prevent the possibility of a traumatic explosion.

# CHAPTER 17

# Ernie King's Beloved Ocean
# (the Strategic Picture)

In 1921 a Marine staff officer by the name of Major Earl "Pete" Ellis made an ominous forecast: the assignment of Germany's former island colonies in the Central Pacific to Japan under the League of Nations mandate would one day make war in the Pacific inevitable. Over two decades later Ellis's prediction came true.

Ellis, however, was not just a doomsayer. After studying islands and distances, he expanded on a plan by the Naval War College (War Plan Orange) and established a groundbreaking blueprint—Operation Plan 712, *Advanced Base Operations in Micronesia*—for defeating Japan. Twenty-three years later the Navy's drive across the Central Pacific followed the essential details of his plan.

Despite Ellis's prescription for success, the invasion of the Central Pacific never would have happened without the persistence and vision of Admiral Ernest King, Commander-in-Chief, United States Fleet and Chief of Naval Operations. The Central Pacific, the blue-water highway to Tokyo, was his baby.

The centerpiece of Admiral King's plan was the Mariana Islands,

a chain of fourteen volcanic islands, including Saipan, Guam, and Tinian, most of which were uninhabited, situated north of the island
of New Guinea and south of Japan in the Philippine Sea. Ellis had
excluded the Marianas from his proposal, but King believed that they
were the key to ultimate victory in the Central Pacific. Other islands
would come first, but upon seizing the Marianas, the United States
could either starve Japan by isolating it from its resource base in the
Southwest Pacific or threaten Japan directly with aircraft carriers,
long-range submarines, and bombers. With a range of 3,500 miles,
and a bomb capacity in excess of four tons, the heavily armed B-29
was America's newest and mightiest weapon. By turning the Marianas
into giant air bases, the U.S. could send bomber crews to the home islands of Japan, only 1300 miles away, and possibly put a quick end
to the war.

Admiral Ernest King's year-long campaign to get the Joint Chiefs of
Staff to recognize the strategic validity of the Central Pacific campaign began in Morocco in early 1943. The first of many top-secret
conferences, during what journalists called the "Year of the Conference," this one took place in the French colonial city of Casablanca.
For King and the Joint Chiefs of Staff and their British counterparts,
Casablanca kicked off a year of horse-trading, arm-twisting, and compromise in which tempers frequently spilled out of the well-appointed
meeting rooms.

In the conference room, King warned against allowing Japan to
consolidate its conquests. Using rough graphs to show that the Allies
had directed only 15 percent of all resources in money, manpower,
and weapons to the Pacific war, he lobbied for greater resources. He
proposed a 15-percent increase, which, though modest, would support a series of campaigns designed to illustrate Allied resolve in the
Pacific.

King irked the Brits. They found him hot-tempered and singularly
absorbed with war against Japan. British general Alan Brooke, chief
of the Imperial General Staff and the top military man in England, insisted that for King "the European war was just a great nuisance that

kept him from waging his Pacific war undisturbed." Prime Minister Churchill called the Central Pacific "Ernie King's beloved ocean."

President Roosevelt, however, regarded King as the "shrewdest of strategists," and a man of extreme competence. After the debacle at Pearl Harbor, he knew that the admiral was the only person who could rebuild the Navy. Secretary Frank Knox agreed. Giving him powers that no other chief of naval operations had ever enjoyed—King was the most powerful naval officer in the history of the country—the executive order that Roosevelt issued made King responsible only to the president.

Reluctantly the British delegates listened to King, though Churchill and his advisers had no intention of giving much ground. Ultimately, however, they made a small though ambiguous concession to the admiral. They prepared a brief compromise document, which the Brits hoped might temporarily placate King. "Operations in the Pacific and Far East," the document said, "shall continue with the forces allocated, with the objective of maintaining pressure on Japan, retaining the initiative and attaining a position of readiness for a full-scale offensive against Japan by the United Nations as soon as Germany is defeated."

In early February 1943, King flew west to San Francisco to meet with Admiral Nimitz, the commander of his Pacific Fleet. Satisfied with his minor victory at Casablanca, King and Nimitz sat down to fashion a plan for the Central Pacific. Nimitz, too, had good news to share. Intelligence reports indicated that the Japanese had abandoned the southern Solomons, and after a battle as savage as the one fought by the Marines at Guadalcanal, MacArthur's troops had defeated Japanese Imperial forces on New Guinea's Papuan Peninsula. Both leaders knew, though, that the Japanese would not rest. Nimitz suspected that already they were planning another attack—on Samoa, perhaps—in order to sever the Allied supply line to the South Pacific. It was not hard to convince King; he had been warning against this threat since the early days of 1941. Though King, as always, wanted to "keep pressure on the Japs," Nimitz cautioned him. A Central Pacific push was ill-advised until war production was at full capacity and they had the ships—and forces—to pull if off.

Several weeks after returning from California, King penned a letter to Roosevelt. King's memorandum to the president again emphasized the importance of securing the lines of communication between the West Coast of the United States and Australia by way of Samoa, Fiji, and New Caledonia. King added that it was essential to protect Australia and New Zealand because they were "white man's countries." Losing them would provide the "non-white races of the world" enormous encouragement. King concluded his "integrated, general plan of operations" with three directives: "Hold Hawaii; support Australasia; drive northwestward from New Hebrides."

Not long after Roosevelt received the admiral's memo, Churchill and more than one hundred advisers and staff members arrived in New York aboard the *Queen Mary* for a series of meetings to be held in Washington. Hard-nosed bargaining marked the conference.

On May 21, 1943, more than a week into the Washington conference, dubbed "Trident," King announced his plan to split the Japanese line of communications, separating the home islands from Japan's southern resource colonies. He proposed to starve the Japanese into submission. The key to doing this, he informed the Brits, were the Marianas. By capturing the islands, especially Saipan, the Allies could cut off Japan's access to its raw materials in the Southwest Pacific and isolate the Carolines and the great base at Truk. They could then move forces westward into the Philippines and China or northwestward into Japan. The offensive, King speculated, might even compel the Japanese navy to challenge the Allies to the decisive naval battle that he wanted. His ideas, King explained, were not novel. The Naval War College had developed them decades earlier, and most naval officers regarded them as articles of faith.

Predictably, the Brits balked at committing to anything that authorized in writing an offensive campaign in the Central Pacific. King's temper flared more than usual when American general Richard Sutherland, MacArthur's chief of staff, seemed to have persuaded the Combined Chiefs that King's plan would constitute a series of "hazardous amphibious frontal attacks against islands of limited value," and that its reliance on carrier-based aircraft operating far from their sources of fuel and ammunition made it unworkable. Seizing the opportunity, Sutherland again argued that the best line of approach, which could make use of Australia as a war base and could be supported by a large reserve of land-based aircraft, was from New Guinea to Mindanao. However, when the Combined Chiefs took the time to study the Army plan in detail, realizing that it would require thirteen new combat divisions and nearly two thousand planes along with landing craft and naval support ships, a colossal undertaking, they cooled. Sutherland's request far exceeded American capacity.

In the end, Trident gave formal agreement to a series of compromises whereby Roosevelt and his commanders agreed to eliminate Italy from the war in return for a firm date—spring 1944—on Marshall's coveted cross-Channel invasion. The other British concession, "Strategic Plan for the Defeat of Japan," formalized the Allied commitment to the Pacific, giving King the green light for his long-sought invasion of the Central Pacific. The caveat? The Combined Chiefs would have final say over the offensive, and King would have to agree to seize the Gilberts before the Marshalls. Nevertheless, King emerged victorious. He had come to the conference intent on establishing the necessity of a "master plan" for the Pacific, and the British had conceded.

In August 1943, five months after Trident, the Combined Chiefs assembled again for the year's third major conference—Quadrant—held in Quebec. Much had transpired during the months leading up to Quadrant. The Allies had captured Sicily, the Italian government had overthrown Mussolini and was threatening to leave the Axis, the Red Army had crushed Germany's last strategic offensive in the east at Kursk, American offensives in New Guinea and the Solomons had gained considerable momentum, and the 7th Infantry Division had recaptured Attu in the Aleutian islands of Alaska. Little, though, had changed between King and the British. King hammered at old themes—more resources for the Pacific theater and the need for a broad strategy—and the British, again, resisted. Undeterred,

King reiterated his plan for the Central Pacific, underlining the importance of the Marianas. Its loss, King said, would constitute an enormous strategic and psychic blow for Japan. For the second time, King outlined a scenario in which the Japanese Combined Fleet would be compelled to challenge the U.S. Navy, which with its new *Essex*-class carriers and F6F Hellcats, would have the chance to administer what might be the final blow to the Japanese.

What also emerged at Quadrant was King's growing support for MacArthur's Southwest Pacific initiative. King explained that he now saw the wisdom of a dual offensive, stretching Japan's defenses and its fuel-starved Imperial Navy to the breaking point. By virtue of their stunning early war victories and an empire that now stretched over one sixth of the earth's surface, the Japanese were especially vulnerable to this two-pronged strategy. King called it the "whipsaw plan," and was convinced that it would keep enemy intelligence wondering where the next American blow would come. MacArthur, however, opposed King throughout the second half of 1943 (and the early months of 1944), and continued to try to make the case for supreme command of the Pacific theater and a single offensive led by the Army.

Ultimately it was President Roosevelt, in consultation with the Joint Chiefs of Staff, who declared that the offensive would be two-pronged and simultaneous, with two separate commanders: MacArthur would fight his way across New Guinea and toward the Philippines while Admiral Chester Nimitz, King's commander-in-chief for Allied air, land, and sea forces in the Pacific Ocean, slashed and pounded across the Central Pacific, capturing tactically important islands, en route to the innermost reaches of the Japanese empire. At the Cairo-Teheran conferences in late November and early December 1943, the Combined Chiefs gave formal approval to the two routes in a master plan titled "Specific Operations for the Defeat of Japan, 1944."

MacArthur, who did not attend the conference, electing instead to send Sutherland, was furious at the outcome. The Central Pacific, Sutherland had argued, should be abandoned for three reasons: it could be carried out only by massive and costly amphibious operations; it relied too much on carrier-based aviation; and finally, because of the distances involved, the Central Pacific offensive would involve an agonizingly slow series of stops and starts. MacArthur's proposal called instead for Nimitz, after taking the Marshalls, to assist the general's forces in pushing on to Mindanao.

In another blow to MacArthur, the Combined Chiefs not only gave their approval to the Central Pacific offensive, but gave seizure of the Marshalls, Carolines, Palaus, and Marianas priority in scheduling and resources. "Due weight," the Chiefs said, "should be accorded to the fact that operations in the Central Pacific promise a more rapid advance toward Japan and her vital lines of communication, the earlier acquisition of strategic air bases closer to the Japanese homeland and are more likely to precipitate a decisive engagement with the Japanese fleet." Based on this decision Nimitz sketched out a tentative timetable for the drive across the Central Pacific: Kwajalein would be invaded on January 31, 1944, Eniwetok on May 1, Truk on August 15, and Saipan, Tinian, and Guam on November 15.

By committing U.S. forces to a two-pronged war in the Pacific, Admiral Nimitz knew that he would be placing enormous pressure on American industry. To outproduce Japan (and Germany, too), the country's war effort would have to reach unprecedented new heights. Dockyards, working round the clock, would be called upon to assemble a steady stream of submarines; amphibious vehicles; large new destroyers; *Independence*-class light carriers; fast, well-armed *Essex*-class carriers, capable of hauling eighty to one hundred aircraft and over three thousand men; and cargo ships. Factories would be ordered to churn out planes and tanks. Arsenals would have to produce huge amounts of ordnance, which West Coast ammunition depots, like Port Chicago, would have to load onto Liberty, Victory, and Navy ships speeding for the Pacific.

In late September 1943, not long after the Quebec conference, Emperor Hirohito met at his Imperial Council Chambers in Tokyo with his prime minister, Hideki Tojo, his chief of the Naval General Staff, Admiral Osami Nagano, his commander of the Imperial Combined

Fleet, Admiral Mineichi Koga, and Baron Yoshimichi Hara, president of the Imperial Privy Council. Although much of Japan was under the illusion that Japanese forces continued to score significant victories, these five men knew the reality of their country's military situation: the tide in the Pacific was turning against them. Soon large numbers of American ground, air, and naval reinforcements would arrive in the Pacific to challenge the Japanese empire.

For Hideki Tojo, a hard-line expansionist, this must have been a particularly bitter pill to swallow. When Tojo seized the positions of war minister and prime minister, and initiated the attack on Pearl Harbor, Admiral Isoroku Yamamoto, who had served as a naval attaché in Washington and was impressed by America's productive capacity, counseled Tojo that Japan had only six months to win the war before the "sleeping giant" of America woke. Now Yamamoto's warning had proved prophetic.

At the Imperial Council Chambers in Tokyo, the Japanese leaders agreed that the borders of the empire were overextended and could not be defended. They produced a chart with a heavy black line that passed east of the Shoto islands (including Okinawa), through the Bonins (including Iwo Jima), south to the Marianas and to Truk in the Carolines, down to the Vogelkop Peninsula at the western tip of New Guinea, west to the Timor Sea, and then through Borneo, Singapore, the Philippines, and Hong Kong. The line represented what Tojo designated the "Absolute Imperial Defense Line."

It was a desperate gamble. Territories outside the line, including Tarawa and the Marshalls, Tojo explained, would be sacrificed. Here Japanese forces would fight a series of delaying actions that would slow the American advance and buy time for the empire to build up its military arsenal, especially its carrier fleet. Possessions inside the line would be held at all costs. Every position, however, regardless of its status, would be defended to the last man.

# CHAPTER 18

# Baptism by Fire

On January 11, 1944, Carl Matthews and Richard Freeby, the Gold Dust Twins, toted their heavy seabags onto the USS *Sheridan* and prepared to ship out for points unknown. Had the 23rd Marine Regiment remained at Pendleton, the Gold Dust Twins would have faced a long stint in the brig. In mid-November the two, having been refused leave by the battalion commander, took matters into their own hands and jumped ship, hitchhiking to San Diego, where earlier Matthews had served as a clerk at base headquarters. After inveigling another clerk to give him the key to the office, Matthews typed up furlough papers for himself and Freeby and forged the battalion commander's signature with an authoritative flourish. Their intention was to make their way to Texas. Without furlough papers, they would be seized at the state line and returned to base under lock and key and thrown in jail. In San Diego the pair split up. While Freeby took a bus home to Quannah, Texas, in the Panhandle, Matthews hitchhiked. Because of the gas shortage, public buses could only go thirty-five miles per hour. Matthews reasoned that if he could catch a ride with a driver who had a heavy foot—people were always willing to pick up a Marine wearing his dress blues—he could get home almost twice as fast.

Matthews spent "twenty-three glorious days" in Hubbard, Texas. He dated, went to church with his family, and even picked up with his old music buddy, Royce Reeves, and his new string band. Mostly, though, he just soaked everything in. Odds were he would never see home again.

Under normal circumstances, when Matthews and Freeby returned to Pendleton, military police would have promptly locked them up. What they discovered, however, was that the brig was full. The very day that Matthews and Freeby fled for Texas, five hundred more men, denied leave, and aware that they would soon be going off to war, went "over the hill."

The Gold Dust Twins were court-martialed, sentenced to sixty days' confinement and sixty days' extra police duty, fined a whopping $136, and had their rank reduced. "Hashmark" Matthews was once again an ordinary private.

Aboard the Sheridan, the two were assigned to clean the officers' quarters for the duration of the journey. The job was meant to be a punishment—in lieu of the sixty days' confinement—but the Gold Dust Twins had the unique ability to make a silk purse out of a sow's ear. Every day, Matthews and Freeby went from the stinky, cluttered enlisted men's quarters with its cold showers and crude toilets to the cooled officers' wardroom. There they would sweep the floors, make the beds, and clean the head. The officers attended hours-long meetings, so after performing their duties, the Gold Dust Twins would linger long enough for a hot shower and a shave. They even took the liberty of including their dungarees with the officers' laundry and were the only enlisted men aboard ship with clean, starched, and pressed uniforms.

Robert Graf was also aboard the Sheridan, and so was Jimmy Haskell. In early 1943, after shacking up with a female acquaintance, Haskell had missed the ship that was leaving Norfolk for sea maneuvers. This time, however, he had used better judgment and resisted the temptation. Bill Jurcsak, another buddy from Ballston Spa, was also aboard.

On the *Sheridan,* water had to be rationed and the heat was stifling. Even when the Navy crew pulled away the hatch covers, the air failed to circulate. Deep in the ship's bowels where the saggy beds were stacked five tiers high, it felt like a boiler room. So the three upstate New Yorkers slept on deck, wrapped in green blankets, preferring the occasional downpour to the suffocation of the holds. There, after the lights were extinguished, they admired the constellations that lit up the sky and the calmness of the dark ocean. Graf, ever the romantic, remarked that the green phosphorescence that swirled around the ship reminded him of a pirate's chest of jewels. But it was Haskell, the biggest scoundrel of the three, who wrote, "On our journey across the vast Pacific Ocean, we usually would be topside. Young as we were, we all remarked what a beautiful scene there was out on the sea. Azure blue skies with high cotton clouds rising miles into the sky. Below us, deep blue water, it was a scene never to be forgotten. I wondered, with all this serene beauty around us, why would there have to be wars?"

Out of earshot of others, the three longtime friends could express their true feelings about war. In the company of other young Marines, war held a bewitching sense of glamour and danger. Occasionally a guy would make a comment about the "fucking crazy Marines" always rushing headlong into battle. It was less a lament than a wisecrack, said with a sense of pride. At night on the ship's deck, however, Graf, Haskell, and Jurcsak could be scared and uncertain. They could wonder whether they had made the right decision, if perhaps they would have been better off going to college or staying in Ballston Spa and raising a family, or buying a farm and getting an agricultural deferment.

The exercises were over now. Graf had written his letters home, explaining that he would be gone for a while, leaving his loved ones to speculate and fill in the essential details. Mrs. Graf, like the other mothers, worried, and the general vagueness of her son's letters gave her little comfort.

Mrs. Graf had reason to be concerned. The Marines' reputation for rushing headlong into battle, while exaggerated, contained an element of truth. It was for their reputed boldness that Robert Graf considered the Marines the best fighting men in the world. The assertion might have contained a touch of recruiter's hyperbole, but there were few Marines who believed otherwise. There was no question about one thing: the Marines were unmatched in their ability to carry out amphibious invasions. Beginning in the years after World War I, planners, hoping to find a role that would justify the Corps' existence (Army commanders were claiming that their own troops could take over the responsibilities of the Marines), fashioned a new doctrine of warfare based on the inevitability of a showdown with the Japanese in the Central Pacific.

Graf knew that Marine landings, even under the best of circumstances, were high-risk affairs. War in the Central Pacific offered little room for tactical tricks, deception, or the element of surprise. The Japanese would be dug in and waiting and would see the ships coming. In the abstract, this approach to war might have been a good one, but even General Holland "Howlin' Mad" Smith, one of the country's leading experts on amphibious warfare, knew that on the islands of the Central Pacific, it was a crapshoot; things could go right, as they had on Guadalcanal, or wrong, seriously wrong, as they had on Tarawa.

As the convoy pushed on and someone on deck broke out into a jolly rendition of "Don't Fence Me In," the men did not have to speculate about their destination. "Operation Flintlock" was no longer a mystery. The twin islands of Roi-Namur in the hundred-island Kwajalein Atoll of the Marshall Islands chain was their objective. The sun-scorched Kwajalein Atoll, 2,100 miles southwest of Hawaii, measured seventy miles long and twenty miles across and contained one of the world's largest landlocked lagoons. Although they were two of the biggest in the chain, Roi and Namur were remarkably small islands. Roi, the larger of the two, rose out of the blue-green ocean, less than three quarters of a mile long—though large enough to accommodate an airfield—and was connected to Namur by a narrow, jungle-choked causeway.

A day out of Maui, someone set up a large mock-up of Roi and Namur on deck. Based on submarine observations and aerial photos, the islands looked well defended. In August 1941, after two years of intensive construction, Kwajalein Atoll, located in the geographic center of the Marshall chain, became a fueling station for the Japanese fleet. In 1942 and 1943, Japan sent in reinforcements to help fortify the Marshalls. However, Allied victories in the summer of 1943 altered those plans. Japan was forced to collapse its defensive perimeter, relegating the Marshalls (and the Gilberts) to delaying outpost status. The 6th Base Force would defend the islands, buying time for large-scale construction projects in the Marianas and the Carolines.

Tactically the picture looked frighteningly similar to Tarawa. The islands were well defended and protected by a coral reef. Guys looked at the maps and photos and swallowed hard. Now the 4th Division was going to get hammered, too.

Lieutenant Roth called it their "baptism by fire." With his men huddled around the diagrams, he went through every detail of the invasion. If it meant saving one extra life, he and his platoon would sit in front of the mock-up every day until D-Day, until the men saw the beaches, trees, fortifications, drainage tunnels, aircraft hangars, and landing strips in their dreams.

On January, 31, 1944, seventeen days after leaving the California coast, and one day before the invasion, Graf climbed over the side of the *Sheridan* into a transport boat that carried him to a waiting LST.

Aboard the LST, Graf grabbed a folding cot and took a spot on the deck under a life raft and listened to the far-off thunder of the big Navy guns. Haskell and Jurcsak listened on a combat radio to scratchy bursts of communication from the 25th Marines. By nightfall the 25th had raised the first American flag in the Marshalls on a coconut tree on Ennubirr Island.

That night Graf witnessed a beautiful sunset, unlike anything he had ever seen before. The sun burned intensely red and then plunged into the sea and Graf heard the command, "Darken ship!"

Reveille came early on D-Day—0400 hours—though in reality, few slept, and no one needed a wake-up call. Soon Graf heard the big guns pounding Roi-Namur and saw the sky light up. The still tropical air smelled of exploded shells. Over the last three days American destroyers and planes had pulverized the islands with 2,655 tons of shells. While men whose stomachs or bowels had not rebelled waited in line for their "condemned man's breakfast" of steak, potatoes, vegetables, eggs, and hot coffee salted by sweat from the cooks' brows, Graf watched planes take off from a nearby carrier. In the distance he located Roi-Namur by the clouds of thick black smoke billowing into the sky. In the stifling heat he lingered on the deck as long as he could, grateful for the slight breeze.

At 7:00 a.m., three hours before the invasion, Lieutenant Roth ordered his men to load up. The loudspeaker blared instructions. In the fetid dimness belowdecks the amtrac landing vehicles were getting revved up, their powerful engines rumbling and coughing diesel fumes. The large fans worked hard to dissipate the smoke, but still it was enough to make Graf choke. Lieutenant Roth waved him over, and Graf joined the lieutenant and his buddy Dick Crerar in a crowded amtrac. Gunners assumed their positions at the mounted machine guns. Then came the signal. The traffic lights changed from red to amber to green, the bow doors of the LST opened, and the amtracs, scraping against the iron ridges of the ramp, lurched forward.

Bobbing like a cork, the amtrac waited for the signal from the control boat and then made its way to the destroyer escort and the line of departure. Spray flew over the bow, and in no time Graf was wet. At least the water was warm. At least it wasn't the Chesapeake Bay.

The attack was scheduled for ten that morning, but as the landing hour (H-hour) came and went, the amtracs circled. *What the hell's gone wrong?* the guys thought. When a nearby battlewagon fired its fourteen-inch naval guns and the shells tore across the sky with the roar of a freight train, Graf felt the amtrac tremble and every muscle in his body clench tightly. When they saw the shell hit, everyone aboard cheered as if they were at a weekend football game.

At just after 1100 hours, Graf's amtrac made for the line of departure. When the command vessel sent up a flare, the coxswain gunned the engines. Graf knew that at top speed the amtrac would cover the two miles in fifteen minutes, provided it was not swamped. Only two feet of freeboard remained. Everyone was thinking the same thing: *If we take on water, we'll go down like an anchor.*

When Lieutenant Roth yelled, "Fix bayonets!" Graf slipped his bayonet from its scabbard and locked it in. He liked the look of the ten-inch blade shining in the sun and hoped that he would remember how to use it. If a Jap soldier rushed him, would he keep his composure long enough to lunge and then slash his attacker diagonally from shoulder to hipbone?

As planes flew over for bombing and strafing runs, Graf slammed the eight-round clip into the breech of his M1 and touched its cold, deadly steel for reassurance. Then the amtrac's machine gunner opened up from his turret, spattering bullets across the beach. As the tread of the amtrac hit the beach and dug into the sand, Graf glanced at his watch—February 1, 1200 hours.

He and Crerar followed Roth over the side. Graf rolled, landed on his feet in ankle-deep water. Roth was waving his arm. "Let's go," he hollered. "Make room for the next wave. Watch your flanks." After unloading the first wave, the amtrac backed up and then spun around, avoiding a number of the sixteen-ton amphibious tanks that had flipped over in the violent surf.

Graf and Crerar crawled onto a small sand dune and surveyed the wreckage ahead of them: shattered palm trees, smashed pillboxes and blockhouses, mangled and twisted steel, a potholed airfield, and demolished planes.

Up ahead, through the smoke and dust and reek of cordite, Graf spotted one of his H Company buddies, Trinidad Arrajos. "Arrajos," he shouted, "what in the hell are you doing out there?" Arrajos was in front of the platoon and was going to get himself killed. "You crazy bastard!" he yelled, and motioned for Arrajos to get back behind the dune. Arrajos was wearing khakis instead of dungarees, and a helmet liner over his head. Then an electric shock shot through Graf's body.

*Jap! Son of a bitch, it's a Jap!* Their eyes met for an instant and then
Graf dove behind the sand ridge, grabbed a grenade, pulled the pin,
and launched it. The blast spattered sand particles through the air.
When he slithered to the top of the dune, he did not see the enemy
soldier. Behind him he noticed that the second wave was coming in.
Marines fired wildly into the companies that had landed in the first
wave until someone got word back to them that they were shooting at
their own men.

Carl Matthews realized that he had forgotten to remove his inflat-
able life vest. As he tried to roll over the side of the amtrac, he
activated the $CO_2$ cartridges. The vest blew up like a big balloon and
Matthews toppled backward. Corporal Mike Mihalek acted fast,
pulling his Ka-Bar knife from its scabbard and puncturing the vest.
Matthews could move now, and slid over the wall of the amtrac without a problem, and he and Mihalek ran to the beach. A Marine in
dungarees that looked as if they had just been dry-cleaned lay in the
sand. His helmet was still on his head, fastened under his chin by a
leather strap. One hand was still wrapped around his rifle.

"Is he dead?" Matthews felt as if he was going to be sick.

"Hell, yes," Mihalek answered, "and you will be, too, if you don't
get your ass off the beach."

Matthews ran forward and located Lieutenant Leary, who sent
him to find the rest of G Company. G Company had landed on the
wrong part of the beach, and Leary could not locate two of his platoon's three squads. Matthews ran down the beach past Navy corpsmen who were tagging the dead. His job was to find the squads and
orient them.

By 12:17, the bulk of the 2nd Battalion had reached the airfield,
its first-phase destination. Matthews and a buddy, Maurice Maness, a
Baptist preacher's kid from Missouri, worked their way to a bombed-
out plane hangar. As they were catching their breath, a mortar landed
and hit Maness, tearing up the flesh just below his knee. Luckily for
him, the hot fragment had expended much of its hitting power. Matthews cut open his dungarees and, gritting his teeth, Maness dug his

Ka-Bar knife into his leg and pried out a piece of shrapnel. Matthews then dusted sulfa powder on the wound and bandaged it.

Using grenades, concussion grenades, and shotguns, G Company investigated every shed, revetment, shell hole, culvert, and drainage ditch. Japanese soldiers, they knew, had an uncanny ability to stay hidden. An officer told them to "flush 'em out like rats." And "no prisoners," he added. "Japs love to die."

By 6:00 p.m. the 2nd Battalion had pushed across to the other side of the island. From a ridge that Graf and Crerar had scouted, Lieutenant Roth instructed the squad leaders to set up a perimeter and machine guns in case of a counterattack. From this low six-foot rise, the battalion watched as the battle still raged on Namur, where most of the Japanese soldiers had taken refuge during the naval bombardment. There the Japanese were fighting a losing battle. Their generals had already decided to sacrifice the island.

Graf and Crerar dug a shallow foxhole. The top layer of sand was easy to dig through, but once they hit the hard coral, it was a lesson in futility. Two feet would have to do. They wiggled into the hole, got situated, and decided it was time to eat. His hand trembling from fatigue, hunger, and dehydration, Graf cut through the waterproof coating on a K-rations box and dined on cold cheese and hash and salt tablets washed down with warm water from his canteen, while Crerar opted for a D-rations chocolate bar.

As darkness descended, Graf waited with his finger on the crescent trigger of his M1. Crerar, soaked in sweat, with his head propped up on his helmet, slept while Graf, eyes and ears straining, watched and listened for infiltrators. Gunnery Sergeant Townsley, who knew as much as anyone in the Marines about staying alive, had warned him about the Japanese banging their grenades against rocks. Japanese grenades were queer things: after pulling the ring, a soldier had to strike the detonator against an object to ignite the fuze.

What Graf got instead of Japanese infiltrators was an onslaught of land crabs and rats scurrying through the sand, palm fronds, crackling leaves, and discarded C-ration tins. Thank heavens for the Navy.

During the course of the night, the Navy shot up flares. Burning phosphorus and hissing, they drifted in the breeze on parachutes, turning night into twilight. Had it not been for the flares, Graf would have assumed that the crabs were lurking enemy soldiers poised to stick him with their bayonets.

Not far away from Graf and Crerar, Lieutenant Leary set up his platoon command post in a shell crater, Matthews at his side. Matthews felt relief, thankful that the fight had not been tougher. A few men had been wounded, but G Company had lost only one Marine, a sweet kid from Mount Airy, Pennsylvania, who, one of the guys said, had a pretty wife, and a baby he had never laid eyes on.

At some point during the night, Lieutenant Leary told Matthews to take a message to the company command post. Matthews was terrified. This was not like running messages on maneuvers. This was the real thing, with the real possibility that some scared, trigger-happy G Company Marine would shoot before asking for the password. The prospect of being killed or wounded by an enemy soldier was bad enough, but what a disgrace it would be to be shot by a fellow Marine.

Matthews delivered the message and lived to see another day. The following morning dawned steamy and bright. By noon the 2nd Battalion had cleared out the north end of the island, disabling every Japanese rifle they found by yanking out the bolt and smashing the stock against a tree trunk or the coral. All that was left to do was to grab a souvenir. Men searched the bushes for whatever they could find. Nambu pistols were the big prize, but Marines also liked the perfectly folded flags that the enemy soldiers kept inside their steel helmets and the personal items they brought with them into battle.

Graf walked past a large trench filled with dead Japanese. What struck him first was the stench of days-old bodies killed in the naval bombardment. Rotting in the sun and bloated with gas, the corpses, he would later write, looked like "small blimps" and smelled like slaughtered hogs. What he noticed next was the size of the Japanese soldiers. These were not little bucktoothed caricatures, but powerful Imperial Marines. From the fat flies surrounding their blood-caked skulls, it was clear that, as loyal soldiers of the Empire, they had blown their heads off rather than be captured.

As for the souvenirs, his fellow Marines had beaten him to the punch. Already they had torn off buttons from the blouses of the corpses, emblems from their lapels, along with their ID bracelets, watches, and diaries. That none of them could read Japanese did not matter a bit. Later, like boys swapping baseball cards, they traded the booty among themselves—a flag with an image of the Rising Sun for a few buttons, an emblem for a family photo.

# CHAPTER 19

# Paradise

On February 16, 1944, following their victory on Roi-Namur, the 4th Marine Division docked in Kahului Harbor, Maui. Gunny Townsley was shouting orders in what Graf affectionately called his "foghorn" voice, and soon the men were boarding trucks. It was comforting to hear Townsley, surly as hell, yelling again. Townsley's presence had a way of restoring order to the universe. With Townsley there, the men knew that nothing was beyond repair. He would let them grieve for lost buddies, but when he determined that their time was up, he would push them again as he always had.

Leaving Kahului, the men got a look at what they thought was paradise—the ocean, towering palm trees that lined the roadway, modest white houses with green roofs, pineapple and sugarcane fields, banana trees scattered across small pastures, and happy-faced locals who waved in welcome. It was not until they smelled the rich scents of plumeria, ginger blossoms, and blooming pikake, however, that they forgot the stench that filled their throats on Roi-Namur.

As they left the coastal road, they began their climb into the hills. Again Graf was filled with the romance of the place and let the names roll off his tongue like music—Lower Paia, Makawao, Haiku. After passing through the village of Kokomo, he saw the gates of Camp Maui. After the beauty of the drive, Camp Maui was a slap in the face, the sloppy roads of red clay and the rows of drab tents, built over wooden platforms. Soon he learned that electricity had not yet been installed, and the showers emitted "the coldest water this side of the North Pole." In the head, "thunder mugs," separated by not even a sheet of plywood, were placed so close together that a guy moving his bowels could punch the fella sitting next to him. The bathroom stank, and so did the weather. The magnificent Haleakala volcano trapped every cloud that floated over the island, obliterating the sun and dumping inches of rain over the camp every afternoon. The dining hall served the worst food east of the Marshall Islands.

At Camp Maui, Graf and his buddies supplemented their food intake with beer from the camp bar. In fact, it did not take long for them to discover that although they could get only two beers at a time, the Marines manning the PX did not seem to care how often they returned as long as they refrained from fighting. Graf, who had cultivated a taste for scotch and soda, became an avid beer man at Camp Maui.

The Gold Dust Twins, too, were drawn to the slop chute like bulls to a red flag. As if the obstacle course at the Army's Jungle Training Center was not grueling enough, plied with beer, they staged nightly raids on a nearby pineapple plantation that their first sergeant said was strictly off-limits. Sometimes they were joined by their tentmates, including squad leader Bill Mihalek, who knew better than to get hung up with the Gold Dust Twins, but couldn't resist the temptation to sink his teeth into fresh pineapple. Even Lieutenant Leary would occasionally join the men in what they called their "refreshments" and never once questioned where, or how, they came by them.

When Matthews realized that he would be sharing a tent at Camp Maui with Wendell Nightingale, he was delighted. They had met at the chow hall at Camp Pendleton over an evening meal where Nightingale teased everyone around him. It was not the kind of sadistic needling that a bully doles out, but funny and good-natured. What

Matthews also noticed was that Nightingale could take it as well as he could dish it out.

The two grew close, which must have struck anyone who saw them together as hilarious. While the Gold Dust Twins, two tiny Texans with oversized, mischievous spirits, were made for each other, "like pigs and shit," according to Sergeant Jack Campbell, Matthews and Nightingale could not have been more different. Nightingale was tall and lanky, with a split-rail-fence physique. He hailed from Skowhegan, Maine, and had a thick, antiquated accent that might have sounded more natural in seventeenth-century England. And Nightingale was as pure as deep-woods snow. In California, while other young Marines were rushing off to bars and prostitutes, he stayed behind, reminiscing about making maple syrup and the team of horses that pulled his sled back and forth across the December pastures. Matthews heard story after story about how Nightingale learned to dance with the pretty "faam" girls at the grange hall and how occasionally he would step outside with one of them long enough to steal a kiss.

It was Nightingale who introduced Matthews to Los Angeles' Riverside Ranchero, a country music club where bands played western swing and whole families came for a night of fun. Nightingale spent most of his time on the floor twirling the beauties. Parents were happy to allow their daughters to dance with such a respectful young man. Matthews studied Nightingale's technique and was soon enjoying the Ranchero as much as his friend.

Liberty at Camp Maui was nothing like liberty at Pendleton. It came once every eight days, and Marines had to be back in their tents by 6:00 p.m. or risk being picked up by the shore patrol. In their sack-pressed khakis (they washed and stuck them under their mattresses to remove the wrinkles), Matthews, Freeby, and Nightingale made occasional trips to Pukalani, Wailuku, or Kahului, but often after a week of intense maneuvers—including thirteen-mile hikes to the Haleakala crater—they were too tired to leave the camp. None of this bothered Lieutenant Leary, who preferred his men to stay behind. Everyone had heard the stories of drunk Marines picking fights with the locals. Some guys could not contain their hatred. "A Jap's a Jap," they would say, ignoring the fact that most of Maui's Japanese were actually Nisei, or second-generation, born in the territory and loyal to the United States.

On those days when he stayed in camp, Matthews read and reread letters from home. He also did embroidery. Matthews was probably the only man in the Corps who knew how to use a needle and thread. He took a lot of heat from his buddies—Lieutenant Leary threatened to expel him from the platoon if he ever caught him squatting to pee—but all acknowledged that he had the best-decorated "piss-cutter" (slang for the Marines' khaki "garrison cap") in the entire 4th Division. A large Marine emblem adorned the cap's left side. On the right Matthews embroidered TEXAS with orange lettering highlighted by bold black outlines. He also stitched the names of places he had been, courtesy of the Corps, into the cap. He included palm trees and an outline of the harbor at Pago Pago in American Samoa. What his tentmates liked best was the native girl in the grass skirt that Matthews had stitched on the right rear of the cap.

Just as they were getting into the swing of things, Robert Graf and his sidekick, Bill More, received some disappointing news. More was being moved to Battalion Headquarters and assigned to a G2 intelligence team. Graf and Crerar were being transferred from H Company to E Company. The silver lining was that Lieutenant Roth was moving, too, and he requested that both join him as runners in his platoon.

Shortly after the reorganization, Colonel Louis Jones, the 23rd's commanding officer, ordered an 81- and 60-mm mortar demonstration. Companies gathered in a field while the mortar squads fired over their heads onto a target. As the mortars landed, an officer explained, via the public address system, how mortars were employed in combat situations.

The mortar round that fell short sounded no different from the others. Bill More saw it land. It happened too fast for him to feel panic. When it hit, he felt the searing heat of the bursting shell and the rush of wind from the explosion. Before the smoke disappeared, it was clear to him that the outcome would not be pretty.

The mortar seriously wounded several men and killed Gunnery Sergeant Emberg Townsley, who was crouched in the grass just feet from where the mortar landed. There was not a dry eye at the funeral. Harking back to their days as "Old Breed" Marines, Colonel Jones said to the assembled men, "With Townsley we cleaned up everything on the China coast . . . his death is not only a blow to the battalion, but a great loss to the regiment." After Jones's words, a firing squad sent three volleys over the grave and then a bugler played taps.

# CHAPTER 20

# Camp Tarawa

While the 4th Division was mourning Townsley's death on Maui, the 2nd Marine Division was months into its training on the big island of Hawaii. After defeating the Japanese at Tarawa, the division dropped off its wounded at Pearl Harbor, where ambulances took them to area hospitals. On a dark night in early December 1943, the convoy arrived in Hawaii's Hilo Harbor. The air hung heavy with humidity. The town was under a blackout, and the exhausted men saw nothing but shadows. They staggered and shuffled off the transport ships, wondering what the division had in store for them. Many of them barely made it to the waiting trucks that transported them sixty-five miles from Hilo Harbor to their tent camp under the giant, snow-capped peaks of the twin volcanoes Mauna Loa and Mauna Kea. Those whom the trucks could not accommodate traveled by narrow-gauge train that was originally built to support the sugar industry.

Upon arriving in camp, some of the men joked that the Marines had delivered them from one hell only to plop them down in another. It was the kind of gallows humor that all of them—veterans of the three-day carnage on Tarawa—now understood. It didn't take long for the newcomers to give their Hawaiian home a name. "Camp Tarawa," they called it.

The men literally had to build the camp from scratch. Piles of cots and tents lay in a pasture waiting to be assembled. Laboring in the gray mist at 6,000 feet, it took until Christmas. The men grumbled that whoever had chosen the site was one sadistic son of a bitch. There were no panoramic views of the blue-green Pacific. Mother Nature had drawn an unsparing line through the middle of camp. To the north lay sodden forests saturated by cold rains, and cloud-covered mountains that caught and trapped the northeast trade winds. To the south lay dry, hilly pastureland, plagued by cacti and dust storms, searing heat and fields of sharp black lava. Only to the west, on the lee of the island, with its quiet, palm-lined beaches, could a wandering Marine escape the climatic extremes.

As much as the men came to hate Camp Tarawa's miserable weather, the Navy physicians rightly insisted that there was no better place for veterans who had also been in the Guadalcanal campaign to recover from the ravages of recurrent malaria attacks. As the atabrine treatments killed the malaria parasites, the fever-addled men recovered their youthful vigor. The officers saw the change and began to push them again. Beginning with forced marches, and maneuvers in the Hamakua and Kan cane fields, they graduated to live-fire exercises. While they scrambled over rock and scrub and fields of knife-edged black lava, machine gunners fired rounds over their heads and artillery shells burst near them.

As a runner for Sergeant John Rachitsky, Frank Borta had gone into Tarawa late on the second day. Just sixteen years old, Borta was as green as they came, a callow young kid with peach fuzz and a sideways grin. But he was in good hands. The sergeant was a consummate Marine, tall, lean, oozing confidence, and nearly indestructible. Prior to the war, he had served in China and survived a number of close calls. Rachitsky, they said, was so rugged he needed a wheelbarrow to carry his cast-iron balls in. But he was no loudmouthed show-off. He preferred a quiet kind of leadership. Every Marine under him knew exactly what he expected: that every man would do his duty. Guys joked that they were less afraid of dying than of letting down the sergeant.

Borta knew that he had gotten off easy on Tarawa. Owing to a series of oversights and mix-ups, the units that had come in early on the second morning were nearly destroyed. That day the tide covering Betio's coral reef was barely two feet high. Japanese defenders on the island's eastern peninsula lowered the long barrels of their dual-purpose antiaircraft guns and hit the Higgins boats as the drivers lowered the ramps. Then gunners along the island's north coast tore into the troops as they waded ashore. The sight horrified correspondent Robert Sherrod, who thought that nothing could be as bad as the initial landing the day before. "This is far worse than it was yesterday," he wrote.

By the evening of the second day, when Borta came ashore, the carnage was over. By November 23, the battle's fourth day, Marines raised an American flag to the top of one of the island's last standing palm trees, and a bugler sounded colors. Borta saluted and thanked God for sparing his life.

Born in late January 1927, Frank Borta was only sixteen when he persuaded his mother that the only thing in life he wanted was to be a Marine. She agreed to lie about his age. When the recruiter called to verify, she assured him that June 1, 1926, was Frank's birthday. His father, a tough Polish-American, wondered aloud why in hell the Marines would want his pipsqueak of a son. "Jesus Christ," he said, "I knew we were losing the war, but not bad enough to take you."

The following day Borta walked down to the station for his weigh-in. Marines had to be 130 pounds, and he came up two pounds short. Winking, the corpsman put his hand on Borta's shoulder while he was on the scale. "This chick is underweight," he said to the gunnery sergeant, "but he's big-boned. We'll put some meat on him."

Tarawa, though, had been a wake-up call. He had gone in dreaming of glory, but after seeing bodies sprawled on the beach and corpses floating like buoys in the surf, he knew the reality of being a Marine. It was not dress blues and adoring women and an easily earned reputation for bravery. For many the reality was death on an obscure atoll.

Borta was assigned to a burial detail, and was among the last Marines off the island. By the time he arrived in Waimea, Hawaii, Camp Tarawa was up and running. In early February his platoon was pulled out and sent back to Hilo. There Sergeant Rachitsky informed Borta and the others that they were now part of a new group called the 2nd Separate Infantry Battalion, under the auspices of the 2nd Marine Division.

In Hilo, Borta and the 2nd Separate Infantry Battalion learned that their home was to be the Kilauea Military Camp, which was still surrounded by barbed wire. Kilauea had housed Japanese-American internees before they were relocated to camps in the continental United States. By day the men guarded ammunition dumps and unloaded ships. Rachitsky assigned Borta to unloading duty. The work was dull and difficult, and Rachitsky pushed and timed the work crews to see how long it took them to unload boxes of hand grenades and 30-mm rounds. Ship-to-shore movement of ammunition—the job had invasion written all over it.

No one, not even Rachitsky, had any idea where the next battleground would be. One thing was for sure, though: wherever they were headed, it was going to be ugly. General Holland "Howlin' Mad" Smith had made that clear. "We are through with the flat atolls," he said. Then he added, "Now we are up against mountains and caves where the Japs can really dig in."

Replacements for the upcoming invasion were coming in from every direction, tenderfeet hustled out of boot camp and regular Marines wearing campaign ribbons. Borta could have been stuck with any number of jerks. But at Hilo he lucked out, sharing a tent with a group of stand-up guys: Glenn Brem, Milt Lemon, William Landers, William Larson, and Richard Carney, a tough Irishman and former Golden Gloves boxer from the Bronx. Carney was also Hollywood handsome. The word around camp was that after being spotted in a Los Angeles bar he had received a letter from a motion picture talent scout. Perhaps after the war, he would make it onto the big screen. Women would howl for his autograph and he would date what Landers, in his Missouri drawl, called "Hollywood sirens." Most important, Carney was the kind of man a guy wanted to go into battle with. Rumor had it that he was up for a Silver Star for taking an enemy bunker on Tarawa. "Stick with Carney," the guys said, "and you'll come out okay."

Lemon and Larson were the greenhorns of the group. Lemon was a naïve country boy from the Panhandle of Texas who loved banjo and fiddle music and talked about going home after the war and striking it rich in the oil fields. Lemon, like Borta, was a runner. Larson was a sweet-natured kid from Wisconsin who had two brothers fighting in the 2nd Division, and was the practical joker. He had been wounded at Tarawa on the first day. Although the wound was not a bad one, it got him out of the rest of the fighting. Larson always said that he had not done anything on Tarawa except get a big scratch on his throwin' arm.

Brem was a farm kid from Gilroy, California. His dad planted row crops and ran a 5,000-acre family spread in the wild hills of Pacheco Pass, a stagecoach route that had once connected Chicago to San Francisco.

The outdoors was Brem's passion. He loved deer and duck hunting best. He was adept at handling a shotgun, but with a rifle he was pure magic. He could shoot as easy as most men draw a breath. In San Diego, on record day, he shot 326 out of 340 bull's-eyes with a twelve-knot wind. They wanted him to stay on as an instructor until they learned that he was only seventeen, two years too young.

Compared to the others, Brem was the quiet one, the independent loner. Landers, who had a penchant for nicknames, dubbed him "Pluto" because he had a funny way of talking, like he had just taken a gulp of helium. The name stuck. Even the officers called him Pluto. Landers hung the name "Chick" on Borta because, even among a bunch of youngsters, Borta, with his baby-smooth skin and affection for Coca-Cola instead of beer, was so obviously the spring chicken of the group. Borta tried to affect a street-smart Chicago attitude, but his buddies knew that he was just a wide-eyed kid. They said he was so young and inexperienced that he would not have a clue what to do if a beautiful girl lifted her dress for him.

As spring approached, Sergeant Rachitsky informed his men that they would soon be headed back to Camp Tarawa for intensive training. Chick Borta and his tentmates were ambivalent about the news. They hated unloading ships. Nevertheless, intensive training meant that soon they would be sent into combat. Would the battles all be as bloody as Tarawa?

Knowing that their days in Hilo were numbered, the tentmates spent as many nights in the bars as they could. Back at camp, they could get Chick Borta's beer ration, but a few cans of beer was not the kind of drinking they had in mind. On one particular night, Landers, Carney, and Borta went into Hilo to drink. They had just sat down when they noticed a black Marine—the first any of them had ever seen—sitting at the bar. *Well, I'll be,* they thought. *A goddamn Negro Marine.* White or black, it did not matter to Borta. If what lay ahead was anything like Tarawa, the Marines could use all the help they could get. As long as they knew how to fight, he did not give a shit if the soldiers were white, black, yellow, or brown. Maybe the Marines were bringing in Negroes as night fighters.

Landers was ordering the first round when a drunk U.S. Army private walked up and began to heckle the black Marine. "Look, dog-face," the Marine threatened. "I'm a United States Marine. I'll kick your ass."

Landers, Carney, and Borta looked at each other. "He sure told that doughboy," Carney said, using the World War I slang for a GI. Then Carney got up, walked over to the black Marine, and bought him a beer.

# CHAPTER 21

# Ernie King's Victory

In the spring of 1944, as Chick Borta and his tentmates prepared to leave Hilo and return to Camp Tarawa, the Marine combat structure was undergoing significant changes. The biggest change, at least for the average Marine rifleman, took place at the squad level. Each squad was split into four-man rifle teams, which were built around a BAR (Browning Automatic Rifle) man. The idea was to free up small teams of men and make them less dependent on squad, platoon, and company supervision. It was the exact opposite of the top-down Japanese command structure. If a Japanese captain or lieutenant died in combat, the men under him found it impossible to implement orders. No one was willing or able to take charge. The Marine Corps was aware of this, and in the process of revising its own command structure for the chaotic fighting ahead, it gave its riflemen greater rather than less autonomy, believing that a decentralized chain of command was the key to victory.

The key to victory, according to Admiral King, was taking the Marianas sooner rather than later. In early 1944, King had flown to San Francisco to meet with Admiral Nimitz and Admiral Halsey,

commander of the South Pacific Area, to try to convince them that
the seizure of the Marianas was the essential piece in the Navy's drive
across the Central Pacific, and should be moved up from its scheduled date of November 15. King left the city with the impression that
the admirals believed similarly. In the ensuing weeks, however, Nimitz wavered. In late January, General Richard Sutherland, Douglas
MacArthur's chief of staff, met with representatives of Nimitz and
Halsey in Pearl Harbor to discuss an alternate plan. Sutherland argued that combining resources, and giving priority to the Southwest
Pacific rather than the Central Pacific, would guarantee the seizure of
the Philippines and provide the quickest route to China. Nimitz's staff
filled him in on Sutherland's presentation, and the admiral seemed
persuaded. Overjoyed, the staid Sutherland wired MacArthur that he
had won Nimitz's support.

Reading the minutes of the Pearl Harbor conference, King grew
furious. How had Sutherland managed to inveigle the admiral? In a
scathing letter, King wrote Nimitz, "I have read your conference notes
with much interest and, I must add, with indignant dismay. Apparently, neither those who advocated the concentration of effort in the
Southwest Pacific, nor those who admitted the possibility of such a
procedure, gave thought nor undertook to state when and if the Japanese occupation and use of the Marianas and Carolines was to be ter-
minated. I assume that even the Southwest Pacific advocates will admit
that sometime or other this thorn in the side of our communications
to the Western Pacific must be removed. In other words, at some time
or other we must take our time and forces to carry out this job. . . ."
Continuing, King wrote, "A number of conferees, particularly Towers [Admiral John Towers, deputy commander-in-chief, Pacific Ocean
Area and deputy commander-in-chief, Pacific Fleet], stated that his
[Sutherland's] statements were allowed to go unrefuted. . . . The idea
of rolling up the Japanese along the New Guinea coast, throughout Halmahera and Mindanao, and up through the Philippines to
Luzon, as our major strategic concept, to the exclusion of clearing out
Central Pacific line of communications to the Philippines, is to me

absurd. Further, it is not in accordance with the decision of the Joint Chiefs of Staff."

Buoyed by Sutherland's report, MacArthur followed up with General George Marshall, the U.S. Army chief of staff, in writing. A dual drive, he said, although already authorized by the Joint Chiefs of Staff (JCS) and the Combined Chiefs of Staff (CCS), would constitute "two weak thrusts" and would inevitably delay an Allied victory over Japan. Addressing himself to King's plan, he argued that seizing the Marianas and the Carolines would be of little value. Neither provided the harbors or airfields to support an eventual assault against the Philippines. MacArthur ended his missive by asking Marshall to make available to him "all ground, air and assault forces in the Pacific."

King, too, pressured Marshall. Irate that MacArthur had decided to flout the decisions of the JCS and CCS at Cairo, King recommended that Marshall chastise the general and command him to obey orders. Marshall, however, demurred, choosing instead to let the JCS decide what to do about MacArthur's proposal. On the very same day King sent his indignant letter to Nimitz, General Sutherland arrived in Washington to again do his boss's bidding.

The jockeying continued. A month after the fall of the Marshall Islands, King wrote to General Marshall, "I am as anxious as you are to have a comprehensive plan for operations against the Japanese, but I feel that we should not put off a decision as to what is to be done in the immediate future, at this time when our tremendously powerful forces can be thrown against an enemy who is obviously bewildered by recent events." Those "recent events" to which King referred were Vice Admiral Marc "Pete" Mitscher's devastating attacks on Truk. After the seizure of the Marshalls, Nimitz had accelerated his Central Pacific timetable. Realizing that he would have to neutralize Truk and enemy airpower before attacking the Japanese base at Eniwetok—350 miles northwest of Kwajalein in the Marshall Islands—the admiral gave Mitscher the go-ahead.

Lying 1,000 miles east of the Philippines, Truk was the operational base of the Combined Fleet, and, according to Nimitz, the Japanese "cojones." Ringed by a coral reef, it consisted of a dozen volcanic islands and thirty smaller ones and contained the fleet anchorage, a bomber airfield, three fighter strips, seaplane bases, docks, and supply installations.

On February 12 and 13, Mitscher's Task Force left Majuro. In a series of attacks on February 17 and 18, the admiral demolished the once-impregnable base, taking out three hundred planes, three cruisers, four destroyers, and 200,000 tons of military and merchant shipping. While roving the islands, Admiral Raymond Spruance, commander of the United States 5th Fleet (originally the Central Pacific Force), and Mitscher's boss, sank a cruiser, a destroyer, a subchaser, and a trawler as they tried to escape the bombardment. The big prize, however, Admiral Mineichi Koga, commander of the Imperial Combined Fleet, was nowhere to be found. Following news of the Allied victory in the Marshalls, the admiral and his fleet fled Truk for the Palaus, 925 nautical miles to the west, at the far end of the Carolines. After destroying Truk, Mitscher headed northwest to reconnoiter the Marianas. On February 23 his carrier planes photographed and then bombed Saipan, Tinian, and Guam.

Two and a half weeks later (March 11 and 12), the Joint Chiefs called an emergency meeting in Washington. Admiral Nimitz and General Sutherland were on hand for the discussions. Realizing that the JCS would no longer find compelling his arguments for focusing the bulk of the Allied thrust on New Guinea and the Philippines, and aware that he might be left behind while the Navy and the Marines charged to glory, MacArthur instructed Sutherland to request permission of the Joint Chiefs to leapfrog his forces four hundred miles up the New Guinea coast to the enemy air base at Hollandia. The Joint Chiefs honored MacArthur's request, and General Kenney's Fifth Army Air Force knocked out Hollandia just over two weeks later.

In the meantime, King's one-man battle to get the Joint Chiefs to recognize the importance of the Marianas was about to end. On

March 12, the JCS reached a decision on the Marianas. The Joint War Plans Committee had advised that the Marianas be excluded from the master plan, but the JCS instead heeded the advice of the Joint Staff Planners and included them. King was elated. The JCS not only authorized the attack on the Marianas, but moved up the assault date by a full five months.

# CHAPTER 22

# Praise the Lord and
# Pass the Ammunition

In late April 1944, Captain Merrill Kinne reported for duty at Port Chicago. Although he was brought on to run the Naval Magazine (his official title was Officer-in-Charge of the Naval Magazine), Kinne, like many of the depot's officers whom he criticized for being book-taught and "too academic" about ordnance, had little experience with ammunition. After graduating from the Naval Academy in 1915, he worked with ordnance for just two years during a seven-year stint in the Navy, and then returned to civilian life. Twenty years later he rejoined the Navy, serving as an officer on a general cargo ship.

The day after Captain Kinne arrived at Port Chicago, Frank Knox, FDR's longtime Secretary of the Navy, died suddenly of a heart attack. Acting Secretary of the Navy James Forrestal announced Knox's death in a dispatch and directed all naval establishments at home and afloat to fly the colors at half-mast until sunset on the day of Knox's burial. Although Knox's death was mourned by many, for Negroes in the Navy, it represented a new day.

When James Forrestal became the Navy's new secretary, blacks got a leader dedicated to providing equal treatment and opportunity for all men regardless of their color. Forrestal was a member of the National Urban League and a proponent of social equality, but he was no moral crusader. As undersecretary of the Navy and then secretary, he saw the issue of using blacks as full combat seamen as one of efficiency and simple fair play. While he accepted the argument of Chief of Naval Personnel Vice Admiral Randall Jacobs's argument that "you couldn't dump two hundred colored boys on a crew in battle," he also agreed with the Special Programs Unit of the Bureau of Personnel that large concentrations of blacks in shore duties lowered efficiency and morale.

One of the first things Forrestal did was to order the Bureau of Naval Personnel to prepare an experimental plan for the integration of some fleet auxiliary ships. In a letter to the president, he explained his motivation. "From a morale standpoint," he wrote, "the Negroes resent the fact that they are not assigned to general service billets at sea, and white personnel resent the fact that Negroes have been given less hazardous assignments." Then he assured the president that his plan would be a gradual one. Initially blacks would be used only on the large auxiliaries, and only at 10 percent of the ship's complement. If the plan worked, then they would be added to other types of ships "as necessity indicates." President Roosevelt responded to Forrestal's proposal, "J.F. OK, FDR." Having received the president's approval, the secretary's victory was sealed when Admiral King gave his conditional okay.

In early May, not long after coming to the depot, Captain Kinne held a meeting of all the division officers. "From all I hear," he said, "it's only by the grace of God that Port Chicago is on the map. I want ammunition handled carefully, and I mean carefully."

Lieutenant James Tobin, head officer of the 2nd Division, approached the captain after his talk. He warned him that with a new attention to safety, there could be a drop in tonnage. Kinne did not even hesitate. "Don't you worry, Lieutenant," he replied. "I will take the brunt on the matter of tonnage."

But with the invasions of Saipan, Tinian, and Guam scheduled for June, and of the Palau Islands and Morotai for mid-September, and under an amphibious doctrine that called for massive naval gun-fire and superior firepower once the troops had landed, tonnage again took top billing at Port Chicago. Contradicting himself, as he often would, Captain Kinne told his officers that "the war could not wait." The depot would operate full blast, twenty-four hours a day, seven days a week.

With the imperious Captain Kinne in charge, the pressure on Port Chicago's 1,400 naval enlisted men and eight loading divisions to push became even greater. Convinced that officers and seamen had to "continually keep in mind the necessity for getting the ammunition out," Kinne posted on the wall of the dock office daily tonnage totals for each division, and each week he awarded the winning division a pennant to fly over its barracks. Some of the seamen adopted the spirit of competition and competed for bragging rights. Most, though, regarded it as child's play. How could a pennant ever make up for poor working conditions, poor pay, and a lack of ratings and promotional opportunities?

Shortly after Kinne arrived, Port Chicago underwent other changes, the most significant being the expansion of the loading dock. On May 10, construction was completed on Pier No. 1, which meant that the pier was not only twenty feet wider than it had ever been, but it had both an inboard and an outboard berth. For the first time, Port Chicago could load two ships simultaneously. The depot was also acquiring land for a permanent magazine for holding ammunition and high explosives. Port Chicago was also slotted to get a number of new buildings, including a recreation building. The improvements, though cheered by the men, did not meaningfully change conditions at the depot, but they did allow Captain Goss to persist in the delusion that at Port Chicago "extreme care and patience" was being paid to take care of the black seamen.

As far as Percy Robinson and Sammie Boykin were concerned, the most important development was the addition of the "Jolly Roger," a training apparatus resembling a Liberty ship, with booms, rigging, and steam winches. The Jolly Roger was fully operational by February 1944, and both Percy Robinson and Sammie Boykin volunteered to train on it. Whenever they could, they practiced bringing empty boxes in and out of the Jolly Roger's holds. Robinson, in particular, was happy about the prospect of getting out of the hold. Increasingly, he had to "coax, threaten, and bully" his men to get them to pull their weight. The new work gave him a sense of purpose and accomplishment. Here was a skill that required more than a strong back, something he could use after the war to get a decent-paying job. Both Robinson and Boykin excelled, and after ten or so days Lieutenant Commander Holman, Port Chicago's head loading officer, moved them down to the pier to serve as hatch tenders and to get a feel for the job. When he thought they were ready, he would move them to the winches for real.

While Robinson and Boykin exhibited natural ability as winchmen, had they been civilian longshoremen they would have spent years working with general cargo before the union allowed them to handle ammunition. Port Chicago, however, had gotten into the habit of taking shortcuts, using inexperienced men to perform extremely sensitive tasks. According to Kinne, Negro personnel or no, "you do the best you can with what you have." Ironically, even as the base flouted basic stevedoring safety standards, Captain Goss—and now Captain Kinne—was generating memos emphasizing the need for the careful handling of ammunition, citing as an example the recent explosion at the Naval Ammunition Depot in Hastings, Nebraska, the country's largest weapons production depot. The blast, which occurred in early April in the bomb and mine loading area, ignited fifty tons of explosives. Tremors were felt 160 miles away in Omaha. Amazingly only eight depot employees were killed. They were buried in a cemetery on depot land. Their monument read, "They gave their lives that liberty might not perish."

Captain Goss worried most about the sensitive, thin-walled bombs and depth charges. "Enough is known," he wrote, "to warrant increased emphasis on the absolute necessity of care in handling all explosives, particularly containers of relatively large amounts of concentrated high explosives within thin walls. In particular, any dropping of bombs, depth charges, etc., upon metal or concrete floors, any bumping against hard substances, and heavy bumps from rolling or swinging are to be carefully avoided. . . . It must be realized by all concerned that explosives are dangerous if improperly handled and that our contribution to the war effort as well as the safety of all individuals engaged in this work is actually dependent upon proper care in handling explosives."

Goss and Kinne issued a joint memo calling for the "unremitting attention" of everyone involved in the loading process. Oddly, though, Captain Kinne still refused to post safety regulations in the enlisted men's barracks. Later he would admit that his opinion of the seamen was so low that he considered it an exercise in futility; they would never be able to understand the regulations anyway.

Goss and Kinne introduced a long-overdue training program for both officers and seamen, with Lieutenant Commander Holman heading up the classes. The goal was an ambitious one: to train hatch tenders and thirty seamen per month as winchmen and to instruct other seamen "who show aptitude" in "methods of stowage and shoring," grooming them as carpenter's mates, riggers, and hold crew chiefs. The lecture program was envisioned as a daily event. The realities of loading for the invasion of the Marianas, however, derailed the series almost before it began. By mid-July, Lieutenant Commander Holman had delivered only two talks.

Despite Goss and Kinne's apparent concern for safety, many of the depot's officers were still betting on the performance of their divisions. Percy Robinson could see it happening—the covert handshake, the wink and smile, the arm around the shoulder, and the mumbling. Once the deal was sealed, the officers would push their men. Delucchi had it down to a science. "C'mon, Robinson," he would say. "Division No. 2 put on 240 tons today. You're falling behind. I got a nice twenty-four-hour liberty pass that says we can catch 'em." Then he would leave the dock, turning a blind eye to the misconduct that followed. Without taking shortcuts and rolling and banging bombs, the loaders could never achieve the kinds of tonnage numbers that officers wanted—often over 20,000 tons of ordnance per month. While there may have been depots putting out more tonnage, none of them were moving a greater variety of ammunition. It was not unusual for Port Chicago's seamen to combat-load 175 different ordnance items onto a ship with a 7,000-ton storage capacity. It was an enormous and often bewildering task, complicated by the need for speed.

With Admiral Nimitz kicking the war for the Central Pacific into high gear, the USS *Mauna Loa* docked at Port Chicago. It left ten days later, carrying a load of 6,400 tons. As if they were not already working hard, Port Chicago's black seamen instead picked up their pace, turning out a succession of Liberty ships every three to five days. In early May the USS *Rainier* berthed at Pier No. 1. By the end of May, she would reach Majuro, where her cargo was transferred to Mitscher's fast carriers for their pre-invasion strikes on Saipan. On May 18, the USS *Shasta* arrived, and two days later the USS *Lynx* tied off at Pier No. 2. For the first time the depot was loading two ships at a time. After taking on nearly 5,000 tons of ordnance, the *Shasta* sailed for Eniwetok, where she took on what remained of the USS *Sangay*'s load (the *Sangay* sailed back to San Francisco) and then headed directly for Saipan.

# CHAPTER 23

# Where Young Men Go to Die

The Northern Attack Force, which was scheduled to invade Saipan on June 15, left Pearl Harbor at various times over a six-day period between May 25 and May 30, the slowest vessels leaving first. The 2nd Marine Division was the last group to go. Frank "Chick" Borta watched as the sailors rushed about, casting off hawsers and lines. Two days outside of Pearl Harbor, he learned that his battalion had a new name—1st Battalion, 29th Marines. Soon after he learned that they would be attached to the 2nd Marine Division's 8th Marine Regiment and would be "taking part" in the invasion. The officer who made the announcement used those very words—"taking part"—as if they were being asked to participate in some kind of celebration.

Chick Borta figured if he ever wanted to see his Chicago home again, he had better listen to Lieutenant Henderson. Henderson was the platoon leader, and every day after an NCO led the men through calisthenics and abandon-ship drills, he presented photographs, relief maps, terrain models, and charts, and took them through the details of the invasion. General Holland "Howlin' Mad" Smith, who would be in charge of the largest force ever to operate under Marine command, had divided the four-mile landing beach on the western shore of the island, extending from Saipan's main town of Garapan to Agingan Point in the south, into four separate beaches: Red Beaches 1, 2, and 3 on the north; then Green Beaches 1, 2, and 3; then, just outside of Charan Kanoa, Blue Beaches 1 and 2; and finally Yellow Beaches 1, 2, and 3, extending to the south. The 2nd Division would hit the beaches north of the sugar dock in the town of Charan Kanoa (actual spelling is *Chalan,* but Marine historians spell it *Charan*) and the 4th Division would hit the beaches to the south. The 29th Battalion's assignment, however, was to execute a feint, faking a landing north of Garapan at Tanapag Harbor. The hope was that the Japanese would commit a regiment to stop the attack on the harbor, distracting it from trying to repel the actual invasion. Amtracs would approach within 5,000 yards of the beach, circle as if preparing to attack, and then return to their LSTs, after which the troops of the 29th would be transported to Green Beach 2, where later on that day they would go ashore. Naval gunfire would be used to make the ruse look realistic.

Lieutenant Henderson's lectures on field sanitation, first aid, and chemical warfare got long and tedious. As a joke, one Marine battalion commander issued his men a "hunting License." "Permission is hereby granted [name of soldier inserted]," the license read, "to hunt Japs on any island, islet, or atoll. . . . Methods or means of exterminating Japs (commonly known as 'Yellow Bastards') are unlimited, as is the bag limit allowed the bearer. Due to the great similarity between Japs and baboons, this license also covers the bearer in the event he shoots a baboon by mistake. Great care should be exercised, however, in distinguishing between the two. This is simple as the Jap is much uglier, smells worse, and sometimes wears clothes. Those wearing colored arm bands get priority. . . . The license expires when the Jap species becomes extinct."

For entertainment, Borta and Brem dealt separate games of blackjack. Brem had a track record as a winner. Back at Camp Tarawa on the Big Island of Hawaii, he had won $300 one night, almost four months' salary, and promptly sent all his earnings to his parents in Gilroy, California. Borta ran a game with a fella named Dajak, who dealt while Borta took the money. En route to Honolulu, after maneuvers on Kahoolawe Island, they had teamed up and won big. On the way to Saipan, they figured that as long as they had Lady Luck on their side, there was no sense in breaking up a profitable partnership.

Robert Patrick Roberts was aboard ship, too. When he took the bus down to Pearl Harbor's West Loch channel on May 22, he had no idea that he would be taking the place of one of the Marines who had been wounded or killed in the explosion. Nor did he know that he would be assigned to a unit that the self-proclaimed "orphans" aboard ship were calling the "bastard battalion." Like so many others in the battalion, he had never been in battle. The 1st Battalion 29th Marines was anything but an elite fighting unit. It had been put together hurriedly, using whatever extras the Marines could find—cooks, bakers, balloonists, antiaircraft gunners, horse Marines, and goof-offs, the kind of guys, as the saying went, who could fuck up a wet dream. Some of the rifle company commanders had been on Guadalcanal and Tarawa, but the battalion's CO and most of the battalion's other officers had no infantry experience whatsoever.

Roberts felt that many of the guys aboard ship had an edge to them. The new ones, especially, were jumpy, distant, and preoccupied, their heads filled with images of battle and death. Considering where they were going, it was inevitable that their nerves were rubbed raw. Many had no experience whatsoever with live fire. Many had never even simulated a landing.

Roberts probably should have been more frightened than he was. He had been to Scout and Sniper School and was one of the best shots the instructors at Camp Elliott had ever seen, shooting 317 bull's-eyes out of a possible 340, but some officer with his head up his ass had made him an assistant Browning Automatic Rifle man, which meant that his job was to carry bandoliers of ammo, sixty to seventy pounds of it, and a tripod. Roberts had been to BAR school and he knew that the Japs targeted the BAR man and his assistant. By taking out a BAR man, the enemy could significantly reduce the automatic firepower of a squad. Roberts wondered if perhaps he should have listened to the doctor at Fort McPherson in Atlanta, Georgia, who gave him his induction physical. When the doctor examined his feet he told Roberts that they were flat and that he should consider going into the Navy instead of the Marines.

"Doctor," Roberts said, "I can walk farther than I can swim."

Had his daddy had his way, Roberts would have stayed at home in Elberton, Georgia, with his middle brother, who had a heart murmur. Mr. Roberts was a carpenter, and although he discouraged his son from going into carpentry, he would have been glad to bring his young son into the business if he had been willing to give up his dream of being a Marine.

"I already got three sons in the service," Mr. Roberts said.

"Daddy," Robert replied, "I wanna go."

The last time Roberts had seen his father was when he left for boot camp. He was sitting in the kitchen and had tears in his eyes. It was the only time Roberts had ever seen him cry.

On June 6, 1944, while his LST was still en route to Eniwetok, the final staging area prior to the assault on Saipan, the heat turned from torrid to unbearable. Robert Graf was hanging over the rails on the weather deck, marveling at the phosphorescence and its "sparkling and glistening symphony of light," when over the PA system the boatswain's pipe sang out. "Now hear this, now hear this," the announcer shouted. "We have just received word that the invasion of Europe has begun." Graf, like everybody aboard ship, listened spellbound. "The landings took place in Normandy, and Supreme Headquarters announced that the landings to date have been successful." Graf felt a lump grow in his throat. Then he heard a deep cheer rumble through the crowd. Seconds later men were jumping, hollering, catcalling, and whooping like Hollywood caricatures of Indian warriors. Graf hugged the Marine next to him.

Admiral Chester Nimitz, who was running the Central Pacific show from his desk in Pearl Harbor, knew that although Operation Overlord was larger than Forager (which included the invasion of Tinian and Guam, as well as Saipan), the Royal Navy's contribution to General Dwight Eisenhower's cross-Channel invasion of Normandy was essential. In the Marianas, however, every soldier, sailor, aviator, and Marine, every piece of equipment and the vast bulk of supplies, would be American. Shipping had to be arranged so that there would be no halt in the flow of materials, which included a colossal supply of ordnance, and nearly 4.5 million barrels of oil, 8 million gallons of high-octane aviation fuel, and 275,000 barrels of diesel oil each month.

Late in the evening on June 6, Graf's LST 84 cruised into Eniwetok's atolls and dropped its hooks in the lagoon. The plan was to remain berthed off the island until the morning of June 9. The USS *Mifflin,* which carried Carl Matthews's Company G, also arrived that evening. The following morning Company G transferred to LST 764. To Carl Matthews it looked as if the entire U.S. Navy had descended on Eniwetok. So many ships had anchored that a man could have hopped across the lagoon from one vessel to the next without ever getting wet. The concentration of ships undoubtedly had Admiral Spruance on edge. Had a Japanese search plane spotted the convoy, it could have spelled doom for the invasion.

On the morning of June 7, aboard LST 84, Lieutenant Henderson briefed his men on what to expect from Saipan. Platoon commanders across the lagoon were giving their own versions of the same lecture. "The water is unfit to drink, and the food could knock you out as fast as a bullet," Henderson said. Then he explained that farmers on Saipan used "night soil," or human waste, to fertilize their fields. He painted a picture of an island where Marines would not only have to do battle with the "yellow vermin" Japanese soldiers but also with a malevolent environment. During the rainy season, which lasted from June through November, the island would be drenched in nearly a hundred inches of rain. Humidity would hang over the island like a wet sock. "The saber grass cuts through the flesh," he added. "The insects carry diseases, and there are snakes that are poisonous and giant lizards. Do not approach the inhabitants. There is leprosy, typhus, dengue fever, and dysentery, elephantiasis, yaws, typhoid, and filariasis."

Henderson's lecture revealed just how little the U.S. military knew about Saipan. Unlike Guadalcanal and New Guinea, Saipan was not covered in jungle and infested with snakes or disease. On Saipan, in June, at the beginning of the wet season, the hibiscus, bougainvillea, and flame and poinciana trees were in exotic bloom, radiating a beauty some of the invading Marines could not help but notice. During lulls in the battle, while watching the fiery sun slide into the Philippine Sea, men had to remind themselves that they were on Saipan to kill or be killed.

The truth was that Saipan was far from primitive. It was the administrative center of Japan's civilian government in the Marianas, and, in many ways, a modern island. It was home to nearly forty thousand Japanese nationals, who, although Tokyo was 2,000 miles away, were determined to remain loyal. Those with electricity devotedly listened to radio broadcasts from the home islands. Saipan's two main centers of Garapan and Charan Kanoa were like towns across Japan with pretty parks, surrounded by concrete fences, sporting cast-iron Buddhas on pedestals. Garapan, in fact, became known as "Little Tokyo." It had a hospital, a school of agriculture, and the largest business district in the South Seas, which locals called the "Garapan Ginza" after Tokyo's famous Ginza. In fact, Saipan was considered such a desirable place that a Japanese commercial airlines company set up a tourist route from Tokyo to Saipan to Palau and back.

Saipan had a prosperous economy, built largely around agriculture, especially sugarcane production. The Nan'yo (South Seas) Kohatsu Kaisha, or NKK, cleared large tracts of timber and connected the fields to refining mills and liquor distilleries via miles of narrow-gauge railway. The NKK brought in Okinawan and Korean farmers as laborers and sent refined sugar, rum, and whiskey back to Japan.

The local government, eager to make devoted citizens of the four thousand Carolinian and Chamorran natives and the Okinawan and Korean workers, initiated a compulsory education system, emphasizing Japanese cultural values and mandating the study of Japanese language and history. It also formed young men's associations (*seinendan*) in which Japanese moral values were stressed. Although intent on inculcating an appreciation for all things Japanese, the government allowed the Carolinians and Chamorros to practice their Catholicism, and for the most part treated Saipan's resident population charitably until February 1944, when the island was taken over by the military. The new heavy-handed administration put the local priest and brother under house arrest, refused to let people attend mass, imposed a curfew, and ordered many Chamorro and Carolinian residents of Garapan to leave their homes. Homes were used as troop billets and comfort houses, where Japanese soldiers could go for sexual gratification, and the islanders' beloved Catholic Church was turned into a military storehouse. The military also pressed all able-bodied, non-Japanese men into labor gangs. It ordered women and children to their farms to tend vegetable gardens in order to feed the soldiers.

Japan's history in Saipan dated back to September 1914, when a naval squadron steamed out of Yokosuka Harbor for the Nan'yo. For years the country had its sights set on German holdings in the Marianas and Micronesia. With Germany preoccupied with a war in Europe, it took what it wanted. In the 1930s, Japan secretly began to fortify the Mariana Islands. Unfortunately the League of Nations and its members were powerless. The terms of the 1921 mandate contained no language permitting League officials to inspect Japan's construction projects. In 1935 an emboldened Japan withdrew from the League, and just two years later the Imperial Japanese Navy assigned its 4th Fleet the task of defending its new holdings in the Philippine Sea. The 4th Fleet used Truk with its deep-water lagoon as its headquarters.

In 1937 the Imperial Navy sent a survey unit to the Marshall Islands to develop plans for airfields, harbors, fueling stations, long-range radio stations, and an outer defensive perimeter. Tokyo also sent engineers to Saipan to reinforce gun positions and to build ammunition storage sheds, communications facilities, troop barracks, torpedo storage sheds, and air-raid shelters. In late 1941, Tojo instructed his island commanders to establish defense plans. Only days later, Japan attacked Pearl Harbor.

With the loss of the Marshalls in early 1944, Prime Minister

Hideki Tojo and his military advisers guessed that an invasion of Saipan was next. In February 1944, only 1,500 soldiers were stationed there. Defense of the Saipan garrison was the responsibility of Lieutenant General Hideyoshi Obata, who was determined to get his hands on as many troops as possible. The first group to leave Japan for Saipan was the 43rd "Glory" Division under the command of General Yoshitsugu Saito. Saito was an aging cavalry officer with no combat experience. Because American submarines prowled the waters around the Marianas, the 43rd made the decision to leave Japan in two separate convoys. The first convoy, which carried General Saito, left Tateyama Harbor in Tokyo on May 14, 1944, and made it to Saipan without incident five days later. When the second one left Japan in early June, American submarines struck, sinking five of seven ships. Still, Japan succeeded in putting thirty thousand troops on Saipan before the American invasion. Pledging to defend Saipan by whatever means possible, they adopted a rallying cry: "We must use our bodies to construct a bulkwark in the Pacific."

Despite the passion of his troops, Obata recognized that without artillery positioned around the island, his forces did not stand a chance of repelling the Americans. The 9th Field Heavy Artillery Regiment had twelve 150-mm howitzers, capable of piercing the thinly armored upper decks of the American amtracs, and 75-mm mountain guns set up on Kannat Tabla Mountain south of Mount Tapotchau, and two miles east of the Green Beaches. At Agingan Point, just south of the Yellow Beaches, defense forces had a battery of two six-inch British Whitworth Armstrong guns with ranges of nearly nine and a half miles. A battery of four six-inch guns defended Nafutan Point at the far southern end of the island. Near each gun was an ammunition magazine. On the eastern slopes of Mount Nafutan was a battery of three 140-mm coastal defense guns. Obata's men hastily camouflaged them with straw and painted canvas. On the south side of Magicene Bay, defenders had a battery of 200-mm coastal defense guns with a range of eleven miles. On the rocky point north of Magicene Bay (Laulau Bay today), the general had two 120-mm guns, surrounded by five-foot-thick walls. On the island's western shore, the Japanese set up two six-inch guns and two dual-purpose 120-mm guns over-looking Tanapag Harbor. A mile east of Muchot Point, just outside of Garapan, they set up four more 120-mm guns.

On the beaches where the Japanese hoped to stop the Americans, Obata placed two antitank guns (a 37-mm and a 47-mm). He also had 7.7-mm machine guns capable of firing six hundred rounds per minute, 6.5-mm Nambu machine guns and emplacements, German-style blockhouses, and rifle pits three feet deep.

The bulk of Obata's defensive strategy rested on his ability to drive the Americans into the sea. As a consequence he devoted little attention to his interior positions where the terrain was ideally suited for a long, drawn-out defense. The task of defending the island, how-ever, would fall to General Saito.

Late in the afternoon on June 7, while the Marines aboard the vari-ous LSTs played pinochle and poker and wrote letters to loved ones, a small group of officers, including Admiral Raymond Spruance and Vice Admirals Marc Mitscher and John McCain (father of the Arizona senator), retired to the Eniwetok Officers' Club for what was the club's grand opening. With its extravagant bar and screened-in porches, the two-story EOC affected a kind of tropical splendor. Whatever relax-ation and conviviality the club offered would be short-lived, however.

Admiral Richmond Kelly Turner did not join them. He stayed aboard the flagship USS *Rocky Mount,* finalizing the details of D-Day. As commander of the amphibious landing, he had the responsibility of organizing the naval gunfire preparation and then getting the troops ashore. To that end, he had divided the island into seven fire-support sections and had assigned battleships, destroyers, and cruisers to each section. Once the troops were ashore, Turner's responsibility was to keep them supplied. Command of the fighting forces, however, was in the hands of General Holland Smith.

On the afternoon of June 11, more than two hundred fighters and bombers, launched from Mitscher's Task Force 58 carriers, hit Saipan, staging what would be Operation Forager's opening salvo. The at-tack caught the Japanese by surprise. For the next three days bombers dropped tons of high explosives on Saipan's airfields and military installations, destroying most of the island's planes before they ever got off the ground. On June 13, Spruance's battleships entered the fray, pounding the western coast of Saipan and the neighboring island of Tinian with a huge amount of ordnance, a portion of which had been loaded at Port Chicago. That night, Task Force 58's destroyers spelled the battleships. A full twenty-four hours of shelling demoralized many of Saito's troops, who watched helplessly while the American ships destroyed airfields, aviation facilities, antiaircraft emplacements, and coastal defense guns. "Where are our planes?" inquired noncommissioned officer Tokuzo Matsuya. "Are they letting us die without making an effort to save us? If it were for the security of the Empire we would not hesitate to lay down our lives, but wouldn't it be a great loss to the 'Land of the Gods' for us all to die on the island? It would be easy for us to die, but for the sake of Japan's future I feel obligated to stay alive." Others remained willfully ignorant of the situation's severity. One Japanese commander sent a message to "all units concerned." "Morale is high," he wrote, "and we are in complete readiness. Although losses, etc., are being investigated, it is expected that they are very slight."

That same day, determined to avoid the mistakes that had cost so many lives at Tarawa, Admiral Turner sent out two Navy underwater demolitions teams (UDTs) to scout Saipan's reef and the waters up and down the 6,000-yard landing area. A third team reconnoitered the Tanapag Harbor area. Battleships provided covering fire for the entire operation. Although the UDTs conducted their reconnaissance in daylight, the teams suffered only seven casualties, and brought back essential information regarding reef conditions, depth of water, surf, tide, and current. Additionally, they planted radio beacons to help direct the amtracs on D-Day and charted the best routes over the reef. They made one other important discovery. Although the Japanese had mined and fortified some of the beaches, especially those to the south and east, where they thought a landing would likely occur, the beaches on the western side, where the Americans would attack, were free of obstructions.

By the time the UDTs were finished with their investigation, the Northern Landing Force had assembled almost eleven miles off the western coast of Saipan, just out of range of Saito's big 200-mm coastal defense guns. For the first time the Marines aboard the LSTs got a glimpse of what they were in for. Despite the lectures from battalion intelligence (G-2), what the men knew about Saipan could have been written on the back of a beer coaster. On maps, it was shaped like a pistol with the barrel pointing north toward Iwo Jima and Tokyo. But from the sea it looked like a giant serpent bursting out of the blue-gray water, its spine pronounced and arcing. At the apex of the spine stood Mount Tapotchau, at 1,554 feet. To the north and south, a series of smaller, interconnected ridges radiated out from Tapotchau. The island was small—12.5 miles long and 5.5 miles across at its widest point—and its mountains so modest that most of the Marines doubted that it could prove an adversary to strong, young men in the prime of their lives. The truth was that while much of the flat western coast had been cleared by the Japanese to accommodate rich green fields of sugarcane and smaller farms, the interior was a jumble of rocky cliffs, box canyons, steep-sided, jungled ravines and gullies where plants battled for sunlight, narrow-mouthed caves that inside opened up into huge, cool chambers, and dense patches of the island's original limestone forests. Razor-sharp coral limestone covered the ground, waiting to tear at the tough, inch-thick cord soles of the Marines' boondockers and slow their advance to a virtual crawl.

Late in the afternoon on June 14, the sun shone brilliantly, and light southwesterly winds rustled the sea. Aboard an LST a Marine carefully folded his American flag, reminding everyone who passed by him that back home June 14 was Flag Day. Another ran a rod and an oil patch through the barrel of his sawed-off shotgun, his weapon of choice. He claimed that the shotgun worked better on Jap snipers hiding in the trees. Pluto Brem sorted through his combat pack. Anyone who knew Brem would have understood that he was stewing. Missourian William Landers, Richard Carney, the dashing boxer from the Bronx, and some of the other guys had taken out a bet on which BAR man would last the longest, Brem or another guy named Wally

Kelb. Carney had put his money on Brem. Still Brem did not like it one bit. The wager gave him the heebie-jeebies.

Brem and Borta had heard the report that Saipan's cane fields were "burning merrily." They also heard about Admiral Mitscher's follow-up dispatch, when Mitscher gushed, "Keep coming, Marines, they're going to run away." Nevertheless Borta was scared and confessed to Carney his trepidation about the next day's events. "Stick with me, Chick," Carney said. "There isn't a Jap mother who has a son that can kill Mrs. Carney's boy."

That evening, aboard the LST, Carl Matthews was doing what he loved best. He and a sailor were making music to the delight of seventy men who were gathered around, sitting on fifty-five-gallon drums of high-octane gasoline. Matthews scraped out a tune on the fiddle and the sailor played the banjo. They did some bluegrass favorites and then a country ballad made famous by the Vagabonds in the 1930s:

> *When it's lamp lighting time in the valley,*
> *In dreams I'll go back to my home,*
> *I can still see the light by the window;*
> *It will guide me wherever I roam.*

As the Southern Cross drifted down near the horizon and Orion appeared, a small group of Marines asked them if they knew any hymns. Matthews had grown up in the Baptist church and could play and sing hymns all night long. The sailor had learned them as a boy, too. They began with "What a Friend We Have in Jesus" and followed up with "In the Sweet By and By." Those who knew it sang along:

> *There's a land that is fairer than day,*
> *And by faith we can see it afar;*
> *For the Father waits over the way*
> *To prepare us a dwelling place there.*
> *In the sweet by and by,*
> *We shall meet on that beautiful shore . . .*

# CHAPTER 24

# The Terrible Shore

June 15, 1944, was only a few hours old when the Marines hit the deck for what each of them knew might be his last day on earth. Once again they were frightened, flustered boys who knew the Japanese would be waiting for them. The previous evening Tokyo Rose had suggested that the invasion was doomed. "You better enjoy these recordings while you can," she threatened, "because tomorrow at oh-six-hundred, you're hitting Saipan . . . and we're ready for you. So, while you're still alive, let's listen." Then she played "I'll Be with You in Apple Blossom Time," an Andrews Sisters tune. The message cast a pall over the men. No one could discount it as a psychological trick. Maybe Tokyo Rose and Tojo really did know something.

Later on she came on again: "Now, what are you boys doing out here fighting us? Wouldn't you like to be home with your wife, dining, dancing, and having a good time? Why don't you just quit this and go on home?" Everyone slept fitfully that night, their dreams filled with images of fire and fast-moving fragments of steel, and loved ones beyond their embrace. When morning came, it was almost a blessing.

As the men aboard LST 84 gathered for breakfast, they learned that the U.S. transport *Monrovia* had almost run over a group of Japanese soldiers whose ship had been sunk. A destroyer had picked them up.

"What the hell?" one of the men asked in disbelief. "Why not run the bastards over?"

On the mess deck, Navy cooks sweated over steaming metal pans and large, sizzling grills. Robert Graf, the former company clerk, tried to wash down his fried potatoes and steak and eggs with black coffee, but the tradition of the last meal puzzled him. Why would you want to fill a man's belly before he went into battle? Likely he would be throwing it up later anyway.

After morning chow, Graf went up on deck. One hundred black Marines from the 19th Depot Company, which had sweated out their journey in the crowded hold of a transport ship, sharing space with essential cargo, were already lugging supplies off the ships and loading them onto amtracs. The all-black 19th had just been activated in February, and this was their first test in a battle zone—the first of any black Marine unit. Nothing in their experience at Montford Point, however, had prepared them for the tumult of war. What they learned to do well in North Carolina was march. The rumor at Montford Point was that once you were assigned to a depot company, all you would ever do again was march and parade and load and unload ships. For the former, all a man needed was rhythm and coordination, and for the latter, a strong back. The question now was, would the men be able to get supplies to the combat troops, or would they crack once the lead started to fly?

From the ship's deck, Graf saw fires burning on the slopes south of Tapotchau. Closer in he could make out the silhouettes of battleships against the dim horizon. At 5:42, Admiral Turner gave his orders to "land the landing force," and at 5:45 the big guns rumbled, and roaring and hissing shells arced through the skies like comets.

Just an hour before the bombing, Major General Keiji Iketa, chief of staff of the 31st Japanese Army, reported that despite the size of the American landing force, "Morale is high. We are waiting." Many others, however, were shocked and bewildered by the sheer number of ships off the western coast of the island.

Aboard LST 764, Carl Matthews, the mischievous Texan Richard Freeby, and Wendell Nightingale, the clean-living kid from Maine, were sorting through their packs. Matthews dressed in his cleanest dungarees and underwear in an attempt to reduce the threat of infection should he be hit by shell fragments. He also made sure he had his copy of the Gideon New Testament. At Roi he had wrapped it in plastic and carried it ashore in his breast pocket. A few days after the incident at the plane hangar, when his buddy Maurice Maness was hit by a mortar fragment, Matthews opened the Bible and noticed that the pages were stuck together. His first thought was that water had gotten into the plastic wrapper. What he discovered, however, was a small piece of shrapnel embedded in the pages. Pulling it out, he noticed that the shrapnel had stopped at a line of Scripture that included the words "from whence cometh wars." From that point on, the Bible assumed for him the character of a talisman. Almost every Marine carried something into battle—a locket, a photo, a letter, a cartridge casing, a rabbit's foot—which he hoped would bring him luck. For Matthews it was the Gideon New Testament.

Nightingale slipped a pack of cigarettes into the pocket of his dungaree jacket. At nineteen, he had taken up smoking to pass the time. The previous evening as he packed his seabag, he picked up a carton of cigarettes that he had bought at the PX back in Hawaii, and held it as if he were contemplating something important. Then somewhat sheepishly he'd looked at Matthews and asked his friend if he would consider putting the cigarettes in his seabag. Nightingale explained that if something happened to him on Saipan, the Marines would send his seabag home, and he could not bear the thought of his mother discovering the cigarettes.

After packing the bulk of his gear, Matthews wrapped his Bible in a new piece of plastic and put that in his pack along with semaphore flags to send signals, and a notebook and pencils. Minutes later,

Lieutenant Leary came through with his checklist. He went from man to man, making sure that none of them had forgotten anything.

Aboard the *Rocky Mount*, during a lull in the firing, the chaplain's voice came over the loudspeaker: "With the help of God we will succeed . . . most of you will return, but some of you will meet God who made you . . . repent your sins . . . those of the Jewish faith repeat after me . . . now Christian men, Protestants and Catholics, repeat after me . . ." Not long after, Admiral Turner got the weather report: "Partly cloudy with cumulus clouds, visibility twenty miles, winds easterly at thirteen knots." Ideal conditions for an amphibious landing.

By 7:00 a.m., the control vessels, charged with organizing the assault, flew flags to identify the beaches to which they were directing traffic. Thirty-four LSTs of the first wave assembled three quarters of a mile behind the line of departure. Barely a minute later the air strikes began. Graf filled his canteens to the top to prevent sloshing, and packed extra toilet paper into his helmet liner. Then he stuffed his pack with socks, an extra pair of skivvies, dyed green back in California (white skivvies poking out of a guy's pants were a dead giveaway), and a poncho. He attached D and K rations to his web belt, and to his pack he affixed his bayonet sheath and an entrenching tool. Then he checked his knives: his personal throwing stiletto that he fixed to his belt, and his Ka-Bar with its seven-inch blade. Finally he hung four grenades from his pockets, fastened his cartridge belt around his waist, and swung two bandoliers, holding forty rounds each, over one shoulder and his gas mask over the other. He felt like a lumbering bear. After all this, he had an urgent need to pee.

His urine was as dark and thick as maple syrup. He knew that he was already dehydrated, and he popped a salt tablet and then returned to the deck, where he watched planes dive out of the sky and drop their bombs. One of the planes disgorged hundreds of packages. Later he learned that they contained leaflets assuring the Japanese soldiers that if they surrendered they would be treated humanely.

Marines were both thrilled and relieved to see the island obscured by billowing clouds of smoke and dust and a fog of burned powder. "Blow 'em into kingdom come!" they yelled. With every bomb that fell, there would be fewer Japs shooting at them. It was a false sense of security that correspondent Robert Sherrod had seen before. On Tarawa he saw firsthand how Japanese defenders survived the merciless pounding. Now, aboard the *Rocky Mount,* he wrote in his notebook, "I fear all this smoke and noise does not mean many Japs killed."

Graf watched as an antiaircraft battery fired at the American planes overhead. "Look," someone yelled. "One of ours got it; it's spinning down. Look, look, there's a chute opening up. He's dropping into the ocean. They'll save him." If the men got a sense of comfort from the belief that the downed airman would be saved, that feeling quickly disappeared when they witnessed Japanese gunners score direct hits on other American planes. As they burst into pieces, Graf fought off a creeping sense of dread. Regardless of America's superior firepower, men were sure to die.

At 7:53 a.m., Admiral Turner postponed the landing from 8:30 a.m. to 8:40 a.m. to allow the armored amphibians and the amtracs more time to assemble at the line of departure. At 8:00 a.m., the battleships—*California* and *Tennessee*—and the cruisers—*Birmingham* and *Indianapolis*—moved in closer to shell the beaches, while the first assault waves of the 4th and 2nd Divisions waited 4,000 yards offshore. Minutes later, twenty-four armored amphibians, or LCI(G)s, made a beeline for the beach, firing as they moved forward. Ten minutes later, at 8:12 a.m., sailors brought down the signal flags from the yardarms. The intolerable waiting was over. The assault was on.

As the wave commander pointed his flag toward the beach, and the coxswain revved the engines of the amtrac that Robert Graf was aboard, the PA system from a nearby destroyer blared, "God bless you all." Although Graf believed that a man's faith was a private issue, he now prayed fervently. "Bless Mom and Dad. Bless my sisters. And please bless Gunny Townsley and my buddy Dick Crerar." As he mumbled his prayers, hoping that he would live to see another sunset, the big naval guns continued firing. The amtrac, belching a blue fog of diesel exhaust, floated with hardly a foot of freeboard. The huge muzzle blasts seemed to pick it up and plop it down into the water, nearly sinking it. With each roar Graf clenched his fists.

Suddenly giant geysers erupted among the amtracs. If at any point Graf believed that the days-long barrage had beaten Saipan's defenders into submission, he now knew differently. The Japanese were firing back with high-angle artillery shells. "Sweet Jesus," someone muttered. Everyone knew how lightly armored the amtracs were. If hit by a big navy gun or a high-angle anti-boat gun, there would be nothing left of them.

Graf looked around at his fellow Marines immersed in their private worlds, some of them experiencing what would be their last minutes on earth. They had shared everything together: sat side by side in the head, chased the same women, joked about their vivid sex dreams, and taunted each other about being the first to grab his pecker after lights-out. But now they refused to share their terror. Some fidgeted, while others closed their eyes and tried to doze.

Seconds later a blast rocked the amtrac. Peering over the gunwales, Graf saw that one had been hit. The shell shattered it, hurling bits of flesh and chunks of steel through the sky. Graf felt the burning taste of bile in the back of his throat, and he thought he might retch. Lieutenant Roth barked at him to get down, and he ducked back in, but not before glancing at the water one last time. Miraculously some of the men were still alive and floating with the aid of their life jackets. What Graf did not see was that most of them were hit and killed by onrushing amtracs.

As the amtracs ground over the reef, the Japanese bombarded them with artillery and mortar fire, automatic weapons, and anti-boat guns. In the hours between the time that the UDTs had done their reconnaissance work and the D-Day invasion, the Japanese had placed mortar and artillery registration flags on the reef and in the lagoon. These markers allowed the enemy defenders to find their range more quickly than American planners ever imagined they would. A Marine aviator observer radioed the *Rocky Mount,* "This is not like the Marshalls. Not at all."

When the amtracs headed into the lagoon, just 600 yards offshore, the big American Navy ships, fearing the possibility of short rounds, ceased firing. That was when the Marine Corsairs and Navy Hellcats strafed the beach and torpedo bombers fired their five-inch rockets. Graf heard the *wuff-wuff-wuff* of enemy flak. As the planes moved inland, amphibious tanks rushed in while their gunners, squatting behind snub-nosed 75-mm howitzers, peered out the open turrets at an island wreathed in smoke. Aboard Graf's amtrac, when the Marine manning the mounted machine gun sprayed the beach, everyone knew that the landing would come soon. Graf slipped some photos into the pocket of his dungaree jacket. He straightened the shoulder straps of his pack and buckled his cartridge belt. Then he heard Lieutenant Roth's voice: "Unlock your pieces. Good luck, keep low, and get off the beach as fast as you can. They're zeroing in on it."

Next came the impact of the island and the sound of the amtrac's treads grinding into the sand. When it hit a tank-trap ditch and stopped, bullets clanged off the steel hull. The plan had been for the amtracs to transport the men to the O-1 (the first day's objective) high ground some 1,500 yards inland, but most of them were stopped 100 to 200 yards in from the waterline.

Light machine-gun bullets clanged off the amtrac's steel hull, and shells burst, shaking the ground. Men were zigzagging across the beach. A Nambu machine gun chattered from the trees, spewing hot casings. Graf knew he had to run, but he could not move. His mind was numb with shock, his pack heavy, and his legs and arms felt as if they had been weighted down with lead. Then, as the terror and adrenaline surged into his limbs, he sprang forward. Sprinting across the beach, he dove headlong into a cluster of tree stumps.

Less than a hundred feet down from Graf, Carl Matthews's amtrac lumbered onto the beach. Mortar shells scattered shrapnel across the sand. Lieutenant Leary shouted, "Get out and move fast." Matthews took a deep breath. Nightingale clutched his BAR. Seconds later they were over the side and in the deep sand. Lieutenant Leary followed. The time was 8:43 a.m. A combat photographer began shooting pictures. One of those, a shot of Leary standing in front of the amtrac while Matthews and Nightingale knelt in front of him—would become famous, the first wave of Marines hitting the shores of Saipan. In Texas, it would make the Waco newspaper, among others, and Carl Matthews would become the toast of Hubbard.

At 8:44, Lieutenant Leary, Nightingale, Freeby, and Matthews scrambled up a little rise, through a grove of soft-needled ironwoods, and into a clearing with a few scattered coconut trees. Behind them, corpses floated on the crests of blue-green waves. Others lay limp on the beach like forgotten dolls. When a shell crashed through the branches and landed twenty feet to their left, Matthews and Nightingale pressed their bodies into the sand. It was a fruitless reaction that, had the shell landed closer, never would have saved either man. Yet Matthews hugged the earth. When the dust subsided, he dared to raise his head and noticed that three men from his company's supply unit lay dead. Matthews had not even had the time to whisper a prayer when a shot rang out. He buried his head again and waited. Sand collected at the edges of his mouth. He licked at it and tried to spit. Then someone yelled, "Witte. They got him. Head shot. He's dead." Matthews knew it was a sniper's bullet. Seconds later someone spattered the trees ahead with his M1, and the sniper came tumbling out with a thud as if he were a stuntman in a movie.

Leary pulled out a small green notebook and entered the name, serial number, and location of Witte, and then he was on his feet, crossing a firing trench, and calling for his men to follow. Hard as it was, the men left Witte where he lay. They had been trained never to mourn the death of a friend. Japanese snipers relished the clean head shots they got when a guy went running to the side of a fallen buddy. Eventually another Marine would come upon Witte, slip off his dogtag, and lay it on his chest. Later, someone from a graves registration crew would find the body and attend to it before the land crabs and the flies found it.

Graf was still lying among the trees. The sun was so intense he could barely breathe. It felt as if the whole world had been reduced to heat and smoke. Glancing back, he saw that amtracs were delivering more assault troops and the second wave of machine gunners, bazooka men, and flamethrower and 60-mm mortar squads, weighted down with bipods, tubes, and awkward base plates. One man, carrying his seventy-pound flamethrower like a great cross, sank to his knees. Another listed as he struggled with a heavy demolition satchel. Off to the side, Graf heard two machine guns open up. Artillery rounds pounded the beach, too. From the explosions he could see that the Japanese had found the range. Despite the intensity of the barrage, by just a few minutes after 9:00 a.m., seven hundred amtracs had landed more than eight thousand Marines.

Still trying to locate the machine gunner, Graf looked left and saw Roth run. When the lieutenant heard the whistle of a mortar shell, he threw his body into the sand. Seconds later he was sprinting again, the weight of his pack knocking against his back. Graf chucked his gas mask—"as useless as tits on a boar," somebody had told him—rose to his feet, and dashed in the direction of Roth. Hurling himself into a shell hole, he nearly ended up in the lieutenant's lap. Shortly after, other platoon members slid in, too. After they had caught their breath, Roth directed their attention to some high ground ahead—Mount Fina Sisu, he told them, their Day 1 objective. Then, with a nod, he barked, "Now!" and jumped out of the hole. His men followed behind, winding and cutting as he did. No one wanted to be separated from the lieutenant. Anyone who had trained with him, or spent any time with him, knew that there was no better man to follow into battle than Roth. When a machine gun opened fire, ripping tree limbs over his head, Graf reluctantly abandoned the group and dove into a gully. There he lay listening to the frantic, high-pitched zing of dozens of .50-caliber bullets. Next came an artillery shell, close enough that he could feel the ground tremble. Then another one, closer yet, which nearly blew out his eardrums. He knew what was happening; enemy gunners were walking the artillery toward him. Soon he would be splattered through the trees.

Drawing in a deep breath, he rushed out of the gully. Twenty feet later he threw himself onto the ground and scrambled for cover. For the first time he noticed it: the sand was murderously hot. He did this two or three more times—running and diving and then running again. He was desperate for air now, breathing in short, irregular gasps, barely getting enough oxygen to keep from passing out. His head spun and it seemed that every muscle in his body was on fire. Grabbing his canteen, he loosened the top and poured water into his mouth, almost choking. Now he knew for certain what he had felt when he rolled out of the amtrac: his pack was too damn heavy. If he was going to stay alive, he needed to get rid of it. He took his bayonet sheath and put it onto his cartridge belt. Then he tucked his poncho under his belt, too. Later it would shelter him from the afternoon downpours. Ripping open his ration boxes, he stuffed what he could into his dungaree pockets and tossed his pack into the brush. By the time he regained his strength, he had no idea how much time had passed. Nor did he know where he was. For the moment, though, no one was trying to kill him.

Surrounded now by cutover jungle and a creepy silence, he felt utterly alone, as he had when swimming through the fiery waters of West Loch. He tried to keep the panic from rising in his throat. Then he saw movement to his left. He held still, trying to make out the shapes. When he recognized Sergeant Max Klein of Company F, he nearly bounded toward him out of relief.

He and Klein decided to keep moving east. When they came upon a large swamp, Klein guessed they were at the edge of Lake Susupe. Figuring they would be better off in the swamp than in the trees, they began to wade. Soon the water rose to Graf's waist. Vines and weeds wrapped around his knees and legs, and the mud bottom sucked at his boots. He knew that if a Jap spotted him, he would pick him off as easily as a kid shooting metal ducks at a carnival.

Eventually Graf and Klein stumbled onto solid ground, their knees folding beneath them with exhaustion. They ripped the vines from their legs, checked their barrels for mud, spread out in a line, and continued east in the direction of a grove of flame trees whose delicate flowers glimmered in the sun. To his right, Graf saw more Marines. One of them nodded in his direction, as if to say, *I see you.* The man moved warily. In front of him Graf heard something in the bushes. The other Marine heard it, too, and lifted his M1 to his shoulder. A mortar round burst between them, sending shell fragments humming and growling through the air. Instinctively Graf threw himself to the ground. When the coral dust cleared, he jumped to his feet and saw that the Marines to his right were dead. Somehow the splintering fragments of steel had missed him.

Racing ahead before another round hit, Graf found himself in the midst of a small group of Marines from Company G. Then he heard a familiar voice—"If that don't beat all!"—and who should be standing in front of him but Bill More. For a moment, Graf was speechless. In the middle of a war, he had run into his old buddy.

"Bunch of dead Marines ahead," More said. "The Japs gave us a good going-over." While More radioed E Company to let them know that Graf and Klein were okay, Graf learned from another Marine that the 2nd Battalion had taken a direct hit from a mortar shell. Bottles of blood plasma littered the ground. Perhaps the Navy corpsmen had arrived in time to save lives.

The afternoon's only positive development was the appearance of the medium tanks. Among those that made it ashore, many were unusable; some were disabled when salt water drowned out their electrical systems. Others were unable to negotiate the difficult terrain. But the few that made it to the 2nd Battalion's zone of combat instantly changed the tide of the battle. They fired on machine-gun nests and enemy strongpoints, clearing out a narrow alley of advance. Nevertheless, few Marines made it as far as the O-1 objective. To shore up their lines, the 23rd Marines' battalion commanders withdrew their forward troops to a position a full 800 yards west of Mount Fina Sisu. The men who had made it to the O-1 line were glad to pull back. Without the support of the rest of the regiment, they would have been sitting ducks.

With twilight approaching, sand crabs as big as mess tins skittered across the ground, and Graf decided that he would wait until morning to find Lieutenant Roth. Later he would learn that it was a decision that likely saved his life.

After executing a fake landing that worked as a deception, tying down a regiment of Japanese soldiers, Frank "Chick" Borta and the 1st Battalion, 29th Marines, prepared to land at Green Beach 2, at the tail end of the Charan Kanoa airstrip, at close to 3:00 p.m. on D-Day. Pillars of smoke rose above the island, obscuring the interior hills.

The 29th had been told that the beach was secure, but when the lead amtracs approached shore, Japanese artillery guns opened up. The first shells were ranging shots, but soon the Japanese had the beach zeroed in. Borta looked at Sergeant Rachitsky for some sign of distress. What he realized was that it was on account of men like Rachitsky that Marine riflemen had such a fearsome reputation. The sergeant was all business. After tucking his mosquito headnet under his helmet—he claimed it worked as a concussion barrier—he tied down his canvas leggings and checked the pocket of his dungaree jacket for the extra spoon he had taken off the LST. Borta did the same and then dug his hand into a pocket of his dungarees to make sure he had remembered the safety pins. Rachitsky insisted that they were an essential part of a Marine's combat gear. When a guy's pants frayed and tore, he could always pin them together. Borta felt them under his fingers and then—wham!—an artillery shell hit, wiping out the nearest amtrac and killing everyone aboard. Years later Borta would say that if fear had a taste, so did hate. It burned in the back of his throat like cheap whiskey.

Borta whispered a Hail Mary. Aboard the LST, he had sung hymns with the Baptists, Presbyterians, and the Lutherans, but now he took comfort in the prayer he had grown up with: "Holy Mary, Mother of God, pray for us sinners, now and at the hour of our death." By the time he reached the word "hour," he was clutching his M1 so tightly that his fingers looked as if the blood had disappeared from them. The M1 felt good in his hands.

Now the treads of the amtrac dug deep into the beach. When it stopped, Rachitsky shouted, "Let's go, men! Let's get the hell out of this coffin." Shell fragments slapped at the hull. Borta jumped to his feet. All he could think about was getting off the amtrac before a shell blast blew it to smithereens. The Marine ahead of him was teetering on the gunwales, ready to roll out, when he fell back, almost knocking

Borta over. Borta reached to help him. Then he noticed blood trickling out of the side of his mouth and saw the hole. A hot piece of metal had gone through his helmet. He reached with his fingers under the man's chin, feeling for a pulse. Seconds later Borta tumbled over the wall of the amtrac and into the scorching sand. Damaged and burned-out amtracs, discarded field packs, maimed trees, and mangled bodies served as reminders of the Japanese strategy to pulverize the invasion force.

Up and down the beach, members of all-black Marine depot and ammunition companies worked among the falling shells and the hammering of Nambu machine guns. They had already set up ammo, water, gasoline, and ration dumps, and were preparing to unload phenomenal amounts of cargo—6,000 tons per day, the equivalent of one jam-packed Liberty ship every twenty-four hours. At Red Beach 2, north of where Borta had come in, a black work crew had taken enough casualties that the 2nd Marines had to call in a backup group. A platoon of black Marines from the 18th Depot Company, attached to the 3rd Battalion, 23rd Marines, fared no better. Landing at Blue Beach 1, two and a half hours after the first assault wave, it was hit by a mortar shell that injured four men. While the wounded Marines were being evacuated, the rest of the platoon moved inland to escape the barrage. Later the commander of the 23rd Marines, Colonel Louis Jones, sent up a squad of black depot company men to replace riflemen who had either been killed or wounded. In the heat of battle, no one bothered to acknowledge the significance of Colonel Jones's order, but it was the first time since World War I that black troops were called upon to face enemy soldiers. Although they had not been trained as infantrymen, Jones desperately needed bodies to patch the holes in his front lines. White Marines were stunned to find Negroes at the front carrying rifles. Many did not even know that black troops were being used to unload supplies. The general consensus, though, was that if they could fight and would not run like cowards, no one cared what color they were. Later Colonel Jones would commend the 18th Depot Company for its hard work and heroism.

Borta was not on the beach long when Rachitsky informed him that their orders had changed. Rather than advancing east, they were to move south toward the sugar factory to assist the 8th Regiment. Rachitsky needed to confirm the change, and sent Borta back to check with headquarters. On his way, Borta was weaving between shell holes and foxholes when he heard a familiar voice. It was Carney. His friend's helmet was tilted low on his forehead, but there was no mistaking the grin. Borta slowed to a trot. Carney pushed his helmet back. "Hot, eh, Chick?" Borta was too out of breath to respond, so he swung his leg, kicked sand into the Bronx-born Irishman's foxhole, and dashed away. "You sonofabitch," Carney called after him.

Borta returned to Rachitsky. "Yup," he said. "The sugar factory." Looking down the beach, Borta could see that it was wide open and completely exposed. Then he turned to Rachitsky, as if to say, "Sarge, are we really going to do this?" Rachitsky nodded. "Ready," he said, and took off at a dead run. Borta was just twenty feet behind when he heard the shriek of a shell. "Close!" he yelled, and he and Rachitsky flung their bodies onto the ground. Rachitsky was back on his feet and ready to run again. "C'mon!" he yelled.

"I can't," Borta groaned. "I'm hit." Rachitsky knelt at his side and seconds later shook his head. "Look," he said. Then Borta realized that his canteen had been punctured, and what he feared was blood running down his legs was nothing more than his hydration mixture, water and salt. Not sure whether to feel like a fool or grateful that he still had the use of his legs, he was back on his feet when another shell hit. The concussion spun him around and momentarily he lost his bearings. When he saw the sugar dock, he was off again at a gallop.

Rachitsky, Borta, and six men from their platoon dove into a ditch just feet from the sugar factory. What none of them knew was that in the chaos they had run through the forward lines of the 8th Marines and were stranded in a no-man's-land between the enemy and Marine forces. They did not discover their mistake until after dark, when machine gunners from each side fired white and red tracer bullets just over their heads, and opposing flares arced slowly across the sky, drenching the battlefield in a yellow light. They were in a fix, and Borta knew it. Reaching into his shirt, he felt for the cross his mother had given him. Back in Hawaii, he had tied it to his dogtags, using telephone wire. When he realized that it was gone, he thought for sure he was a dead man.

# CHAPTER 25

# A Long, Bitter Struggle

"Fix bayonets," Rachitsky whispered. "The Japs are probably going to attack before it gets light."

Borta heard the click of bayonets being checked and refitted onto rifle barrels. He was glad that he had whetted and sharpened his before leaving the LST. Every Marine knew the reputation of the Japanese. They were superb night fighters. They could slither through the forest and disembowel a man or slit his throat without being detected. Yet Borta was ready for them. He had his M1, whose hitting power he loved, instead of the lighter .30-caliber carbine that most runners used. "Let 'em come."

When Borta felt the morning sun, he knew that the Japanese had missed, or passed up, their chance to counterattack. Rachitsky looked at Borta. The sergeant's eyes were bloodshot from lack of sleep. "Let's get the hell out of here," he grumbled.

The first thing that Borta noticed at the beach was the smell of burning flesh. He clenched the muscles in his throat to keep from gagging. Farther ahead, bodies lay strewn across the sand, baking in the hot sun. Although most were covered with ponchos, hordes of fat flies moved sluggishly from one to the next. Later someone from the graves registration detail would puncture the bodies with a hypodermic needle to reduce the swelling. One Marine with a large hole in his belly lay on his back with his arms and legs spread wide like a child making a snow angel. The walking wounded, in their blood-splattered dungarees, wandered around like blind men with glazed, wide-open eyes. Corpsmen hustled among the injured, stuffing ruptured chests with cotton balls, and putting on and tightening dressings and tourniquets and whispering words of encouragement. They had to act fast; in the heat and humidity as thick as grease, it didn't take long for open wounds to become infected, even gangrenous. One corpsman, with a sad smile, stood over a moaning man, holding a bottle of plasma.

Borta found Landers lying among the dead and wounded. A piece of shrapnel had done a number on his leg. Ashen-faced, Landers told Borta that a corpsman had decided that he could wait. There were too many others losing blood too quickly to treat a leg wound. *To hell with that,* Borta thought. Wrapping Landers's arm over his shoulders, he took him to the battalion aid station.

When Borta returned to Sergeant Rachitsky, he overheard someone tell the sergeant that thirty-two men from Company A were killed or injured in the D-Day shelling. Many of the wounded had lost arms and legs, including the company's executive officer. Borta had just one question: Where in hell was Carney? For a moment he remembered what Carney had told him: *There isn't a Jap mother who has a son that can kill Mrs. Carney's boy.* He had believed it, too. Carney had not just made it out of Tarawa with his hide intact, he had been nominated for the Silver Star, and returned with a reputation for bravery and good luck. Surely Carney was okay. Whoever broke the news to Borta did it with the tactlessness that often accompanies war. "Carney," the Marine said. "He had his head blown off. Larson got it bad, too. A shell cut him in half. Dajak's dead, too."

The other side of what had been the sugar factory now lay in rubble, its vats of sugar rotting in the sun and attracting millions of

flies. Nearby, Graf and Bill More huddled in a shell hole. Two former
II Company buddies, Sergeant Morris Lipfield, who had loaned Graf
the money to get back to Ballston Spa on his first furlough, and a
corporal joined them. The shell holes were the only good things about
the bombing. Those who tried to fashion a foxhole, scratching at
the earth, discovered that the coral was as hard as concrete. By evening most of the men, stained with sweat, had given up their digging and slid into the crowded shell holes. More urged everyone to be
on alert: reports were that the Japanese knew that a gap existed on
the 4th Division's left flank between the 23rd Marine Regiment and the
2nd Division's 8th Marines. Enemy soldiers would be probing that
gap, searching for ways to get in behind the Marines.

If, after enduring a day of shelling, Graf believed that the Japanese would let up and conserve their ammunition, he was mistaken.
The Japanese pounded the 2nd Battalion's positions. Graf gritted his
teeth against the noise, but each shell still made him shudder. Lipfield
did his best to talk him down. "Hell," the sergeant said, "if it's got
your name on it, it will get you no matter where you hide." Graf
knew that Lipfield meant to reassure him, but he wavered between
being comforted and disturbed by the sergeant's fatalism. The corporal, on the other hand, had turned the shelling into kind of a game.
He had convinced himself that he could time the pattern as well as tell
the size and direction of the flight of a shell just by the sound, and he
provided a kind of running commentary. "No need to worry, boys,"
he would say, as a mortar howled and curved through the sky. "This
one will miss us by a mile," or "This son of a bitch is close. Hit the
deck!" When, not long after dusk, the 14th Marines' 4th Battalion,
which had come ashore on Blue Beach 2 at 5:00 p.m., began to answer the Japanese with its own artillery, the corporal turned enthusiastic. "Yeoww!" he yelled. "There goes one of ours; there goes a
whole barrage of ours. Give those gooks hell!"

Enemy artillery shells shrieked and whistled throughout the night,
and Graf's mood turned reflective. What determined whether a man
lived or died? Maybe, he thought, it was fate. If that was the case, it
would not matter whether or not he hugged the inside of a shell hole.

If the Japanese lobbed in a mortar, and his number was up, there was not a damn thing he could do about it. More likely, though, it was just dumb luck. It was not as if God had painted an X on some sucker's back. The God he prayed to would not have a hand in this man-made foolishness; he would take no part in this or any other war.

That night on the 4th Division's left flank, Japanese infiltrators probed the gap that More had warned the men about. Again, had it not been for the 18th Marine Depot Company, whose members shot and bayoneted enemy soldiers trying to penetrate the security perimeter, the Japanese might have gotten through and wreaked havoc. If initially Colonel Jones had been opposed to using blacks in a war zone, he had become a convert, and again lavished praise on the "colored units forming part of the Shore Party."

When the first strands of light wove through the trees, Graf was overjoyed to see another sunrise. Darkness added a horror to war that not even the Navy, launching five-inch star shells that lit up the night, could lessen. During a 6:00 a.m. lull in the enemy shelling, Graf decided that he was going to have to find Company E. Bill More pointed him in the right direction, and the two old friends parted ways, each wondering if and when they would see each other again.

Graf walked west toward the beach. As he passed the battalion command post, someone recognized him and yelled out, "You're still alive?" There was something about the man's voice that stopped Graf in his tracks. "What do you mean?" Graf asked. The guy shook his head as if he would prefer not to be the one to break the bad news. "Company E got hit hard last night," he said reluctantly. "There's not much left of it. Some gook observer called in artillery right down on top of them."

Graf bit his lip as if trying to prevent himself from inquiring further. But then he blurted it out. "What about Lieutenant Roth?" Graf had been with Lieutenant Roth since his training days at Camp Pendleton when he first became the lieutenant's runner.

"Dead."

"You're certain?" Graf asked. "Absolutely certain?"

"Yup," the man answered. "I saw it with my own eyes. Killed instantly."

Difficult as D-Day was for the 23rd Marines, farther south at Agingan Point, the situation resembled the debacle at Tarawa. The 25th Marines barely got ashore. Japanese artillery pounded the invasion beaches. If not for the Army's Amphibian Tank Battalion, which absorbed a large portion of the artillery fire, the 25th would have been decimated. Those Marines who made it off the beach found the going especially treacherous. The Point was littered with spider holes. The Japanese defenders waited until a Marine unit passed by and then jumped from their holes to fire into the rear of a passing platoon. Later, in the early-morning hours of the second day, Japanese soldiers used civilians, mostly women and children, to lead their counterattacks.

At Agingan Point, the black Marines again showed their mettle. Prior to reaching the shore, the 20th Depot Battalion's commanding officer, Captain William Adams, gave his men a pep talk. "You are the first Negro troops ever to go into action in the Marine Corps," he proclaimed. "What you do with the situation that confronts you, and how you perform, will be the basis on which you, and your race, will be judged." Upon reaching dry land, the 20th was hit by some of the fiercest D-Day artillery fire that American troops on Saipan saw. Adams and his men raced for cover, but Kenneth Tibbs, his orderly, did not make it. Killed by an artillery shell, he became the first black Marine fatality of World War II, and a hero to every Marine entering or leaving Montford Point.

If the men of the 20th, who had never trained for the situation in which they now found themselves, were demoralized over the death of one of their own, Captain Adams did not see it. Over the next few hours, despite the savage enemy artillery barrage and the snipers, the 20th succeeded in setting up cargo dumps without losing another man. If the 20th Depot Company had good fortune on its side, a platoon from the 3rd Marine Ammunition Company enjoyed a bit of it, too.

While unloading an amtrac in the early afternoon, the amphibious vehicle took a direct hit. Though dazed and frightened, every member survived. That night, while defending the beachhead perimeter, the ammunition company beat back an enemy counterattack, taking out a .50-caliber machine gun in the process.

At Afetna Point, north of the sugar factory, the 6th and 8th Marines were fighting not to achieve their O-1 objectives, but merely to capture the beach. Strong currents had pulled their amtracs a quarter of a mile to the north, causing battalions to bunch up and mingle. Instead of pushing far inland, units struggled to reunite, and then fought fiercely just to cross the coastal road and secure a beachhead seventy yards in from the water. Small groups of Japanese soldiers used the chaos to their advantage, probing the gaps between the companies.

The 8th Marines met with especially stiff resistance. Japanese riflemen fired from pillboxes, and as the Marines advanced, enemy soldiers rushed them, shouting "Banzai!" and brandishing swords and bayonets. The Marines shouldered their shotguns—Company G had the 8th Marines' entire allotment of shotguns—and blasted the Japanese at point-blank range. The seizure of Afetna Point proved critical. An open channel off Green Beach 3 meant that incoming vessels could reach shore without having to cross the reef.

At 3:00 a.m. in the 6th Marines' zone, the Japanese launched a counterattack. Shattering the calm that had fallen over the battlefield, a Japanese bugler sounded his horn, and nearly one thousand enemy troops from Colonel Takuji Suzuki's 135th Infantry pushed forward. According to one member of the 6th Marines, they sounded as if they were "souped up on sake," waving flags, yelling, and swinging their curved, two-foot-long katana swords like eleventh-century samurai warriors. Destroyers responded to the Marines' calls for illumination shells, and two Marine companies, using the light, cut down the attackers. At dawn, Marines counted hundreds of enemy dead.

Aboard the *Rocky Mount,* Admiral Turner and General Holland Smith discussed early dispatches announcing that the Marines had carved out beachheads from outside Garapan south to Agingan Point. Smith, in particular, was heartened by the news. He considered Saipan "the decisive battle of the Pacific offensive." In his opinion, the island was "Japan's administrative Pearl Harbor . . . the naval and military heart and brain of the Japanese defense strategy." Meanwhile, Admiral Spruance mulled over submarine reports indicating that the Japanese fleet was heading at top speed for the Marianas from its anchorage at Tawi Tawi in the southern Philippines. Admiral Toyoda, commander-in-chief of the Combined Fleet, saw a naval showdown in the Marianas as Japan's last best chance of turning the tide of the war, or, at the very least, negotiating a favorable surrender. Although Admirals Spruance and Turner had anticipated Toyoda's aggressive response, they were now confronted with a series of crucial decisions. Spruance did not deliberate long. On June 16 he canceled the Southern Attack Force's June 18 landing at Guam. He also directed the old battleships and cruisers, and some destroyers of the Joint Expeditionary Force, to a point twenty-five miles to the west of Saipan to guard against a surface attack. By the end of the day he ordered the Fast Carrier Task Forces to withdraw from the island. Finally he announced that all unloading of transports and LSTs would cease by darkness on June 17. What this meant for the Marine African-American depot and ammunition companies was that they would be forced to get as much material off the boats as they could in the next two days.

As Spruance left the *Rocky Mount* to return to the *Indianapolis,* his flagship, General Holland Smith pressed him. Was there any chance that Admiral Toyoda "would turn tail and run?" "No, not now," Spruance answered. "They are out after big game." Spruance knew that if the Japanese had wanted an easy victory, they would have disposed of the relatively small naval force covering MacArthur's operation at Biak. The attack on the Marianas, however, was "too great a challenge for the Japanese navy to ignore."

With the Navy terminating its support of the landing force, Holland Smith had his own decisions to make. Should he use his reserve force—the Army's 27th Division? Smith did not deliberate long. Reasoning that it was "always better to get them [the reserves] on the beach rather than have them sitting out at sea on ships," Smith made the decision to land the 27th Division's troops—with the exception of the 106th Infantry—throughout the day on June 17. What also convinced him were the conditions on the ground. Just one day into the campaign, with the casualty count pushing six hundred, he realized that he was up against perhaps as many as 32,000 troops—twice as many as intelligence analysts expected—charged with defending the island at all costs. Saipan would not be pacified quickly. His men were in for a long, bitter struggle.

On the beach, Sergeant Rachitsky gathered his platoon and explained their Day 2 task: to push on past Lake Susupe and to clear out any enemy stragglers in the process. He warned his men to be ready for an ambush and to watch for snipers. "No daydreaming," he said, "or they'll come in and slit your throats."

Moving forward was the last thing in the world that Borta felt like doing. He wanted to find his buddy Landers and make sure he came out okay. If it meant that Landers would live, he would gladly be the butt of one of his practical jokes. He would give anything to hear the Missourian's unmistakable drawl: "We sure pulled one over on you, Chick."

The day was unbearably hot, and despite Rachitsky's warning, Borta's mind drifted. It was the height of the Depression, and his dad was between jobs. Later he found work at a Ford factory on Chicago's South Side, putting together tank engines, but before the war, to make ends meet, he brewed and sold beer. On Friday and Saturday nights, people would buy a growler and sit in the Bortas' living room. Mrs. Borta would serve homemade pretzels. Now he wondered if he would ever make it back home to Chicago, if he would ever be able to thank his mother for working so hard, or to take his father down to the corner tavern.

By late afternoon, Rachitsky's platoon had made it to a point along Lake Susupe's western shore. In a small ironwood tree that had somehow escaped the shelling, Borta discovered a Marine helmet hanging from one of the branches. An enemy soldier had apparently detonated a grenade in it and hung it from the tree as a sign of disrespect. Everyone else in the platoon saw it, too, and all of them swore that when the time came they would get their revenge. One of the new riflemen announced that before the battle was over he was going to make himself a necklace of gold Japanese teeth and pickle a gook ear.

Not long before Rachitsky ordered the men to dig in, a shot echoed through the hills just north of the lake. The next thing Borta knew, someone yelled his name. It was Lemon. "D-d-dammit, Chick," he stuttered in his Panhandle drawl, "I got shot in the bee-hind." Before Borta could respond, Lemon had his pants down around his ankles. Pointing his bare ass at him, Lemon asked, "Tell me, Chick, how bad is it?" Borta could not help but laugh. All Lemon had was a purple streak as big as the state of Texas running from his lower back across the right cheek of his buttocks, a scratch that would not even qualify as a "million-dollar wound." His pride more injured now than anything else, Lemon defended himself, "Dammit, Chick, it hurts."

By 6:45 the dimming sun cast a dull blush of light over the Lake Susupe hills. Rachitsky was cursing his contour map, which showed the territory east of Lake Susupe as a rolling plain. "They're big goddamn hills," he said in disgust. The swamp north of the lake was much bigger, too, than the map showed.

While drinking from his canteen, Borta noticed a smudge of white near the bank on the lake's north side. He studied it for some time, but could not detect any movement. Borta was no souvenir hunter. He had heard of too many men losing their lives while pilfering dead Japanese bodies for a knife, a sword, or a necklace. Sometimes they were booby-trapped, and sometimes an enemy sniper waited nearby, eager to put a bullet in the back of a distracted Marine's head. But there was something about the white form that bothered Borta. Could it be a nun's habit, or a child wrapped in a cloth? Stories were circulating among the Marines about persecuted priests and nuns and civilian mothers who had fled with their babies and young children to caves across the island. Borta drew Sergeant Rachitsky's attention to the white shape.

"Whaddaya think, Sarge?" he asked. "Can I go give it a look?"

Rachitsky squinted his eyes and then turned to his runner. "If you want," he said skeptically. "Be careful. Curiosity killed the cat."

Borta crept along the edge of the lake. When he was forty feet away, he knelt down and watched. Finally, certain that it was not a trap, he moved forward and knelt again. What he saw was a dead Marine lying on a stretcher. A corpsman was sprawled out next to him, dead too, half his head blown away by a bullet, his mouth black with swarming flies. His first-aid kit sat next to him, open. The thing that Borta had spotted from a distance was a large white bandage that the corpsman had been reaching for when the bullet ended his life. Borta could not help but be moved by the corpsman's selflessness. His was a gesture of compassion that seemed to have no place on the battlefield: to risk one's life in order to save another human being. If Saipan had any room for God or goodness or Jesus, he had just laid his eyes on it. Borta reached for the necklace that his mother had given him, and realized again that it was gone. He pulled his hand out of his blouse, said a brief prayer, and then double-timed it back to the platoon.

It neared dusk, and a fog settled over the swamp. As water seeped into their foxholes, the men grew cold and uncomfortable. "Stranded in a goddamn swamp," Borta heard one of the guys say with disgust. Then he heard the Marine leave his hole and the crunch of huge, green Great African snails being crushed under his field boots.

Until the early-morning hours, the night was quiet up and down the front. Sharing a sopping foxhole—two hours on, two hours off—Borta and Lemon even managed to sleep. At 3:40 Borta heard what he thought was the rusty rattling of tanks, and he nudged Lemon awake. Lemon opened his eyes and shivered. Then Borta heard voices in the nearby foxholes. "Tanks," someone said, confirming his suspicion. Minutes before, the commanding officer of B Company, 6th Marines, had called the battalion CP to notify Colonel William Jones that he heard enemy tanks approaching from the east. Jones immediately alerted a nearby tank company and the 1st Battalion of the 10th Marines. In addition he requested naval illumination fires.

Borta shook his leg to get the blood back into a foot that had fallen asleep. When he realized that the tanks were moving to the north, he was relieved. He knew that among the elements of the

29th dug in near Lake Susupe there were no bazookas or artillery. If the tanks had ventured into their sector, they would have been unable to stop them.

General Saito's goal in sending out the tanks was for them to push 400 yards behind the 6th Marines' lines and to recapture the radio station. Although the station had no strategic value, it was a prominent landmark that Saito knew the island's defenders would recognize. The motivation for the counterattack was in keeping with Saito's strategy to "destroy the enemy at the water's edge." Had he been able to execute the assault on the night of June 15 or the morning of June 16, he might have caught the Marines off guard. By the early morning of June 17, however, they had solidified their hold on the beachhead and were prepared to fight.

When the destroyers off the coast fired their five-inch star shells, Colonel Jones's men saw the attack unfolding. For the Japanese, who were counting on the cover of darkness to confuse and unnerve the Americans, the star shells were dispiriting. According to one officer, they turned "night into day" and made the "maneuvering of units extremely difficult."

Saito's tanks advanced in groups of four or five. The Americans were dug in and determined to hold. When several of the tanks broke through the front lines, the well-drilled riflemen merely pivoted and, using bazookas, mortars, rifles, and machine guns, subjected the Japanese to a withering onslaught. Reinforced by the pack howitzers of the 10th Marines and 75-mm halftracks, the Marines repulsed the first major tank attack of the Pacific War. By 7:00 a.m., over two dozen Japanese tanks sat smoldering on the battlefield. Colonel Jones's 1st and 2nd Battalions suffered ninety-seven casualties. In beating back the enemy tanks, however, they had delivered a tremendous blow to Saito's plans for defending Saipan.

Although General Saito's plans to cripple the Marine invasion before it had a chance to move inland had failed, in the first two days his troops had inflicted heavy losses on the Americans. Aboard the *Rocky Mount,* General Holland Smith's wall chart told a disconcerting story: casualties in some of the assault battalions pushed

40 percent, and the 6th Marines had already lost six top-notch officers. Losses south of the sugar dock were "very heavy, especially in
the 23rd." Overall, U.S. forces had already suffered 3,500 casualties,
and hospital ships were filling up fast. Most of the wounds were not
clean bullet wounds, either, but the nasty work of shell fragments that
tore, ripped, and gashed their victims.

# CHAPTER 26

# A Healthy Spirit of Competition

As the morning sun flowed into the barracks hall, Seaman Second Class Joe Small was still lying in bed. Small usually rose early for breakfast and then returned to the barracks to wake the guys sleeping off hangovers before the petty officer burst in, but on this morning he needed the extra shut-eye. In Pittsburg, the night before, he had met a woman and barely made the 1:30 a.m. bus, the last one back to Port Chicago.

Joe Small was born in 1921 in Savannah, Georgia, but spent most of his childhood in Middlesex County, New Jersey, where his family moved in 1927. When his father, a part-time Baptist preacher and a farmer, died in 1936, Small became the family's mainstay. Like his father, who could wield a hammer and a welding torch as well as he could quote from the Bible, young Joe was a gifted handyman. He liked to swim and play baseball, but there was often too much to do for him to devote any time to either pursuit. He, his mother, three brothers, and a sister made do, working a small farm where they grew corn and wheat for sale, and tending a large garden plot of tomatoes, lettuce, cabbage, and collards for their own use. In 1939, realizing that the family needed cash money, Small entered the Civilian Conservation Corps. An officer saw that he had leadership potential and that the other men respected him, and soon promoted him to lieutenant. Rather than spending his money on beer and entertaining women, Small sent the bulk of his paycheck home to his mother. After putting in a year with the CCC, he took a number of jobs, learning to operate heavy equipment—cranes, backhoes, and bulldozers—acquiring skills he would put to good use at Port Chicago. He worked hard, but manged to find time to be the lead voice in the church choir. In 1943, while making thirty dollars a week driving a truck for a flour company (at the time the average weekly salary for a white driver was forty to forty-five dollars), he was drafted.

Small had not chosen the Navy, nor had it chosen him. He ended up there because he and a buddy got their physicals at the same time. When the doctor asked them which one wanted to go into the Army, neither of them responded, so his buddy got the Army and Small got the Navy.

At Port Chicago, Small became a section leader and a hold boss. By January 1944 he was the division's official "cadence caller," the man assigned to summon the division to attention so that the petty officer could call the roster. As a cadence caller, he always marched outside the ranks, and regardless of rain or mud, he kept his men moving at a regulation sixty-two steps per minute. At twenty-three, he was a few years older than many of the men in his division. He was tough, bull-necked, and strong-shouldered—though, at five feet seven and a half inches, and 170 pounds, not physically imposing— sometimes cantankerous, and a tireless worker. More important, the guys looked up to him and some feared him, too. He had no patience for malingerers and was not shy about his dislike for the white officers or a good portion of the all-black enlisted crew. Although he had only an eighth-grade education, he was exactly the kind of person whom the officers at the October 1943 "Conference with Regard to Negro Personnel" had in mind when they talked about the importance of finding a respected "Negro" boss or a "headman" to keep the others of his race in line. The black petty officers, whom many of the loaders considered to be Uncle Toms, did not mess with him. Even the white commissioned officers treated him with respect.

Eventually Small got transferred to the winches. He was undoubtedly delighted about the move. Working in the cargo holds, fourteen to twenty-seven feet down in the belly of the ship, was dangerous work. Small knew that there was "no place to run or hide in the hold of a Liberty ship," especially when a winchman, waiting for instructions from his signalman, held suspended in the air a wire net filled with bombs. The seamen in the hold wanted their best men up above—one at the levers and the other giving him instructions. When the winches started to hum, just short of burning up, the man running them had better know what he was doing, especially if he was trying to stop a big load from free-falling. The waterfront union had strict regulations that required its winchmen to have many years of experience with various kinds of cargo before graduating to ammunition. If the Navy Bureau of Ordnance had similar regulations, Port Chicago did not observe them.

Small started on the winches without any kind of special training; he just "picked up" the skill by closely observing other operators, filling in when one needed to use the head, playing with the levers over his lunch hour. He was good with machines and loved to watch the way the winches worked, a design as practical as it was simple. A winch consisted of two steam engines connected to a crankshaft, which, in turn, was connected to a drum. One end of a wire runner (cargo lifting line) was wound around the drum while the other was run up a cargo boom or crane—which was anchored to a mast—and was used to move loads from the dock to the hold of a ship. Each Liberty ship had five five-ton booms and two jumbo booms (one fifty-ton boom and one fifteen- or thirty-ton boom) rigged to three masts. As long as a winch was cared for properly and greased often, it might run forever.

Lieutenant Ernest Delucchi rode Small hard, but Small saw through his power plays. From his first day on the base he could tell that the lieutenant was a "short fat man . . . who was making a desperate attempt to change the color of his bars." What Small meant was that Delucchi was bucking for a promotion, trying to trade in a lieutenant's two silver bars for the gold oak leaf of a lieutenant commander. Consequently, little holdups pissed him off, and he could be a vindictive SOB, wielding liberty passes to deliberately inflict pain. If the division made its tonnage goals, he might reward it with a free movie or a twenty-four-hour pass. If he was in a really good mood, and a ship was not scheduled to come in for a few days, he might give the men seventy-two hours off. Tick him off, though, or fall short of his tonnage targets, and he would be as "hot as a peppermill," florid-faced and unforgiving. A guy might have a beautiful woman on the line in Berkeley or a hot date at the USO club in Oakland, but if Delucchi decided that he wanted the men to stay on base, they were not going anywhere. If he were really ticked, he would assign the men to extra duty handling explosives.

Joe Small was still sleeping when the barracks petty officer stormed in, shouting at the top of his lungs, going from seaman to seaman, and inspecting the bunks. Those men who lingered under their sheets got a rude awakening when he grabbed their mattresses and pulled the whole works onto the floor. Near Small, a small group of guys was telling tales about their night on the town. Outside the barracks, one of the guys was pitching horseshoes in his skivvies with his sneakers wrapped around his neck, as he had every day for the last two months. The fella wanted out of Port Chicago, even if it meant that he had to settle for a Section Eight discharge to get it. In the background Lieutenant Delucchi's voice boomed over the intercom, "Now hear this, now hear this. Division Four, Barracks B, fall out, fall out!"

Small could already see the day unfolding. There would be another ship at the dock, and everybody would be pushing to load more tonnage. The lieutenants and inspectors would be sounding off. The black enlisted men, trying to earn a night's liberty pass, would be racing, too, rolling bombs out boxcar doors, down ramps, and across the dock until they clanged against the ship's hull and nearly ricocheted into the bay.

After leaving the barracks and slopping through the mud, Small stood with the petty officer and called the division to attention. After the men settled in, the petty officer shouted roll call. Then the cattle car pulled up, waiting to take the division to the docks. When Lieutenant Delucchi stepped out of the bachelor's officer's quarters, Small barked, "Right face, forward march." The men boarded the cattle car reluctantly. It seemed that the driver was always deliberately popping the clutch, sending men sprawling across the floor.

When the truck reached the docks, the men, some of them limping, exited and lined up in columns. When Small took his position, he saw Kong break ranks. Long-armed and wide-shouldered, he was a powerfully built man. And he was livid. Flying across the back of the truck was the last straw. The previous night he had gotten tanked and picked up a woman who turned out to be a man. Kong did not find out until he was up in a room and almost naked. That was when the guy tried to rob and kill him. Now Kong not only had a king-sized headache, but he had a bad case of blue balls, and his body felt as if he had been hit with a sledgehammer.

Kong started for the truck driver, fully prepared to tear him apart and then accept a long bread-and-water stay in the brig. The petty officer, however, stopped him and ordered him to get back in ranks. He obeyed, walking back to his spot in the column, all the while shaking his fist at the driver. One day he would get him.

The 3rd Division had arrived at the docks first, and the division officer was already briefing his men on the day's work. Then he called over his petty officer and said in a hushed tone, "This hull needs two hundred fifty ton to sail. Tell the boys if we get it by 1530, they can hit the beach at eighteen hundred."

When Delucchi walked up, he and the division officer greeted each other like two friends meeting in a saloon. "Ernie [Ernest Delucchi], you want to kick that another fifty?" the officer asked. Delucchi did not even pause. "Sure," he said. Small was standing near enough to overhear them. It did not take a genius to figure out what they were talking about. Each was wagering that his group of guys could put on more tonnage than the other's. Although Captain Goss probably would not have approved of the betting, he encouraged a rivalry

between the divisions, what he called a "healthy spirit of competition." Delucchi's bet with the other officer sealed, he turned to Small.
"Okay," he said. "Move them out."

Small gave the cadence call, but his mind was elsewhere. Unlike
his buddy Kong, on the previous night he had met the sweetest girl
he had seen in a long time. Small had been with his share of women,
but this woman, this "Lou," had really "hung one on him." Pittsburg,
California, had never been his favorite liberty destination. Because
of Camp Stoneman, it was an Army town, and a sailor, especially a
black one, walked around with a bull's-eye on his back. But on the
night of February 13, Small took the bus to Pittsburg anyway and ran
into Lou at a little place called the Tender Rib Café. He had walked
her home and now he could not get her out of his mind.

The clang of metal on metal snapped Small from his reverie in
time to see the Liberty ship coming into the bay. She was empty, drawing only a few feet of water. Small had been hoping that the ship was
a new one with state-of-the-art electric winches. Old-fashioned steam
ones, with their old leaky valves, were a bitch. The last few ships had
been steam, and Small's hands were blistered from weeks of manhandling the long iron handles.

When the ship pulled up to the dock, Small was not disappointed.
This one had obviously just come off the yard, a brand, spanking new
Kaiser Liberty. Her winches would be electric and as smooth as silk.
The men would load her down with 6,000 tons, and if all went well
they would send her on her way seven days later so full of ordnance
that her decks would be awash.

As Small approached the ship, the graveyard shift was walking off
after a tough night. Small stopped the petty officer. "How much did
you get?" The petty officer muttered that they had fallen short. "A
hundred ninety." Then he added that the lieutenant in charge of the
division was mad as hell.

Walking toward the gangplank around a huge wire net packed
full of one-ton bombs, Small moved now with a skip in his step. He
could not wait to get at those electric winches. The hold crews were
descending the ladders. The way it worked was that the division

was broken up into five "platoons," one per hatch, each comprising twenty to twenty-four men. The platoons were then divided in half; one squad worked the pier, while the other worked the hold.

Small saw that Hoppy was going to be his signalman. From the time a load dropped below the rail until the time it came back above the edge of the hold, Hoppy had to function as Small's eyes, guiding him with a series of hand signals. The winchman handled the levers, pulling back on the inboard control a few clicks, taking up the outboard line a click or two, but the safety of the load depended on the alertness of the hatch attendant. He was the one who determined how quickly or slowly Small raised or lowered the bombs. If Hoppy was not on his game, things were not going to go well.

Hoppy and Kong were standing at the edge of the hold, shooting the shit. When Small saw the cable tighten, he knew that the crew, three decks deep in the ship, was in place and the net was ready to be lifted. "Better get to work," he yelled to Kong, and then he grabbed the winch handles. Six inches long, belt-high, they felt comfortable in his hands.

By holding his right hand in front of him and moving his left index finger in a spiraling motion like water washing down a drain, Hoppy gave Small the signal to lower the outboard line. Two clicks forward, and Small set the wire net on the dock. When Hoppy clenched his left fist, he knew that the dock crew was unhooking the empty net and attaching the loaded one. Small's mind drifted for a moment, perhaps to Lou and the previous night and the memory of her smooth brown skin, until a sharp clap focused all of his senses on the moment. Hoppy rubbed his palms together as if he were rolling something between them, and Small knew that he wanted him to move slowly. Small watched him like a hawk. When Hoppy extended his left index finger, Small pulled back on the outboard winch control just one click. Hoppy wanted a little more power, and waved his finger. Small added one more click to the winch and heard the net dragging across the dock. When it came into his field of vision, directly under the outward boom, Hoppy made a fist, and Small moved the lever to neutral. Now Hoppy wanted speed, and touched the tips of his fingers

together. Small added two clicks to the slack line. The inboard line became taut and he raised the net over the ship's rails, stopping it above
the hold. He held it there while he and Hoppy did a quick inspection,
making sure the net was intact and the load was balanced. If anything
spilled out, the guys down in the ship were in deep shit.

The load looked good. Small swung it over the hold. Suddenly
Hoppy yelled, "Hot!" What in the hell was going on? Then Small saw
it, too. Some newly commissioned officer was kneeling at the edge of
the hold. Another second and he would have been tumbling to the
bottom deck. Fortunately for him, Small had reversed the outboard
winch and brought the load straight up full speed. All the ninety-day
wonder had to show for his stupidity was a bloody mouth from being
hit by the net.

Delucchi had heard the valves singing and was sprinting. With
both winches running under a five-ton load, the sound was unmistakable. Anxiously he examined the lines and valves. The last thing he
needed was for a winch to go down and put him days behind schedule. When everything checked out, he patted Small on the shoulder.
"Make it up, Randy. We need three hundred tons." Delucchi always
called Small by the short version of his middle name, Randolph, and
Small had never liked it.

Small was raising his twenty-fifth load when the ship's bell sig-
naled 1200 hours—chow time. Lowering it to the deck, he knew he
was twenty-five tons down and would have to make up the extra five
lifts before the end of the day.

The guys lined up at the chow wagon. Down in the hold, Percy Robinson and his crew had been hauling loads like mules all morning. He was glad that he had spent the night at the base studying
his catechism—his goal still was to be baptized a Catholic—especially
when he saw the guys who had been out drinking all night. The hold
was no place to nurse a hangover.

Robinson enjoyed a night on the town as much as anyone. The
Black USO Club in East Oakland was one of his favorite haunts.
There was something there for everybody: pool tables, a boxing ring,

a basketball court, cards, food and women, and sometimes music, too. Robinson loved to shoot pool and play bridge, but he never had enough money to gamble. A Port Chicago seaman's pay was a paltry sum. Like Boykin and a lot of the guys, Robinson would supplement his meager salary by grabbing extra work at the Shell Oil Refinery in Martinez. The refinery always needed men to clean up oil spills and to break up saltpeter for agricultural fertilizer. Often Robinson could pick up an extra eight hours, and sometimes, when he had a twenty-four-hour pass, he could put together back-to-back eight-hour shifts. Afterward, he would hustle to Port Chicago and fall exhausted into his bunk, getting a little sleep before the day's loading began.

When he landed a seventy-two-hour pass, which, given the depot's beefed-up schedule, was harder to come by, he and the Hawks would go into San Francisco. A trip into the big city could be dicey, though, and Robinson and his buddies would carry razors just in case. The members of the Hawks were what Robinson called his "cut brothers," guys he could rely on when a situation got tense. They would watch one another's backs, especially at the bus station when they were entering or leaving town. In San Francisco, white and black servicemen would self-segregate, but at the bus station they mingled whether they wanted to or not, and fights sometimes broke out.

In San Francisco, Robinson and the Hawks loved to go into the Fillmore, the coolest square mile west of Chicago, an exciting, multicultural melting pot, where many of the businesses were owned and run by African, Japanese, and Filipino Americans. Here blacks could hang out at the Subway Nightclub, Club Alabama, or Jack's Tavern on Sutter Street, the neighborhood's first black-owned music venue, and listen to Johnnie Ingram, Billie Holiday, Dizzy Gillespie, and many other up-and-coming musicians who were not allowed to play clubs east of Van Ness Avenue. Those (like Duke Ellington) who did perform at the big hotels could not stay downtown, so after their gigs they would often return to the Fillmore to jam with other black musicians. Like the Stroll in Chicago, Harlem in New York, and Detroit's Paradise Valley, the Fillmore swung from dusk till dawn. Because white servicemen also cruised the neighborhood, the Hawks frequented a two-to-three-block area of nightclubs and saloons called the International Settlement that catered especially to blacks. Whether or not there was mixing, the bars were rough places. Reasoning that it was better to avoid trouble than tempt fate, Robinson and his crew stuck mostly to the nightclubs where they could absorb the music and enjoy the promenade of finely dressed women.

While the Hawks enjoyed the fresh air, Joe Small, having passed up breakfast, eyed the food the cooks had laid out. Given a choice of liver and onions or bacon, Small took the bacon and then added two pieces of bread and a piping-hot cup of coffee to his tray. Then he joined Hoppy and Kong down at the water. As Small sat down, Kong spotted the cattle-car driver. Small put his hand on his buddy's shoulder to calm him, saying, "The beach is better," urging him to get his revenge at another time.

A KP brought over some apple pie. Small wolfed it down and then walked over to the chow wagon. A Marine guard stood over the GI can, like some mother superior, inspecting the trays to make sure no one was wasting food. Just then Small caught sight of Delucchi and walked over to him. The lieutenant asked how things were going.

"Rough," he replied. "I think we're pushing too hard." Small had confronted Delucchi before about the rushing. Delucchi's stock reply—in fact, the response of all the officers—was that the bombs were harmless without the detonators. Small, though, knew that detonator or not, the bombs were packed with TNT. As a winchman, sometimes swinging five-ton loads across the quarterdeck, he was especially conscious of the dangers. One slipup and he could send a whole bunch of men to the undertaker.

Delucchi looked at his watch again. Then he asked, "Do you think you can lift thirty by 1530?"

"Sure," Small responded, "if this place doesn't blow up, and someday it will."

"If it does, neither you nor I will be around to know about it." Delucchi laughed.

Lunch was over and the work began again. It did not take long for Small to figure out how Lieutenant Delucchi was going to make up the morning's tonnage shortfall. He felt the winches drag and realized that the petty officers, obviously under orders from Delucchi, had added another bomb, another ton, to the net. Now the winches would be straining to lift six tons instead of five.

Small put the load in the hold, and Hoppy waved him up and out. *What the hell's going on?* he thought. *What's Hoppy doing?* Then he got his answer. Delucchi had added another net in addition to the extra ton. Now there was always a loaded net ready to be set in the hold and an empty one to bring back up. No resting. In order to get his tonnage by quitting time, Delucchi was willing to risk the safety of every man out there, or at the very least burning up the winches or frying the brake bands.

At five-thirty the cattle car returned with the night division, and the crew members of Division 4 assembled on the dock. They were tired and hungry. Their only consolation was that since the 183 men from Great Lakes arrived in late December, they were putting in two to four hours less per shift.

Small was getting ready to march the division, when Delucchi put his arm around his shoulder. "Thanks, Randy," he said, holding the day's tally sheet. "You did a fine job. We got five ton over."

Small marched his men to the cattle car and watched them board. Then he, too, climbed on. He had not been joking when he told the lieutenant that the place was going to blow. As the winchman, he knew better than anyone else how hard they were pushing. An extra ton per net, with no break between loads, was not a pace that could be maintained without courting disaster. Small hoped like hell that when that day came, he would be far away from Port Chicago.

# CHAPTER 27

# The Devil's Backbone

Now that the 6th Marines had fought off the early-morning tank attack and the beachhead was secured, General Holland Smith could begin to implement his master plan. The 4th Division would push across the island, while the 2nd Division held the pivot, waiting until the 4th made it across the interior spine and swung north, before it began its own movement up the west coast. What that meant for Matthews's Company G was that it would fight its way through the swamps along the southern edge of Lake Susupe, past Aslito Field, over the "Devil's Backbone," into the shallow valleys with their small farm plots and bellowing cows, toward the wild cliffs of Magicene Bay. Lieutenant Leary knew it would be a risky proposition for his 2nd Platoon. From the ridgeline, which ran parallel to the beach and looked down on the lake, Japanese artillery observers could see and target the advancing Marines.

Carl Matthews felt as if he had not eaten in days, but it was not hunger for food that burned in his belly; it was a desire for vengeance. First for Witte, a fellow Texan from Desdemona. Leaving Witte behind was the sensible thing, but it went against all his instincts, and gnawed at his gut. He knew that a halo of flies had probably discovered the body. He knew, too, that more soldiers would die that morning as Company G walked into the teeth of the Japanese artillery.

The moment the men of Company G stepped out into an open field, hidden machine guns tore into them, and a Japanese artillery unit atop Kannat Tabla Mountain opened up with its 150-mm howitzers, laying waste to the forward platoons. A Marine halftrack answered, firing its 75-mm cannons, but Leary called for his men to retreat. Everyone was sprinting in the direction of a small ravine when Richard Freeby, Matthews's Gold Dust Twin, noticed that Wendell Nightingale had been hit. Freeby stopped, threw down his rifle, and headed back into what Matthews saw was a "hail of bullets." Matthews and every member of G Company dropped to their bellies and opened up on the brush behind Freeby, hoping to provide him with enough covering fire that he and Nightingale might escape. With enemy bullets spattering around him, Freeby dragged and tugged at his friend. For a moment it seemed as if they might get out alive. Then Nightingale was hit again. Freeby continued to pull at him, until he felt the weight and knew that Nightingale was dead. Then, as if realizing for the first time that every Japanese rifle was trained on him, he ran for his life, racing and zigzagging across the field to safety.

Every man who had watched him knew what an extraordinary act of courage he had witnessed. What each of them also knew was that nothing short of a miracle had saved Freeby. The Japanese had him dead to rights. His pack was riddled with bullet holes. Why he was not lying out there spouting blood from a dozen holes, they could not say. Lieutenant Leary said that if he lived beyond Saipan, he would recommend Freeby for the Silver Star. From the moment he rolled into the ravine, however, Freeby knew he had failed and knew, too, that not being able to save his friend was something that would stick with him for the rest of his life. Nightingale would never again lay his eyes on his beloved Maine. While Marine artillery and mortarmen hammered the enemy command post, Freeby put his face in his hands and cried like a baby.

At three o'clock that afternoon, the company learned that its job was to cross the field and set up a bivouac shelter in a cluster of palm trees on the far side. If the men were surprised by the order, they should not have been. Since D-Day they had made little forward movement. Now that they had begun the push across the island, battalion commanders wanted to see progress.

When Leary gave the signal, his 2nd Platoon moved out. Every man hoped that the mortar and artillery barrage had done a job on the command post. When they reached the clearing, they began to run. It was an obstacle course, littered with dead Marines. Matthews dodged and jumped over corpses, cursing under his breath, determined to use his long-thrust bayonet training and gut every Jap hiding in the trees ahead. To his right a group of Marines dropped concussion grenades into every gap and gash they found, and riddled the bushes with bullets. Matthews heard the sound of empty clips popping out of rifles. When a man jumped out of a hole, the Marines shredded him with fire. Only later did they realize that they had killed an old Chamorro farmer.

By evening Leary's platoon had made it into the hills. The lieutenant ordered his men to dig in, and then he and Matthews went out in search of Nightingale's body. They found him facedown where Freeby had left him. Lieutenant Leary wiped the dirt off Nightingale's cheek and forehead and then removed one of his dogtags, leaving the other so that the burial detail could identify him. Then Leary stuck Nightingale's rifle, bayonet first, into the ground and placed Nightingale's helmet over the butt. It was standard Marine procedure, but he performed the work tenderly, as if it were a benediction. When he finished, Matthews stood over his friend's body. He avoided Leary's eyes. No one had ever told him it could be like this, that after such a short life it could come to this. Before leaving, Leary whispered a few words. Then he and Matthews hustled back to the platoon.

As Matthews climbed into his foxhole that evening beneath the gray monsoon clouds, the energy and hate seeped from his limbs. He felt old, homesick, and weary of war.

• • •

Back at the beach, Robert Graf sat in the sand in the blinding late-afternoon sun. He had barely moved for two days. He, too, was done with war. After the deaths of Lieutenant Roth, for whom he had been serving as a runner since his early days at Camp Pendleton, and Sergeant Lipfield, he had checked himself into the battalion aid station. Later he would admit that he had lost faith and cracked up. Perhaps he thought of home, pinching his eyes to sharpen the view, to see the mid-autumn trees streak the blue sky with color, to feel the half-moon curve of a girlfriend's hips. He was watching the sea when a long shadow fell over him. Looking up, he saw an officer, and rose slowly until he realized that he was face-to-face with a major.

"Your name Graf?" the officer inquired.

When Graf answered yes, he thought, *Jesus, I'm gonna be court-martialed.*

"My name is Fought," the major said. "I'm taking over Company E and I want you as my runner."

Stunned, Graf almost asked if the major could repeat himself. Then he exhaled as if he had just been saved from a firing squad. Sticking out his chest and squeezing his shoulders together, he said, "Aye, aye. Thank you for the vote of confidence."

The major explained to Graf that Company G's mortar section had been hit so bad that battalion was sending them a new squad. He had barely walked away when Graf saw the men approaching. Two of the mortar men were none other than Bill Jurcsak and Jimmy Haskell, his old Ballston Spa buddies. They were a sight for sore eyes. Just a day before, Graf had been almost paralyzed with grief. Now he felt happiness, and as that happiness grew, so did the hate. He would avenge Lieutenant Roth's death by killing every bucktoothed Jap he could.

Later that morning the 1st Battalion, 29th Marines, had orders to take the ridge in front of them. Realizing that Japanese spotters were watching the bare hills and the meadows, Rachitsky pulled out his compass and took a bearing and then charted a course through the swamp and along the north shore of Lake Susupe. The route enabled his men to avoid being destroyed by Japanese artillery. Hugging the bank, the men sloshed and stumbled through the waist-high water. When a shot rang out and a man near them slid into the coffee-colored muck, Borta and Lemon held their rifles over their heads and crouched as low as they could until the lake was lapping at their chests.

The crossing took hours, and when the men reached the far bank, they flopped in the mud. The hot sun beat down on them, and the air was thick and wet. Even Rachitsky, who was the toughest man Borta had ever known and never allowed himself a break, lay there until he caught his breath. Then he rose to his feet and wobbled. He grabbed the branch of a tree to steady himself. Borta watched as the sergeant studied his map. Tucking the map in its case, he waved the men in. Enemy snipers had picked off a few guys in the lake, but most of the men had made it across. Clicking his fingers to get their attention, Rachitsky pointed to a grove of trees 200 yards in front of them.

"That's our target," he said.

None of the guys knew for sure what lay between them and the trees ahead. Would they make it across, or would they walk into a slaughter? Had they been following another man, they might have thought twice about moving forward. With Rachitsky in the lead, however, they did not hesitate. They set out, bending low at the waist, dropping to a knee every ten yards. At every sound their fingers tightened on their triggers. At each stop Rachitsky grabbed his field glasses and scanned the woods. When they were sixty feet away, he studied the grove. Seeing nothing, he waved the men forward. Borta and Lemon were on his right at the front of the platoon. Borta's eyes were so clouded with mud and sweat that he could hardly see, and his feet, raw from jungle rot, burned with every step. Still, he had to suppress the desire to break into a mad run, covering the distance between him and the grove as fast as he could. He took a few more steps, cursing the water that sloshed inside his canteen. Then gunfire burst from the trees ahead. He and Lemon were on their bellies when they heard a Japanese *juki* machine gun. They could tell it was a *juki* by its slow, heavy thud.

Rachitsky was yelling now, "Hand grenades! Throw your grenades."

Borta and Lemon rolled on their sides and whipped their grenades as if they were throwing a roundhouse punch. Rolling back to his belly, Borta saw the flash of an Arisaka rifle barrel and then he heard the sickly smacking sound of a bullet entering flesh. He prayed that it was not Lemon or Pluto Brem or Sergeant Rachitsky. Then he realized that he did not know where Brem was. He had not seen his buddy for an entire day. Had a sniper got Brem back at the lake? When he heard the sharp bark of a Browning Automatic Rifle to his right, he knew Brem was still alive. Then, off to his left, he heard Robert Roberts open up with his BAR. Roberts had been an assistant, but when his BAR man was killed on the second night, the rifle became his possession. Borta slammed in a new magazine. Suddenly the grove was quiet. Neither Borta nor Lemon dared to move. Everyone, it seemed, was waiting for fire to erupt again from the trees.

Then Borta heard it, Rachitsky's voice. "Borta," Rachitsky growled. "You there?" *Thank God,* Borta thought, *the old man is alive.* Before he could respond, Rachitsky wriggled on his forearms and belly to his runner's side. "I want you to go to the beach and get some hand grenades," he said. "And take Pluto with you."

By late afternoon they had made it. Borta saw bodies sprawled across the beach: exhausted stretcher-bearers who, after delivering wounded Marines to the aid station, collapsed in the sand, and young men who had died in combat. Some of them looked as if they were napping, as if they might wake from a dream and curse him for disturbing their sleep. Among them were Japanese soldiers who had staged an early-morning raid after the tank attack had failed. Ultimately they would be thrown into a deep trench and buried, but for now they rotted in the sun. A few were Japanese marines, their caps decorated with a cherry blossom superimposed over an anchor.

Dusk was setting in by the time Borta and Brem, each carrying a crate of hand grenades, made it back across the lake. At Susupe's eastern edge, they lay on their backs, resting against an embankment.

Their legs and arms ached and their lungs felt as if they were on fire. Borta wondered if he had the strength to carry the grenades for the last eighth of a mile. Caked with mud, Brem wondered if he could stand the smell of himself. He had spent the night of D-Day in a foxhole that turned out to be a septic tank, and wading back and forth through the mud of Lake Susupe only seemed to make the stench worse.

Both Borta and Brem had let their guards down. When they heard a high-pitched crack, and a bullet struck the dirt between their heads, they froze, waiting for a second shot. Brem pointed in the direction of a shack. "From there," he whispered. Then he and Borta formulated a plan. Borta's job was to get around behind the shack and throw in a grenade and flush the sniper out. Brem would be hiding in front and would spray him as he ran.

Borta crept into some bushes in back of the shack and noticed that a rear window was shattered. Pulling the pin on a grenade, he let the spoon go. Despite the adrenaline slamming through his veins, he calmed himself long enough to count, "One one thousand, two one thousand, three one thousand." It seemed to last a lifetime. When the grenade sparkled, he heaved it. Only it never came close to the window. It flew over the roof and exploded. Borta heard Brem cursing him, "Dammit, Chick, you nearly killed me." Then he heard Brem running, firing like a madman, and showering the shack with bullets. The sniper was probably so full of holes that he looked like a piece of cheesecloth.

Walking back to their unit, they chortled like boys. Man, would Brem have a story for the guys. They would double up with laughter when he told them about Chick hurling a grenade over the roof of the shack. If only Carney and Larson were alive. They would laugh themselves sick.

It did not take them long to reach the spot where they had left the platoon earlier that day. When they spotted movement in the grove, they lay down and watched. Then Borta heard voices, American voices. Company A had taken the grove! As they approached the trees, they realized that something was wrong. Men shouted for corpsmen and stretcher bearers. One badly wounded Marine, who had obviously been injected with morphine, lay in the grass like a zombie, smiling while the man next to him, whose hand had been shot off, moaned in pain. Brem spotted a four-by-four section of dirt that was saturated with blood. It reminded him of hunting in the Pacheco Pass, of hanging and bleeding out a big deer.

Borta was wandering through the grove looking for Rachitsky when he saw a man lying on a stretcher. Someone had laid a poncho over him and pulled it up to his nose. As Borta walked by, he thought, *Rachitsky?* Then he thought, *Nah, Rachitsky is too goddamned tough to die.* Borta was just about to move on when someone walked by. "Sarge," the Marine said, pointing to the body. "Poor sucker."

Borta knelt down and pulled back the poncho. Rachitsky appeared to be taking a siesta. Soon he would pop up and give him that steely stare that made a man's knees shake and his heart flutter. Rachitsky had never said anything to Borta that was remotely personal, but as his runner, he had come to love and respect the sergeant. Other than his father, there was not another man whom he thought more of.

Borta searched his memory for an appropriate prayer, something from Revelation or Romans or Isaiah. All he could come up with was, "Our Father, who art in heaven . . ." He clenched his jaw as he said the words, fighting back the tears. Dead or alive, Rachitsky would never tolerate crying. Borta finished the Lord's Prayer and then studied Rachitsky's watch. Not a scratch on it. He could take the sergeant's and put it to good use. Rachitsky would forgive him. A runner who did not know the time was worthless.

Slowly Borta reached for Rachitsky's hand, and then stopped. He felt like a crow feeding on roadkill, only the roadkill in this case was his dead sergeant. He pulled back his arm and turned away. Then he looked at Rachitsky and began to slip the watch off his wrist. The expandable band made it easy. He stopped again, and arranged the poncho over Rachitsky's body as if he were covering a sleeping child, and then rose and made the sign of the cross. *Rest in peace, Sarge.*

A bunch of guys from Company A, their hair matted with rifle oil, their dungarees torn and bloody, sat together Indian-style in the grove, wolfing down cold C-rations: dehydrated eggs, potatoes, and canned meat. From them Borta learned that after their CO, Lieutenant Colonel Tannyhill, had been wounded, his replacement CO, Lieutenant Colonel Tompkins, had led the push. Intent on taking the grove before dark, he had come up to the front lines to assess the situation and then called in four Division 2 tanks. After the tanks pummeled the grove, Tompkins personally led the infantry attack.

"Yeah, we got the grove," one of the guys said, "but we lost Lieutenant Henderson and a bunch of other guys." Moreover, Henderson's platoon, of which Rachitsky was the senior NCO, had taken such a beating that the remaining guys were being assigned elsewhere. The following day Borta learned that he would be going to company headquarters.

As Borta was standing there among badly wounded Marines whose collapsed veins refused to take plasma, Lemon walked up and nudged him. *Jesus Christ,* Borta thought, *I forgot all about you.*

"Doin' okay?" Borta asked.

Lemon looked at him blankly. "Right as rain."

At 4:30 a.m. on June 18, the 10th Marines spotted thirty-five Japanese barges, packed with soldiers, off Flores Point north of Garapan. The Marines had no idea where they had come from, but it was obvious that the Japanese were trying to reinforce General Saito's garrison, hoping to land the slow-moving barges under the cover of darkness. Their plan, however, failed. The Marines, together with Navy vessels, sank thirteen of the barges, while the other twenty-two reversed course to escape harm.

At sunrise that same morning, the troops discovered that Admiral Spruance's fleet had left the previous night. For the men who had been in the Solomons, the explanation was an easy one: the Navy bastards had hauled ass again, just as they had done at Guadalcanal.

The reality was that Admiral Spruance was 200 miles west of Saipan, preparing to meet the challenge of Vice Admiral Jisaburo

Ozawa, who, upon implementing Operation A-Go, was planning to destroy the U.S. Pacific Fleet with "one blow." Because Admirals Ozawa and Toyoda did not know the damage that Admiral Mitscher's Task Force 58 had done to its land-based planes (Ozawa was counting on five hundred planes from Yap, Guam, Tinian, and the Palaus), the Japanese high command was confident that the showdown could be won.

MacArthur's efforts to the south in New Guinea, however, complicated the Japanese response. In April, American pilots had destroyed the Japanese air base at Hollandia, and on May 27, MacArthur's forces invaded Biak Island, off New Guinea's northwest coast. Uncertain about where the United States would execute its major thrust— would it be Biak, or would it come somewhere else?—Japanese admirals committed vital naval resources, including two battleships, cruisers, troop-carrying destroyers, and fighter planes from its First Air Fleet, to defend the island and its airfields. Admiral King undoubtedly took a measure of satisfaction from Japan's indecision. He had been preaching that a two-pronged approach would keep enemy intelligence guessing as to where the major American blow would come.

On June 11, with the carrier strike on Saipan, Toyoda and Ozawa no longer had any doubts about where the U.S. advance would take place. Temporarily suspending "Operation KON," the defense plan for Biak, Toyoda green-lighted A-Go. From his flagship at 8:55 on June 15, he sent out a message to all his commanding officers. "On the morning of the 15th, a strong enemy force began landing operations in the Saipan-Tinian area. The Combined Fleet will attack the enemy in the Marianas area and annihilate the invasion force. Activate A-Go Operation for decisive battle." He ended his address by invoking the words of Admiral Heihachiro Togo, who in 1905 defeated the Russian fleet in the Tsushima Strait between Korea and southern Japan. "The fate of the Empire rests on this one battle," Toyoda said. "Every man is expected to do his utmost." Admiral Ozawa transmitted his words to every ship in the Mobile Fleet. Two days later, Ozawa's forces massed in the Philippine Sea. On the following morning, the admiral addressed the ships under his command, relaying the message he had received from the Emperor through the chief of staff of the Imperial General Headquarters' naval section: " 'This operation has immense bearing on the fate of the Empire. It is hoped that the forces will exert their utmost and achieve as magnificent results as in the Battle of Tsushima.' "

Although the Japanese navy was still formidable, Spruance's force was superior in almost every way—and the admiral knew it. Nevertheless, Spruance saw his mission as twofold: he had to meet Ozawa's naval offensive while first protecting the forces on Saipan. Although he was eager to engage the enemy, by venturing too far from the island he risked the possibility of a Japanese "end run" that would expose his ground troops there to danger. Lending credence to his fears was a document that MacArthur sent him detailing Japanese carrier doctrine. It instructed carrier force commanders to occupy the enemy by feinting in the middle, while sending detachments around the flanks to execute a pincer movement. The Japanese had used the strategy effectively in the Coral Sea and in battles around Guadalcanal, in addition to attempting it at Midway, where Spruance defeated the carrier force's center before the flanks could close in.

Not everyone agreed with the admiral's decision. A frustrated Admiral Mitscher lobbied repeatedly for an aggressive pursuit of the Japanese fleet, arguing that the Expeditionary Force, which remained around the island, had enough warships and escort carriers to protect the Marines and soldiers. Spruance, however, remained firm. His orders, he said, were clear: to protect the invasion force, "proceeding west in daylight and towards Saipan at night."

By June 18, Spruance's fleet was 200 miles west of Saipan, and 300 miles from Ozawa. Although Spruance did not have a fix on Ozawa's position, the Japanese admiral knew where the Americans were, and was eager to strike the first blow, knowing that his carrier planes had a greater range than their American counterparts.

Back on Saipan, General Saito had just received a message from Hideki Tojo: "Because the fate of the Japanese Empire depends on the result of your operation, inspire the spirit of the officers and men and to the very end continue to destroy the enemy gallantly and persistently; thus alleviate the anxiety of the Emperor." It was not Saito, however, who responded to Tojo. That task was left to the chief of staff of the 43rd Division. "Have received your honorable Imperial words," he replied, "and we are grateful for boundless magnanimity of Imperial favor. By becoming the bulwark of the Pacific with 10,000 deaths we hope to requite the Imperial favor."

Had Imperial Headquarters in Tokyo learned of the day's events on Saipan, nothing could have quelled Hirohito's fears. Driving toward Aslito, the Army's 165th Infantry Regiment captured the vital airfield before noon on June 18. General Holland Smith was cheered by the Army's progress. Later that day in a radio recording, an enthusiastic General Ralph Smith, commanding officer of the Army's 27th Division, said, "This is an appropriate point to emphasize the perfect teamwork that has existed between the Navy, Marines, and the Army. It irritates me a little to read these stories. . . . Nothing could be farther from the truth out here in the field. . . . One of the 165th's officers remarked to me this morning that Saipan has sealed the brotherhood between the services." Unfortunately for Ralph Smith, the harmony would not last.

On the following morning, in the Philippine Sea, 100 miles west of Guam, American Hellcats attacked and shot down thirty-five Japanese air reinforcements. Unaware of the loss, Ozawa sent sixty-nine planes toward the American fleet for the first of four air strikes. It was a clear day with unlimited visibility, and once radar spotted the enemy planes, Admiral Mitscher launched his Hellcats. American pilots had an easy time finding the enemy fighters. A Japanese-speaking lieutenant aboard the carrier USS *Lexington* monitored the radio chatter of the approaching pilots and passed on vital information to the American crews. With the lieutenant's reports and superior numbers, the Americans sent most of Ozawa's planes spiraling into the sea. Antiaircraft fire took care of the few that made it past the barrage. Because they were heavy with bombs, they were easy targets for the gunners. At 9:00 a.m., Ozawa launched a second wave of 110 planes, a third wave an hour later, and a fourth wave of eighty-two at 11:30 a.m. Outclassed and outmaneuvered, Japanese pilots succeeded in damaging the USS *South Dakota,* a battleship, but not a single American carrier, and by the end of the day, Ozawa had lost nearly four hundred planes. Triumphant American pilots referred to their lopsided victory—and the greatest carrier battle of the war—as "the Great Marianas Turkey Shoot."

While American pilots chalked up kills, American submarines also entered the fray. The submarine *Albacore* fired on Ozawa's flagship, the *Taiho*—at 33,000 tons and 850 feet, the Taiho was the newest and biggest carrier in the Japanese navy—hitting her with one of six torpedoes and rupturing one of her oil tanks. Six hours later she exploded. Although a lifeboat rescued Ozawa and his staff, much of the *Taiho*'s crew was lost. The *Cavalla,* which had sent Admiral Spruance the first warning about the Japanese fleet leaving Tawi Tawi, also got in on the action, hitting the carrier *Shokaku* with three of six torpedoes at noon that same day. Fumes, fed by ruptured oil tanks, leaked through the ship and fires broke out. Three hours later a bomb magazine exploded, and the *Shokaku* broke apart.

That night Mitscher deliberated about whether or not to send out night-fighting Hellcats with mounted belly tanks to search for Ozawa. Although the belly tanks enabled the Hellcats to extend their reach to 400 miles, Mitscher held them back, believing that his pilots were exhausted. Had Mitscher sent out his planes, they might have caught and surprised Ozawa and decimated his carriers. The admiral and his staff were aboard the cruiser *Haguro,* still trying to reach the other carrier divisions and to get some sense of the day's losses. While Ozawa knew that he had lost two big carriers, he knew little about the damage to his air groups. Based on the exaggerated reports of pilots who had made it back from the "Turkey Shoot," and despite the fate of his two big carriers, Ozawa believed that June 19 had been a success. The official Tokyo broadcast boasted that Japanese pilots had sunk eleven U.S. carriers. So instead of fleeing north, the admiral made plans to refuel the following day and then to resume his search for the American fleet.

At 3:40 p.m. on June 20, after one of his pilots sighted the Japanese, Mitscher made plans to strike Ozawa. Twenty minutes later the pilot confirmed his report: the Japanese fleet was apparently refueling, moving slowly and heading west. Now Mitscher put his plan into action, knowing that a portion of it would take place at night, and that "to destroy the Japanese fleet was going to cost a great deal in planes and pilots." Later, in his after-action report, he wrote that he was launching his planes "at the maximum range" and "at such a time that it would be necessary to recover them after dark." Most of his pilots, he added, "were not familiar with night landing and would be fatigued at the end of an extremely hazardous and long mission." Nevertheless, Mitscher believed that the risk was worth it.

At 6:10 p.m. he gathered his pilots and gave them a pep talk. "Give 'em hell, boys," he said. His pilots did just that, disabling two oilers, damaging the carrier *Junyo,* and sinking the carrier *Hiyo.* Then, realizing their fuel was running low, they disengaged and began their return trip.

At 7:45 that night the sky turned completely dark, and clouds obscured the moonlight. An hour later, with his returning planes circling, Mitscher turned his carriers east into the wind. Then, disregarding the safety of his fleet and naval procedure, he ordered his carrier commanders to turn on their lights. Truck lights, red and green running lights, signal lights, and glow lights, outlined the flight decks, and star shells pierced the coal-black night. Having dreaded the landing, his pilots realized that they might now get back alive. One described seeing the lights as equal parts "Hollywood premiere, Chinese New Year's and Fourth of July." By eleven that night, carriers had gathered, and destroyers, using huge searchlights and aided by a calm, flat sea, looked for the pilots who, unable to land, had splashed down. When the search was called off days later, only sixteen pilots and thirty-three crewmen were unaccounted for.

The following morning, June 21, Spruance ordered Admiral Mitscher and his carriers to pursue the retreating Ozawa. Although Spruance had given his vice-admiral the okay to strike Ozawa's fleet if contact was made, the primary reason for giving chase was to comb the ocean for crippled enemy ships. At 7:20 that night, Mitscher had not yet sighted the Japanese, and after Spruance called off the search, he reversed course and headed for Saipan.

That evening, 300 miles south of Okinawa, a chastened Ozawa summoned his senior staff officer and dictated a letter to Admiral Toyoda, accepting responsibility for the defeat, and offering his resignation. Toyoda refused to accept it, although he understood the full implications of Ozawa's defeat, as did everyone at Imperial Headquarters, including the Emperor: Japan's carrier-based airpower was finished. Now they could only hope that General Saito was able to hold Saipan, for they understood that if they lost Saipan, too, the Philippines and the home islands would be the targets of long-range bombing raids.

Back on the island of Saipan, General Saito's men clung to the idea that their powerful navy had driven off Spruance's Fifth Fleet. The fantastic Tokyo broadcast, which stated that Japanese pilots had sunk eleven U.S. carriers, served only to confirm their unreal expectations. By June 21, even as the noose was tightening around their necks, the island's defenders, like their general, still believed that reinforcements were on their way.

Reinforcements or no, Saito's men had pledged to defend the island until the end. "We will fight hand to hand," said one of his soldiers. "I have resolved that if I see the enemy, I will take out my sword and slash, slash, slash at him as long as I last . . ."

# CHAPTER 28

# Valley of the Shadow of Death

Although General Holland Smith was "determined to take Saipan and to take it quickly," the reality was that when he left the USS *Rocky Mount* and came ashore, setting up the Northern Troops and Landing Force command post in Charan Kanoa, he knew that Saipan would be a war of attrition. On June 22, Navy pilots dropped another thirty packages of propaganda leaflets informing the enemy that because of the Japanese navy's loss at the Battle of the Philippine Sea, no one would come to their rescue. "The American Navy," it said, "has complete sea and air superiority."

After a week of combat, the men of the 4th Division, with the 25th Marines on the right, the 24th in the middle, and the 23rd on the left, had driven east across Saipan, severing the southern third of the island from the north. Yet they had put little distance between themselves and the invasion beach. They were still short of what Smith called the "O-4," or Day 4, objective. The sluggishness of the American advance disturbed the general, for Smith believed devoutly in the dictum of the great German military theorist Karl von Clausewitz: "For the victor, the engagement can never be decided too quickly; for the vanquished, it can never be decided too long. The speedy victory is the higher degree of victory; a late decision is, on the side of the defeated, some compensation for the loss."

The good news was that Spruance's victory in the Philippine Sea meant that transport ships would be returning to the island, and the supply channel could once again kick into overdrive. Marine depot companies would soon be working round the clock, landing tens of thousands of tons of cargo.

For Smith's men it would be a blessing. They were contending with a dwindling supply of everything from water to medicine to star shells and artillery rounds. Worse yet was the problem of where to put the wounded. The hospital ships *Relief* and the *Samaritan* had left for Guadalcanal, following the route taken by transport ships, which had already delivered thousands of wounded soldiers to the Solomons. That left only the *Solace* and the *Bountiful* and an assortment of cargo vessels to take on men. Many wounded Marines had nowhere to go. Admiral Turner's flagship was being used as a floating hospital. Men wearing casualty tags lined the corridors, waiting for a doctor's attention. More than a quarter of these were badly injured mortar or artillery victims. Another 7 percent had knife and bayonet injuries sustained in hand-to-hand combat.

The health of the men, in general, was deteriorating quickly. Marines and soldiers alike were suffering from lack of sleep, heat exhaustion, prickly heat, and, despite sulfa therapy and opium derivatives, diarrhea, too. Dehydration was a major concern. The men found the water, sometimes stored in fifty-five-gallon drums that had once held aviation fuel, undrinkable. So they resorted to catching rain in their helmets, and when it did not rain, they popped salt tablets as if they were gumdrops. When they came upon cane fields that had not been burned, they sucked on sugarcane as if it were ambrosia.

The men's feet were burning with jungle rot. The coral tore at their boots, and without foot powder or fungicide, their feet were swollen, raw, and blistered. For some men, even for those who cut slits in the sides of their boondockers to let their feet breathe, every step became a chore. Although most of them had tossed their underwear, the upper legs of many of the Marines were already infected with crotch rot and beginning to run pus where their pocket edges and trouser seams rubbed against their thighs. An opportunistic infection, brought about by poor nutrition and the compromised immune systems of the men, the crotch rot migrated down the men's legs, causing them to grimace in pain and to walk like bowlegged cowboys.

The flies were maddening, and the men came to loathe them. Black flies, green blowflies, and bluebottle flies descended in thick clouds. More than a nuisance, they were a health hazard. Medics resorted to spreading the pesticide sodium arsenite on dead bodies, and company commanders punished men for not observing proper field sanitation. A common practice when they were in foxholes was to shit on their entrenching tools and throw the mess out. The following day, few bothered to bury it or cover it up in a cat-hole latrine. They pinched their noses and shut out the smell, and moved on.

It being the rainy season, the mosquitoes were a curse. They came out every day in the early morning and just after sunset, and descended upon the men, attracted by the smell of their sweat. The air hummed with them. Still, most of the men refused to wear their head nets. The head nets made it hard to see, and, given the choice of being bayoneted by a Japanese soldier who had been able to creep in close because one's vision was obscured, or being eaten alive by mosquitoes, the Marines chose the latter.

What concerned the medics and Navy doctors was the "unusually high" incidence of tetanus and gas bacillus (gas gangrene). Because resident farmers used night soil, or human feces, to fertilize their fields, the ground was heavily seeded with the spores of both bacteria. Gas gangrene, which could spread from wound to wound, had a mortality rate of 50 percent, even when treated with penicillin.

The push across the island had taken its toll on the men's spirits, too. Platoon leaders, artillerymen, even General Smith, were operating with inadequate maps that inaccurately estimated both vertical and horizontal distances. On some days the troops covered lots of ground and on others they moved at a snail's pace. No one seemed to know the extent of Japanese casualties, either. The Japanese continued their practice of hiding their losses by carrying away their dead and wounded.

Nothing, however, could compare with war's unending brutality. Somewhere near Magicene Bay, on Saipan's eastern coast, Graf came upon a dying Marine, no older than he. Graf sat beside him and quickly realized that he had no miracles in his first-aid packet, only sulfa powder and a compress. The young Marine had a look of amazement about him. He could feel his life ebbing away, and he could not quite believe it. He was dying here, thousands of miles from home. He asked Graf to reach into his helmet and find the picture he carried there. Graf slipped his fingers inside and gave it to him. The young man held it in his hand familiarly, as if he had studied its details many times. Then his eyes grew blurry and his breath quickened. When he began to choke, the photo fell from his hand to the ground. Graf picked it up and looked at it. It showed the young man standing with two women: one, perhaps his mother, and the other, his wife or girlfriend. They were smiling into the camera.

Leaving the body there, Graf moved on, fully aware that Japanese soldiers regularly mutilated dead Marines, cutting off their heads and smashing in their faces until they were unrecognizable. Believing that their campaign was a sacred one, they did not consider the violence untoward. Their goal was "to extend the light of the Imperial power" over the "Greater East Asian Co-prosperity Sphere" and to eliminate the "White Race from Asia." Mothers, bidding farewell to their sons, encouraged them to commit suicide rather than be taken prisoner. A Japanese soldier would perform seppuku, gutting himself rather than allowing himself to be captured. If captured, he expected to be tortured, because that was what he would do to a captured enemy. Though they had signed the Geneva Convention of 1929, which articulated a policy for the humane treatment of POWs, the Japanese never ratified it. At the onset of the war, Prime Minister Tojo boasted that "in Japan, we have our own ideology concerning prisoners of war . . ."

American Marines were appalled by the Japanese atrocities, but no one had a monopoly on hatred or rage. When American Marines

smelled blood, they could be just as brutal, shooting Japanese soldiers, even prisoners, as if they were rats at a dump. Some killed prisoners and then pissed in their mouths. Platoon commanders took to
rewarding their men, most of whom believed that the Japanese were
less than human, with beer and whiskey to bring in prisoners. A secret
U.S. intelligence memo reported that only the "promise of ice cream
and three days' leave would induce American troops not to kill surrendering Japs."

As the 23rd Marines crossed the Devil's Backbone, they encountered caves for the first time. The Marines' procedure was to shout
into a cave, promising food and water, especially if they believed that
noncombatants had taken refuge there. One of the phrases they practiced was *"Korosanai yo,"* or, roughly, "We won't murder you." But
often caves held both Japanese soldiers and civilians, and platoon
commanders could not take any chances. Graf saw it countless times:
a shot would come from a cave, and a platoon would lay down a wall
of cover fire while a specialist, holding a satchel charge, crept toward
the mouth. When he got close enough he would heave the charge and
back off before it blew. Sometimes they threw in fragmentation grenades, scattering metal throughout the cavern, and other times they
hurled phosphorous grenades that burned everybody inside. As for
flamethrowers, when a sheet of fire reached the depths of the cave,
Graf heard screams that made his skin crawl. Japanese soldiers and
civilians ran out as their bodies melted from the heat. Later in life,
Graf would write, "When men could not get near the entrance, we
would call upon the tanks and these monsters would get in real close
and pump shells into the opening. Other times we would call for the
monster to end all monsters . . . the flamethrowing tank. These grue-
some weapons sent a mighty flame into the caves, a hundred times
more destructive than the back carrying type."

Graf understood that it was kill or be killed—by June 22, total
American casualties reached 6,000, with 3,800 of those coming from
the 4th Division—but he could not help reflecting on the fact that
just a couple of years before, most of the Marines had no conception
of war. Like him they were "civilized" kids whose worlds consisted of

sipping malts at the drugstore, watching Andy Hardy on the silver screen, going to high school, studying, playing ball, and holding their girlfriends close at weekend dances. But now they were killers, delighting in the sight of dead Japanese, never imagining, even for a moment, that they were human beings with homes and families. Later Graf would write, "They were devils, bastards, the one who killed our best buddy, the one who had raised his hands in surrender and upon approaching dropped a live grenade at our feet. It was he that infiltrated our lines and cut our throats while we slept. Or he who would pump machine gun rounds into our guts or blow off our arms with his mortar fire. Having no feelings, his only desire was to maim and kill. That was the infamous Japanese soldier. How ironic, that was also us."

Late in the afternoon on June 22, as the 23rd Marines moved north in the direction of Hill 600, a civilian woman approached Graf. She was probably the wife of an Okinawan farmer. As she got closer, Graf could see that she was crying. When she started to hit him and point to his pack, he was taken aback. What the hell was she doing? An interpreter who had been watching explained to him that the woman wanted food and water for her baby. When Graf looked at the basket of woven bamboo that she carried on her back, he could see that her baby was dead. Giving her food and a canteen anyway, he watched as she delicately placed them in the basket next to the child.

More and more civilians were being lured out of caves by the testimonies of others who had agreed to put their lives in the hands of the Americans. Some walked out holding crucifixes so that the Marines knew they were Christians and did not pray to Shinto gods. The Americans gave them water, cigarettes, and chewing gum, and sometimes carried those too small or too weak to walk. They escorted the civilian internees to two stockades not far from the invasion beaches, where they turned them over to the civil affairs section. Graf's heart ached for them. They emerged half mad with fear, smelling of sweat and rot, and choking of thirst.

The 25th Marines discovered a cave holding more than one

hundred people, mostly young women and their children and old grandfathers and grandmothers. They had stayed alive by licking the moist cave walls where the dew formed every morning. These people were the real victims "of civilized man's method of settling their differences." In thousands of years of living, Graf thought, man had not progressed much. The true savages were the ones who persisted in settling their disputes with blood.

The only consolation was that Easy Company had captured a Japanese storage dump that day. Haskell had found some beer, Jurcsak some brandy, and Graf had managed to abscond with a few bottles of sake. Later, after digging their foxholes, the bottles made the rounds, and by nightfall the three men, joined by other members of the company, drank until they were numb.

Buffeted by the wind and slowed by cold hands that made holding entrenching tools difficult, G Company was just getting settled for the night on the 23rd Marines' far right flank, not far from E Company. Only the 25th Marines separated them from the island's eastern coast.

Matthews knew that the push across the island had been a costly one. Official statistics revealed that companies had been reduced to just 50 to 60 percent of their original strength. His own depleted battalion, the 2nd, had to be reinforced by the 3rd Battalion's rifle companies and its 81-mm mortar platoon. If not for the ability to call in bombing strikes, the Marines would have gained less ground and lost even more men.

Matthews was one of those who made the strikes possible. Before the planes arrived, his job was to set out the panels. In his field pack he carried two large sheets of colored cloth, one red and the other yellow. These were the pilots' targets. He placed the red one directly in front of the advancing Marines and the yellow, pointing toward the enemy. The pilots knew that it was not safe to strafe or bomb behind the yellow panel. Setting them out, however, was dangerous. It required that Matthews creep out in front of the forward platoon, exposing himself to enemy fire. Statistics showed that no group among all the services had so high a casualty rate as Marine Corps second lieutenants, and Matthews knew that runners assigned to them rarely fared better. They were often called upon to perform the least desirable assignments, like putting out the panels. So, all things considered, it was nothing less than a miracle that he was still alive, especially when he considered what had happened to so many of his comrades. First there was Witte, and then Robert Howard, a likable, seventeen-year-old New York native, who, after taking a sniper's bullet, told Lieutenant Leary, with tears in his eyes, that he was too young to die. Matthews wept when Howard's breathing grew tenuous. Lieutenant Leary was also shaken. He stayed with the private until he died, and then disappeared behind a farmhouse. Minutes later he returned, and Matthews could tell that the lieutenant had been crying.

Other friends, too, had died, but nothing could match the loss of Nightingale. Among all the deaths, the young man from Skowhegan, Maine, was the one who least deserved it. Unlike a lot of guys, who drank and whored and gambled, Nightingale had no shadows. He was light and goodness. Had he lived, he would have returned home, married, raised a family, taken over the "faam," and lived the life that he loved, a model of constancy and kindheartedness. Ever since his death, Freeby had not been the same, still faulting himself for failing to save his friend.

On the 23rd Marines' right flank, Matthews had been digging a foxhole big enough to accommodate himself and the lieutenant. Racing to get it done before the light faded, he had not noticed the smell. Then it came to him, an overpowering stench of human excrement. When Lieutenant Leary walked up, he blurted out, "Count, what in the world is that smell?" Leary always called him "Count." He had picked it up from a corporal in the platoon, but Matthews never knew how it began.

"Not sure, Lieutenant," Matthews replied. "I can sleep with it, if you can." He was exhausted and did not relish the thought of having to dig another hole. Leary shrugged, climbed in, curled up, and fell asleep in seconds. Matthews had the first watch, but he knew that when his turn to sleep came, he would do exactly what Lieutenant Leary had done, stench or no.

The following day, in the dim light of early morning as the flies began to stir, they saw that they had been sleeping in the farm's garden amid the night-soil fertilizer. By the second week, most of the men were so sour with sweat, they could hardly stand the smell of each other. But now Matthews and Leary had the distinction of reeking like a sewer. Matthews had come to dislike the nighttime rains, the soggy clouds that reached down to touch the earth, and the cool winds that came in off the coast. Often he would huddle in his foxhole, nearly freezing to death, while waiting for the sun to come up. But now as they moved out and marched into the hill country, he prayed for rain.

At daybreak on June 23, while the various companies waited for orders, Leary said, "Hey, Count, why don't you read us something from that New Testament you carry." Since discovering that his little copy of the Gideon New Testament had saved his life on Roi, the book had taken on a special meaning for him. But Matthews was no Bible-beater. Like many of the guys, he had a private, largely uninformed faith. Nevertheless, he was a believer. But what should he read? He thought for a moment. He had always loved the 23rd Psalm. As he began to read, everyone stopped what he was doing and fell silent: "Yea, though I walk through the valley of the shadow of death, I shall fear no evil: For thou art with me."

If the Lord was listening that morning, he was occupied elsewhere that afternoon. The 23rd Marines' goal for the day was to capture Hill 600, with the 2nd Battalion leading the way. The Japanese battled like men possessed until forward units crawled within twenty feet of the enemy position and eventually ousted them with grenades. Once on top of the hill, Company G discovered the bodies of the men who made up the previous day's patrol. They were members of the 24th Marines, and included a radio operator who destroyed his SCR 300 two-way radio before the Japanese could capture it.

By midafternoon the 2nd Battalion had captured the peak and dug in to prevent a counterattack. Ideally they would have moved on, but they were ordered to wait until the 27th Division's 165th Infantry could catch up. The Army had been assigned the center of the Corps' northbound front. The 165th was ordered to tie in with the 4th Marines on the right, while the Army's 106th Infantry tied in with the 2nd Marines on the left.

The 27th Division inherited the territory just east of Mount Tapotchau and just west of a low chain of hills that the division's soldiers called "Purple Heart Ridge," which fell off toward Kagman Point. It was a pocket of land, thick with undergrowth that tore at exposed skin, and jagged limestone formations, nearly three quarters of a mile across. Because it formed a saddle-shaped corridor to the northern section of the island, the Japanese guarded it with large numbers of ground troops, tanks, and strategically positioned snipers and machine gunners. Members of the 165th and 106th Regiments named the passage "Death Valley."

Despite the difficult terrain and a tactical situation that favored the enemy, Holland Smith was distressed that the Army division had not made better progress. The delay created large gaps and left his adjacent Marine units with dangerously exposed flanks. The Marine general confessed that if he thought he could avoid a political typhoon, he would have immediately relieved General Ralph Smith, the 27th Division's CO. Ralph Smith was not any happier with his troops. He held his regimental commanders responsible for the lack of progress, and promised that on the following day, June 24, he would "personally see to it that the division went forward."

Late that afternoon, Holland Smith received a report that enemy units planned to counterattack. At six-thirty that evening, the Japanese struck, sending tanks to pound the boundary between the two Army regiments. With bazookas and 37-mm guns, the American soldiers held them off, taking out five of the six tanks. An hour later five more tanks crashed into the 106th Infantry's lines. The regiment's cannon company destroyed four of them, but one penetrated the 3rd Battalion's perimeter, setting fire to an ammunition dump and attacking an aid station. Another five tanks tried to break through the area between the 165th Regiment and the 23rd Marines, attempting to climb Hill 600 via a road on its western side, but the troops held them off. Although the tank attacks failed, small bands of Japanese tried to break through the Marine and Army lines.

It was a hellish night for the members of the 23rd Marines' 2nd Battalion. Matthews heard the Japanese on the opposite side of the ridge, talking. He looked into the dark, watching for vague forms slipping through the trees and the high grass, focusing his eyes, and trying to steady his thumping heart. If a branch snapped or a bayonet struck a slab of coral or a rock, he wanted to be able to hear it. Then he would slink down low in his foxhole, his finger brushing the trigger of his rifle. He would wait until the enemy soldier got close enough to smell, and then he would pump a clip into his chest.

Graf heard them, too. They sounded like they were drinking, and as the night wore on they grew louder. To Graf they sounded like "demons from hell," like "movie Indians prior to an attack on the wagon train."

Like Matthews, Graf waited for them. He had set out clips of ammo and his knife where he could reach them. Next to him sat Major Fought, scanning the trees, trying to pick up movement by the light of the flares. In the days since Fought had found him on the beach, mourning the loss of Lieutenant Roth, Graf had grown close to the major. He was the consummate gentleman and soldier. Rather than punish him for what some might have called cowardice, he had given the young private another chance to prove that he was a Marine. From that moment on, Graf determined that he would never give the major cause to doubt him. Fought recognized that, and as they battled their way across the island, he took Graf under his wing as he might a son, and their friendship blossomed. They studied maps together and discussed battle strategies, and Fought seriously considered Graf's recommendations and opinions. Huddled together in a foxhole, they shared their personal stories, too.

The morning of June 24 came early as the sun clambered above the horizon. Graf turned his face toward the light and felt the first rays of sunshine. Then he sat for a moment and looked out over the beautiful cliffs of the Kagman Peninsula. From another foxhole he heard someone say, "Jesus, that was one helluva night." That was Graf's cue to get moving. June 24, he sensed, was a day of big expectations.

On the 2nd Battalion's left, General Ralph Smith's 27th Division was ready to move out, into the heart of Death Valley, as he had told Holland Smith they would. At 8:00 a.m., just before the division pressed forward, Ralph Smith received a dispatch from the Marine general. The dispatch read, "Commanding General is highly displeased with the failure of the 27th Division on June Twenty Third to launch its attack as ordered. . . . It is directed that immediate steps be taken to cause the 27th Division to advance and seize objectives as ordered." Minutes later the Japanese pummeled one of the battalion command posts with mortar fire, chopping up men who had just put on their field packs and picked up their rifles.

Only 100 yards in, the 27th Division walked smack into a wall of machine-gun and mortar fire. The 165th wheeled to the right, to the northeast, but the 106th was caught. To its left was a cliff face pockmarked with holes and caves that held Japanese snipers, machine gunners, and mortarmen. The 106th soon discovered that short of direct artillery and mortar strikes, those positions were nearly indestructible. Unable to advance, the regiment hammered the cliff and sent out small units to probe the valley. All returned with casualties and the same report: forward movement was impossible.

By midafternoon the handwriting was on the wall: the 106th would retreat to its line of departure, leaving—except for one company that had been able to tie into the right flank of the 2nd Marine Division—a dangerous gap of 300 to 400 hundred yards on its left flank. Ralph Smith was angry and embarrassed for his men. In the meantime, a livid Holland Smith was now more determined than ever to make the command change. He went to the *Rocky Mount* to discuss the issue with Admiral Turner, who advised that they both go see Admiral Spruance, who, as commander of the 5th Fleet, had the ultimate say over the entire operation. Smith argued, as he later wrote, that Ralph Smith should be relieved, that he was slowing the advance because he lacked "aggressive spirit." Turner agreed, and Spruance assented to the Marine general's wishes.

Not long after, Spruance followed up with an official message to Holland Smith, authorizing him, as commander of the Northern Troops and Landing Force, to dismiss General Ralph Smith. At 4:00 p.m. that day, the 27th Division's commanding general received a message from Holland Smith ordering him to turn over his command.

On the evening of June 24, the 23rd Marines dug in again on top of Hill 600. The drive north had ground to a halt, the Kagman Peninsula remained to be taken, and now individual Marines cursed the 27th, stranded in the valley below. "Goddamn dogfaces," one of the Easy Company Marines said. "They're leavin' us out to dry." Graf wanted to come to the division's defense. The 27th was made up of lots of men from his neck of the woods. They were tough soldiers from Troy, Albany, and Schenectady, brave and reliable men, from good upstate New York stock. It was their commanders who deserved the criticism. They had apparently forgotten that their troops were what Graf knew to be "damn good fighters."

Although the 27th certainly deserved criticism, it was also being scapegoated for the slow, costly grind that Saipan had become. Perhaps no one should have been surprised that the island had exposed the fundamental differences between the Marines and the Army and the way they waged war.

In combat, the Marines drove hard. They believed in speed and hitting power, in getting in and getting out as fast as possible. The Marines' basic premise was to apply unremitting pressure on a concentrated objective. They fought till sunset and then dug a line of double foxholes with no flanks. The Army, on the other hand, advanced more methodically and cautiously, often behind an artillery barrage, stopping one hour before sunset to establish a series of mutually supporting foxholes—even if that meant giving up ground gained during the daylight hours. Two forward companies dug in with a full perimeter defense while a third, situated some distance behind, covered the gap between them. In the eyes of tacticians, each method had advantages and disadvantages. The Army claimed that this alignment discouraged nighttime infiltration, a favorite ploy of the Japanese. The Army also asserted that its way preserved men. The suggestion was that the Marines ignored casualty counts and recklessly threw its men into situations that clearly favored the enemy. Countering, the Marines alleged that the Army's method encouraged timidity. They may lose more men in the early days of a battle, but in the end, they contended, the Army lost more because its campaigns were longer than they needed to be.

On Saipan, Holland Smith's strategy for a relentless drive north posed problems for the Army. First, from the Army's perspective, General Smith failed to consider the nature of the terrain. Death Valley resembled a canyon and left little room for the 27th to maneuver. To make matters worse, Holland Smith's orders often arrived late in the day, which gave the 27th little time for reconnaissance or to position its troops and artillery or to develop a scheme for advancing. The Marine general also seemed unwilling to alter his battle plans. Although he was concerned about gaps between the Army units and his Marines, he did not instruct the 2nd Division to move to its right or the 4th Division to move to its left to fill those gaps. Instead he expected his ground troops to push the battle until late in the day, and discouraged withdrawal even to consolidate lines.

Whatever Holland Smith's and Ralph Smith's respective shortcomings and whatever mistakes the two of them might have made, by the evening of June 24, with the American forces stranded in the middle of the island, the interservice "brotherhood" that Ralph Smith had extolled just days before was over.

# CHAPTER 29

# Tapotchau's Heights

On June 18, Major General Keiji Iketa drafted a message to Tojo. "The army," he told the prime minister, "is consolidating its battle lines and has decided to prepare for a showdown fight. It is concentrating . . . in the area east of Tapotchau."

When the 1st Battalion, 29th Marines, wheeled north, Chick Borta could tell that Mount Tapotchau, the island's highest ground and ultimate prize, was the goal. Tanks and jeeps would be useless. The mountain would have to be taken on foot. The problem was how. A valley that ended in a deep gorge ran along the mountain's eastern flank. The front, south-facing side was nothing but sheer cliffs. The western side was a tangle of gulleys, ravines, and thick forests. The inability of the 27th Division to push through Death Valley proved problematic, too. "We cannot attack Mount Tapotchau until the Twenty-seventh Division moves up," complained a staff officer, "and we've got to have that high ground so we can look down the Japs' throats instead of them looking down ours."

As much as he dreaded the push toward Tapotchau, Borta's

more immediate concern was his foxhole partners. The night after Rachitsky was killed, Borta was dug in with a cook who had been sent in as a replacement. The guy had a fierce appetite, and when he finished his rations, he was still hungry. "I need food," he told Borta. "I gotta go find something to eat."

"You're an idiot," Borta told him. "If you don't get killed by your own men, the Japs will get you." The guy left anyway. Borta wondered if the shit-for-brains even bothered to learn the password. Hours later he was alone in the foxhole as flares lit up the area, bright white ones that the Marines sent up every eight minutes, and yellow ones that the Japanese used. The flares meant that something was up. Japanese soldiers might be trying to get back to their lines, or infiltrators, clad only in loincloths, might be sneaking in on the Americans. Another possibility was that the Japanese were trying to hit the supply lines.

Borta listened to the rain spatter against his poncho and watched the flares, wondering if some Jap had already cut the cook's throat. When he slid back in the foxhole, Borta was astounded. The cook was the luckiest damn Marine on the whole island of Saipan. He had not returned empty-handed either. He had brought back a five-gallon can of fruit salad. Borta opened it with his trench knife. After spooning half the can into his mouth, he spent the rest of the night vomiting. By morning the cook was gone.

That day the 29th pushed farther north in the direction of Tapotchau through a patchwork of small farms and burned sugar-cane fields. It was the cane fields that really scared Borta. Cover was nonexistent, and when the spotters atop Tapotchau called in artillery strikes, individual Marines could do little more than sprint and zigzag and hope. After one crossing, Borta and a number of others came across a farmhouse. They moved forward, edgy with adrenaline, fingers on the thin metal of their triggers, ready to snap off shots at the slightest movement, the faintest sound.

Borta crept up to the door, kicked it open, and dove to the side. Before he could shout *"Kosan se yo!"* ("Surrender!"), or *"Detekoi!"* ("Come out!"), a BAR man rushed in and sprayed the room with bullets. The walls were riddled with holes, and on the floor, drenched in blood, lay an old man, a woman, and a young child. The BAR man stood with his rifle hanging from one hand, staring straight ahead, as if hypnotized. Borta turned, walked out of the shack, and sat down in the dirt of the farmyard and gulped at the oily water in his canteen.

That night, as the air was chilling off, Borta huddled in a fox-hole with another stranger. It was a shitty way to go through the war, never knowing if your foxhole buddy would be another joker or someone you could depend on. If only he could find Lemon or Brem. He needed to talk to someone to get the image out of his head—the dead Chamorros, especially the child.

The cook the night before had been bad enough, but now his foxhole partner was a smoker who could not go an hour without a cigarette. Most guys who smoked refrained from doing it at night; it was too dangerous even if covered by a poncho. Jap observers would catch the flicker of flame from a Zippo lighter or the glow of a deeply inhaled cigarette. They would listen, too, for the coughing. Then a mortar would come whistling in.

While Borta silently cursed him, the man had a smoke and then fell asleep. Early in the night a Japanese soldier jumped into the fox-hole. Borta found his knife and lashed out, catching the intruder in the belly. He felt the blade enter and then he ripped, yanking his arm back as hard as he could. The enemy soldier's body grew slack, and in one motion Borta tossed it out of the hole. The Marine sleeping next to him never so much as stirred.

The following night, after a long, hard push toward Tapotchau, Borta again shared a foxhole with a Marine whose name he did not bother or care to learn. He cared about only one thing—staying alive. *Does this asshole have the chops to save his own hide, much less mine?* he wondered. *Can I depend on him and catch an hour or two of sleep?* The lack of sleep, the shelling, the dead civilians—all were beginning to take their toll on him and his fellow Marines. Borta saw it during the day—the lifeless eyes, the robotlike movements. The guys were wearing out, and the toughest part of the battle had not even begun.

Hours later someone slid into the side of Borta's foxhole. It might have been a Marine who had gone to the bushes for a shit, but neither Borta nor his partner waited to find out. They slashed with their knives. Seconds later a flare went up, and Borta saw from the glistening viscera that he had caught the intruder in the belly and his foxhole buddy had stabbed him through the throat and smashed in his face with his rifle's buttplate. As the light dimmed, Borta pulled off the Japanese soldier's watch and pushed him out of the hole. If the goddamned land crabs wanted him, they could have him.

Three days passed before the 29th made it into Tapotchau's foothills. Shortly after midnight on June 23, the battalion took a direct artillery hit. Because it came from the rear, they shot up green flares to indicate to the artillery that short rounds were landing on American troops. Less than a minute later they were hammered again. Shells were dropping in on top of them, both ground and treetop bursts. White-hot shrapnel ripped across the field. One of the pieces, after bouncing off a trunk, struck Borta in the stomach. This one, though still hot, had expended most of is energy. Instead of being ripped open, it felt to Borta as if he had been shot with a BB gun. He rolled the fragment between his fingers. Just seconds later another shell fell, and cries for corpsmen came from every corner of the camp. Company C was getting chewed up. Before the next one hit, before the detonation's wave and tearing blast, Borta had an instant of clarity that made him feel as if he had been kicked by a horse. Earlier in the day, the battalion was making a push. He and a BAR man from Company C came upon a Japanese field howitzer. Borta wanted to stick a grenade in the barrel in hopes of disabling it. He and the other Marine, however, decided to keep moving. A team of engineers would knock it out. They were wrong. The engineering unit passed it by, and the Japanese returned to it that night. For Company C, which lost more than forty men, it was the worst night of the entire battle. For Borta, it was an incident that would haunt him for the rest of his life.

Other units had been hit hard, too. Casualties were mounting across the island. A frustrated Holland Smith knew what the enemy

**CARL MATTHEWS**
*(right)*

**SAMMIE BOYKIN**

EDGAR HUFF

Secretary of the Navy (1940–44) FRANK KNOX

**PERCY ROBINSON**

**GEORGE BOOTH**

**RICHARD FREEBY**

**Lieutenant JAMES LEARY**

*From left:*
Admiral
CHESTER
NIMITZ,
Admiral
ERNEST
KING,
and
Admiral
"BULL"
HALSEY

*From left:*
ROBERT
GRAF,
BILL
JURCSAK,
and
WALT
HASKELL

FRANK BORTA

*From left:*
MILT LEMON,
FRANK BORTA,
and
RICHARD CARNEY

GLENN BREM

Secretary
of the Navy
(1944–47)
JAMES
FORRESTAL

General HOLLAND SMITH *(center)*, FLANKED BY TWO MARINES

LIEUTENANT JAMES LEARY *(standing)*, CARL MATTHEWS, and
WENDELL NIGHTINGALE on invasion day, Saipan

PERCY ROBINSON stooping over a box of ammunition

THURGOOD MARSHALL

was up to. "The Japs are being smart, so far," he told correspondent Robert Sherrod. "They are fighting a delaying action, and killing as many of us as possible." That same day, Major General Iketa assured Prime Minister Tojo that he intended to hold the high ground, that the Americans would risk losing their entire army if they tried to take it. "The 43rd Division units," he reiterated, were "in the midst of disposing so as to hold Tapotchau firmly." Hours after the "showdown fight" had begun, he drafted another, less optimistic message to his prime minister. "In this sector," he explained, "the enemy has infiltrated and broken through our positions. . . . The raging battle is pressing in the area of the CP. The fighting strength of the units have fallen to less than two infantry battalions. Though our forces have called on all kinds of methods to hinder the enemy advance, we are regrettably reduced to the condition where we cannot carry out this plan with our present fighting strength. It is recommended that plan [for reinforcements] be executed with all haste."

He followed this message with another one to the commanding officer of a regiment stationed on Tinian: "Prepare to send one company of infantry by landing boats to Saipan." The order betrayed his desperation. U.S. naval vessels closely guarded the waters around the island. Although Tinian lay just across the Saipan Channel, only five miles to the southwest, the hope that defenseless boats or barges, loaded with troops, could break through the blockade was a chimera.

To the east, on the Kagman Peninsula, Japanese troops trying to hold back the 23rd and 24th Marines fared no better. General Saito fled his command post above Chacha Village, east of Purple Heart Ridge, assuming that the plunging white cliffs on the northeast side of Tapotchau were safe. What he did not know—Japanese wire communications had been destroyed—was that the once-impregnable mountain was under siege.

At 7:30 a.m. on June 25, the 29th shoved off with Tapotchau looming above them. The plan that Colonel Tompkins and the 2nd Battalion of the 8th Marines had worked out was basic. The two battalions would approach the crest of the mountain via two routes: Tompkins's "bastard battalion" would attack frontally by way of a wooded valley; and the 8th Marines would drive along a ridgeline on the right flank.

When Borta and Pluto Brem reached the end of the woods, they hesitated. Ahead they could see more trees, but to get there, they needed to make it across an opening that offered little protection. Snipers nestled into the rocks above had already taken out a number of men from the company.

Brem volunteered to go first. He had no sooner exited the woods than a Japanese machine gunner opened up on him. Brem threw himself to the ground just in time. Bullets sprayed dirt over him. Though he could not see the machine gunner, Borta fired blindly into the hills. Those few seconds allowed Brem to slither forward. The gunner let loose again, kicking up dirt and scattering stones. Then Borta heard Brem yelling, "I can't see! I can't see!"

Borta took a deep breath and dashed across the meadow, cutting one way and then the next, expecting to be met by a hail of bullets. The gunner, however, was silent. Reaching Brem, Borta discovered another wounded Marine. He grabbed him by the arm and hoisted him onto his back. Then he told Brem to grab hold. Brem reached out, and Borta guided his hand to his web belt. Nearly buckling under the weight of the wounded Marine, it took Borta what seemed an eternity to make it back to the woods. He dropped to a knee and rolled the Marine off his back and called for a corpsman. Then he took Brem by the elbow and sat him down against a tree. Brem flushed his eyes with water from his canteen.

By 10:00 a.m., it was obvious to Colonel Tompkins that his battalion was not going anywhere, at least not without losing a lot of men. At just 50 percent of its original strength, the battalion was walking into the teeth of the mountain defense force. The 8th Marines' 2nd Battalion was having an easier go of it. By nine-thirty, it found itself at the base of a fifty-foot cliff that protected Tapotchau's highest peak. Moving around the face of the cliff, the men advanced slowly, trying not to hyperventilate, fearing the whip-crack of a .25-caliber Japanese Arisaka rifle or the heavy thud of a *juki* machine gun. What they discovered, however, stunned them. The top was empty.

Held up in the valley at the front of the mountain, Colonel Tompkins called on the help of a platoon from the division reconnaissance company. Using the path pioneered by the 8th Marines, Tompkins and the platoon picked their way to the top of the mountain, where they discovered the platoon from the 8th Marines dug in on Tapotchau's right shoulder. Since no one had explored Tapotchau's highest point, Tompkins decided that he and his men would reconnoiter it. What they found was a flat observation area, perhaps thirty feet in diameter, where the Japanese had dug a long trench that stretched across the mountain's top. The plan now was for Tompkins to fetch his men while the lieutenant and his platoon held the trench. They knew that at some point the Japanese would realize that they had forfeited the most important observation post on the entire island and would attempt to regain it.

Tompkins asked the lieutenant before he parted, "Think you can hold it?"

"We'll do our best, sir," the lieutenant responded.

An hour later the Japanese rushed the trench. Holding their fire, the men of the recon company waited until the enemy soldiers were on top of them before they cut them down. Wounded Japanese soldiers detonated grenades. It was the first time the lieutenant had ever seen anything like it. They had pulled the pins knowing they would die.

In the valley below, Colonel Tompkins was trying to move his men up the mountain. Leaving Company B on the line as a deception, he led Companies A and G up Tapotchau while the battalion's 81-mm mortar crews blasted the slopes and the 8th Marines' 2nd Battalion pounded the enemy positions on the ridges. On top of the mountain the lieutenant and his men watched the sun melt into the ocean. It was a strange feeling to admire a sunset in the midst of war. Minutes later the lieutenant heard the sound of men scaling the backside of the mountain. Then he heard the colonel's voice and saw a long string of Marines walking single file.

At his command post among the cliffs on the northeast side of Tapotchau, General Saito received the news that the mountain was now in American hands. In the face of unyielding setbacks—his front-line strength was less than 20 percent, his artillery and communications had been virtually destroyed, and most of his top commanders were dead—Saito had been able to keep his composure. But the news that the Marines had Tapotchau drained him of whatever hope he had left.

That night the general sent a message to Tokyo: "Please apologize deeply to the Emperor that we cannot do better then we are doing. . . . The Governor General of the South Seas [Saito was speaking of himself] . . . will retreat to the north end of Saipan Island and the army will defend its positions to the very end, though that be death, to guard the Treasure. . . . Praying for the good health of the Emperor, we all cry, 'Banzai!'"

Back in Tokyo, Hirohito's chief aide, General Hasunuma, had just delivered a sobering report to the Emperor. Saipan, he said, was already lost. An angry Hirohito insisted he put those words in writing and abruptly left the room.

On the western edge of the mountain, Chick Borta scraped out the best foxhole he could, given the conditions. Everybody knew that the Japanese were going to strike at some point during the night.

Just before midnight, A Company sent up a flare. The mountain glowed. In that glow, the Marines caught the Japanese, bare from the waist up, their torsos painted black, creeping in on their positions. Many carried nothing more than long poles with bayonets or knives tied to the end. The ensuing battle was a blur. Men lunged for each other, bayonets flashed, bullets fired at point-blank range ripped through flesh, and men screamed. From his foxhole, Borta saw a Marine get stuck in the back and topple over the side of the cliff.

Minutes later, another flare went up. Bodies, mostly Japanese, were scattered across the rocky ground. Borta checked his bayonet, clutched his rifle, slunk down, and waited for them to come again. Then he heard the Japanese below, calling out, "Maline, you die; to-night you die."

Hours later, someone called his name: "Borta, Borta, the captain wants to see you." At night the Japanese were full of tricks, moaning "Corpsman," or "Help me, Sarge," in order to get a Marine to respond and give away his position. But this was an American voice; Borta was sure of it. Besides, he thought, how could a Jap know my name?

Borta had always disliked the captain. Now he mumbled to himself, "Shit, what does he want now?" When Borta reported to the foxhole, the captain explained that he wanted him to make contact with C Company and bring back a crate or two of grenades. "It's a damn death mission," Borta almost blurted out. He bit his tongue, but he knew he would be lucky to get across the mountaintop alive. A bunch of tense Marines, expecting a banzai, would shoot first and ask questions later.

"Yes sir, Captain sir," Borta said. Another officer might have given Borta a tongue-lashing or worse for addressing him as "captain" or "sir" while in battle. An alert sniper might be listening. But if this captain wanted to hear it—which he did—Borta was happy to oblige. If a Japanese rifleman overheard—well, then, so be it.

Borta went off into the dark, moving from one foxhole to the next, repeating, "Borta, it's me, Borta," every few seconds, fearing that at any moment a bullet from a fellow Marine would tear open his chest. By the time he made it to C Company, his voice was so choked with fear he could barely say his name.

"Hey, you guys got any extra grenades?" he said to no one in particular. "We're gettin' low over in A Company."

"What, are you kidding?" came a response from the dark. "We're fighting for our lives here."

Borta tried as best he could to retrace his steps. "It's me again,

Borta," he said, as he moved along, hoping that his fellow Marines would let him pass. When he found the captain, he reported that C Company had no hand grenades to spare.

When he got back to his foxhole, he discovered another Marine in it. The man was groaning. "Who is that?" Borta asked.

Whoever it was answered in a raspy voice, "It's me."

Borta recognized it. "Chief, is that you?"

"Yeah, I got bayoneted," answered Wallace "Chief" Quarta.

Borta felt around for the wound. When he pulled his hand back, it was sticky and full of blood. He knew that it would be dangerous to try to move Quarta, so he gave him some water from his canteen and left him there while he went to tell the captain.

Five minutes later he was out on the flank, sharing a foxhole with a greenhorn BAR man who had been sent to the front that morning as the battalion was driving toward Tapotchau. The captain had told Borta that he would send a corpsman to treat Quarta. Now, confined to his foxhole, Borta wondered if there even was a corpsman among the Marine units on top of the mountain. He had his doubts whether Quarta would make it out alive.

During the early-morning hours Borta was drifting in and out of wakefulness when he heard the bark of a Browning Automatic Rifle. In an instant he was on his belly, looking out over the rim of the foxhole.

"What the hell happened?"

"I heard something," whispered his partner.

"You heard something?" Borta mocked him. "I'll take over." His Chicago street smarts told him that he might not live to see another day if he left his life in some panicky pup's hands. Then he wondered about the kid's "sound shots." The kid said he had heard something. What would they discover the next day—a Marine with his pants down around his ankles and a bullet in his belly?

The following morning, Borta was flabbergasted to find four dead Japanese outside his foxhole. One burst from the BAR had taken all of them out. Now, instead of cursing the greenhorn, he wanted to kiss him. Borta thanked him and then left to find another foxhole buddy.

A novice BAR man might get lucky once, but the likelihood of it happening again was next to nothing.

Shortly after sunrise the Japanese mortared the mountaintop. Companies A and C held tight, but took enough casualties to worry the captain, who was also concerned about the worsening water situation. Most of his men were already down to half a canteen. Another day, and they would be sucking on stones to keep their saliva circulating.

Before the shelling began, Borta found another foxhole partner, a guy he knew vaguely from his Hilo days who seemed eager to have a seasoned Marine in his hole with him. Borta was happy, too. It was good to be dug in with someone who had been in the battalion for more than a few days. Later that morning, during a lull in the bombing, Borta left the foxhole to check in with the captain. It was the last thing he wanted to do. The captain might send him off on another fool's errand. Borta had taken a few steps when he heard a mortar whistle in. By the time it hit, he was on the ground with his head buried in his arms. He waited for a minute without moving, and then rose to a knee. When the dust disappeared, he saw that the mortar had hit directly in his foxhole, dismembering his partner. Borta grimaced, but he did not grieve. It seemed to him that he no longer had the capacity to mourn. He had seen men torn apart by mortars so many times. Now he was simply concerned with saving his own hide. He needed to find someplace safe.

Borta scouted the mountaintop and found a small opening in a jumble of rocks. A mortar would have to fall straight from heaven to hit him here. Bone-tired, he lay on the ground, curled up, and fell asleep. Then he heard the captain's voice: "Borta, Borta, where the hell are you?" He had no idea how long he had been there; it could have been minutes or hours.

When he crawled out, so exhausted he could barely focus his eyes, he saw the hazy figure of the captain standing in front of him. "Goddammit," the captain said, "the lieutenant was looking for you for a patrol. He couldn't find you. Now, I want you to go out and locate the patrol and tell the lieutenant that if he makes it as far as the next mountain, he should hold it." Borta walked away, still half asleep, thinking the captain had completely lost it. *How are we going to hold two mountains when we can barely hold one?*

Borta descended Tapotchau and proceeded east into Death Valley. He had not gone far when he saw three men walking toward him. Borta dropped to a knee and was prepared to open up when one of the men yelled, "Don't fire—Marines!" Borta lowered his rifle, knowing that a split second later and he would have killed them. The men explained that they were the tail end of the patrol. They had been ambushed and somehow managed to escape. Their best guess was that they lost a handful of men, including the lieutenant and his runner. When they said "runner," Borta felt an electric shock radiate through his hands and up into his shoulders. He should have been the dead runner.

Borta pushed on. Along the trail he saw evidence of the ambush— bodies scattered in the knee-high grass. He could tell that one of the men had only been wounded. He followed the blood trail. Like a half-dead rabbit, the man had crawled through the field on his belly. When Borta came to the body, he tested the pulse. Nothing. Before the sun fell, he hurried back up Tapotchau.

The mountain was quiet that night. A steady rain fell, and Borta shivered in his foxhole, pressing his body against its walls, and wondered what had become of Lemon and Brem. Word was that Lemon was somewhere on top, but none of the guys whom Borta questioned had actually seen him. Brem, he heard, was still below, recovering from his eye injury.

The night passed miserably. By morning the rain had stopped, and some of the guys were actually whistling. Borta had been collecting cigarettes, and now he tried to trade them for a swig of water. The only problem was that no one had any water left. After going from one foxhole to the next, Borta found a Marine who had collected rainwater in his helmet. For two cigarettes he agreed to allow Borta a pull from his helmet.

About midmorning, Borta learned that the captain wanted to see him. As usual, he dreaded what his next order might be. When he reached the foxhole, he was stunned. The old captain was gone. In his place was a new one just up from the beach. Captain Leonard introduced himself. He struck Borta as a decent fella. After introductions, Captain Leonard explained that the battalion had orders to push to the northern edge of Tapotchau with the help of Company B, which had joined the battalion late the previous day. In order to do that, he needed to get the lay of the land. He had been briefed at the beach and had seen various maps, but what he wanted now was a firsthand picture of the battalion's position.

As the sun climbed high and turned hot, Borta led the captain along the rim of the ridge, pointing out landmarks. For the first time it became obvious to him why Tapotchau was so important. He felt as though he could see all the way to Guam. There was Tinian to the south, the Navy ships on all sides of the island, the invasion beaches, Lake Susupe, the rubble that was once Charan Kanoa, and the soaring cliffs at Saipan's northernmost point. He could also see below the movements of the American forces, and every detail of the land— the burning cane fields, farmers' shacks, tanks, and command posts.

After about thirty minutes they took a break. The captain was wearing a pressed uniform right off the quartermaster's shelf, with his sleeves rolled up neatly. He looked like someone important, and Japanese snipers loved to take out the big shots with the shiny boots. So Borta sat with him against some rocks that protected them on three sides. Leonard took off his helmet, wiped his forehead with a handkerchief, and offered Borta a drink from his canteen. He took just enough to moisten his mouth, and in that time a sniper spotted them. When Borta pulled the canteen from his lips, Leonard was lying on his back with a bullet hole through his throat.

Borta walked back to where the company was dug in and explained to a new corporal that the captain had been killed. He was standing next to the corporal when he radioed the 8th Marines' headquarters. "Goddammit," someone at headquarters said, "isn't the captain there yet? "Yes, sir," responded the corporal, "but he's dead."

Then Borta heard headquarters say, "Well, Corporal, it looks like you're in charge now."

Borta returned to where the captain had been shot. He had been gone no more than fifteen minutes, but when he reached the spot he saw that Marines had already stripped the captain of his clothes down to his skivvies. Early on in the battle, Borta might have been offended by the act. But now he knew that the men meant no disrespect. They were not scavenging hyenas. They were desperate. Some wore nothing but rags. Others were covered in dried blood and reeked of night soil. Even if they belonged to a dead captain, new boondockers or socks or a dungaree jacket were too good to pass up. Nearly every other Marine there would have done the same thing.

# CHAPTER 30

# Gyokusai

By late June the American casualty count hit nearly ten thousand, and Holland Smith knew that the Japanese were hoping to win a war of attrition, or to prolong the war long enough for reinforcements to arrive. The doctors who treated the wounded recognized this, too. "The thing that impresses me is this," one physician remarked. "These Japs know they can't win. They have nothing left except some small arms and a few mortars, and we've got a world of everything. But the Japs fight on and on and on, and we're going to lose ten thousand men before we win this damned little island."

The doctor's assessment was right. General Saito was once again on the run, moving his command post one and a quarter miles north of Mount Tapotchau in the midst of a rainsquall. His army had been reduced to "chewing the leaves of trees and eating snails," and had little drinking water or medical supplies left. Nevertheless, the Japanese soldiers vowed that they would hold back "nothing in the service of the Emperor."

With the battle dragging on and no end in sight, General Holland Smith had to find fighting men. He had already landed his reserve force, the Army's 27th Division, which he committed to some of the island's trouble spots, where they met fierce enemy resistance. The 106th Infantry's 3rd Battalion had fewer than one hundred men and was reorganized into a single rifle company.

Smith had also mobilized the two-hundred-man 2nd Division Shore Party, comprising blacks from Marine depot and ammunition companies. Although he may have supported the Corps' long-standing opposition to using blacks in battle, troop shortages necessitated desperate measures. The black servicemen had already proved their reliability, landing an unprecedented 75,000 tons of supplies, including TNT, rockets, parachute flares, carbines, and thousands of rounds of small-caliber cartridges, diesel fuel, and water, in just ten days. Seeking to strengthen some of his harder-hit units, Smith distributed hundreds of men from the 18th, 19th, and 20th Depot Companies as well as the 3rd Marine Ammunition Company among the 6th and 8th Marines. He used others to help transport casualties and to establish a guard company to protect the observation post atop Mount Tapotchau.

Back at Montford Point, Edgar Huff had just been promoted from gunnery sergeant to first sergeant. His rise through the ranks had been meteoric, but, to his frustration, he was still right where he had started. He wanted to fight, and repeatedly asked Colonel Woods to transfer him overseas. Woods was sympathetic to his requests, but reluctant to let him go. Huff argued that as first sergeant of a malaria control unit, he was not serving any purpose. He should have been fighting Japanese on Saipan with the men he had trained, instead of battling mosquitoes in North Carolina.

In late June the 4th Division was well north of the Kagman Peninsula. While it waited for the 27th Division to come abreast, it mopped up rear sections in the vicinity of Donnay and scouted the terrain to the north. The real action, though, was still in the middle, in the area just east of Tapotchau, where the 27th had finally established contact with the 8th Marines on its left and the 24th Marines on its right. The Army division was still behind, but as soon as it caught up, the 4th Division would begin what might be its final push north.

On Tapotchau, Chick Borta learned that he would be working as a runner for a new lieutenant and soon would be getting off the mountain. Borta dreaded answering to a wet-behind-the-ears second lieutenant, fresh out of officers' candidate school, with a bronze suntan and spotless khakis. But when First Lieutenant Bradford Chaffin introduced himself, Borta knew he had lucked out. Chaffin, who hailed from Adrian, Michigan, a straight shot east of Borta's Chicago, struck him as a thoroughly decent guy, the kind of leader, like Sergeant Rachitsky, who could inspire loyalty without really trying. If Chaffin was disappointed with the battalion, he did not let on, though he would have had good reason to: the entire 29th Battalion numbered just 284 men, with fewer than ninety to each infantry company.

From the peak, Chaffin pointed out four hiccups of land to the north, the Pimple Hills, the next target for the 8th Marines and Borta's "bastard battalion." The 29th's goal would be Tommy's Pimple, the second one from the right.

The following morning the battalion began its descent via a narrow crevice that dropped off at an angle that would have been difficult for a mountain goat to negotiate. To Borta it looked like an invitation to an ambush. But by midday on July 1, the battalion had made it down Tapotchau and occupied the top of Tommy's Pimple—without a fight. The battle that Chaffin and others had predicted never materialized.

Somewhere near midmorning on July 2, Borta and a squad of men came upon a bunker. Everyone was jumpy. For the first time, many believed that they might actually get off Saipan alive, and they were not about to take any chances. One of the guys wanted to lift the lid and throw in a hand grenade in case the bunker contained Japanese soldiers. Remembering the trigger-happy BAR man and the dead mother and child, Borta asked him to wait.

As he walked up, the rest of the men stood at a safe distance. Borta hesitated. Who gave a shit about a bunch of starving civilians? Pulling the lid off the bunker, he had the urge to drop in a grenade, but then he said, *"Detekoi!"*—"Come out!" Stepping back from the hole, he saw a small hand. *"Korosanai yo,"* he said—"We won't murder you." Seconds later, a frail, shriveled-up old woman crawled out. *"Mizu,"* she said, pointing to her mouth—"Water." When a Marine gave her his canteen, she gulped at it. When she finished, she wiped her lips with the back of her hand and walked to the edge of the bunker and said something. A long string of people filed out, civilians all of them. Lieutenant Chaffin chose a group of men to escort them to the stockade, and then the battalion pressed on.

By early afternoon, after moving unimpeded for hours, the 29th cut through a meadow flanked by two small hills. There for the first time since Tapotchau, they confronted Japanese machine gunners and mortarmen. Chaffin and Borta dove behind some rocks, and Chaffin yelled to his men to stay put. After a few minutes a squad of Marines tried to move forward. Spotting them, Chaffin tugged on Borta's arm. "Stop the point."

Borta ran to reach them. He had not gone farther than twenty yards when a mortar hit. For a moment Chaffin thought Borta was dead. But then he moved and the lieutenant charged out from behind some rocks and dragged Borta to safety.

While a medic attended to Borta, two tanks pounded the enemy's position. Then Chaffin, following a flamethrowing tank, led his men on a dead run across the open field and up a hill as a rainstorm that had swept over the sea hurled itself against the landscape. As the tanks rumbled up the hill, they followed. Shortly before dusk, a large group of Marines, led by Chaffin's platoon, reached the top. With what little light remained, they shot the retreating Japanese soldiers. According to one Marine, it was a heck of a good time, like "shooting jackrabbits."

July 2 was a good day for Holland Smith. The 2nd Division made its greatest push since the D-Day landings and moved into the heart of Garapan's Little Tokyo, which weeks of shelling had reduced to little more than a pile of rubble. The Seabees, working day and night, had lengthened and widened the Aslito airstrip. It was now big enough for fighters to take off and land. Soon B-24 Liberator bombers could start using it. With more improvements, the larger B-29 bombers could as well.

On July 3, much of General Saito's island garrison crumbled. Forfeiting the Pimples, the general had moved his command post farther north, to a secluded cave in what the Americans called "Paradise Valley," a thousand yards inland from the northern village of Makunsha (or Matansa). Here, during the uprisings of the late 1600s, Spaniards massacred the local Chamorro inhabitants. The Chamorros called it the Killing Place. The general ordered his troops, fighting just north of the Garapan-Tapotchau-Kagman Peninsula line, to withdraw, too. Now, nearly two weeks behind schedule, the 2nd and 4th Marine Divisions and the Army's 27th Division were taking huge chunks of territory. Outside of Garapan, the 2nd Marine Division pushed into the O-7 area (Day 7 objective), near Mutcho Point, and cut down large numbers of fleeing enemy soldiers.

For the 4th Division Marines, who had reached the O-6 line, north of the village of Hashigoru, turning to the northwest as the island narrowed, the going was much tougher. On July 3 they encountered a succession of hills that the Japanese seemed determined to hold, despite the division's use of tanks and 75-mm halftracks. Hill 721 (named for its elevation) proved especially difficult. That night the Marines subjected it to unending fire and, after taking it the following day, renamed it "Fourth of July Hill."

On the fourth of July, Holland Smith gave many of his troops a rest, ordering the 2nd and 6th Marines detached from the 2nd Marine Division, and assigned them the role of NTLF (Northern Troops and Landing Forces) reserve. He also removed the 8th Marines from the fighting. Even the beleaguered 27th Division got a break after reaching Flores Point on Saipan's west coast.

Chick Borta's "bastard battalion," which had not enjoyed a day of rest since the battle began, was assigned to patrol operations under the Saipan Garrison Force. Borta almost could not believe it. He had been on hand days before when Colonel Tompkins had told General Merritt Edson, CO of the 2nd Division, that the battalion had nothing left as a fighting unit. "Hey, Red," Borta had heard the colonel say, "this battalion has had it." Now, looking around at his fellow Marines, Borta was taken aback by what he saw. Their dungarees were spattered with blood. They were gaunt and hollow-eyed, and shuffled, as if shackled, on feet burning with jungle rot. Pluto Brem, tall and thin before the battle had begun, looked like a scarecrow. But at least he was alive. Lemon was nowhere to be found. A photographer, Keith Wheeler of the *Chicago Times,* caught the battalion pulling back. Even for his hometown paper, Borta could not muster a smile. He walked head down in a fog of fatigue, conscious of the fact that he and the others looked like the dregs of humanity.

That evening General Holland Smith circulated a message to his troops: "The Commanding General takes pride on this Independence Day in sending his best wishes to the fighting men on Saipan. Your unflagging gallantry and devotion to duty have been worthy of the highest praise of our country. . . . Your fight is no less important than that waged by our forefathers who gave us the liberty and freedom we have long enjoyed. Your deeds to maintain these principles will not be forgotten."

Admiral Spruance, too, was in high spirits. On July 3, Admiral Mitscher reported that two of his carrier task force groups had hit Iwo Jima. U.S. fighters had shot down fifty Japanese Zeros and demolished dozens of planes on the ground. The following day, Mitscher's pilots pounded Iwo Jima again and followed up with raids on the Chichi and Haha Jima island groups.

On July 5, Holland Smith set his sights on the northern part of the island. Splitting it in half, he gave the west side to the 27th Division and the east to the 4th Marine Division. Together the divisions would advance all the way north.

Morning came early for the 23rd Marines' 2nd Battalion atop Hill 767. Hoping to prepare the way for the day's push, artillery sent up a spotter. Joining the spotter, Lieutenant Leary and Carl Matthews, still stinking of night soil after their night in the farmer's garden, crawled to the highest point on the ridge.

Everyone heard the initial rounds as they whooshed overhead. Seeing that they had landed too far out, the spotter called in the co-ordinates and began walking the rounds in closer, hoping to drop the next one in the middle of the enemy outpost. When Matthews heard it, he knew something was wrong. The shell fell short, failing to clear the crest of the hill. Matthews felt as if he had been slammed against a concrete wall. His ears rang as if someone were holding his head up against a screaming teapot. Although he did not appear to notice the injury, Lieutenant Leary had been hit by a piece of shrapnel that had ripped his jacket and grazed his side. The spotter's dungaree jacket was in tatters and his back covered in blood, but he continued to direct the artillery until the rounds were landing on top of the Japanese on the far side of the hill.

An hour later the 23rd Marines moved forward. Dead and wounded enemy soldiers covered the ground. The odor of blood mingled with the smell of rain. Some Marines walked among the bodies, plunging their bayonets into the bellies of the half-dead Japanese, while others rested in the grass and licked at the water that dripped from the lip of their helmets.

By the morning of July 6, Holland Smith was already fed up with the 27th's lack of progress and what he considered its persistent timidity. Smith ordered the 4th Marine Division to move west and squeeze it out. His Marines would execute the final sweep of the island. The Army could busy itself mopping up the coast near Tanapag.

Thanks to Smith's decision to relieve the 27th, the 23rd Marines were again on the move. Held in reserve for just a day, they would now assume a position on the left flank of the advancing Marines, expanding the 4th Division's coverage of the island from the west coast to the east.

Despite their new assignment, there was a growing sense of optimism among the Marines of the 4th Division. After weeks of fighting, the battle seemed to be winding down. Huge numbers of Japanese soldiers were said to be fleeing north. Civilians, perhaps sensing the imminence of the Japanese defeat, were surrendering en masse. Hundreds turned themselves over to the American troops on July 6 alone.

On its two-mile hike from the divisional bivouac to the day's line of departure, Company G came upon a Chamorro man. Through gestures, the man made the Marines understand that a large group of people was hiding in a nearby cave. Lieutenant Leary feared a trap and ordered his men to advance with rifles at the ready. One shot from the cave was all it would have taken for Company G to release a torrent of fire.

The old man yelled into the cave and then waited. Soon people began to creep out, shielding their eyes from the glare of the sun. Once outside, they gathered together in a tight circle, like frightened cattle. A Marine interpreter spoke to them and directed them to a nearby trail.

Carl Matthews watched as a woman struggled to carry two children up the trail's steep incline. Walking up to her, he held out his arms, as if to say, "Let me help." The woman eyed him suspiciously and then shook her head, perhaps remembering what the island's Japanese administrators had told her about the barbarous Americans. Matthews watched her as she trudged on. Then he offered again. This time she handed over a child. Dizzy and weak himself, Matthews labored up the hill with the child in his arms. Although he did not know it yet, the artillery shell that had fallen short the previous day had ruptured his left eardrum and blood vessels in his brain, causing it to swell. He had been fading in and out ever since.

To the east, along a coast pitted with caves and knotted with forest and thick underbrush, the 25th Marines encountered civilians, too. At first they tried to coax them out. However, after Japanese soldiers, hiding among them, shot and killed a number of Marines, the regiment abandoned all charity and blew the caves, civilians or no.

That evening the 25th Marines bivouacked on top of Mount Petosukara amid lashing rains. Shivering in their foxholes, they endured repeated attacks from small groups of Japanese riflemen. Armed with what the Marines called "idiot sticks," poles with bayonets and knives attached, and grenades, and uttering bloodcurdling cries, enemy soldiers staged small banzai raids throughout the night.

On the coastal plain north of Tanapag, the Japanese were

preparing for their biggest raid yet. Holland Smith had been warning his officers for days that the enemy would either "fight a withdrawing action ending in complete annihilation on the northern tip of the island, or attempt to muster their disorganized and crumbling forces into one all out 'banzai' charge." Smith felt that a banzai attack was the most likely scenario. A Japanese prisoner, captured by the Army's 105th Infantry and sent to G-2 for interrogation, confirmed General Smith's fears—General Saito was rallying his troops for one last charge.

The intelligence that General Smith had from G-2's interrogation of the Japanese prisoner was accurate. On July 4 General Saito had sent an aide on an inspection trip of the front lines. He returned with a grim message: the Americans could not be stopped. The following day the Americans pounded Paradise Valley so fiercely that Saito feared that he and his advisers would be buried alive in their command-post cave. The very next day the general, his chief of staff, and a handful of officers held a conference to discuss their options: "to starve to death or secondly, to make a last attack and fight to the finish." They chose the latter, but not before General Saito contacted Tokyo by radio and requested permission to stage a *gyokusai*.

A *gyokusai* was the ultimate banzai, a final act of sacrificial self-destruction. Made up of two ideographs, which translate into English as "jewel" and "smashed," the word *gyokusai* derived from an ancient Chinese parable about a man who chose to destroy his most precious possession rather than compromise his principles. The Japanese had used it only once before: on the island of Attu on May 29, 1943, when one thousand Japanese Marines, realizing that defeat was inevitable, charged the Army's 7th Infantry Division, penetrating the American front line. Shocked rear-echelon troops rallied, and, after hours of hand-to-hand combat, succeeded in killing nearly every enemy fighter.

Saito chose July 7 for the historic event. Then he dictated his final instructions. An assistant made three hundred copies and then messengers went out to deliver the news to unit commanders.

The message read:

For more than twenty days since the American Devils attacked, the officers, men, and civilian employees of the Imperial Army and Navy on this island have fought well and bravely. . . .

Heaven has not given us an opportunity. . . . Our comrades have fallen one after another. Despite the bitterness of the defeat, we pledge "Seven lives to repay our country."

The barbarous attack of the enemy is being continued. . . . Whether we attack or whether we stay where we are, there is only death. However, in death there is life. We must utilize this opportunity to exalt true Japanese manhood. I will advance with those who remain to deliver still another blow to the American Devils, and leave my bones on Saipan as a bulwark of the Pacific.

As it says in the *Senjinkun* [the Japanese military code], "I will never suffer the disgrace of being taken alive" and "I will offer up the courage of my soul and calmly rejoice in living by the eternal principle."

Here I pray with you for the eternal life of the Emperor and the welfare of the country as I advance to seek out the enemy.

Follow me.


That evening, as the last rays of sun left the valley, General Saito, Admiral Nagumo, and Brigadier General Keiji Iketa, chief of staff of the 31st Army, dined with their aides on squid, rice, and a few remaining tins of crab meat. Although there was little food for the men to pass around, all enjoyed plenty of sake. The next morning the general decided he was too old and sick to join the *gyokusai*. Instead, he, Nagumo, and Iketa retired to a small cave. Sitting cross-legged and dressed in their military finery, they unbuttoned their blouses and exposed their chests and stomachs. They shouted, *"Tenno Heika! Banzai!"* as they plunged their swords into their bellies and ripped from left to right, disemboweling themselves. Then, as instructed, their assistants shot them in the head, dragged their bodies out of the cave, and burned them.

In the early-morning hours of July 7, Colonel Takuji Suzuki, commanding officer of the 135th Infantry Regiment, whom General Saito had chosen to lead the *gyokusai*, waited for the troops to gather at the rendezvous areas. In a terrific thunderstorm thousands came, carrying rifles, knives, swords, clubs, poles with bayonets attached, and spears fashioned out of bamboo. At Makunsha they shared sake and beer. Those physically unable to join the *gyokusai* were given the option of taking their own lives or being shot.

# CHAPTER 31

# Red Flags

Lieutenant Paul Zacher from the Port Director's office had inspected the *E. A. Bryan* and given the Liberty ship the green light to be rigged and loaded. Although her winch bearings had been greased and her piston rods and valve stems oiled, just hours later problems surfaced. The driver on the No. 1 winch was lowering a net of bombs when he realized the brake was stuck in the off position. A greenhorn operator would have panicked and sent the bombs free-falling. Fortunately he had been running the winches long enough not to have to depend on the brake. If he kept his cool and the steam pressure lasted, he could bring the load down without smashing it on the deck of the ship or dropping it on top of the men working in the hold.

After bringing the load down safely, the winch operator alerted the ship's third mate, who was charged with keeping the ship, its crew, and its cargo safe, about the problem. He, in turn, relayed the message to the *Bryan*'s chief mate and engineer, who evidently never followed up. Some of the division heads may also have been notified. If they were, they decided that the problem was not an urgent one. As long as the winch was semifunctional, there was no point in losing valuable loading hours by shutting it down.

On the *Bryan*'s No. 4 winch, Lieutenant Richard Terstenson, one of Lieutenant Commander Alexander Holman's two assistant loading officers, discovered that a valve (the petcock) was loose on the compression regulator. So much hot steam was escaping that the winch driver found it difficult to do his job. The steam burned his skin and created such a fog that he could not see his signalman on the deck of the ship. Terstenson immediately alerted the ship's engineer, the same man who earlier had chosen not to attend to the defective brake on the No. 1 winch.

Still, the loading did not stop. For two solid months in the lead-up to the invasion of Saipan and the Marianas, the pressure at Port Chicago had been intense. The autocratic Captain Merrill Kinne, the depot's head officer, constantly reminded his division heads of daily tonnage goals, and they in turn reminded the seamen. The port director's office warned Kinne, as it had warned his boss, Captain Goss, that loading ten tons of high explosives per hour was beyond Port Chicago's capacity. But Kinne, like Goss, wanted nothing to do with anyone looking over his shoulder, and banished the Coast Guard from the pier. "Explosives," he said, "will be quite safe so long as one realizes that they are dangerous." The expectation was that the *Bryan* would be topped off and sent downstream as quickly as possible.

Later that day Lieutenant Terstenson told Lieutenant Commander Holman that he did not approve of the way the seamen rolled and skidded Mk-47 Torpex-loaded aerial depth bombs from the second tier of the boxcar down a wooden chute to the dock. Terstenson knew the hazards of working with ordnance, especially Torpex, a mixture of highly combustible RDX, TNT, and aluminum powder that packed an explosive power one and a half times greater than TNT and was sensitive to bullet penetration and, more important, impact. The Navy Bureau of Ordnance warned of "'container dent' sensitivity . . . new to the literature of explosives." If, in the interest of speed, one was going to cut corners and ignore safety precautions, Torpex was definitely not the stuff to do it with.

"It's dangerous, sir," Terstenson told Holman. "They [the bombs] have a tendency to bang against other bombs laying on the dock." Terstenson suggested using a forklift with a pallet on which to lay and lower the bombs, or at the very least putting a mat on the pier to cushion their fall as they slid off the chute.

That afternoon, Lieutenant Tobin, the 2nd Division's commanding officer, was on the loading platform near the No. 4 hold of the *Bryan,* watching his men break out a boxcar packed seven tiers high with fragmentation bombs. Farther down the pier, near the *Bryan*'s No. 2 hold, Tobin saw what Lieutenant Terstenson had seen—men struggling to move high-explosive Mk-47 bombs off the boxcar. The sight made him nervous, but instead of reporting it, he climbed down into the Bryan's No. 2 hold as if ignoring it would make it disappear. What he witnessed there alarmed him even more. The seamen pushed the 325-pound bombs around as if they were moving crates of oranges, banging them against each other and into the bulkhead.

"Dammit!" Tobin shouted over the din of the clanging bombs. The men stopped working and looked up, startled. "Take it easy with those bombs," Tobin warned. "You're going to blow us all to hell."

When Tobin returned to the deck of the *Bryan,* he was frightened and furious. Had none of the loading officers talked with the seamen about handling Torpex-filled bombs, or was that another depot rule that would go unenforced? Tobin was convinced that Port Chicago was pushing the envelope, and later would admit to one of his fellow loading officers an "apprehension of danger."

Tobin felt that what was missing from Port Chicago was a uniformity of procedure. Everyone seemed to have different expectations and preferences. There were officers who discounted rough handling because they thought it came with the territory. Others, like Lieutenant Richard Terstenson, insisted that there should be "no rough handling of any kind."

In defense of Port Chicago, the West Coast's main port and storage point for ammunition and high explosives, the demands of the war effort left virtually no time for implementing depot-wide standards. Lieutenant Commander Holman could do little more than show his officers and seamen a training film called "Safe Handling of Explosives." Transferring those methods to the dock was something that everyone intended to get to—someday.

The Navy Bureau of Personnel was not of much help, either. It did not issue a comprehensive "ammunition handling" textbook until 1945, meaning that no standard practice for handling high explosives even existed. The Port Chicago Naval Ammunition Depot had to rely on an impractical Coast Guard manual titled *Regulations Governing Transportation of Military Explosives On Board Vessels During the Present Emergency* and the perfunctory *U.S. Naval Magazine, Port Chicago, California, Manual of Loading and Dock Procedure*. The manuals were kept on file but rarely consulted. Some of the officers did not even know that they existed.

Days later, after ninety-six hours of round-the-clock loading, a bleeder valve on the problematic No. 4 winch blew. A petcock could be overlooked, but a blown bleeder valve needed immediate attention. A civil service plumber was brought in to repair it. He replaced a worn-out nipple on the valve and then watched as the ship's engineer tested the winch. Picking up his tools, the plumber began to leave.

"Where are you going?" the engineer asked.

"Well, I'm through," the plumber said. As he turned to walk away, he saw seamen rolling huge bombs out of a boxcar. One bomb got away from them and fell two feet from the car onto the deck.

The plumber looked up at the engineer and shook his head. "I don't like the looks of things around here."

# CHAPTER 32

# Island of the Dead

At 4:00 a.m. on July 7, Colonel Suzuki raised his sword. After bowing in the direction of the Imperial Palace, his troops began to move south down the Tanapag Road. To the Americans, it sounded like a stampede. The Japanese covered the three quarters of a mile in ten minutes and ran smack into the 105th, one of the 27th's regiments, which earlier Holland Smith had relieved of frontline duty. Men fired at each other at point-blank range, and slashed and lunged with their bayonets. A small group of Americans dashed back to the regimental command post half a mile south of Tanapag to sound the alert. In the meantime, the enemy found a gap between the 105th's battalions. They poured through. Then they turned back north and attacked the Americans from the rear. Marine artillery units, observing from the surrounding hills, fired on their own men.

At sunrise the Japanese came across a field and stormed the position held by the 3rd Battalion, 10th Marines. Setting their fuses at a dangerous four tenths of a second, the Marine artillerymen fired at will. The shells exploded so close that they sprayed their own positions with shrapnel. To avoid being killed by flying fragments from their own shells, they bounced them off the ground fifty yards in front of the gun tubes.

Pushing forward, the enemy soldiers ran up against the 105th's regimental command post, half a mile south of Tanapag. Members of the Headquarters Company heard the advance and were waiting. They cut down the Japanese as they swept across an open field. By early afternoon, Headquarters Company, joined by units from the 106th Infantry, counterattacked. Although other enemy units staged smaller attacks throughout the day, the *gyokusai,* the largest and most vicious of the Pacific war, had finally foundered.

After leaving the front lines on the morning of July 6, the remnant troops of the 1st Battalion, 29th Marines were treated to ten-in-one rations, powdered C-ration coffee, and fruit cocktail. Chick Borta's mouth watered at the mention of hot food. Had he been a smoker, like so many of the other men, he might have relished that first long drag of a cigarette. Many of the smokers had gone days without a puff.

Although Borta had planned to eat himself sick, by the time the rations were distributed, he was so exhausted and his temperature had soared so high that he could barely sit up. His legs felt like dough. So, instead of eating he spent the night in the 2nd Division hospital in Garapan, riding out a 103-degree temperature.

That night, woozy with fever, he heard the distant sounds of the *gyokusai:* the cries of the charging Japanese; the machine guns raking the fields; and the roar of artillery. It was not until two days later, however, that he knew for sure that he had not been suffering from auditory hallucinations.

On the morning of July 9, a group of Marines came into the hospital. They were short on men and needed anyone capable of walking and holding a rifle to join their patrol. Borta had already gone through a cycle of fever and chills and knew he had a window of time before his temperature spiked again, so he volunteered.

The first thing Borta noticed were fat clouds of flies moving heavily through the air. Then the patrol came upon a tidal creek choked with dead soldiers. He could have walked across without getting his feet wet.

Reaching the Tanapag Plain, Borta reminded himself that what he was seeing was real and not a fever-induced vision of hell. Dark blood stained the ground. Hundreds of Japanese corpses lay strewn across the dirt with maggots swarming over them. Some looked as if they had died happy, their mouths curled up and teeth bared in a macabre grin. Samurai swords, knives, pistols, rifles, and spears were everywhere. Men assigned to burial details—the lucky wore gas masks—searched through the piles, trying to identify the Americans, puking and retching as putrid gas escaped from the bloated bodies, whose skin was the color of coconut meat. Bulldozers clawed and scooped out trenches and holes and then filled them with dead Japanese doused in kerosene. Years later, what Borta and his fellow Marines would always remember about the battle for Saipan was the stench of the dead. They would smell it on the breeze, at ball games, as they drifted off to sleep, even on their wedding days.

The post-*gyokusai* statistics were mind-boggling. Burial crews handled over 4,300 Japanese bodies. The Americans, too, suffered heavy casualties. The 105th lost a total of nine hundred, with four hundred killed. The 3rd Battalion, 10th Marines lost a total of 140 men, including seventy-five dead. Eighty percent of the men in its H Battery were either killed or wounded.

Although the 27th Division units had fought heroically during the *gyokusai*, General Holland Smith would never forgive it or its disgraced general for slowing his advance through the center of the island. He called it "the worst division I've ever seen," adding that its soldiers were "yellow." In his report to Admiral Spruance, he dismissed the Japanese attack, asserting that it had amounted to nothing more than "300 enemy supported by two or three tanks."

The combat correspondents would have disagreed with him. "This is an island of the dead," wrote one reporter. "The dead are everywhere," scribbled another. "They are thicker here than at Tarawa."

• • •

On July 8 the Marines of the 23rd Regiment prepared to move. Their task for the day was to clear out the cliff line that flanked the Kalaberra Pass (Marine Corps historians called it "Karaberra," but the locals called it Kalaberra) and then to search the caves on the island's north coast. Rather than giving the Army the satisfaction of securing the island, Smith sent his rested 2nd Marine Division to the front and assigned it and the 4th Division the task of mopping up enemy groups.

Carl Matthews could barely stand, much less walk. While his brain swelled, he faded in and out of consciousness, blacking out for seconds at a time. He continued to perform his duties, but he functioned more like a robot than a human being, hardly aware of what he was doing.

Matthews's G Company was following a trail that fell off into a valley. He and Lieutenant Leary picked their way down a steep slope. Before reaching the bottom, they stopped in order to give Companies E and F time to negotiate the descent. On a flat rock outcrop, Leary and Matthews filled their lungs with the bracing air and admired the island's chalk-colored cliffs that plunged into the sea. The two had been through hell together. But now they could see the end.

No one said a word. The lieutenant might have been thinking about what it would be like to be back home in his parents' big house in the center of Ahoskie, North Carolina. He had been blessed and he knew it. That day when the short round hit might have been his last. He had seen so many men die.

Or perhaps he was thinking about Nightingale. A week after Nightingale was shot, Matthews and Leary walked back to see where he was killed, assuming that a burial detail had removed his body. But Nightingale's body was still there, baking in the sun. Leary shook with anger. Later that day he reported the body to battalion headquarters. The following morning he planned to visit the site again, but the company was summoned back into battle. Never again would he or Matthews return to the spot where their friend had died.

Ten minutes passed before Leary broke the silence. "Count," he said, "I don't think the Japs got much fight left in them." Matthews responded that that was just the way he liked it. He was tired of war.

When word came to move out, Matthews stood first, leaning into the wind, and then Lieutenant Leary got up, too. Seconds later there was a machine-gun burst from below. Matthews hurled himself to the ground. From a rock above, someone yelled for a corpsman. Matthews shouted back that it was no use; Lieutenant Leary was dead.

Machine-gun fire continued to rake the slopes, and Company G retreated. At the top of the ridge, Matthews wandered around collecting grenades. No one paid attention until he walked in the direction of the cliff. As he neared the drop-off, several Marines called out to him. When it looked as if he were about to step off into the abyss, a buddy dashed out and grabbed him.

"What the hell do you think you're doing?" he asked. Matthews responded that he was going to knock out the machine gun that had killed Lieutenant Leary. "You're crazy," his friend said. Matthews struggled to free himself, but his friend, who weighed fifty pounds more than he did, held on, dragging him back to safety. Matthews fought like a wild tiger.

The 23rd did not move again until the following morning. That afternoon it arrived at the beaches on the northwest coast, where the sea flaunted its power, crashing against the rocks. When Major Fought's men saw the blue-green water of a small, semiprotected cove, their first impulse was to stampede into the breaking waves and wash off three weeks of dirt, night soil, blood, and grime. But they restrained themselves. Each of them knew that the cliffs held more snipers, and that together with the amtracs of the 2nd Armored Amphibian Battalion, which would spend the day hammering the rock walls, their job was to clean out the caves. Demolition squads were already busy, using ropes to rappel down the wall and drop charges into likely hiding holes.

When Robert Graf saw the high ridges of Marpi Point, he allowed himself to imagine what it would be like when his unit was finally relieved of duty. He had not seen Jimmy Haskell or Bill Jurcsak, his fellow upstaters, in days, but he knew that if they all made it, they would have one hell of a reunion.

At 4:15 that afternoon, the first American Marines reached Marpi Point and radioed Admiral Kelly Turner. They were fifteen days behind schedule, so Turner wasted no time announcing the good news that at 4:16 on July 9, 1944, Saipan was secured. The next morning General Holland Smith presided over a flag-raising ceremony at his Charan Kanoa headquarters. That night a 4th Marine Division chaplain read from Matthew 5: "Here Jesus says, 'Ye have heard that it hath been said, An eye for an eye, and a tooth for a tooth: but I say unto you, That ye resist not evil: but whosoever shall smite thee on thy right cheek, turn to him the other also. . . . Ye have heard that it hath been said, Thou shalt love thy neighbor, and hate thine enemy. But I say unto you, Love your enemies, bless them that curse you, do good to them that hate you, and persecute you; that ye may be the children of your Father which is in heaven: for he maketh his sun to rise on the evil and on the good, and sendeth rain on the just and the unjust.'"

Neither the chaplain's words nor the fact that the American flag now waved over Saipan could have meant anything to the Japanese soldiers or the hundreds of civilians who had fled to the cliffs on the island's north coast. It was here that Robert Graf and countless other American servicemen would witness scenes that would be forever etched into their memories. Graf would later write that "Saipan was filled with horror, but it was during these securing days that we came upon the worst of the nightmares."

At an interior hilltop that the Americans would call "Suicide Cliff," Japanese soldiers held grenades to their bellies, or tossed them back and forth, laughing madly, until the grenades exploded, spewing razor-sharp shrapnel in every direction. Others, realizing that their life was "fluttering away like a flower petal," threw themselves off an 800-foot peak. It was a good death—*okuni no tame ni* (for the country's sake)—their spirits returning to the Yasukuni Shrine where even the Emperor would one day pay them homage. From the beach, Graf saw them fall. What he could not see was that some of these people were civilians.

Later, at Banzai Cliff, which loomed 265 feet above the blue-green waters of the sea, Graf watched the horrible spectacle up close. At another time the sight would have been a beautiful one, the stark cliffs where white terns soared through a cloudless blue sky. But on July 10, Japanese and native Chamorro and Carolinian families, told for years about the devil Americans, held hands as if playing a children's game and dove onto the huge rocks below or into the surging surf. Mothers, grasping their babies, jumped rather than turn themselves over to the Marines. Japanese soldiers shot or prodded at gunpoint those who resisted. Some who were already on the rocks below simply walked out into the crashing waves and were sucked down by the current or bashed against the cliff wall. From a distance, Japanese snipers shot those who appeared reluctant to commit themselves to the sea.

The Americans had anticipated the civilian suicides. They had dropped notices, written by military intelligence translators, explaining how to surrender. "All non-combatants, whether Japanese, Korean or natives," the notice said, "will come down the Banaderu Road on the NE coast of Saipan toward Tanapag, at 9 o'clock, Friday 7 July. They will come unarmed and carrying white flags held high. If they do this, the American forces will receive them and save their lives. Americans do not want to kill non-combatants. 7000 civilians of Saipan are already safe in American hands." The Marines set up PA systems and, using interpreters, pleaded with the people not to jump. Boats offshore employed civilians to broadcast messages promising kind treatment in the internment camps. In some cases their appeals worked. But still, over the course of the next few days, many hundreds leaped to their deaths.

Bill More was there, too, and like Graf, his longtime buddy, he was powerless to stop what he saw. He watched as a group of people, including children, gathered around a man as if he were a respected leader about to impart a message of wisdom. When the grenade went off, and body parts flew through the air, any hope that the children might be spared was shattered.

As for reporter Robert Sherrod, who had been on Saipan since D-Day, what he saw convinced him to write an article, titled "The Nature of the Enemy," for the August 7, 1944, issue of *Time* magazine. "Saipan," he wrote, "is the first invaded Jap territory populated with more than a handful of civilians. Do the suicides of Saipan mean that the whole Japanese race will choose death before surrender?"

Days later, Seaman First Class James Fahey wrote in his diary, "After supper while we were out patrolling Saipan the fellows passed the time running from one side of the ship to the other, watching the Jap bodies float by. . . . Some were on their stomachs, others on their backs, they floated along like rubber balls. . . . They were bloated." Two days later he returned to his diary: "There must be thousands of Japs in the waters near Saipan. The ships just run over them." A lieutenant on a minesweeper confessed, "The area is so congested with floating bodies we simply can't avoid running them down. I remember one woman in khaki trousers and a white polka-dot blouse, with her black hair streaming in the water. I'm afraid every time I see that blouse, I'll think of that girl."

When word came that the 23rd Marines were being relieved, Robert Graf was glad to go. Watching babies die was more than he could stomach. Now the question was whether or not he could make the march back to the invasion beaches. Like the others, he was battered and gaunt, and his lower legs were a patchwork of sores and cuts. Some of the guys had lost so much weight that their shoulder blades poked out of their dungaree jackets. But as they neared Charan Kanoa, they rushed the beach like wild horses and flung themselves into the water. Then they sat in the sand and dried off in the hot sun.

A day later their seabags came ashore. Graf stripped out of his rotting clothes and waded back into the sea, where he washed his hair and scrubbed himself as if he were going to Sunday church. Back on land he put on a clean, new uniform, enjoying the feeling of it against his skin. Then he took his old one and tossed it onto a giant pile. Using a camera that one of the guys had stolen off a Japanese corpse, Graf, Haskell, and Jurcsak posed for a photograph. Later that afternoon, they looked on and clapped when a quartermaster unit doused the hill of clothes and bleached-out boots with gasoline and set it on fire. For chow that night, a group of corpsmen caught thirty-two chickens, which the cooks fried. Before turning in, the men learned that they would be invading Tinian in two weeks. Graf joked that it was their "reward for taking Saipan."

Just two days after the American invasion of Saipan began, Emperor Hirohito told Japanese Prime Minister Tojo, "If we ever lose Saipan, repeated air attacks on Tokyo will follow. No matter what it takes, we have to hold there." Now, realizing that the heartland of Japan was within reach of the American bombers, the Emperor despaired, "Hell is upon us."

The American victory on Saipan and Japan's defeat in the Philippine Sea (in which the United States wrested control of the air and the seas throughout the Pacific) brought about a crisis in Tokyo that even the Emperor could not escape. Members of the imperial family, including Hirohito's brother, criticized him. Tojo, however, absorbed most of the blame for what he himself had called a "national crisis." A small cabal of statesmen and naval officers had been trying to undermine Tojo since the defeat in the Solomons in early 1943. Hirohito's unwavering faith, however, protected the prime minister. With Saipan now in American hands, they saw their chance to force the prime minister out of office. On July 18, 1944 (July 17 in the United States), Tojo and his entire cabinet resigned.

On the same day, Admiral Ernest King, seated in his cramped office on the third floor of the Navy Department building, penned a letter regarding the West Loch disaster in Pearl Harbor, which had occurred just weeks before the invasion of Saipan. He had fought for over a year to convince the Joint Chiefs, the Combined Chiefs, and Admiral Chester Nimitz of the wisdom of invading the Marianas, and the explosions at West Loch had threatened to derail the plan. As it was, the assault on Saipan came off as scheduled. The disaster was kept from the enemy—and the American public—for another sixteen years.

"It is noted," Admiral King wrote, that "the organization, training, and discipline in the LSTs involved in this disaster leave much to be desired. The lack of proper understanding and compliance with safety precautions when handling ammunition and gasoline . . . is also noted." Then, evidently still irritated by the Naval Board of Inquiry's failure to assess responsibility for the incident and Admiral Nimitz's magnanimity (on June 29, 1944, Nimitz wrote that the explosion was not the result of "misconduct . . . or negligence"), King added, "It is perfectly apparent that this disaster was not an 'Act of God.'"

# CHAPTER 33

# Hot Cargo

The evening of July 17 was cool and nearly windless. By 7:00 p.m., the *E. A. Bryan,* facing downstream, squatted low in the water. After four days of nonstop loading, she was half full, carrying 4,379 tons of ammunition and explosives: antiaircraft projectiles and igniter charges in the lower portion of her No. 1 hold, and in her No. 2 hold, Torpex-loaded aerial depth bombs and 500-, 1,000-, and 2,000-pound bombs. These general-purpose bombs introduced by the Bureau of Ordnance in late 1943 were loaded with a TNT or an Amatol charge. The 2,000-pounder stretched ninety inches long (with its fin assembly) and was one of the largest bombs that would ever pass through Port Chicago.

The seamen had already loaded the *Bryan*'s No. 3 hold with over 1,000 tons of the Torpex-loaded aerial depth bombs. The No. 4 hold held another 790 tons. The No. 5 hold contained antiaircraft projectiles and 40-mm cartridges. The schedule called for an approximate load of 8,179 tons, meaning that if all went well, the *Bryan* would be ready to sail in another three days for Richmond, California, where her deck would be loaded with more cargo. In case of trouble, there was a Coast Guard fireboat tied to the pier with its hoses connected to the depot's hydrants. Another Coast Guard vessel, the *Mia Helo,* was patrolling the river, as it always did during loading operations.

The SS *Quinault Victory,* a brand-new Victory ship, just out of Portland, Oregon, was moored at the outboard side of the pier with her bow into the current. That morning she had her diesel tanks topped off at the Associated Oil Company fueling dock in Martinez, eight miles upriver. For the time being, she was empty and rode high in the water. Lieutenant Commander Glen Ringquist watched as the 6th Division hoisted dunnage aboard, lifted the hatch beams, and rigged the vessel for loading.

Ringquist was a Navy man with thirty-five years of service, who had come to Port Chicago in early June 1944 as the senior of Lieutenant Commander Holman's two assistant loading officers. He had spent much of his career working with explosives, and for the three and a half years just prior to coming to Port Chicago, he was the cargo and ammunition officer of the USS *Lassen.* Ringquist was a real stickler. Together he and Holman should have formed a crack team of inspectors.

On the three railroad tracks that separated the ships sat sixteen railroad cars waiting to be unloaded. One of the cars opposite the *Bryan*'s No. 1 hold was packed with thirty tons of incendiary cluster bombs, or firebombs, from the Hawthorne, Nevada, Navy Ammunition Depot. They were considered "hot cargo," and extremely dangerous because they came with their fuzes installed. The fuzes were sensitive enough to be ignited by shock waves. Another carload of incendiary bombs was parked on the approach wing of the pier. Next to it was one containing 1,000-pound armor-piercing bombs filled with TNT. Although TNT was more stable than Torpex, impact, friction, sparks, and shock were known to ignite it. Opposite the *Bryan*'s No. 2 hold were two cars carrying Torpex-loaded depth bombs. Loads did not get any more volatile than this. Aerial bombs were thin-walled and known to detonate en masse in the event of fire. On the inside and outside tracks across from the *Bryan*'s No. 4 hold were two cars of general-purpose bombs, what the depot loading document called

"Mk4 fragmentation clusters." Near the middle of the *Quinault Victory*, on the inside track, sat two cars holding more general-purpose bombs and, near her No. 4 hold, one car of armor-piercing bombs.

Despite the fact that it violated his own safety orders, Kinne allowed the cars to collect on the dock. The practice—like shipping bombs with fuzes—was all about the demands of war. Moving cars on and off the pier could leave a division idle, delaying the loading process for as much as an hour. Just one month before, Kinne had posted his new rules for the widened pier, warning that the "accumulation of explosives," especially "trains of explosives must be carefully avoided under all conditions." The captain may have paid lip service to safe handling in his correspondences, but in countless other ways he had made it clear that safety at Port Chicago would be sacrificed for speed. When loading got fast and furious, he was willing to overlook regulations—even his own.

If any group of men could handle the tension, the 3rd Division could. Its head officer considered the 3rd the best, from its junior officers—Lieutenants Raymond "Bob" White and Thomas Blackman—on down to its petty officers, winchmen, and ammunition handlers. The head of the other division on duty, the 6th, did not have the same kind of confidence in his men. It had some good winchmen and petty officers, but its seamen were largely inexperienced Great Lakes graduates and transfers from other divisions.

The newer seamen had never seen such a concentration of ordnance, and the sight left them uneasy. Even the old hands on the dock, who had been at the depot since its early days in late 1942, were stunned to see so many railroad cars waiting to be unloaded. Some half-joked that if there was a fire, there was enough ordnance sitting on the tracks to make a small island disappear into dust.

By 8:30 p.m., the pier was lit up like a carnival, and cluster lights, attached to poles, flooded the cargo hatches. Lieutenant Ringquist was on the dock. He had been keeping an eye on both the *Bryan* and the *Quinault* for the last two hours, watching to make sure the winches were running properly. At 8:45, accompanied by Lieutenant

Commander Holman, he boarded the *Quinault* and examined her No. 2, No. 3, and No. 4 holds. Satisfied that the *Quinault* was ready for loading, he moved back over to the *Bryan* forty-five minutes later. After "peering down into her holds," where the 3rd Division had been working since 4:00 p.m., moving and hoisting large loads of 40-mm shells and incendiary, aerial, cluster, and armor-piercing bombs, he had brief conversations with Lieutenants White and Blackman and then returned to the dock office. Twenty minutes later, Captain Kinne checked in on the *Quinault*. Holman assured him that the ship was in tip-top shape and would be ready to take on ordnance by 11:00 p.m. Loading on the *Bryan,* he said, was going smoothly. Ten minutes later, Kinne and Holman drove to the officers' quarters to turn in for the night, leaving the operation in Ringquist's capable hands.

Back on the pier, Ringquist pointed out to one of the loading officers on duty that the *Quinault*'s propeller ("the screw") was turning over and informed him that it would have to be stopped before loading began. After giving the *Bryan* a quick once-over, he left the dock at 10:15 p.m., intending to go to the dock office to talk with Lieutenant Bob White. When he saw the base station wagon making its regular rounds, he changed his mind and asked the driver to take him to the administration building. His change of heart undoubtedly saved his life.

# CHAPTER 34

# End of the World

Ten o'clock was lights-out, and Percy Robinson was lying in his top bunk with his hands under his head, staring out one of the big bay windows at a sky bright with stars. He was feeling good about himself for almost the first time since coming to Port Chicago. As part of his training program he had been assigned to a number of ships as a backup winch driver, but as of Monday, July 17, he was a full-fledged winchman. It was the kind of skill that one day might allow him to return to Chicago and make a good living down on the lakefront docks. He would not have to wander the streets of the Black Belt selling produce or peddling bootleg whiskey or running numbers.

Earlier in the day, he and a handful of other seamen had boarded the *A. E. Bryan* to watch the crew top off the No. 1 hold, paying particular attention to the winchman on duty as he picked up, swung, and lowered loads of incendiary cluster bombs down into the hold. He was filled with excitement. No longer would he have to slave in the hold of a ship. After leaving the *Bryan*, he and his closest buddies—the Hawks—gathered at the recreation hall, only recently opened, with its lunchroom, bowling alley, gymnasium, swimming pool, exercise room, and movie theater. Together they toasted Percy's good fortune with a beer.

Sammie Boykin, too, was lying in his bunk, trying not to think about the night ahead of him. His Division No. 1, and the 2nd Division, had the graveyard shift, midnight to 8:00 a.m. He had been working night and day as long as he could remember, running the winches at the depot, then grabbing forklift jobs for extra money at the Crockett Sugar Plant, the Shell Oil Refinery, the Del Monte Cannery in Oakland, and the Avon Refinery.

Robert Edwards had been reading in his bunk for much of the night. When he first arrived at Port Chicago in May, all he wanted to do was to see "Frisco." Having grown up in Brooklyn, New York, he was no stranger to big cities, but San Francisco held a special spot in his imagination as a kind of melting pot where Chinese-Americans, black Americans, and whites, too, lived in relative harmony. But one day on Sutter Street, his imagined paradise turned ugly when he ran into six white sailors looking for trouble. "Ah," the ringleader said as Edwards approached, "look at that nigger there in the Navy. Let's teach him a lesson." Edwards was pint-sized, barely five feet six, a petty officer with a good head on his shoulders who could type and file. He was no fighter, especially when he knew that the odds were stacked against him. So he bolted. Even after he no longer heard their shouts or the thumping of their feet on the pavement, he sprinted until his chest heaved and his legs felt as if they would give out. When he stopped, he made himself a promise—he would steer clear of San Francisco.

Robert Routh had arrived at Port Chicago from Mare Island just three months before. A callow nineteen-year-old who was still treating his pimply face with cream, he had to admit that things were looking up for him. When he shipped out of Mare Island, he was told that in ninety days he would get an increase in rank, and in early August would be up for leave. On the night of July 17 he could have gone to Oakland or Berkeley or San Francisco, but instead he stayed behind to wash clothes, write a few letters, and save money. At 10:15 that night, not long after taps sounded, he climbed into his top bunk.

Dewhitt Jamison had just lain back in his bed, when an explosion rocked the depot. Seconds later came another, more massive one, and then a series of sharp cracks like blasts from a machine gun. Shortly before 10:19 p.m., seismograph machines at the University of California, Berkeley, forty miles away, registered two tremors, seven seconds apart, with the force of a small earthquake. The second blast lifted Jamison out of his bed and smashed him against the ceiling. When he hit the floor, the barracks building crumbled down on top of him.

"Lie flat and don't move!" he yelled out. "Don't move!" Then he covered his head with his hands. Minutes later he opened his eyes and discovered that the building was gone. The ceiling and walls had collapsed. All that remained was the floor. Pieces of wood, hot steel, and glass fragments hissed through the air.

Jamison got up, yanked a piece of wood out of his side, and walked past what had been the front door of the barracks onto the grass. A nauseating chemical stench assaulted him. The first person he saw was Captain Kinne. "What was it?" he asked.

Kinne shook his head. "I don't know. I think the ships blew up." As Jamison and the captain walked in the direction of the pier, Kinne noticed a fire burning near the railroad tracks close to town. When he saw that the bachelor officers' quarters building was still standing, for a moment he hoped that a boxcar of explosives had detonated on the tracks outside the magazine. Then he heard someone say, "There's nothing left."

Lieutenant Glen Ringquist was en route to the administration building when he heard a terrible crash and a "breaking of timbers." Realizing that the second sound was probably made as the Bryan's fifty-ton jumbo boom toppled over, he jumped out of the car that only a few minutes earlier had picked him up at the pier and ran back in the direction of the waterfront, fearing the worst. He did not have to wait long before he saw a flash of color followed by a violent discharge as the entire *Bryan*, with its 4,379 tons of ammunition and explosives, blew. A column of smoke and fire shot thousands of feet into the air, producing a brilliant flame that rose even higher. Then red-hot fragments, chunks of molten steel, and body parts cartwheeled through the sky.

An Army Air Force plane flying at 9,000 feet from Oakland to Sacramento was over Port Chicago. The frightened copilot noted that from above it looked as if the depot blew in one colossal explosion. He saw a ring of fire three miles in diameter burst from the ground. It seemed to shoot straight up. As it rose, garage-sized chunks of metal tore past the plane. Seconds later the pilot felt a concussion, as if one of the slabs of metal had collided with the aircraft.

At the Roe Island lighthouse, one and a half miles away from the depot, on the opposite side of Suisun Bay, the explosion smashed every window. As the lighthouse shook violently, the keeper dashed up to the second floor while his wife attended to two of their children below. From the second floor, he saw the giant red cloud across the bay, and the thirty-foot tidal wave filled with diesel fuel, ammonium nitrate, hydrochloric acid, and potassium chlorate, on a collision course with the lighthouse. He grabbed their baby and ran downstairs.

Lieutenant Ringquist jumped back into the car and drove toward the barracks. Electricity to the depot had been lost, and men were running through the dark. Exiting the car, Ringquist instructed his driver to turn on his high beams, and then the lieutenant flicked on the lights of the trucks that had survived the blast. When a civilian from Port Chicago asked if he could help, Ringquist told him to rush back to town and alert Mare Island, the Twelfth Naval District, and the Army and to tell them that the depot needed lights, water, and medical assistance.

• • •

Lying in his bunk, Joe Small was dozing off when he heard the first and smaller of the two blasts. He had little time to make sense of it or to react. The second one demolished the building. Small was thrown to the floor. He had had enough sense to grab his mattress and cling to it. When he saw a funnel cloud of thick, black smoke surging into the sky, he knew that what he and so many of the seamen had feared for so long had finally become a reality.

Just a few bunks down from Small, Percy Robinson saw a flash and the stars disappear and the sky light up as if it were a cloudless summer day. Moments later he felt a tremendous explosion. The shock wave sucked the air out of the room, and pressed down on his chest and lungs until he could not breathe. Then he heard another roar, an apocalyptic howl. The second of the two blasts felt as if the earth were splitting apart. It lifted him out of his bed and threw him to the floor. While everyone around was screaming, Percy lay on the ground too stunned to move. It felt like someone was drilling into his skull. The first voice he heard was Joe Small's. "Where's Percy? Is Percy okay?" Then he heard someone else yell, "The upper deck is going to fall!" and he scrambled to his feet and ran out the barracks door.

Outside he saw an officer shouting, "It's the ships! It's the ships!"

Men were rushing around aimlessly. Joe Small, who was now outside, spotted a man whose feet were covered in blood and gave him his shoes. Another man had a gaping cut that ran the length of his arm. Small knew he had to stop the bleeding, and applied a tourniquet to it.

Percy Robinson heard Small calling for volunteers for rescue duty and ran up to him, but Small did not recognize him. When he realized who it was under the tattered clothes and blood, he ordered Robinson to get aboard an ambulance that was taking men to Camp Stoneman.

Claude Ellington had been on the docks just hours before. When the pier blew, he was standing by the clothesline. The next thing he knew he was lying in the dirt, uncertain of where the ground ended and the sky began. When he got back to his feet, his first thought was to get the hell off the base before it exploded again. But then he heard one of the lieutenants say, "West of the dock, a lot of people are hurt down there." So instead of fleeing, Ellington ran toward the pier.

When Robert Routh heard the first explosion, his initial thought was that the Japanese had staged another sneak attack. Seconds later he heard a larger blast, like hundreds of railroad cars roaring into a station. Every window exploded, and glass flew through the barracks like tiny missiles, cutting and slashing everything in its path. He felt a searing pain and then his eyes went dark. *I'm blinded,* he thought. He called out for someone to take him to sick bay. Then he heard a seaman yell that sick bay had been destroyed.

George Booth was standing beside his lower bunk. The explosion ripped through the air with hurricane-force winds (the *San Francisco Chronicle* reported winds of 150 mph) and blew him through what had been the back wall of the barracks. He ended up outside, pressed against a Cyclone fence. His first reaction was to run, but then he noticed that the stars seemed to be falling from the sky. He thought that he was experiencing the end of the world, Judgment Day.

Getting up, he ran to a jeep and turned the key. He was scared, and all he wanted to do was to get away from the noise and the tumbling sky. Then he realized pieces of glass and red-hot fragments of metal were raining down on him. Leaving the base he thought, *I'm gonna get the hell out of here. I'm gonna drive home to Detroit.*

When he had made it halfway to Pittsburg, he pulled over to the side of the road, turned off the key, and tried to calm himself. Minutes later he was racing back to Port Chicago.

The explosion had finally happened as some of Booth's buddies had been telling him it would. As the editor of the depot paper, he had ignored Port Chicago's dark side, instead writing lighthearted and encouraging stories, telling the seamen to keep their spirits up, and to remember the importance of their role: they were the men behind the men who were doing the fighting, he wrote, reiterating what Lieutenant Delucchi had told him and his group from Great Lakes when they first arrived at Port Chicago. Booth had no intention of rocking the boat. Lieutenant Delucchi had promised him that he could go to Hampton University to learn a trade.

Booth had been back at the depot for just a few minutes, helping out with the wounded, when Army vehicles from Camp Stoneman began arriving, lighting up the night with their headlights. Then, for the first time, he saw the destruction. Much of the depot no longer existed. The mess hall and his beloved recreation building, which was as big as a city block, were gone.

At the revetment area, which had been built to prevent an explosion on the pier from igniting the hundreds of boxcars waiting to be unloaded, a fire had broken out. By the time five Port Chicago seamen arrived, it had enveloped two cars. Black smoke coughed out of the doors. Recognizing the danger of a chain-reaction explosion, the men grabbed water hoses and fought to keep the fire from spreading.

In the town of Port Chicago, one mile from the pier, Morris Rich and his buddy, armed guards from the *Quinault Victory* who were in town on liberty passes, were thrown from their restaurant booth and against the far wall. Like Routh, Rich's first reaction was that the Japanese were bombing. Worried that the ceiling might fall, Rich crawled under a table. Pieces of steel and wood flew through the air. By the time Rich made it outside, injured people lay in the street. Some wandered aimlessly with wet handkerchiefs pressed to their mouths, their eyes wide open as if frozen in shock. Then he noticed that he had a piece of shrapnel embedded in his nose and another in his leg.

After a wall buckled and the roof threatened to cave in, people poured out of the adjacent theater, some screaming and crying. When they reached the outdoors, they were accosted by a tower of fire and smoke rising from the river.

Rich and his buddy helped to load the injured into cars and then made their way back to the depot. The town looked as though it had been the scene of a pitched battle. Hundreds of homes and businesses were damaged or destroyed, and none had light or water or heat. Undetonated bombs and smoldering debris from the ships and pier lay scattered in the streets. Where the Santa Fe depot had stood lay a pile of rubble. When Rich and his buddy reached Port Chicago's main gate and were stopped by a Marine guard, Rich realized that his shirt and pants were wet with blood, his own, and that he needed medical attention. The guard pointed them in the direction of what once had been a barracks hall. Men lay on the ground moaning. Others, with perforated eardrums, grabbed at the sides of their heads. A few looked as if they had been chewed up by a threshing machine.

Spencer Sikes, who, the first time he ever saw a net of bombs feared he would never again lay eyes on his family, was in a movie theater in Berkeley. At 10:18 he heard a boom that sent tremors through the building. Everyone assumed that it was one of the Bay Area's frequent small-scale earthquakes. Later an announcer came on the intercom: "All military personnel at Port Chicago, please report back immediately." After dropping off his date at home, he took a streetcar to the San Pablo Greyhound station. Soldiers and sailors milled about, wondering what had happened. Someone mentioned the dreaded word "sabotage." Then Sikes heard someone say that Port Chicago had blown up and everyone was dead.

He and some other seamen caught a bus as far as Concord. There, almost twenty miles from Port Chicago, he saw debris scattered in the streets. An emergency call went out for all medical workers, and Sikes caught a ride to the base with a doctor and his wife, a nurse. By the time he arrived, the Salvation Army had already set up lights and a triage unit. Sikes could not believe his eyes—much of the base had been wiped out. Then he saw men wandering about with blood dripping from their heads, feet, arms, and hands. The more seriously wounded, he learned, were being taken to the Navy hospital in Vallejo.

The night was a blur. Seamen and officers alike organized teams to treat and carry the wounded. Relief organizations delivered blood plasma, morphine, chlorinated water, and blankets. Ambulances, trucks, cars, and even a Greyhound bus were brought in to transport the injured to Pittsburg's Camp Stoneman Army Hospital for medical attention. The army arrived with diesel generators and searchlights. Soldiers were summoned to protect government property and to guard against looting in town. One group patrolled the area in an armored car with an antitank gun mounted in back.

The following day, Inez White sent a telegram to her husband's brother alerting him that Bob—Lieutenant Bob White, who was in the dock office at the time of the explosion—had been declared missing and that she was awaiting official notification. While some men searched for bodies to put into coffins, Spencer Sikes was assigned to a detail that was ordered down to the river to look for body parts. It was a grim task. He would never forget what he saw that day: severed heads bobbing in the water; bodies charred beyond recognition and others swollen with tissue gas; a bloody hand; a shoe with a foot in it. One of the rescue teams discovered a civilian carpenter nearly dead under a pile of rubble in what had once been one of the depot's machine shops. The carpenter had been working in the shop, using a band saw, when the ships exploded. The saw landed on top of him, slicing him from his left eye down his back and arm, lopping off a portion of his ear.

Later that day, Sikes stopped in to check on his living quarters. Since he had been promoted from a boxcar inspector to shore patrol, his room was in the jail. Although much of the building was destroyed, the room was still standing. What he saw nearly made his legs buckle. Stuck in his pillow, blanket, and mattress were dozens of razor-sharp shards of glass. Had he not made the last-minute decision to shave and shower and head for town, he would likely be a dead man.

Sammie Boykin had much the same feeling. He knew that had the explosion taken place an hour or so later, he, too, would have died and the list of those killed or wounded would have been nearly twice as high as it was. By 11:30 p.m., the 1st and 2nd Divisions would have been assembling at the pier, preparing to relieve the 3rd and 6th Divisions. Four divisions would have been down at the river instead of two.

In the days after the explosion, many of the seamen who had survived the blast without injury were taken to Camp Shoemaker in Dublin, California, thirty miles east of Oakland. By that time, the picture of what had happened had become fairly clear: the blast that had destroyed much of the Port Chicago Naval Ammunition Depot detonated with the force of nearly two and a quarter kilotons of TNT (one fifth the explosive fury of the atomic bomb that would be dropped on Hiroshima just over a year later), carving out a crater under the *Bryan* that measured 600 feet across. The *E. A. Bryan*, the boxcars sitting on the pier, and the locomotive had all disintegrated, and the 1,200-foot pier ceased to exist. The force of the explosion broke the *Quinault Victory* into a number of large pieces, hurled her twenty-ton stern through the air, and dumped it upside down 500 feet from the dock. The blast lifted the Coast Guard fire barge into the sky and flung it two hundred yards upriver.

Had the explosion occurred above the waterline rather than below, which reduced the blast output, the damage would have been massive. Had it spread to the revetment area or happened closer to a busy seaport like San Francisco or San Diego, the loss of life would have been incalculable. Comparing the Port Chicago explosion to the Halifax disaster of 1917, Captain William Parsons, who, shortly after the disaster, investigated the incident for the Office of Chief of Naval Operations and the Los Alamos Laboratory, said that the loss of life would have been far greater if not for the Navy's choice of an isolated site for the depot. "Port Chicago," he said, "was designed for large explosions."

As it was, everyone on or near the pier, including Lieutenants White and Blackman, and on the *E. A. Bryan,* the *Quinalt Victory,* and the Coast Guard fire barge, died within seconds of the two explosions. Three hundred twenty men were killed, including 202 black enlisted men. Another 390 military personnel and civilians were injured. Two hundred thirty-three of them were black.

# CHAPTER 35

# Down the Barrel of a Gun

The day after the explosion, Morris Rich, whose injuries had amounted to a collection of cuts, was sent out to sea. He had no idea how many of his buddies aboard the *Quinault Victory* had died in the blast, but guessed that none of them had survived. In the ensuing months he was transferred so often that he became convinced that he had been shanghaied, that the Navy did not want him anywhere near California, where he might tell what he knew about the explosion.

Power and telephone linemen strung new wires, and Army demolition squads searched the area for unexploded ordnance. Meanwhile, two hundred black seamen who volunteered to remain at the depot assisted with the monumental cleanup effort, which included transferring ammunition from damaged boxcars to certified cars under the guidance of bomb-disposal officers. Dewhitt Jamison, who had survived the blast, did not like the work one bit. He had finally been able to reach his parents in South Carolina to let them know that he was still alive, but now he wondered if that phone call might have been premature.

For Spencer Sikes, the days after the disaster were a time of mourning. Although he was grateful to be alive, the explosion that he had dreaded since coming to Port Chicago in late 1942 had taken many of his good friends.

On July 19 the *San Francisco Chronicle* opened with the headline BLAST DEATH TOLL NOW 377; 1000 INJURED! The story quoted Captain Goss, who said, "We have no basis for giving any cause of the explosion, as there are no survivors to give evidence of what happened."

Another *Chronicle* article titled CHRONICLE PLANE SURVEYS DESTRUCTION: RECONSTRUCTION ALREADY IS IN EVIDENCE began, "Less than twelve hours ago, the burned and blackened scene was a site where thousands of men labored and sweated to load war materiel for the fighting fronts on the Pacific. Now all such activity is halted. . . . The desolation is hard to describe."

Two days later, Captain Kinne was informed that he had been awarded the military's fourth-highest award, the Bronze Star, for "heroic or meritorious achievement." In turn, he issued a statement praising all the seamen of Port Chicago for their response to the disaster. "Under those emergency conditions," he wrote, "regular members of our complement and volunteers from Mare Island displayed creditable coolness and bravery."

The new commandant of the Twelfth Naval District, Rear Admiral Carleton Wright, who had come to California directly from the war in the Pacific, where half his cruiser flotilla had been lost to Japanese destroyers, echoed Kinne's sentiments: "I am gratified to learn that, as was to be expected, Negro personnel attached to the Naval Magazine Port Chicago performed bravely and efficiently in the emergency at that station last Monday night. These men, in the months they served at that command, did excellent work in an important segment of the District's overseas combat supply system. As real Navy men, they simply carried on in the crisis . . . in accordance with our Service's highest traditions." Of the men who perished, he said, "Their sacrifice could not have been greater had it occurred on a battleship or a beach-head."

On July 21, at 10:00 a.m., a Naval Court of Inquiry, made up of three naval officers and a judge advocate, met for its first session to "inquire into the circumstances attending the explosion." Captains Goss and Kinne were forced to join the proceedings as "interested parties," which meant that, although Kinne had been awarded the Bronze Star, he and Goss were under suspicion of dereliction of duty.

Meanwhile, teary-eyed wives of Port Chicago men feared lost in the blast waited at the depot pass gate for word about their husbands. Some carried babies and begged the guards to let them go to the barracks and find out for themselves if their husbands were alive or dead. The women, according to the black-owned *Pittsburgh Courier*, which was one of the first newspapers on the scene, "faced a dark future."

Nine days later, on July 30, memorial services were held for the men who died in the explosion. Captain Goss brought in swing bands and USO shows to comfort the survivors. Meanwhile, nearly 3,000 miles to the east, Congress was considering a proposal to compensate the families of the victims. Eventually it decided on a maximum allowable benefit of just $3,000. The surviving seamen were outraged. Their lives were worth only a measly $3,000?

Many of Port Chicago's residents were similarly disappointed by the Navy's response. They had hoped that the Navy would cover the cost of repairing the town's houses, stores, restaurants, and other businesses in addition to a payment for physical and emotional suffering. Instead, the Bureau of Ordnance, having set aside $20 million, publicly announced its plan not to close the ammunition depot, but to initiate an expansion program that would make Port Chicago not just a loading and transfer center, but one of the largest ammunition storage bases in the country. The undertaking would add two additional ship piers, which, together with the reconstructed Pier No. 2, would give the depot six berths and the capacity to load 100,000 tons of ordnance per month. The plan also envisioned the construction of twenty high-explosive magazines and fifteen gun ammunition magazines in addition to eleven five-car barricaded sidings. Ironically, in the eyes of the bureau, the explosion had raised Port Chicago's status, justifying the bureau's original decision to "locate an ammunition loading station at a relatively isolated locality, in contrast to the congested lower San Francisco Bay Area or Mare Island."

On that same day, July 31, as the *Oakland Tribune* ran photos of the memorial assembly at Port Chicago, many of the black seamen billeting at Camp Shoemaker were transferred. The 1st and 2nd Divisions, minus Sammie Boykin, who was still in the hospital, went back to Port Chicago, and the 4th and 8th Divisions were sent to the Mare Island Naval Barracks (formerly the Ryder Street Naval Barracks) in Vallejo, the site of the April 1943 race riots in which armed Marine guards opened fire on a group of black seamen. Until their transfers, many of the seamen had hoped—and expected—that like the white officers and enlisted men who survived the blast, they would be granted survivor's leave. They also believed that they would be sent to other stations or ships or even overseas to fight. Most of them agreed that anything would be better than loading ammunition again.

At the Mare Island Naval Barracks, a group of men approached Joe Small seeking his advice: What was he going to do—what should they do—if ordered to handle ammunition again? Small made it clear that he would refuse. The group sought out other leaders and received similar answers: to work under the same conditions and under the same officers was suicidal.

A petition listing the names of those unwilling to handle ammunition and requesting a transfer of duty circulated among the men. Sixty seamen had included their names, but when it came to Joe Small, he may or may not have destroyed it. One thing was for sure: he wanted no part of putting his name on any piece of paper that the Navy could later use against him.

Meanwhile the Court of Inquiry proceeded. Although it would eventually hear testimony from 125 witnesses, including Port Chicago personnel and ordnance experts, only five black enlisted men were called before the court. The court examined the possibility of sabotage, equipment malfunction, organizational inadequacies, rough handling by inexperienced black enlisted men, and the characteristics and dangers of various ordnance, but speed versus safety became the real hot-button issue, with Captains Goss and Kinne going toe-to-toe with Captain Davis, Captain of the Port for the Port of San Francisco. Captain Davis reiterated for the court what he had told Goss in late October 1943. Worried about safety lapses at Port Chicago, Davis had informed Goss that if there was an accident, he would be held accountable.

When the court discovered that no Coast Guard observers were present on the night of the explosion, it pressed Captain Goss for an explanation. Goss did not attempt to conceal his contempt for either the Coast Guard personnel or representatives of Captain Davis's office. In his opinion they had little experience with loading operations—especially with wartime turnaround schedules—and were incapable of assuming even an advisory role.

The court also pressed Kinne regarding the posting of tonnage figures on the blackboard. Kinne responded that it was no different from displaying scores at the rifle range, dismissing the opinion of officers who contended that it encouraged an unhealthy spirit of competition. The court was not buying his explanation, and scolded Captain Kinne, contending that the "loading of explosives should never be a matter of competition."

On Monday, August 7, the day Percy Robinson was discharged from the Mare Island Hospital, a petty officer handed out work gloves to the 4th Division. What the men did not know was that Secretary Forrestal and Bureau of Personnel heads had decided that sending the seamen back to load was the "preferred method of preventing them from building up mental and emotional barriers which, if allowed to accumulate, become increasingly difficult to overcome." Surely they were also concerned about the upcoming Marine assault on Peleliu and MacArthur's plan to take Morotai. Other California depots, at Seal Beach, Fallbrook, and Long Beach, might be able to pick up the slack. Indian Island in Washington's Puget Sound might, too. The fact was, however, that much of the ordnance for Morotai and Peleliu had already been shipped from depots across the country to Mare Island. Rerouting those boxcars to other depots would take time.

On August 8 the ammunition carrier USS *Sangay* docked at Mare Island's Pier 34 East and was rigged for loading. Her holds were empty.

The following morning, Wednesday, August 9, just twenty-three days after the explosion at Port Chicago, the men of the 4th Division were ordered to fall in. The petty officers called muster, and then Joe Small marched the division off, as he always did, at sixty-two steps per minute. When the division reached a juncture in the road, Lieutenant Delucchi, who had survived the explosion, gave the command "Column left."

Every man in the division had been hoping that Delucchi would order them to march right, in the direction of the parade ground. To the left rested the ferry, the *Oakland,* that would take them across the Napa River to the Mare Island loading dock, where they would load ships as if the explosion never happened. Now they knew that nothing was going to change. Delucchi would send them back to work and was going to push them as he always had.

Percy Robinson stopped dead in his tracks. In the hospital he had formally requested a survivor's leave. When it was denied, he made up his mind that he would never load ships again.

When Delucchi shouted, "Forward march—column left!" for a second time, not a soul moved.

Delucchi stomped off to the administration building to report to the personnel officer at Mare Island that his division had "refused to obey his lawful order." In turn, the personnel officer called Lieutenant Commander Charles Bridges, Mare Island Naval Barracks' executive officer, who informed Lieutenant Delucchi that he was again to give his men the order to load. Then Lieutenant Commander Bridges found Commander Joseph Tobin, head of the Mare Island Naval Barracks, who was in a meeting with Captain Goss. Tobin had given the division heads the original order to begin loading the *Sangay.* Together Bridges and Tobin made their way to the parade ground.

Meanwhile, an officer climbed up to the platform on the parade ground and called out Joe Small.

"Front and center," he said. All eyes were on Small as he walked to the platform.

"Are you going back to work?" the officer asked.

"No, sir," he answered.

"Why not?"

Small answered that he was afraid.

Then another seaman shouted from the ranks, "If Small don't go, we're not going, either." Whether Small wanted it or not, the men were now looking to him for leadership.

At 11:40 a.m., Commander Tobin and Lieutenant Commander Bridges arrived, and Tobin talked with Lieutenant Commander Jefferson Flowers, the base chaplain, and asked him if he could speak with the men.

At noon, Lieutenant Commander Flowers addressed the seamen in front of their barracks. When Flowers walked up, the men were milling around, talking among themselves, obviously frightened and confused.

"Gather round me," he said. "What's the trouble?"

Percy Robinson and a number of others spoke up. "We don't want to load ammunition. We're scared."

Lieutenant Commander Flowers tried to be gentle but matter-of-fact and told them that they did not have a choice; it was their duty, and failure to do that duty meant dire consequences, likely a court-martial.

Flowers could see that the men were not persuaded, so he tried a different tack, appealing to their "race pride," telling them that they were "letting down the loyal men of their race" and abandoning the men overseas whose lives depended on the ammunition they refused to load.

Percy Robinson saw right through the chaplain. He was trying to shame them into going back to work, but the seamen "stood tall and strong." They would obey any other order, but they would not go back to toting bombs.

Chaplain Flowers then told them that he, too, was afraid of ammunition, but that he and the other officers would go down to the ship with them and would remain there while they loaded. He was grasping at straws now. The men knew that the offer was a ruse; the officers would come down and then they would leave as soon as they could. They had seen it before.

Recognizing that he had "exhausted his arguments," Lieutenant Commander Flowers reported back to Commander Tobin, adding that he believed that in private some of the men would agree to go back to work.

Two petty officers again assembled the men on the parade ground. They were standing there when Lieutenant Delucchi ascended the platform. "We have never had any trouble like this," he said. "You are letting your people down. Besides, you took an oath to obey orders." Delucchi reminded them that there were many people fighting for the Negro cause who might withdraw their support if they found out how the seamen were acting.

At 1:00 p.m., the seamen were ushered into the recreation hall, where Commander Tobin and Lieutenant Commander Bridges hoped to interview them one by one about why they would not load ammunition. Delucchi and Flowers also participated in the interviews. By the end of the day they had only questioned a small portion of the men in the division.

Lieutenant Carleton Morehouse, commanding officer of Division No. 8, was up against much the same. Having assembled his men, he ordered them to go to work. His division then became, in his words, a "milling, talking mob." Thirty minutes later he mustered the division on the base's outdoor basketball courts and asked each man to step forward in alphabetical order. "I order you to load with me," he said to each of them. "You may answer yes or no. Think carefully. A no means severe disciplinary action. Will you load with me? Yes or no?" Ultimately, 87 out of 110 refused.

Meanwhile, Lieutenant James Tobin was en route with his Division No. 2 to Mare Island from Port Chicago. Earlier he had ordered the division members to pack their seabags, inspect the barracks, and prepare to load ships when they arrived at their destination.

Tobin and his men reached the base an hour and a half later, whereupon Tobin was informed that there had been a "mass refusal of duty" by two other divisions. The lieutenant then lined up his division.

"Many from the other divisions have refused to obey orders," he told them. "Refusal to obey orders in a time of war is a serious offense. You have been told that we came here to resume our regularly assigned duty of loading ships. I know some of you are afraid, but fear can be conquered. Fear is no excuse for disobeying orders. I am ordering you men to 'turn to' for the purpose of carrying out your regularly assigned duty of loading ships. Those men obeying this order, stand fast, those men refusing to obey this order, fall out!" Then he added, "All cowards, fall out!"

When half his division moved off to one side he addressed the group, reminding the men of the seriousness of their actions. Lieutenant Clement, the assistant division officer, recorded in a notebook the names of those who would not return to work. Many of them made it clear that although they did not wish to disobey an order, they were afraid of handling ammunition.

That night the men from Divisions 2, 4, and 8 who refused to load ammunition—258 out of a total 328—were declared "prisoners-at-large" and were marched under guard and confined to barracks aboard an old barge tied to the pier.

For Carl Tuggle, the Cincinnatian who came to the Great Lakes Naval Training Center with a dream of becoming an aviation mechanic, only to have that dream extinguished by the reality of Port Chicago, his objection to handling ammunition again was less about fear than disrespect. In the wake of the explosion he had hoped that perhaps the Navy would change the way it treated blacks. Now he realized that he was hoping for a miracle.

The barge was cramped and stifling, with three tiers of bunks, spaced no more than a foot apart. To Percy Robinson, one of those who refused to handle ammunition, the barge felt like a slave ship.

Nearly everyone aboard was scared, confused, and angry. Some wanted to go back to work, while others grabbed butter knives and forks to defend themselves in case things grew violent. The majority, though, felt that there was power in numbers and wanted to stick together.

On the morning of August 10, a fracas broke out between a guard and an enlisted man. As the day wore on, tempers flared and fights erupted. Joe Small tried to bring order to the barge and cohesion to the group, but it was no easy task. Things were growing increasingly volatile. Small foresaw the worst—the men might riot and guards might turn their rifles on them.

That night Small and a handful of group leaders met on the upper deck of the barge to calm what he called the "general state of rebellion." Although Small did most of the talking, he was hardly the picture of an insurgent. Small encouraged the men to be on their best behavior, to act like proud and disciplined Navy seamen, and to show the officers that they were willing to obey any order short of loading ammunition. Perhaps then they might be transferred to other duties, or sent overseas, or at the very least receive dishonorable discharges. On a practical level, he organized meal-hall teams to cook, serve, and clean.

When Small finished his impromptu speech, some of the men, including Percy Robinson and George Booth, gave him an ovation. A leader was what they had needed, and now Small confidently assumed the role.

On August 11, the day after the meeting, guards ordered the men off the barge and marched them to the base's baseball diamond. They were standing in formation as a jeep carrying Rear Admiral Wright drove up.

The admiral had only just received Captain Goss's report on the situation. Ever paranoid about the influence of conspirators, Goss insisted that "agitators and ringleaders" who had been exposed to "outside propaganda" and union organizers had instigated the rebellion to seduce the seamen from their proper allegiance and advance a radical black and socialist agenda. According to him, the men involved had previously been compliant, exhibiting "the normal characteristics of negroes," but had recently shown a "persistent disposition to question orders."

When Percy Robinson spotted Wright, he knew that things had gone from bad to worse. In the days after the explosion Wright had come to Port Chicago to praise the men. Now he was paying them a visit of a different sort.

"They tell me that some of you men want to go to sea," the

admiral began. "I believe that's a goddamn lie! I don't believe that any of you have enough guts to go to sea. I handled ammunition for approximately thirty years and I'm still here. I have a healthy respect for ammunition; anybody who doesn't is crazy. But I want to remind you men that mutinous conduct in time of war carries the death sentence, and the hazards of facing a firing squad are far greater than the hazards of handling ammunition."

"Like hell!" George Booth shouted out from the crowd of men. Wright was bluffing. No way he could have over two hundred men shot dead. Wright heard the remark and reiterated his threat. "I will personally see to it," he countered.

The admiral's words struck Percy Robinson like a hard blow to the belly. He remembered his mother's warning: "Don't let the white man lynch you. He will lynch you if he can." Now, here was the admiral fulfilling his mother's prophecy.

The ultimatum devastated everyone present. Could they really be staring at the possibility of death by firing squad, or was Wright trying to intimidate them? Percy Robinson had been willing, if need be, to go to jail to get a change of duty, but now he was scared.

The admiral left and Lieutenants Delucchi, Tobin, and Morehouse instructed the men to divide themselves into those willing to handle ammunition and those who would not. Some moved back and forth between the two groups, aware that this one decision might determine the course of their lives.

After what seemed like hours of agony, the lines were finally drawn. The entire 8th Division, which was largely made up of graduates recently delivered from the Great Lakes Naval Training Center in Illinois, indicated that it would be willing to return to work. George Booth and Percy Robinson joined those willing to work, too. Robinson saw that some of his friends were standing their ground, but he did not feel a sense of responsibility to them. One thing he had learned from his father was that every man had to take care of himself. Only a total of forty-four men in Divisions 2 and 4 still refused to load ammunition. The following day, six more joined the forty-four, making a total of fifty. Inexplicably, John Dunn, a seventeen-year-old mess cook in Division No. 2, and Charles Hazard got thrown in with the group. A Port Chicago Naval Ammunition Depot doctor had declared months before that Dunn, five feet two and just 104 pounds, was "too light to work" and Dunn had never done any loading of any kind. Hazard was a soft-spoken chaplain's assistant.

On August 12, Marine guards took the fifty men to Camp Shoemaker and put them in the brig. As the alleged leader of the group, Joe Small was separated from the group and thrown into the "hole." If any punishment could break Small, perhaps solitary confinement could. He was confined to a seven-by-seven-foot cell with no human contact except the prison guards. He would be allowed to leave the cell only one hour a day to stretch.

For the 208 men who, faced with the possibility of a death sentence, decided that they would be willing to load ships, it was too late. They were informed that they would receive summary courts-martial and then would be taken to the naval stockade at Camp Shoemaker.

On August 13, Commander Joseph Tobin signed Percy Robinson's court-martial. The specification of offense, like the others, was straightforward. It read: "In that Percy Robinson, seaman first class . . . U.S. Naval Reserve, while so serving at the U.S. Naval Barracks, Naval Ammunition Depot, Mare Island, California, having on or about August 9, 1944, at said barracks, did then and there refuse to obey and did willfully disobey said lawful order, the United States then being in a state of war."

If Robinson hoped that the Navy would go easy on him and the 207 other men, the stockade extinguished those hopes. The men were given coveralls with a big *P* on them. Then guards marched them to the South Prison. Surrounded by ten-foot-high fences of barbed wire and gun towers at twenty-foot intervals, and patrolled by a jeep with a mounted machine gun, it looked to Percy like an internment camp. The Navy could let them rot there, and no one would ever know.

While they waited to hear what their further punishment might be, guards marched them to the administration building, where Navy officers interrogated them about their roles in the so-called uprising. In violation of Navy law, none of the men was allowed to consult an attorney. Because armed guards were present during the questioning, many of the seamen felt threatened.

During the interrogations the men were encouraged to implicate the leaders of the protest, especially Joe Small. Wielding sentences of fifteen years' hard labor and bad-conduct discharges, Navy officers pressed the men for answers. What the investigators wanted more than anything else were the details of the meeting on the barge. From the day Percy Robinson arrived at Port Chicago, the officers had been using the same tactic—trying to pit one black man against another. They would choose their Uncle Toms, pile on the praise and the liberty privileges, and then ask them to rat out other seamen. Some of the informants just made things up because officers told them that the Navy would "go lighter and easier" on them if they did. The lieutenant who questioned Percy Robinson asked him repeatedly if he had been subjected to coercion. Robinson gave him the same answer every time: no one had forced him into anything. Others, however, seeking to save their own hides, were happy to scapegoat Joe Small. Some said that during his speech on the barge, Small had grown feisty. "We've got the officers by the balls," some of the seamen recalled hearing him say. "If we stick together, they can't do anything to us."

In the end, interrogators prepared individual statements, based on the testimonies of the seamen, and insisted that they sign them. Some of the seamen protested that their words had been twisted, but most eventually gave in. Days later, Robinson and the others learned that they would each be fined $198—a fortune for most of them—and sentenced to three months' hard labor.

Captain Goss had already delivered his report on the "mutinous action" to Admiral Wright. After describing the events of mid-August, he informed the admiral that steps were being taken to recommend the fifty seamen for a general court-martial. Wright promptly forwarded Goss's summary to Secretary of the Navy James Forrestal and the chiefs of Naval Personnel and Naval Operations. He included two and a half pages of remarks, adding that "pains must be taken to ensure that there is no justification for an opinion that any type of hazardous work is assigned exclusively to negro personnel." He further added, "It is necessary that there be set up a system of rotation of duty that will ensure that Negro enlisted personnel at the Naval Ammunition Depot, Mare Island and the Naval Magazine, Port Chicago, be not retained indefinitely."

On August 26, even before the court of inquiry released its findings and recommendations, Vice Admiral Randall Jacobs, chief of Naval Personnel, wrote Secretary Forrestal that the Bureau of Personnel "concurred with the disciplinary action to be taken." Following Admiral Wright's suggestion, Secretary Forrestal authorized the transfer of white loading units to both Mare Island and Port Chicago in order to "avoid any semblance of discrimination against Negroes."

Secretary Forrestal also sent President Roosevelt a report on the situation. Two days later, Roosevelt responded. Borrowing the phrase used by Admiral Wright to describe the situation at Mare Island, Roosevelt agreed that the 208 men "were activated by mass fear" and should be treated leniently. He failed, however, to say anything about the fifty men who persisted in their refusal to handle ammunition, although they, too, were certainly motivated by the same fear. This omission, whether deliberate or unintentional, undoubtedly helped to seal their fate.

By late August the naval court of inquiry was ready to deliver its final report on the explosion. The *San Francisco Chronicle* had already weighed in on the disaster, which it called "the worst disaster of its kind in the American record." "What caused the explosion," the editorial continued, "is to date a mystery that may never be known. It is a sort of thing that can happen in an operation with highly dangerous materials in such a volume as occurs only in war, under the pressure of war and with hasty expansion of personnel in both production and handling."

The blast, however, was too big for the Navy court not to try to assess some measure of blame, and in the end, it placed responsibility squarely on the shoulders of the black seamen. "The consensus of opinion of the witnesses," it announced, "is that the colored enlisted personnel are neither temperamentally or intellectually capable of handling high explosives . . . sixty percent of the lowest intellectual strata of men sent out of Great Lakes were sent to Port Chicago. These men could not understand the orders which were given to them and the only way they could be made to understand what they should do was by actual demonstrations. . . . It is an admitted fact, supported by the testimony of the witnesses, that there was rough and careless handling of the explosives being loaded aboard ships at Port Chicago."

Although it did cite a "general failure to foresee and prepare for the tremendous increase in explosives shipments," the comment was more of an observation than an indictment of the Navy Bureau of Ordnance, the Bureau of Personnel, or Port Chicago's leadership. In fact, no mention was made of the officers' role in the disaster. Their carelessness and silence went largely unaddressed. Port Chicago's regulations stated that if an officer was concerned about safety or observed the "rough and careless handling of explosives" or the buildup of ordnance on the pier, his obligation was to shut down the loading process. In practice, however, no one attempted to enforce the rule.

Rather than criticize the depot's officers, the report, in fact, commended them for working "loyally, conscientiously, intelligently, and effectively to make themselves competent officers and to solve the problem of loading ships safely with the men provided." It stated further that "a very sustained and vigorous effort was made to train these men [the black seamen] in the proper handling of munitions."

On other matters, the findings of the court were patently false. The report claimed that "there was no unnecessary concentration of explosives or personnel on the pier at the time of the explosion." It also maintained that "the loading procedures and the gear used at Port Chicago were safe and in accordance with standard naval practice and did not violate naval safety precautions." The report said nothing about Captain Kinne's board, despite chiding him during the investigation for encouraging competition among the divisions. The court went on to argue that "the few practices . . . which were contrary to the Coast Guard shiploading regulations were not dangerous and did not increase the hazards."

Nowhere did it mention the ongoing battle between Captains Goss and Kinne and the Coast Guard over the observance of safety regulations and who should enforce them. Nor did the court address Goss's decision to remove Coast Guard observers from the pier, though it was certainly aware that the various shipbuilding yards that dotted the Bay Area had good safety records. Their records could be attributed not only to the excellent training the workers received under the guidelines of the Maritime Commission, but also to the Coast Guard inspectors who were stationed at each yard. Although the explosion undoubtedly tarnished the careers of Captains Goss and Kinne, the two officers escaped without any sort of punishment or formal reprimand.

The same could not be said of the fifty seamen. Just days after the court of inquiry released its statement, a legal officer showed up at Camp Shoemaker. He told the seamen, "You failed to obey orders, that's mutiny and is about the same as looking down a gun barrel."

# CHAPTER 36

# Proving Mutiny

In early September 1944, Admiral Wright formally accused Joe Small and the forty-nine other seamen of "having conspired each with the other to mutiny against the lawful authority of their superior naval officers duly set over them, by refusing to work in the operation of loading ammunition aboard ships and unloading ammunition from ships, did, on or about 11 August 1944, at said Naval Barracks, make a mutiny . . . in that they . . . did then and there willfully, concertedly and persistently disobey, disregard and defy [a] lawful order [to work] with a deliberate purpose and intent to override superior military authority; the United States then being in a state of war." Adriral Wright reiterated what he had told the men before: To be convicted of mutiny during wartime carried the maximum penalty of death by firing squad.

Next, Wright appointed a seven-member general court-martial, comprised of senior naval officers, with the distinguished Rear Admiral Hugo Osterhaus, a career officer and winner of the Navy Cross in World War I, at its head. In the military tradition, Osterhaus would act as both judge and jury and was assigned his own attorney to help him interpret and enforce Navy law. Judge advocate Lieutenant Commander James Coakley took the helm of the prosecution team. Coakley was a former Alameda County, California, assistant district attorney under Governor Earl Warren, and was a supporter of Republican presidential candidate Thomas Dewey. Short and nearly bald, Coakley was not a physically imposing man. But he had a forceful, exacting nature that he would display throughout the course of the trial. Lieutenant Gerald Veltmann led the defense. A tall, lean Texan with a pronounced drawl, Veltmann was under no illusions about the seriousness of the charge of "making a mutiny" or the Navy's intention to prosecute the case as aggressively and publicly as possible. He was literally fighting for the seamen's lives.

Historically the Navy had fiercely guarded its reputation, hushing up incidents of rebellion because of their implication of failed authority. Near the end of World War I, thirteen seamen aboard a cargo ship, the USS *Robert M. Thompson,* assembled to protest the ship's living conditions. When an ensign ordered them to go belowdecks, they refused and were accused of mutiny. When the ship reached the Brooklyn Navy Yard and the case went to trial, however, no mention was made of mutiny. The men were charged with nothing more than disobedience.

But now, curiously, the Navy's public-affairs arm was doing everything in its power to promote the case to newspapers, distributing photographs of the men and describing it as the largest mass trial in the history of the Navy and the first of its kind during World War II. Although it was wartime, the Navy opened the trial to the public. Perhaps it was eager to showcase what it hoped would be the propriety and transparency of its judicial methods. Maybe, too, it wanted to prove that its resistance to integration had been justified. Black sailors, like the ones at Port Chicago, could not be trusted. Their carelessness had led to the worst home-front disaster of World War II. Following that tragedy, they had willfully committed an unthinkable act of mutiny during a time of war.

Lieutenant Veltmann's pretrial strategy was to assign to himself and each of his four attorneys ten of the defendants. Each attorney would conduct detailed interviews and, based on those interviews, prepare a defense. After questioning each man, Veltmann and his team seized upon a defensive strategy that they believed could derail the trial before it even began. In his "Objection of Accused to Charge and the Specification," Veltmann cited the definition of mutiny from *Winthrop's Military Law and Precedents* and asked to have the charges dismissed on the grounds that the men had not conspired together to "usurp, subvert or override superior military authority." He conceded that although they might have disobeyed an order, their conduct did not amount to what *Winthrop* called "the gravest and most criminal of the offenses known to the military code." Theirs was a case of "dereliction of duty" since their intention was not to seize command from their superior officers—the "essential element" of mutiny, as defined by *Winthrop*.

Veltmann believed that the refusal to obey an order, even by a group of men, was not always the same as a conspiracy to overthrow and seize control. Winthrop called these incidents "disorders." In his opinion they did not "constitute in general the legal offense of mutiny." Winthrop added further that it was the intent that distinguished mutiny from other offenses with which it had often been confused.

Meanwhile, Lieutenant Commander Coakley argued that historically the mere act of insubordination—"murmurings and mutterings"—absent any violence, had sometimes been considered enough to warrant mutiny charges. He pointed out that in 1923, with the publication of *Naval Courts and Boards,* the Navy, in fact, had attempted to broaden the definition of what constituted a mutinous offense.

Understanding that the definition of mutiny was conditional and based on the shifting sands of circumstance, Coakley opposed Veltmann's brief with a brief of his own, stating, "Evidence showing a joint, collective and persistent refusal by two or more men in the military or naval service to work after a lawful order to do so, or what might commonly be called a 'strike' by a group of military or naval personnel, constitutes sufficient proof of conspiracy to subvert or override military authority and consequently sufficient proof under the law of the charge of making a mutiny." What Coakley was saying was that the required motive was implicit in the men's disobedience.

Admiral Osterhaus's court agreed. Refusal to work might be termed a "strike" in the civilian world, but in the military those same actions were evidence of mutiny. Although the burden of proof rested with Coakley, the court had made it clear that the prosecution simply had to prove that the men had engaged in a conspiracy to strike, which implied a desire to mutiny. It was a generous ruling that clearly favored Coakley's team.

Although it was billed as the largest mutiny trial in U.S. history, when it opened at 10:00 a.m. on Thursday, September 14, it took place in a small, unassuming Marine barracks building, which had been hurriedly converted into a courtroom, on Yerba Buena Island. Situated in the middle of San Francisco Bay, the 100-acre island with its steep and rocky shores and scent of eucalyptus commanded million-dollar views of Oakland and the tawny colored hills of the East Bay. To the west it looked out on the city of San Francisco and the Golden Gate Bridge. At Mare Island to the north, the bustle of war continued. Men were still loading Liberty ships, which would steam their way across the Pacific, where American forces awaited their precious cargoes. In the western Caroline Islands the 1st Marine Division would soon be locked in a bitter battle for the island of Peleliu, and off the northwest coast of New Guinea, General MacArthur's forces (along with Australian troops) would soon invade the island of Morotai, which the general needed as a base for the liberation of the Philippines.

In the stuffy barracks building, the defense and prosecution teams sat in straight-backed chairs at tables cluttered with papers and books. The fifty seamen sat shoulder-to-shoulder against a drab wall behind Lieutenant Veltmann and the defense team and to the right of the court. Each seaman wore his undress blues—standard-issue black shoes, straight-leg wool trousers, and a blue, V-neck jumper with a white T-shirt underneath. Despite the open window at the back of the barracks, they were hot and nervous and wanted to fidget, but Lieutenant Veltmann's defense team had counseled them to project a positive image and to be as calm and courteous as they could. If the court was struck by anything, it was the size and age of the seamen. Barely five feet, six inches tall and not much over twenty years old, many of them still looked like boys.

One by one the defendants came before the court to be arraigned. Without hesitation, all registered pleas of not guilty, including Joe Small, whose time in the hole had not weakened his resolve.

Later that morning, Lieutenant Commander James Coakley called to the stand his first witness—Commander Joseph Tobin, head of the Ryder Street Naval Barracks. The Commander had been on hand almost from the beginning of the dispute. Shortly after being alerted to the problem by Lieutenant Commander Charles Bridges, Mare Island's executive officer, Tobin left his office and hustled down to the parade ground. It was Tobin who, hoping to avert more trouble, had asked Chaplain Flowers to talk to the men.

Coakley asked the commander to recite for the court the events of August 9. Veltmann objected often to the commander's testimony. When Coakley finished, Veltmann moved to have Tobin's testimony struck from the record because he could not identify by sight most of the men implicated in the alleged mutiny. Osterhaus overruled the objection.

Under cross-examination after the lunch recess, Lieutenant Veltmann skillfully attempted to dismantle Coakley's conspiracy case by getting Tobin to admit that he had only interviewed twenty-four of the so-called mutineers—none of whom he could identify in court—and that none had expressed a desire to seize command of anything. Although Tobin was the one who had recommended the court-martial, he acknowledged that he had given a formal work order to only six or seven of the seamen, and those men were quiet and respectful.

Following Tobin's testimony, Coakley called Lieutenant Delucchi to the stand. Since Delucchi's Division No. 4 was at the heart of the demonstration, Coakley saw him as his ace in the hole, and the vindictive lieutenant was happy to comply. Delucchi wanted nothing more than to pin the crime of mutiny on the fifty men. He strode to the front of the court. When asked to identify the men from his division, the lieutenant pointed to twenty-five of the fifty sailors seated against

the wall. Then he proceeded to tell how on August 9 he had heard
some of the men from Division No. 8 make a threatening remark.

"And what was that remark?" Coakley asked.

"Don't go to work for the white motherfuckers," Delucchi replied. If the reporters in the audience wanted a bombshell article, here
it was. Delucchi was implying that a potentially violent conspiracy
to subvert the authority of the officers was hatched that morning.
It began with Delucchi's 4th Division, but quickly spread to the 8th
Division.

Veltmann was furious. As a former prosecutor, Coakley should
have known that Delucchi's remark was hearsay and inadmissible as
evidence. At the time, Lieutenant Delucchi had been standing with his
back to the 8th Division. Could he really identify the man, or men,
who uttered the words? Veltmann also pointed out that every member
of the 8th Division had gone back to work.

Coakley jumped in, arguing that just because Delucchi could not
pick out the men, did not mean that the threat had not been made.
The lieutenant was testifying under oath that he had heard the words
"Don't go to work for the white motherfuckers." Admiral Osterhaus
sided with the prosecution, overruling Veltmann's objection, as he
would time and again throughout the course of Delucchi's testimony.

On Friday, September 15, the court-martial's second day, page one
of the San Francisco Examiner captured the significance of the trial.
The headline read, MUTINY TRIAL OF 50 MARE IS. SAILORS OPENS. The
article continued, "With death the maximum penalty under the law,
the Navy yesterday opened court-martial proceedings here against
fifty Negroes charged with mutiny for refusing to handle ammunition
in the loading of a naval vessel. It marked the first time in American naval history that so many defendants had been simultaneously
tried during a single courtmartial, and records similarly failed to dis-
close a formal American Navy courtmartial in which mutiny was the
charge."

At Yerba Buena Island, Lieutenant Commander Coakley and Lieutenant Veltmann debated whether or not declarations made by one
member of an alleged conspiracy are admissible against all members

of a conspiracy. If, for instance, one man said, "Don't go to work for the white motherfuckers," was he speaking for the group? Did that statement reflect the feelings of everyone, or just the man who uttered it? It was a battle that the defense did not want to lose.

Reinvigorated by a night of rest, Veltmann again took up the issue of Lieutenant Delucchi's September 14 testimony. "Sir," he said, addressing Admiral Osterhaus, "a statement that applies to a particular accused cannot possibly apply to all the accused. I again ask that Lieutenant Delucchi's comments be stricken from the record. Only the lieutenant's comments regarding the men he had personally ordered to load ammunition are relevant."

Judge Advocate Coakley then asserted that the testimony was admissible as part of *res gestae* (a Latin phrase meaning "things done"), which established exceptions to the rule against hearsay evidence. Coakley argued that Lieutenant Delucchi could not have misunderstood the meaning of "Don't go to work for the white motherfuckers," or the speaker's intentions. It was reasonable to assume that whoever uttered the words was speaking for the group.

Coakley and Veltmann then argued back and forth about what the charge was. Was it the defense's responsibility to defend the seamen against the charge of "making a mutiny" or "*conspiring* to make a mutiny"? Finally, Admiral Osterhaus got fed up with the legal jousting and ordered the court to be cleared.

When the trial resumed, Osterhaus ruled against Veltmann's objection to strike Lieutenant Delucchi's remarks from the court record, although he did allow for the possibility that they might be removed upon conclusion of the prosecution's case. It was a clear triumph for the prosecution that would profoundly affect the course of the trial.

When Delucchi returned to the stand that morning, he testified that after Admiral Wright's speech of August 11, he had walked over to his division just as the men were absorbing the full impact of the admiral's words. That was when he heard someone seethe, "The motherfuckers won't do anything to us; they are scared of us." Then another man chimed in, "Let's run over the motherfuckers."

The fifty defendants looked on stolidly, but Lieutenant Veltmann, fed up with Delucchi's testimony, interrupted. Lieutenant Delucchi, he said, was again quoting anonymous speakers who were not part of the trial and, therefore, not part of the alleged conspiracy. The prosecution's intention was obvious. By repeatedly mentioning the statements, he hoped to portray the seamen as crude and undisciplined in addition to being rebellious, and prejudice the court against them. Veltmann was again overruled.

If Veltmann resented the admiral's decision, he took his anger out on Lieutenant Delucchi during an hour of cross-examination, interrogating the lieutenant about every aspect of the alleged mutiny, pressing him for exact answers, and forcing the lieutenant to choose his words with extreme care.

At 10:00 a.m. the following day, when the court reconvened, Lieutenant Commander Coakley called Lieutenant Commander Charles Bridges, Mare Island's executive officer, to the witness stand. Bridges testified that he had ordered the men back to work. During his brief cross-examination of the witness, Lieutenant Veltmann established that, from where he was sitting, Bridges could not identify any of the fifty seamen as men whom either he or Commander Tobin had ordered back to work. At Admiral Osterhaus's urging, Commander Bridges left the witness stand to get a better look at the men. He approached them reluctantly, making a pretense of studying the men, aware that even up close he would not be able to recognize any of them. A number of them were clearly older than the others, but beyond that, they all looked the same in their undress blues.

When the commander returned to his seat, Veltmann asked him if he had given a "personal order for them to go to work."

"That is correct," Bridges answered.

Now Veltmann seized his opportunity. "Can you identify any of the men in this group of fifty that you ordered to go to work?"

"No, I cannot," responded the commander.

Under cross-examination, Bridges also admitted that although he was just ten to fifteen feet from the divisions when Admiral Wright made his speech, he had not heard the men make the vulgar remarks or the threats that Delucchi had mentioned. The first two days had gone poorly for the defense, but here was a glimmer of hope. If no one else had heard the remarks that Delucchi claimed he had, it would be hard for Coakley to maintain that the men were working themselves into a state of mutiny.

When the court met next on Monday morning, September 18, Chaplain Flowers took the stand. In contrast to Lieutenant Delucchi's depiction of the seamen, Lieutenant Flowers, a South Carolinian who had been at Mare Island since the spring of 1943, described them as frightened but resolute, respectful, and "close-mouthed." He also mentioned that a number of the men inquired about survivor's leave. In addition, Flowers testified that on August 9, after he described the fear that frontline soldiers in their foxholes must fear, the seamen responded, "You can fight back in that case, but you can't fight back . . . if it blows up." Flowers might have been paraphrasing, but the men's message was unmistakable: a man could defend himself against an enemy, but was powerless against an explosion like the one at Port Chicago. It was an issue of dignity for the seamen. They were willing to give their lives for their country, but they did not want to die as hapless victims.

Under cross-examination, Flowers also admitted that the men did not say, "I refuse to handle ammunition," but rather "I am afraid to handle ammunition." Veltmann was not just splitting hairs. The defense attorney's objective was clear: to prove the passivity of the seamen's resistance. Their intent was not to challenge or to usurp anyone's authority, but only to express their fear of working with explosives.

Over the next few days, Coakley examined (and Veltmann cross-examined) a handful of the black seamen who had agreed to go back to work. In a major victory for Lieutenant Commander Coakley, the court ruled that the prosecution could use as evidence the statements that the men made under duress to Navy-appointed interrogators. Coakley's tactic then was to furnish the witness with his signed statement, ostensibly to refresh his memory, and then to ask him leading questions based on it. Lieutenant Veltmann objected that the statements were inadmissible, arguing that the testimony should come from the witness and not from a piece of paper, but the court overruled.

On September 21, Seaman First Class Edward Stubblefield, a black petty officer with the 8th Division, testified that Joe Small had spoken to the men on August 10. Coakley asked the seaman to tell the court what Small had said. Stubblefield seemed uncertain of himself and how to answer the question. He told the court that Small had said that "the boys was in enough trouble" and should "obey the shore patrol and the officers," and that "if we stick together, they couldn't do anything with us [because] we had the officers by the ass."

Coakley could see that Stubblefield was not going to say anything more.

"What else, if anything, did he say at the time?" the lieutenant commander asked, noticeably frustrated with his witness.

Stubblefield again seemed confused. "Well, at that time I—after he got through making the speech I didn't hear them say anything else."

Coakley interrupted. "Now, just to refresh your recollection, I will call your attention to your signed statement," he said, and showed the statement to Stubblefield.

The seaman now realized what he had omitted. "Oh, yes," he said. "If any guys back out, [they] would beat them up."

Over the next few days, Coakley summoned to the witness stand a number of junior-grade lieutenants who had been on hand between August 9 and August 11, and a host of seamen, most who were from the 8th Division, which had agreed to go back to work. The prosecution's goal was to establish incontrovertible evidence for conspiracy by eliciting from them that a "no work" list had circulated around the barge; that some of them were threatened with physical violence if they did not sign the list; that a meeting in which the men were encouraged to stick together had taken place on the barge; and that the alleged rebellion had a ringleader in Joe Small.

What might have been the most emotional part of the four days of testimony came when Lieutenant Commander Coakley called Joseph Gray to the stand. The events of August 11 had divided the Gray brothers. A member of the 4th Division, Joseph Gray, like his brother Charles, also a 4th Division seaman, had signed, a "don't work" list aboard the barge. Sixty other men had signed the list, but after Admiral Wright's speech, Joseph Gray lost his nerve. The image of being shot before a firing squad was too much for him. Unlike his brother Charles, Joseph did not remain with those who would not load, and pleaded guilty to disobedience in the summary court-martial. In doing so, he deserted his brother. Now he was a prosecution witness in a trial in which his brother was one of the defendants.

Lieutenant Veltmann could tell that Gray was not a particularly responsive witness, so, when he cross-examined the seaman, he posed a number of basic questions. Could the "don't work" list, he asked, have said, "We, the undersigned men, don't want to handle ammunition"? Gray admitted that it could have. Then Veltmann asked him about his initial decision not to load ammunition, and Gray testified that no one had forced him to say no. It was a line of questioning that the defense had used with the other prosecution witnesses, attempting to prove that the seamen were motivated by fear and not by an insidious plan to wrest power from the hands of Mare Island's officers. Even in their petition, the seamen had tried to strike a compliant tone.

The following day, the *San Francisco Examiner*, reporting on the trial, focused not on the discrepancies in the seamen's testimony, but on Edward Stubblefield's accusation. The paper's headline read: THREAT TOLD AT SAILOR TRIAL: BEATING PROMISED FOES OF MUTINY.

On Friday, September 22, Lieutenant Commander Coakley, having finished with his arguments for the prosecution, prepared to turn over the courtroom to Lieutenant Veltmann, who would open his defense fully aware that Coakley had won some of the trial's biggest battles. Veltmann hoped to reverse that tide by calling to the stand each of the fifty defendants and allowing them to testify on their own behalf. The strategy was a dangerous one. How would the men hold up under what was sure to be aggressive interrogation? They would either come across as dedicated Navy men who, after the explosion, had become victims of fear, or Coakley would undermine their testimony during cross-examination, depicting them as subversives acting together to deliberately disobey a direct order.

The following day, Lieutenant Veltmann addressed the court regarding the hearsay evidence it had allowed into the record over his frequent objections. He noted that the judge advocate, without first having proved that a conspiracy existed, introduced the evidence of alleged co-conspirators, unidentified co-conspirators, and even more brazenly unidentified seamen who were not alleged to be part of the conspiracy. "I wish the record to show," Veltmann said, "that the defense wishes to reserve the right to submit in writing objections to the entire record when it is finally completed." The motion was granted, and at 11:15 the court adjourned.

On Tuesday, September 26, the defense called Division No. 2 Seaman Second Class Edward Longmire to the stand. In the immediate aftermath of the blast, Longmire had been transferred to Camp Stoneman. By late July, however, he was back at Port Chicago. On August 9 he was bused with the rest of his division from Port Chicago to Mare Island. Although no one had told the men why they were being moved, many guessed the reason: once again they would be loading ships. Only three weeks after the explosion, everyone was still traumatized. Upon arriving at Mare Island, they left the bus, mustered, and then Lieutenant James Tobin explained why they were there and asked them if they were planning to obey orders. When they hesitated, he told them to separate into two groups: those willing to load, and those unwilling. When Tobin spoke to Longmire, the seaman confessed that he was "afraid of ammunition." Tobin then instructed him to give his name to the assistant division head. Coakley's witnesses had said that some of the seamen had grown cocky and unruly and were congratulating those who were brave enough to submit their names. Longmire, however, contradicted their testimony. Their mood was anything but brash.

On the night of August 10, Longmire heard Joe Small speak aboard the barge. According to Longmire, the seamen were subdued, and a composed Small spoke but never said anything about "having the officers by the balls" or "the tail," as a number of prosecution witnesses, including petty officer Stubblefield, said he had. Instead Small cautioned the men, exhorting them "to watch their conduct and co-operate with the shore patrol officers." The meeting was brief, and at no time did Small or anyone else force Longmire to say that he would disobey orders. Unlike Stubblefield, Longmire depicted Small not as a ringleader, bullying the others into rebellion, but as a responsible and respected spokesman who encouraged the men to stay out of trouble.

In a deep Alabama drawl, Longmire also testified that after Admiral Wright's speech, he had tried to join the men who were willing to load ships, but was told by Lieutenant Tobin that it was too late for a change of heart. Afterward, he was taken to the stockade at Camp Shoemaker, where a lieutenant pressed him for details of the barge meeting. "If you want us to help you, you have got to help us," he said. "There is a side for the sheeps and a side for the goats." Longmire insisted that he did not have the kind of information the lieutenant wanted. He had not coerced anybody into not working, nor had he been coerced himself. After questioning him, the lieutenant read what he called Longmire's "statement." The seaman was taken aback. He had not said those things. When Longmire objected, the two got into a shouting match, and the officer informed him that he would not change a word.

When Veltmann asked the seaman if anyone had told him that he had to make a statement, Longmire answered, "No, sir, no one told me that I had to make a statement, but they put it to you so funny . . . anyway after they was talking about shooting I was afraid."

The day's most shocking testimony came from Ollie Green of the 4th Division, who had suffered multiple lacerations in the explosion and almost lost an eye. A thirty-seven-year-old Washington, D.C., native who had made his living before the Navy as a special delivery man and cardplayer, Green might have been the oldest seaman at Port Chicago. He was also one of Lieutenant Delucchi's favorites, a man who could be trusted to do a good day's work. Judge Advocate Coakley, however, was determined to break Green down, and hammered him about whether Lieutenant Delucchi had given him a direct order to load ammunition. Although Green had only a grammar school education, the lieutenant commander's tactics did not intimidate him.

At one point, Lieutenant Commander Coakley asked him, "And before you broke your wrist on the eighth of August, did you intend to say no if you were ordered to load ammunition?"

Green replied, "If I was ordered to, I would have had to load it."

Then Coakley said, "Answer the question, please. Before you broke your wrist on the eighth of August, did you intend to say no if you were ordered to load ammunition?"

Green was resolute. "If I was ordered to, I would have had to load it, sir."

Coakley persisted, "But—"

Green interrupted him: "I had never been *ordered* to load ammunition."

Green's claim that he had never been given a direct order might have sounded deceitful. But at the time Delucchi and the other officers might have deliberately avoided ordering the men to load out of fear for their careers in the event that they might have to go on record with the mutiny charge.

Coakley continued to grill the seaman, not about Delucchi, but this time about Chaplain Flowers. "You testified on direct examination that the chaplain asked you if you were going to work and that you said no."

Green corrected the lieutenant commander. "He asked me was I *willing* to go to work and I said no."

Angered by what he felt was Green's obstinacy, Coakley fired back, "You heard him testify that he gave you an order." Perhaps he thought that the seamen would not be bold enough to contradict a chaplain, but Green held his ground.

"No, sir," he responded. "The chaplain asked me was I willing to work and I told him, 'No, sir.' He didn't give me no order."

After Coakley realized that he could not break Green, he announced that he had no more questions. Admiral Osterhaus then asked the seaman if he had any comments before leaving the witness stand.

"I got a couple of things to say, sir," Green replied. "The reason I was afraid to go down and load ammunition [was because] them officers [were] . . . racing each division to see who put on the most tonnage, and I knowed the way they was handling ammunition, it was liable to go off again. If we didn't work fast . . . they wanted to put us in the brig."

No one had dared to say it. The naval court of inquiry had addressed the issue and arrived at the benign conclusion that the "loading of explosives should never be a matter of competition," but no one had come out and made the link between the constant pressure to move ships in and out of Port Chicago as fast as possible and the explosion. Green was accusing the officers of having precipitated the disaster.

In the courtroom there was silence, except for the sound of newspaper reporters scribbling in their notebooks. Green continued, "That is exactly the way—put it on fast; if we didn't put it on fast they want to put us in the brig. That is my reason for not going down there."

On Wednesday, September 27, one day after Ollie Green's testimony and nearly two weeks into the trial, Marine guards escorted Joe Small from solitary confinement at Camp Shoemaker to Yerba Buena Island, where he was called to the stand. Small was the witness that everyone was waiting for, especially Lieutenant Commander Coakley, who hoped to portray him during cross-examination as the chief agitator.

Small, like many of the men before him, testified that in the weeks after the blast the seamen were terrified. Many, like Douglas Anthony, one of the accused, who had suffered a concussion and had cuts on his legs, face, and also his left eye, were injured when the ships exploded. Others, like John Gipson and Charles Hazard, two of the fifty defendants, were forced to handle the mangled bodies. So the explosion was all they talked about. They prayed for survivor's leave and new assignments, even if those assignments involved loading ammunition somewhere else. They just wanted to put as much distance between themselves and Port Chicago as they could.

While being questioned by Lieutenant Veltmann, Small told of an incident that had happened at Camp Shoemaker before the seamen were transferred to Mare Island. It was after taps, and the barracks were dark, when one of the men dragged his bunk across the floor. To the men who had survived the Port Chicago blast, the rumble sounded like a precursor to another explosion. It woke them from their sleep and they scrambled for the door, tripping over bunks and banging their shins. When they realized that it was nothing more than a practical joke, they cursed the man. Some wanted to beat him. If Small had not stepped in, they might have made good on their threats.

Following the story, Lieutenant Veltmann questioned Small as he went through the events of August 9. After the men balked at the prospect of loading another ship and were interviewed in the recreation building, Small testified that Lieutenant Delucchi had him muster the men who were unwilling to work. The lieutenant then made it clear to Small that he and Ollie Green, Myrle Wylie, one of Percy Robinson's Hawks, and another seaman were in charge. They would have to make sure the men got their gear and made it to the barge. Once there, it was their job to maintain discipline. "Keep things straight," Delucchi told Small. If it seemed an odd order to be giving the ringleader of an alleged mutiny, Veltmann chose not to make an issue of it.

On the night of August 10, not long before taps, Small and a number of other men called a meeting on the lower deck of the barge. Under oath, Small testified that he told the men to knock off the rough stuff. Then he encouraged them to be on their best behavior, to obey the shore patrol guards so that white Marine guards would not be brought in. Then he urged them to "pull together."

Veltmann interrupted. "What did you mean by that?"

"I meant to pull together in keeping themselves straight," Small explained. "If one got off wrong, it was up to his shipmate, his pal, whoever it might be, to tell him to 'straighten up and fly right.'"

Veltmann again interjected. "In other words, you meant to keep order?" Veltmann's strategy was to show that Small had taken Lieutenant Delucchi's order seriously. Veltmann was taking a risk. To highlight Small's role as the primary speaker that night could be ruinous.

Next, Lieutenant Veltmann drew Small's attention to August 12, the day that he and the others were taken to Camp Shoemaker. Small was placed in solitary confinement and then interviewed by a lieutenant. At no point did the lieutenant reveal that he was drafting a statement. When he brought the copies in for him to sign, Small was surprised.

"Did you sign them?" Veltmann inquired, to which Small answered, "I did sign them, yes, sir."

"Why did you sign them?" Veltmann asked.

"Well," Small answered, "he told me to sign them. I was under orders from him; he just shoved them and said, 'Sign them,' and so I signed them."

Having achieved his goal of depicting Small as anything but uncooperative, Veltmann sat down at the defense table and turned over the courtroom to Lieutenant Commander Coakley. In an attempt to find discrepancies in Small's testimony, the judge advocate went over much the same ground as Veltmann. At times Coakley bordered on antagonistic, most especially when he was grilling Small about calling the meeting on the barge.

"Now, then," said Coakley, "you called it, didn't you?"

"Well, that's where all the petty officers come in," said Small. "One is as much to blame as the other."

Coakley then referred to Small's interrogation at Camp Shoemaker. "In that conversation . . . I will ask you whether or not these questions were asked of you and these answers given: 'Q. Who called the meeting? A. I did, sir. Q. How was the meeting called? A. I just went through the barge and asked all the men to gather on the lower deck.' Were these questions asked you and those answers given?"

Small paused. "Well, they were asked, but it wasn't exactly that way, that is not exactly the answer."

"Answer the question yes or no," said the lieutenant commander. "Either you did or you didn't."

When Lieutenant Veltmann objected, Coakley answered that he was "laying a foundation for impeachment," attempting to destroy Small's credibility as a witness.

"I will ask you again, when you were asked the question who called the meeting, did you say, 'I did, sir'?"

"I did," Small yielded. But then he added, "I had a part in calling it."

Osterhaus called for a lunch recess. After everyone returned to the courtroom, Coakley again bore down on Small, referring frequently to the statement he had made at Camp Shoemaker in order to highlight holes and half-truths in his testimony. It was a grueling cross-examination for both Small and Judge Advocate Coakley, but no matter how much the lieutenant commander hounded him, Small would not recant. He had not called the meeting in order to organize the men to take over the base. Nor had he or anyone else engaged in a conspiracy to undermine the authority of the officers at Mare Island.

As for the mutiny charge, Small testified that he and the others were well aware of what mutiny meant. The Great Lakes Naval Training Center required that all recruits, black and white alike, read the 1940 edition of the *Bluejackets' Manual*, which was the one used throughout World War II. Chapters Four and Five of that manual were devoted to "Rules and Regulations" and addressed issues related to misconduct and punishments.

After Small, Lieutenant Veltmann called upon a number of other witnesses to testify. Then he recalled Ollie Green to the stand. Admiral Osterhaus reminded the seaman that his oath was still binding. The only question that Veltmann asked Green was whether or not Lieutenant Delucchi had made him one of the bosses of the barge.

"Small and me and Willie Gray and Myrle Wylie," Green answered.

Then it was Lieutenant Coakley's turn. Green had frustrated the judge advocate earlier in the trial, and now that the seaman was back on the witness stand, Coakley seemed determined to exact some kind of revenge.

"By the way, Green," Coakley asked, "what was your occupation before you were drafted—you were drafted, weren't you?" The lieutenant commander was trying to impugn Green's character by insinuating that the seaman had no interest in serving until he was forced to by Uncle Sam.

"Yes, sir," Green replied.

Then Coakley asked again, "What was your occupation before you—"

But Veltmann cut him off; what Green did before the Navy was immaterial. When the court sustained Veltmann's objection, Coakley announced that he wanted to continue to pursue the same line of questioning. This time Osterhaus allowed it, and the lieutenant commander rephrased his questions. Green was evasive and uncharacteristically intimidated. Then, finally, he confessed that before entering the Navy he had "made a living on the game of chance."

Coakley saw his chance and, raising his voice, confronted the seaman. "Green, you were one of the leaders in this thing, weren't you? You were one of the leaders in this refusal of the men of the Fourth Division to work, weren't you?"

No one was more surprised by Coakley's outburst than Lieutenant Veltmann. It was more than the judge advocate trying to prejudice the court against the witness. Clearly things had become personal between him and Green.

On September 28 the two largest San Francisco daily papers, the *Chronicle* and the *Examiner,* ran articles on the trial. Under the headline ORGANIZED RESISTANCE TO ORDERS DENIED, the *Chronicle* concerned itself largely with Small's denial of having instigated a mutiny. The *Examiner* ran the headline TERROR TOLD IN MUTINY TRIAL. A story run by the *Chicago Defender* also focused on Small's story about the panic at Camp Shoemaker. The paper's correspondent, John Badger, wrote that Veltmann's key witness had painted a "vivid, terrifying picture of fear that gripped [the men] after the fatal Port Chicago blast."

• • •

Over the next few days, Veltmann questioned and Coakley cross-examined some of the defense witnesses. Veltmann succeeded in establishing that most of the defendants had signed the written statements prepared by the interrogators at Camp Shoemaker under stressful circumstances. Some felt that they had been forced to give their signatures against their will, while others maintained that the statements were only rough approximations of what they had really said. In a number of cases it had been Lieutenant Commander. Coakley who had recorded their admissions.

On Wednesday, October 4, Veltmann called Alphonso McPherson, a seaman in the 2nd Division, to the witness stand to testify about being interrogated at Camp Shoemaker. The nineteen-year-old McPherson was from Columbia, South Carolina, where he had been a model student and social club chairman of his high school. He loved sports, especially basketball, and liked to sing and play the piano. At Port Chicago his job was to handle ammunition and rig the winch booms. He was not a particularly good worker, though, and apparently had a wild streak that was often exacerbated by liquor. On April 21, 1943, he was charged for "disturbing the peace and assault on another person in the Navy with a dangerous weapon," for which he received a court-martial punishment of ten days' bread and water and a loss of pay in the amount of eighteen dollars.

Veltmann established that on the night of July 17, McPherson had been taken to the hospital, where he remained for ten days, to be treated for severe cuts to the head, leg, and feet. Afterward he was transferred to the Mare Island Barracks, where on August 9 he confessed to Lieutenant Tobin, head of the 2nd Division, that he was afraid to load ammunition again. On August 11, after the admiral's speech, he again told the lieutenant that he was afraid. Like Small and Green, he, too, was taken to Camp Shoemaker, where he was questioned by a lieutenant about the "don't work" list.

"I don't know nothing about no list," McPherson answered him.

"You better come clean," the lieutenant pressed him. Then he bluffed, "I know all about the meeting."

McPherson replied innocently, "Sounds like you know more about it than me."

Angered, the lieutenant called McPherson a "professional liar" and dismissed him.

Later he had the seaman brought back in by a Marine guard. "I am going to give you another chance, but if you don't come clean this time, I'm going to see that you get shot."

After relating the incident to the court, McPherson told Lieutenant Veltmann that another lieutenant had then entered the room. McPherson looked up and pointed at Judge Advocate Coakley; Coakley was the one who had come into the room. McPherson then described how Coakley also told him that if he did not cooperate, he would be shot.

# CHAPTER 37

# Putting the Navy on Trial

The trial had already attracted considerable national attention, but on Monday, October 9, the NAACP upped the ante. Sitting in the audience was Thurgood Marshall, chief counsel of the NAACP's Legal and Educational Defense Fund, and future Supreme Court justice. Marshall had just arrived by plane from New York on Navy priority, with permission from Secretary Forrestal to observe the trial. The NAACP's San Francisco branch, which had initially alerted the main office about the implications of the trial, had already briefed Marshall on the specifics: the men were up against a spurious mutiny charge, which the Navy intended to make stick. Although they may have been guilty of individual acts of insubordination, mutiny suggested a conspiracy of which the San Francisco office saw none.

Although his career was still young, by the time he arrived on Yerba Buena Island, Marshall had already argued a case before the Supreme Court. In 1940, in *Chambers v. Florida,* Marshall contended that the confessions of four black men who admitted that they had killed an elderly white man, a crime for which they were sentenced to death, had been compelled by the police and were therefore inadmissible as evidence. In a unanimous decision, delivered by Justice Hugo Black of Alabama, the Supreme Court agreed with Marshall and overturned the convictions.

Late in the day on October 9, following the trial, Marshall met with Veltmann and his defense team as well as the defendants. He was already suspicious of the mass mutiny charge, but when he discovered that a number of the men had been thrown in with the alleged mutineers against their will, he knew then that his instincts had been right. Others, he learned, had valid medical reasons for not loading. The interviews confirmed his belief that the Navy had chosen to try them not individually but as a group. Then it tried to link the men who had very little interaction with each other via a conspiracy charge. The number fifty had been chosen for its symbolism. Fifty black men conspiring to defy the authority of the Navy was memorable.

Although he had only attended the trial as a bystander, having witnessed the day's events, he was convinced of the defendants' innocence and was contemplating representing them. That evening he wrote Walter White, executive director of the NAACP, "Defense counsel are good and know what they are doing. Prosecutor is vicious and dumb. . . . Most of the accused testified that they told the lieutenant that they were willing to obey orders but that they were afraid of loading ammunition after the Port Chicago incident. . . . There is no evidence of mutiny and we should be able to beat this in the reviewing board."

The next day, October 10, Marshall held a press conference. Eager reporters awaited him. None of them had ever laid eyes on Marshall before, but they knew his reputation as an ardent defender of the civil rights of black people who was willing to do battle with the white establishment and was not afraid of using the law to promote social change.

At six feet two inches tall, Marshall towered over them, and the way he carried himself made him look even larger. "The men actually don't know what happened," he said, his voice slow and precise. "They were asked whether they would load and they replied that they were afraid. . . . They had no idea that verbal expression of their fear constituted mutiny. This is not an individual case," he challenged. "This is not fifty men on trial for mutiny. This is the Navy on trial for its whole vicious policy toward Negroes. Negroes are not afraid of anything any more than anyone else. Negroes in the Navy don't mind loading ammunition. They just want to know why they are the only ones doing the loading! They want to know why they are segregated; why they don't get promoted." On just his second day, Marshall had already seized upon the Jim Crow aspect of the case. It was an angle that Veltmann had either felt unprepared to address or, as a Navy officer, wanted to avoid. But it was a line of attack that Marshall was determined to pursue.

The following day, the *San Francisco Chronicle* put Marshall's accusation on page one. The headline read, PREJUDICE IS CHARGED IN MUTINY TRIAL.

Meanwhile, the National Negro Council pushed President Roosevelt to end discrimination against Negro members of the armed forces, "especially returning [black] veterans being banned from rest and redistribution centers . . . provided for all other soldiers."

By Tuesday, October 17, the day on which Lieutenant Commander Coakley summoned the first of his twenty-five rebuttal witnesses, Marshall began his campaign to discredit the Navy, insisting that the Navy formally investigate: "The policy of the Twelfth Naval District, which, with only a few minor exceptions, restricts the use of Negro seamen, regardless of their training and qualifications, to shore duty in the capacity of laborers and in segregated outfits; the inefficient and unsafe manner in which ammunition was handled at Port Chicago prior to the explosion, and the fact that Negroes working on it are given absolutely no kind of instruction or training in the proper handling of it; the inconsistent, haphazard and utterly unfair manner in which the fifty accused seamen now on trial for their lives were singled out from [other] men, whose actions with regard to the loading of ammunition after the Port Chicago explosion were identical in almost every respect to those of the fifty accused."

The following afternoon he continued his attack. "I want to know why," he said, "the Navy disregarded warnings by the San Francisco waterfront unions—before the Port Chicago disaster—that an explosion was inevitable if they persisted in using untrained seamen in the loading of ammunition. I want to know why the Navy disregarded an offer by these same unions to send experienced men to train Navy personnel in the safe handling of explosives. . . . I want to know why the commissioned officers at Port Chicago were allowed to race their men. I want to know why bets ranging from five dollars up were made between division officers as to whose crew would load more ammunition."

Just nine days after arriving on Yerba Buena Island, Thurgood Marshall was already looking at the bigger picture. By October 18, it was clear that he intended via the press to defend the fifty seamen and to put the entire Navy on trial.

# CHAPTER 38

# Punishing the Seamen

On Saturday, October 21, as the court-martial concluded, Judge Advocate Coakley began his closing argument. "In a trial of one or two days, much reviewing of the facts is not necessary. But in a case that has taken as long as this, I believe that [the closing] argument can be of considerable assistance. Rather than spend too much time arguing facts and attempting to impress the court with my views or interpretations of the evidence, I believe that I can be of more assistance by reviewing the evidence and recalling it to the court's attention. Now, the case might be generally divided into two phases: the events preceding 1100 on the ninth of August; and . . . the events which transpired from that time on."

Coakley then hammered home the points he had made time and again during the trial: The conspiracy was hatched in the days after the explosion, when the men who had survived the blast were taken to Camp Shoemaker. Gradually the notion picked up steam. Those who wavered were presented with an ultimatum: you're either with us or against us. In its second phase the rebellion became a reality when the seamen were ordered to load ammunition and they refused.

Although Admiral Wright convinced most of the men of the seriousness of their actions, fifty mutineers decided to defy the authority of
the Navy.

Coakley reviewed the evidence for the better part of two hours.
Before the court adjourned for lunch, he left it with this: "I submit . . .
that under the law applicable to this case, there is ample evidence to
sustain a conviction of all of these fifty men under the charge and
specification. . . . Collective insubordination, collective disobedience
of lawful orders of a superior officer, is mutiny. . . . A conspiracy to
disobey the lawful orders of a superior is mutiny. . . . You do not have
to prove in any conspiracy case that men actually got around a table
and agreed to commit a crime . . . men who conspire and confederate
together to commit crimes do it in such a way and under such circumstances that people don't see them doing it, and they do not shout it
from the housetops."

When the court reconvened, Coakley explored the terms *mutiny*
and *conspiracy* and for fifteen minutes explained why the allegations
in the case of the fifty seamen were appropriate. Before the court adjourned until Monday, October 23, Coakley concluded, "Here, we
have ample proof of a specific intent, a deliberate purpose to override
superior military authority."

On Monday, October 23, it was Lieutenant Veltmann's turn. Like
Coakley, the lieutenant began by defining a number of words: *mutiny,
usurp, subvert,* and *override.* Then he addressed the prosecution's witnesses and the contradictions in their testimonies. He called one of the
witnesses "the comic of the trial, glib of tongue and sharp of answer,"
and not at all credible. Why, he asked, were all but four of Lieutenant
Commander Coakley's seventeen enlisted witnesses from the 8th Division? Why did he avoid calling to the stand the seamen of the 2nd and
4th Divisions? The answer, Veltmann said, was clear: because the men
of the 4th Division would have "burst beyond repair the bubble of
conspiracy . . . and destroyed the fantasy of concert of action."

Veltmann argued that the seamen acted individually and without intent to conspire, and were motivated by "uncontrollable" fear.
Many of them were lucky to have escaped the blast with their lives.

Many had lost friends. Never before had they flinched about loading ammunition. These men, in other words, were not shirkers. Prior to the explosion, they were reliable and hardworking. But following the explosion, they were in a state of shock. "These fifty men," Veltmann pointed out, "had been at Port Chicago from three to twenty-five months . . . They had loaded ammunition, handling all types of explosives, large and small. . . . They were all subjected to the danger and uncertainty of that work without an opportunity to fight back. The repercussions from that catastrophe," he added, "linger in this court today—the damage wrought by that explosion is well known."

The lieutenant then painted a vivid image of the July 17 tragedy. "When you cannot see or hear the danger until after it bursts in your face, until after the flames envelop your surroundings, until after the concussion has shaken your world and wiped out the lives of your fellow workers without warning, when you see them picked up in baskets and pieces—an arm, a leg, or a head and shoulder—or you pick up the remnants of human bodies, as some of these men did, when you can't see your opponent you must fear him—fear him the more for the reason he can wipe your name from the slate of life with one sweep and you are powerless to resist his move."

Continuing, he said, "There was no scheming or plotting toward a conspiracy or mutiny. There was talk of ammunition at Shoemaker, so the prosecution insists—yes, there probably was, but there is no reliable, recorded evidence of the type of talk the prosecution would have you believe took place. . . . If there was conversation among the men, it must have been of the specific incident of the explosion . . . the fear that it imposed in the minds of the men. What would be more natural for these men . . . to exchange comments along these lines?"

Then he invited the members of the court to explore their own experiences. "Have you ever discussed with a friend, with whom you witnessed an unusual scene or accident, the details involved? Didn't you gentlemen, in fact, discuss with your acquaintances the explosion at Port Chicago? That is not conspiracy; that is not scheming; that does not provide the essential elements of mutiny or conspiracy. . . . The record shows that the state of the men at Shoemaker was free of contrivance, free of meetings, free of prearrangement. . . . And the record shows conclusively that the men of the fourth and fifth (formerly the second) divisions were at no time after the explosion, until and including the 9th of August, within immediate proximity of each other."

Regarding the varying testimony about whether or not the seamen had been given an order to load ammunition, Veltmann reiterated that even if such orders were given, "collective insubordination" did not constitute mutiny.

By many accounts, the defense's performance throughout the course of the trial had been excellent. Now, after thirty-two days of hearings, and after delivering a final, impassioned appeal for the innocence of the fifty seamen, Lieutenant Veltmann put their futures in the hands of the court.

Walter McDonald, NAACP San Diego branch secretary, had already cautioned the Osterhaus court to resist the temptation to make an example of the men. "Every effort should be made," he said, "to impress the Navy with the fact that a heavy-handed sentence in this case will not make any contribution to discipline, but will, in fact, only arouse resentment among the Negro people . . . and will be very damaging to the national unity of the white and Negro people in behalf of the war effort."

Following the defense's closing remarks, Lieutenant Commander Coakley stepped forward to make his final rebuttal argument. He began with a lengthy discourse on the history of mutiny. An hour later, Admiral Osterhaus called for the court to adjourn. Coakley would be allowed more time the following day to complete his argument.

On Tuesday morning, October 24, at 9:30 a.m., Lieutenant Commander Coakley continued. First he called into question the veracity of the defense's witnesses, explaining that they had good reason to "distort," to "color," and to "twist" their testimonies. Then he addressed what was perhaps the defense's most precarious argument: that the officers had asked the defendants if they were "willing to obey orders." Coakley reminded the court that every officer had testified that he had given a direct order. "This is the Navy," Coakley said.

"Do you think that any of the officers were in any mood to fool with them [the seamen]? Were they in any mood to ask questions? Or do you think they gave them a direct order and put them up against the proposition of obeying or disobeying it?"

Next, Coakley addressed the element of fear and the way Lieutenant Veltmann used it to explain the defendants' disobedience. "The reason they drag it in," Coakley cautioned the court, "is because they have no confidence in the testimony of the accused with respect to the order issue. They probably have a feeling that the court won't believe that after three days, they were still being asked a question, so they hang their hat on two hooks."

Coakley paused. He knew what he was about to say had to be done just right, in order to elicit the kind of response from the court that he hoped it would. "There is a war on," he said. "There was an ammunition ship to be loaded . . . and fear was no excuse. Under the circumstances I cannot understand how any man in uniform could be so depraved mentally as to come into a court of law in a time of war and under oath say, 'I was afraid to handle ammunition.' A man . . . who is so depraved as to say that is capable of giving testimony that is false."

Still indignant over Alphonso McPherson's accusation that he had threatened to have the seaman shot, the judge advocate surely fastened his eyes on the defendant and then on the brazen Ollie Green and then on Joe Small, who, despite Coakley's attempts to break him, had testified with quiet defiance. These were three men, he felt, who deserved to be punished to the full extent of the law.

Coakley ended on a solemn note. "What kind of discipline, what kind of morale would we have if men in the United States Navy could refuse to obey an order and then get off on the grounds of fear?"

On Tuesday, October 24, on the trial's thirty-third day, after 1,435 pages of single-spaced transcript typed on legal-size paper, and following the testimony of nearly one hundred witnesses, the court emerged from its quarters having deliberated less than an hour and a half, a period of time that, because it fell over the noon hour, also included a lunch break.

Admiral Osterhaus instructed Joe Small and the forty-nine other seamen to stand. Small's heart felt as if it would jump from his chest. The admiral adjusted his reading glasses and cleared his throat and instructed Lieutenant Commander Coakley to record the court's findings. Then he read the verdict for each of the fifty seamen: "The specification of the charge proved. And the accused [name of seaman] is of the charge guilty."

By the time Osterhaus reached Seaman Second Class Freddie Meeks, it must have been obvious to Lieutenant Veltmann that the court would find all of the seamen guilty. Perhaps he had hoped for too much. Perhaps it was too much to expect that a decorated World War I veteran would view the seamen as anything but cowards.

Charles Gray surely regretted his decision to cast his lot with the fifty mutineers. Perhaps he should have joined his brother Joseph and avoided the confrontation. In the end, the Navy had asserted its might, and what had he, or the others, gained? Now their only hope was that when the court sent the findings to Admiral Wright, he would find an ounce of mercy in his heart and not follow through on his promise to have them shot.

Alphonso McPherson feared that his reputation as a malingerer and a troublemaker had come back to haunt him. Perhaps he should have restrained himself when the Admiral asked if he had anything more to say. What good could come from impugning the integrity of a Navy officer, especially the judge advocate?

For Joe Small the verdict was hardly unexpected. He felt that from the moment it began, the trial was rigged. Fifty black men could not get a fair hearing in a military court.

Before adjourning, Admiral Osterhaus announced the seamen's sentences. Although no one would stand before a firing squad, the punishment was extreme. Each man's rank was reduced to apprentice seaman; each one was sentenced to a period of confinement and hard labor of fifteen years; and finally, each, after serving his sentence, was to be dishonorably discharged from the United States Navy and, as Admiral Osterhaus said, made "to suffer all the accessories of said sentence, as prescribed by Section 622, Naval Courts and Boards."

Fifteen years was a chunk of life, but some of the men were young enough that perhaps they were able to comfort themselves with the fact that even after a decade and a half in a military prison, they would have something to look forward to. For the few who were married or had children, the sentence tore out their hearts. Eventually they would be released. In the meantime who would support their families?

But it was the last phrase—"to suffer all the accessories of said sentence"—that haunted each of the fifty men. They would lose all their rights and benefits as veterans. And what employer would hire a man who had been dishonorably discharged from the Navy? Had they also disgraced black America? In every practical sense, their lives were over.

# CHAPTER 39

# The Sins of a Nation

Following the trial, five Port Chicago seamen who had risked their lives to keep a fire from spreading on the night of the explosion received the Navy and Marine Corps Medal. The irony of five black seamen being awarded the United States Department of the Navy's second-highest noncombatant medal just days after fifty black seamen were convicted of mutiny was not lost on Thurgood Marshall, who penned a scathing piece on the trial for the November issue of *The Crisis,* the NAACP's official magazine. In the editorial he called the mutiny charge a "frame-up" and accused the Navy of charging the men "solely because of their race and color." He also criticized Admiral Osterhaus for his prejudicial handling of the case and the mere eighty minutes it took his court to reach a verdict. Did fifty black men mean so little to him and to the other Navy officers that they devoted a mere one and a half minutes to the fate of each defendant?

Now that the verdict and sentences had been handed down, black publications and civil rights groups vented their outrage. The president of the San Francisco branch of the NAACP fumed, "The Negro people are well aware of the pattern of discrimination practiced by the Navy, and they are very much concerned about this trial. I feel that a general investigation of the policies which led up to this thing should be made at once."

*The Crisis* and other black publications ran scathing editorials of the mutiny trial, highlighting the second-class treatment of blacks in the military and its courts. The NAACP organized protests, circulated petitions, and contacted prominent public figures, including Eleanor Roosevelt. Mrs. Roosevelt was keenly aware of the situation and wrote Secretary Forrestal a brief note, making it clear that her sympathies lay with the men. It "seems a sad story," she said. "I hope in the case of these boys special care will be taken." She enclosed the "Mutiny" pamphlet that the NAACP's Legal Defense Fund had written about the case.

Even the editors of the *San Francisco Chronicle,* which had been reporting on the trial since it began, felt impelled to comment on the severity of the sentences. "We have been mulling this matter over for several days," they wrote. "These Negroes who refused to load the munitions ships . . . were plainly overcome by fear. They were not per se mutineers except to the extent that their fear overcame whatever responsibility they had. Considering then that fear and failure to do a duty because of it, cannot be encouraged in war-time, we still believe that the sentences imposed on these men were altogether too severe. We do not believe that the honor of the United States Navy . . . would have been impaired by sentences ranging from one-half to one-third of those given."

For Percy Robinson, George Booth, and the other 206 men who agreed to handle ammunition after Admiral Wright threatened to put all resisters before a firing squad, the two and a half months between the time they were imprisoned at Camp Shoemaker's South Stockade and the end of the trial passed painfully. Some who had been called to testify at the trial of their fellow seamen brought back news of the proceedings, but for the most part Robinson and Booth and the others heard nothing. Assigned to work crews, they fashioned cargo nets from rough, one-inch-thick hemp fiber ropes. Daily quotas were steep, and the men worked mind-numbing ten-hour shifts, twisting and lacing the rope until their hands grew sore and bloody.

On October 26, two days after Osterhaus's court reached its verdict regarding the mutineers, and ninety days after they were first imprisoned, Percy Robinson and the other 207 men were transferred from Camp Shoemaker to Treasure Island. At the island's de-embarkation camp, they awaited their orders. Soon they learned that they were being sent to the Pacific for the "duration of the war." Some of the men were thrilled that they were going to the combat zone and might finally see some action. Percy Robinson was sensible enough to know that the Navy had no grand plans for a bunch of court-martialed black seamen. None of them would serve aboard a destroyer or a battleship or a cruiser. They would be assigned to munitions ships or to bases where they would perform the mule work that white servicemen wanted no part of.

That same day an article appeared in the *San Francisco Chronicle*. NIMITZ'S SECRET WEAPON, the headline read. PACIFIC FLEET SERVICE SENDS MUNITIONS, FUEL AND FOOD OVER TREMENDOUS DISTANCES TO OUR SHIPS. The gist of the story was that without the extraordinary efforts of America's military and civilian workers to meet the staggering demands of the U.S. Fleet and its ground troops, the war in the Pacific could not have been waged successfully. The story quoted a staff member for the Service Squadron for the Pacific Fleet who boasted that the Saipan invasion alone demanded more fuel (and more of everything else) than the entire Pacific Fleet used in 1943.

In mid-November, Admiral Wright, who had been reviewing the findings of the Osterhaus court, acknowledged that there had been "erroneous rulings on questions of evidence present in the record." Nevertheless, he determined that they "did not affect the validity of the proceedings, and did not prejudice the rights of the accused." In view of "their youth, clear records, and short periods of service," Wright reduced the sentence to eight years for five of the defendants. For eleven others, including Edward Longmire, who had butted heads with the lieutenant at Camp Shoemaker over his statement, he reduced the sentence to ten years. For another twenty-four of the seamen, including Charles Gray, he took off three years. But for Small and another nine seamen, including Ollie Green and Alphonso McPherson, Wright would not budge.

Thurgood Marshall was determined to stick with the case, and when he returned to New York he made his report to Secretary Forrestal. He had only attended the trial for twelve days, but in that short time he had developed a disturbing picture of the situation at Port Chicago. Why, he asked the secretary, was all the loading done by blacks, and why were they not sufficiently trained? Why, also, after suffering through such a traumatic event, were the seamen not allowed survivor's leave?

Forrestal's answers were ambiguous and evasive. Regarding the denial of survivor's leave, he said that "requiring men to immediately return to handling ammunition, after an explosion, is the preferred method of preventing them from building up mental and emotional barriers which . . . become increasingly difficult to overcome." He did not say why many of the white officers who had survived the blast were given leave.

In early December, the editors of the *Pittsburgh Courier* wrote an article titled "Fifty New Martyrs."

> The *Pittsburgh Courier* is not disposed to ever condone crime or disobedience of military orders. Men and women in the Armed Services promptly should obey the orders given them, no matter how distasteful or repugnant those orders may be, especially when the Nation is at war.

> But we cannot dismiss the feeling that the fifty Negro sailors in California, who have just received sentences ranging from eight to fifteen years on one specification of mutiny for refusing to load ammunition after scores of their comrades had been killed and injured in the disastrous Port Chicago explosion, are, in a sense, martyrs. The boys went into the Navy expecting to receive the same treatment as other seamen and hoping to be able to strike a blow for democracy. Instead they found themselves doing the

arduous, unsung, undistinguished and dirty work of laborers and
stevedores with no hope whatever of getting transfers to active,
military service. Their experience taught them that they were
not in a democratic institution, but a jim-crow institution where
colored men could do only the dirtiest and most dangerous work
without any of the compensation derived by white boys of their
same age and rank. It is easy to understand their state of mind
when they saw their buddies blown to bits and were asked to take
the same chances they took. Fed up with their status as second-
class citizens fighting in a first-class war, they could see no reason
why they should risk their lives for little or no reward. True, they
should have done as they were ordered, as all good sailors and
soldiers should, but all of us can understand why they balked, and
to that extent they are martyrs, paying the penalty for the sins of
a Nation. This sorry case should be a warning to the Navy to
change its racial policy and to give colored youths the same
opportunity to serve as white youths and alongside them, rather
than in jim-crow units.

Days later, Joe Small and the forty-nine other mutineers were
jailed at the Terminal Island Disciplinary Barracks in San Pedro, California, just outside of Long Beach, to serve out their sentences. The
men were put in separate cells to discourage any sense of unity that
might develop among them. Nevertheless, they were often assigned to
the same work details and stuck together as best they could. Guards
and other prisoners referred to them as the "Port Chicago Boys," presumably with a mixture of awe, pity, and fear, as if to say, "Here are
the men who had the guts (or the temerity) to take on the United
States Navy." Rather than being sullen and bitter, the seamen held on
to a ray of hope that Thurgood Marshall and the NAACP, which they
had given written permission to file an appeal brief, might succeed in
their efforts to have the convictions reversed or the sentences reduced
further when the case came up for review before the judge advocate
general (JAG) of the Navy.

In early 1945, Thurgood Marshall and the NAACP stepped up
their pressure on the Navy. Marshall filed a twenty-four-page appeal brief in which he charged the Navy with initiating a "mass

prosecution . . . calculated to dispose of a large group of men with one swoop." The trial of fifty men, he argued, "militates against our whole traditional concept of personal guilt." Then he accused the Navy of "callous disregard of even perfunctory justice," suggesting that "the prosecution in an effort to establish the requisite intent necessary to sustain the charge of mutiny was permitted over objection of accused (Lieutenant Veltmann) to introduce [inadmissible] testimony as to certain statements made by unidentified individuals."

Secretary Forrestal's office asked Admiral F. L. Lowe, the assistant judge advocate general, to review Marshall's appeal. In a letter that underscored the Navy's nagging uncertainty about whether the Port Chicago incident constituted mutiny, and whether the case had been prosecuted justly, the secretary's office impressed upon Admiral Lowe the importance of being "painstaking and thorough so that the secretary's action will be unassailable." Then it posed a series of questions that it wanted Lowe to investigate: "Can disobedience of one order, but obedience to all others constitute mutiny?" "Can there be mutiny when guards are not overridden?" "Did the giving of an individual order to each accused have the legal effect of terminating the 'conspiracy' or 'concerted action'?" "If 'concerted action' or 'conspiracy' is an essential element, was such first made out prima facie before statements and acts of co-actors were admitted?"

That spring, Thurgood Marshall met with Admiral Lowe in Washington. Now in person, he asked, "Why is it that whenever more than one Negro disobeys an order, it is mutiny?" Then he pointed out that the fifty seamen had obeyed all other orders. "At best," he told the admiral, "it is a refusal to obey an order." He also accused Lieutenant Commander Coakley of having "misled the court—deliberately." His conduct, Marshall said, amounted to a "complete violation of Navy Courts and Boards." Before leaving Admiral Lowe's office, he suggested that justice could only be achieved by overturning the convictions.

Admiral Lowe may have been sympathetic to Marshall's argument. But the Navy's reputation was on the line. How could it not uphold the convictions of what it had billed as the largest mass trial in the history of the Navy and the first of its kind during World War II?

On May 17, 1945, six and a half months after the Osterhaus court reached its verdict, the Department of the Navy sent a memorandum to Admiral Wright instructing him to order Admiral Osterhaus to reconvene his court for the purpose of reconsidering the findings and sentences in the Port Chicago mutiny trial. "The Secretary of the Navy," the letter began, "notes that in a number of instances throughout the case for the prosecution evidence was admitted concerning alleged declarations made by various unidentified individuals." It then went on to cite over forty occasions on which Judge Advocate Coakley, under the principle of *res gestae,* introduced hearsay testimony for the purpose of proving the existence of a mutiny. "The admission in evidence of the testimony," the letter continued, "was in error . . . and therefore should have been stricken by the court from the record. . . . You will inform the court that in its reconsideration of its findings, wholly disregarding the above evidence, the court will reconsider whether the prosecution has proven beyond a reasonable doubt . . . the existence of the specific intent to usurp, subvert, or override superior military authority. . . . Simple violence or disobedience of orders . . . is not mutiny."

The Osterhaus court met for a total of five hours, and then, on June 12, 1945, it declared that it would change neither its findings nor the sentences. A spokesman for the secretary of the Navy defended Osterhaus, saying, "The trials were conducted fairly and impartially. . . . Racial discrimination was guarded against."

After the Osterhaus court insisted that it would adhere to its verdict, Thurgood Marshall demanded a face-to-face meeting with the secretary, but Forrestal refused. The trial had clearly become a "hot potato for the Navy" and had generated enough bad publicity. Port Chicago was best forgotten.

Just over two months later, Emperor Hirohito announced to his nation Japan's surrender, and voices inside Secretary Forrestal's Department of the Navy encouraged clemency for all of America's imprisoned servicemen. Now that the war with Japan was over, they argued that many of the sentences, especially in the case of Port Chicago seamen, seemed unjustifiably harsh.

The following month the Navy acted, reducing all the mutineers' sentences by one year. Lester Granger, Secretary Forrestal's special adviser on race relations, however, was not satisfied with what he considered a pro-forma cut. He continued to push for leniency for the Port Chicago fifty, while arguing that the Navy needed to resolve its racial problems in general by providing equal treatment and opportunity for blacks. Chief of Naval Personnel Admiral Louis Denfeld backed Granger, pointing out that the admission of Negroes to the auxiliary fleet had caused few problems. Denfield reminded Secretary Forrestal that he and Admiral King had agreed to use Negroes throughout the entire fleet if the preliminary program proved practical. The time, he said, had come to honor that agreement.

In mid-October 1945, a confidential memo regarding the Port Chicago sentences circulated throughout the Navy Department. The author affirmed the convictions, but advised reducing the sentences "to three years for those with previous record of minor misconduct, and two years for those with previous clear records." The author also urged the Navy to regard the Port Chicago incident as an object lesson underscoring the importance of discipline in the labor battalions.

In January 1946 the efforts by men like Lester Granger paid off. Quietly the Navy Department agreed to release the Port Chicago men from prison and to erase the remainder of their sentences. The seamen were then broken into small groups and assigned to vessels bound for the South Pacific for what was called a "probationary period." The move both pleased and irked Thurgood Marshall. He would later say, "The conclusion of that case was extremely interesting, because there was no official notice of what happened. The records of the final disposition were never entered, but I happen to know . . . that all of the men were released, and put back onto active duty in the Pacific. But there's no record in the Navy Department about it."

On February 27, Secretary Forrestal officially abolished the Navy's Jim Crow policy in favor of complete integration. "Effective immediately," said the edict, "all restrictions governing types of assignments for which Negro personnel are eligible are hereby lifted. Henceforth they shall be eligible for all types of assignments, in all ratings in all facilities and in all ships of naval service. In the utilization of housing, messing, and other facilities no special or unusual provisions will be made for the accommodation of Negroes."

One week after being moved from Camp Shoemaker to Treasure Island, Percy Robinson and a small group of black seamen he had served with at Port Chicago boarded the USS *President Monroe*. Robinson was sent to a series of bases throughout the Pacific, where, despite volunteering for combat duty, he was assigned to a variety of menial work details. In December 1945 he returned to the United States. The Navy offered him a promotion to chief petty officer, but he refused, and was discharged in early 1946.

George Booth, too, went to the South Pacific. Eventually he ended up on Espíritu Santo, where he ran the post office and supply store. Days after President Truman announced Japan's surrender, black sailors on Espíritu Santo were ordered to dump everything—ammunition, jeeps, even trousers and boots—into the bay. Rather than discard unused clothes, Booth distributed them to the local people. The picture of South Sea islanders walking around in pea coats in the sweltering heat would amuse him years after he left the Navy. In late 1945, Booth was discharged in Detroit, Michigan.

When he was released from the hospital, Sammie Boykin returned to Port Chicago and active duty. He heard rumors of what had happened in mid-August at Mare Island and was grateful he had not been there and faced with the decision of whether to return to handling ammunition or side with the fifty mutineers. At Port Chicago there was little for him to do while the depot was being rebuilt, and most days he picked up work at the Shell Oil Refinery in Martinez, California.

In July 1946, Joe Small received a general discharge from the Navy "under honorable conditions." Neither he nor any of the other mutineers, however, was granted veteran's benefits, and the Navy never reversed the felony conviction for mutiny.

• • •

In 1990, George Miller, whose district includes Port Chicago, and three other northern California congressmen petitioned the then secretary of the Navy, Henry L. Garrett, requesting a review of the Port Chicago mutiny trial cases. Three months later Garrett rejected the petition, suggesting instead that the survivors apply for presidential pardons. Joe Small wanted no part of it. "We don't want a pardon," Small insisted, "because that means 'you're guilty, but we forgive you.' In January 1991, with the backing of forty members of Congress, Miller again asked Secretary Garrett to review the Port Chicago convictions. Three years later, Secretary of the Navy John Dalton maintained that the trial was influenced neither by racial prejudice nor by other "improper factors." Secretary of Defense William Perry also weighed in on the issue. "Sailors," he said, "are required to obey the orders of their superiors, even if those orders subject them to life-threatening danger."

Forty-plus years after leaving the Navy, Joe Small would still remember a dream he had on the anxious night before the trial began. In that dream he was bitten by a poisonous snake. He survived and the wound healed. The scar, however, remained.

# EPILOGUE

Saipan was a battle whose significance cannot be overestimated. The historian Donald Miller called it "as important to victory over Japan as the Normandy invasion was to victory over Germany." For the Americans, the cost of taking the island was 16,525 casualties, including 3,426 killed or missing. The Marines lost more men on Saipan than in any previous Pacific campaign, including Guadalcanal and Tarawa. The death toll for the Japanese was staggering. Out of a garrison that some estimated at 32,000, Marine and Army forces took only 921 Japanese soldiers prisoner. Except for two thousand–plus stragglers who roamed Saipan's jungle-clad hills, the rest died in combat or martyred themselves in the largest banzai charge of the Pacific war.

On the night of July 17, 1944, as Admirals Ernest King and Chester Nimitz were celebrating the battle's end aboard the cruiser *Indianapolis*, within sight of the devastated island, on the very day General Tojo Hideki announced the loss to the Japanese people and was forced to present his resignation to Emperor Hirohito, the Port Chicago Naval Ammunition Depot exploded.

These two seemingly disparate events are linked together by a fate explained by the eminent World War II historian Samuel Eliot Morison. He wrote, in *New Guinea and the Marianas: March 1944–August 1944*, that the expenditure of ammunition by American forces in the battle for Saipan and in the Battle of the Philippine Sea was "colossal." The invasion of Saipan placed demands on the Port Chicago Naval Ammunition Depot that prior to the spring of 1944 would have been considered fantastic. The depot was ill equipped to handle such an onrush of ordnance, and the longshoremen's union warned that Port Chicago was a powder keg waiting to blow.

In the lead-up to the battle for Saipan, the Navy still had not issued a comprehensive "ammunition handling" textbook. In fact, it was not until 1945 that the Bureau of Naval Personnel released a 256-page training manual titled *Ammunition Handling* that provided a uniform code of loading and unloading procedures for an array of ordnance ranging from depth charges to torpedo warheads and ship-mounted rockets to 1,000-pound, armor-piercing bombs. When it finally published the textbook, the bureau insisted that its new standards be "rigidly enforced."

Whether this new attention to safety could have prevented the worst home-front disaster of World War II and one of the largest explosions in American history, we will never know. What we do know is that what happened in the aftermath of the July 17 blast highlighted the inequities of the Navy's benighted policy on race.

When Port Chicago's seamen learned that the officers had been given survivors' leaves that had been denied to them, they grew bitter. Many felt like lambs being led to slaughter. Black servicemen, in general, had always done the work that no one else wanted. They were the ones who buried the dead, built bridges and airfields, cleaned latrines, drove trucks, peeled potatoes, handled toxic chemicals, and loaded ammunition.

By mid-August 1944, all of black America was fed up. Adam Clayton Powell Jr., the pastor, politician, and civil rights leader from Harlem, New York, attributed the anger in the black community to "the whole, sorrowful, disgraceful bloody record of America's treatment of one million blacks in uniform." General Douglas MacArthur, no supporter of integration, knew the importance of morale. He warned that it could "quickly wither and die if soldiers came to believe themselves the victims of indifference or injustice."

By initiating the Port Chicago mutiny trial, the Navy heaped injustice upon misfortune. If it hoped to discourage future unrest by using the trial as an example of what could happen to disobedient blacks, its plan backfired. The trial became a cause célèbre.

In the wake of the guilty verdict and the extreme sentences handed down by the Osterhaus court, a wave of discontent swept through the Navy. A deadly race riot in which white and black Marines fired on each other broke out on Guam (120 miles south of Saipan) in the Mariana Islands. White and black Marines died during two days of gun battles, but it was the black Marines of the 25th Depot Company who were court-martialed and sent to prison. At Camp Rousseau in California, one thousand black members of a naval construction battalion (the Seabees) staged a two-day hunger strike against racial discrimintaion.

To his credit, Navy Secretary James Forrestal recognized that segregation had to end, and in late 1944 he ordered the Bureau of Personnel to lift restrictions on where blacks could serve, announcing that the Navy was "making every effort to give more than lip service to the principles of democracy in the treatment of the Negro." Just over a year later he officially abolished the Navy's Jim Crow policy in favor of complete integration.

Unlike the Navy, the Army and the Marine Corps resisted integration. Secretary of War Kenneth Royall defended the Army, arguing that it "was not an instrument for social evolution." Meanwhile the Marines' General Vandegrift asserted that "the assignment of Negro Marines to separate units promotes harmony and morale and fosters the competitive spirit essential to the development of a high esprit."

Disgusted with the glacial pace of change in the armed services, A. Philip Randolph and the black press threatened a campaign of civil disobedience, including a black boycott of the draft. How could a Fair Employment Practices Commission (FEPC), Randolph asked, presume to condemn unfair labor practices in industry if the government was discriminating against blacks in the armed services?

Confronted with a black backlash, President Harry Truman used Executive Order 9981 to desegregate the entire military on July 26, 1948. "It is hereby declared to be the policy of the President," the order read, "that there shall be equality of treatment and opportunity for all persons in the armed services without regard to race, color, religion or national origin. This policy shall be put into effect as rapidly as possible, having due regard to the time required to effectuate any necessary changes without impairing efficiency or morale."

While the president had not explicitly called for an immediate end to segregation in the military, his action represented an extraordinary victory for the civil rights community. A full decade before Martin

Luther King Jr.'s crusade, black leaders had brought to bear the new-found power of African Americans across the country.

Change, however, came slowly. Not until the North Korean People's Army almost drove the American-led United Nations forces off the Korean peninsula did commanders on the ground accept black replacements for white units. When integrated combat units proved that they could perform under fire, the Army high command took notice, and on July 26, 1951, exactly three years after President Truman's Executive Order 9981, the U.S. Army formally announced its plans to desegregate. By the end of the Korean War, 90 percent of black soldiers served in integrated units. What's more, interviews with servicemen indicated that the more contact white and black soldiers had, the more favorably they felt about racial integration.

It had been ten years since the Port Chicago explosion, but the forces unleashed by that incident had transformed the military. Despite its long history of resistance and neglect, the United States military proved itself a progressive force in the fight for racial justice. No civilian industry could claim such an accomplishment. By 1954 a quarter of a million blacks were serving side by side with whites in the armed services. By October 30, 1954—three years before the "Little Rock Nine" entered Little Rock Central High School—the last racially segregated unit in the armed forces had been abolished, and all federally controlled schools for the children of servicemen had been desegregated.

Forty years later, despite the efforts of Congressman Miller, the Navy still refused to clear the names of the Port Chicago fifty, standing by a three-page statement released in January 1994. That statement, which followed a review of the case ordered by Congress, stated that although "racial discrimination did play a part in the assignment of African-American sailors . . . racial prejudice and discrimination played no part in the court-martial convictions or sentences."

In 1999, one Port Chicago survivor—Freddie Meeks—accepted a pardon from President Bill Clinton.

Today, almost seven decades after the Port Chicago explosion and the subsequent mutiny trial, few Americans who read about the Good War and the Greatest Generation know anything of the Good War's ugly underbelly, a largely untold story about the struggle on the home front for justice and equality by black servicemen who, desiring to respond to their country's call to arms, were denied that right. It is an American tragedy best not forgotten.

On October 17, 1944, on the day Thurgood Marshall stepped up his legal counterattack on the Navy, accusing it of having disregarded the myriad danger signs at Port Chicago, the first B-29 arrived at Isley Field on Saipan. Five weeks later, ninety-three B-29s made the first attack on Japan's home islands, unloading their bombs on the Nakajima aircraft factory, just ten miles from Emperor Hirohito's palace. The "hell" that Hirohito had predicted on July 17, 1944, was now a reality.

The "precision bombing" of Japan continued until early 1945, when General Curtis LeMay, who had been the head of the 8th Air Force in Europe, came to Saipan to take over the bombing campaign. By March, LeMay had radically changed the 21st Bomber Command's tactics. Not in his darkest nightmares could Emperor Hirohito have imagined the horror that LeMay would unleash. No longer would the B-29s go in at 30,000 feet. They would fly in at night, at 5,000 feet, and they would use napalm, a new weapon of warfare. When dropped on Japanese cities, the napalm clusters—LeMay called them "fire sticks"—broke apart above the target, and each separate stick ignited on contact, setting off thousands of small blazes that together became an inferno. The napalm killed not only by fire, but also by heat and suffocation, as hot flames sucked oxygen out of the air. Bombardier and poet John Ciardi recognized the new strategy for what it was. "We were in the terrible business of burning out Japanese towns," Ciardi wrote later.

On the afternoon of March 9, 1945, 334 bombers took off from Saipan on one of LeMay's "burn job" attacks. The planes hit Tokyo at 3:00 a.m. on March 10, and in less than three hours dropped almost 250,000 incendiaries, leveling sixteen square miles of one of the most densely populated areas on earth. By sunrise the B-29s had killed 100,000 people, injured another million, and left another million homeless. In Tokyo, where most buildings were constructed of wood, straw, or paper, the fire sticks left nothing standing. The city was a bed of ashes. Those who had fled to smoldering waterways were boiled alive. Thousands of feet above, American bomber crews covered their mouths and noses to shut out the smell of burning flesh.

The Japanese called LeMay's B-29 raids "slaughter bombing." Later LeMay admitted that had Japan defeated the United States he would have been tried as a war criminal. Part of his strategy was to wipe out the people who were part of the war effort, and in Japan that meant everyone. "It was their system," LeMay said. "Entire populations got into the act and worked to make those airplanes or munitions of war."

Night and day, America's incendiary bombing campaign laid waste to Japan's major cities. With Japan's air defense system all but gone, there was little to fear. On June 15, 1945, Lemay turned his attention to small and medium-sized cities like Hiroshima and Nagasaki. In the meantime, American submarines, operating out of the Marianas, initiated Operation Starvation, mining the country's harbors. The submarines closed the ports of Nagoya, Yokohama, and Tokyo, cutting off most of Japan's imports. Admiral Bull Halsey got in on the act, too. Task Force 58 cruised up and down the coast, shelling port cities and military installations. Admiral King's vision had come true—the Marianas *were* the key to victory in the Central Pacific. By seizing Saipan and Tinian, the United States could both starve Japan by isolating it from its resource base in the Southwest Pacific and threaten it directly with aircraft carriers, long-range submarines, and the B-29 bomber.

While American air and sea forces pounded Japan, military officials assembled plans for a massive land invasion of the country. "Operation Downfall" called for General MacArthur and Admiral Nimitz to assemble 750,000 assault troops and the largest fleet of warships ever assigned to a single campaign. Military intelligence officers anticipated a "titanic confrontation" with potentially "unbearable" losses. All of Japan, they knew, would be mobilized to defend the "divine homeland."

The world's first nuclear explosion, at the remote Alamogordo Air Force Base in New Mexico on July 16, 1945, allowed President Truman and American military officials to contemplate an alternative to a costly land invasion. On that same day a heavily guarded railroad car shipment, carrying a top-secret four-foot-tall canister, arrived at the Port Chicago Naval Ammunition Depot. There it was moved to another pier, loaded on a barge, sent down the Sacramento River and then across San Francisco Bay to Hunter's Point Naval Shipyard. At the shipyard it was transferred to the heavy cruiser USS *Indianapolis*. Unescorted, the Indianapolis covered the 5,000 miles to Tinian in a record-setting ten days. It anchored 1,000 yards off the shore, where the canister containing the radioactive components (probably the fissionable uranium bullet—U-235—and the firing mechanism) for "Little Man" was moved to an onshore shed and assembled by atomic scientists. On that very same day, July 26, emboldened by the successful test at Alamogordo, Allied leaders at Potsdam, Germany, issued an ultimatum calling for "the unconditional surrender of all the Japanese armed forces." "The alternative for Japan," they warned, "is prompt and utter destruction."

When Japan did not respond to the president's ultimatum, Truman gave the order to drop the bomb: "Release when ready but not sooner than August 2." Although the president confessed in his diary the fear that "machines are ahead of morals," the mission was on. Bad weather canceled the first flight, on August 3, but on the morning of August 5, meteorologists called for days of clear skies.

At the briefing on Tinian, Captain William "Deak" Parsons, the Manhattan Project's chief of weapons development, told the crews that they would be delivering the most powerful weapon in the history of the world. The flight surgeon distributed cyanide capsules. If the mission went awry, crew members were encouraged to use them. The B-29 *Enola Gay* and the two planes accompanying it left Tinian at 2:45 a.m. on August 6. Afraid that the plane would crash on takeoff,

Parsons waited eight minutes before he crawled into the bomb bay and inserted the explosive propellant powder into the bomb's firing mechanism and hooked up the detonator.

Forty-three seconds after it was dropped, the bomb, known as "Little Boy," detonated at 8:16 a.m. Hiroshima time, 1,900 feet above the ground. Just seconds later the city ceased to exist. When Armed Forces Radio announced that the bomb had been dropped, service-men across the Pacific shouted with joy, many believing for the first time that they would now survive the war.

President Truman again gave Japanese leaders the opportunity to surrender, warning that if they did not accept our terms they could "expect a rain of ruin from the air, the like of which has never been seen on this earth." But Tokyo remained silent. Orders were already in place to drop the second bomb, so when Japan's leaders did not respond, Truman saw no reason to amend the schedule. "Fat Man" was detonated over the secondary target of Nagasaki (Kokura, the "Pittsburgh of Japan," was the primary target, but the bombardier could not see the aiming point through the smoke and clouds) at 11:01 a.m. on August 9. Little Boy killed a minimum of 100,000 people, and Fat Man another 74,000.

Truman and General George Marshall again waited for word from Japan's leaders. Hearing nothing, on August 14 they ordered a two-thousand-plane bombing attack. It was the last raid on Japan and the largest of the war. The following day, Japan surrendered. After a failed attempt to kill himself, Hideki Tojo was placed on trial before the International Military Tribunal for the Far East and was found guilty of war crimes and crimes against humanity. He was executed by hanging on December 23, 1948.

In 1968, with congressional approval, the Navy bought the town of Port Chicago for $20 million. The residents' efforts to resist that sale, and the subsequent razing of the town, are detailed in Ken Rand's book *Port Chicago Isn't There Anymore*. Not long after, the Port Chicago Naval Ammunition Depot, which was shipping 100,000 tons of munitions every month to American forces in Vietnam, became the scene of antiwar demonstrations. Years later an investigative reporter by the name of Stephen Talbot produced a public television documentary film called *Broken Arrow* in which he argued that Port Chicago, which was now part of the Concord Naval Weapons Station, had become a storage and transshipment facility for nuclear weapons. The Navy refused to comment on Talbot's charge.

In Peter Vogel's 2001 book, *The Last Wave from Port Chicago,* he makes an even bolder claim than Talbot. In 1980 Vogel discovered a document written in late 1944 by Los Alamos mathematician Joseph Hirschfelder and physicist William Penney titled "History of the 10,000 ton gadget." The document is a mathematical model of an atomic bomb detonation at the Trinity site in New Mexico on July 16, 1945. The bottom line forecasts a "ball of fire mushroom out at 18,000 ft. in typical Port Chicago fashion." The discovery launched him on a twenty-year investigation of the Port Chicago explosion.

Relying on primary documents and correspondence between General Groves, James Conant, Robert Oppenheimer, Rear Admiral W. R. Purnell, and Captain W. S. Parsons, the director of the Ordnance Division at the Los Alamos Laboratories, Vogel argues that the explosion at Port Chicago was caused by the deliberate detonation of a low-yield nuclear fission weapon called the Mark II in a test conducted jointly by the United States Navy and the Manhattan Project Los Alamos Laboratories. In *The Last Wave from Port Chicago,* Vogel attempts to prove that enough U-235 isotope had been separated in sufficient degree of enrichment to enable detonation of the Mark II bomb.

One of the documents Vogel cites as evidence is an August 3, 1944, letter from Oppenheimer to Conant in which Oppenheimer writes, "We have had the first positive indications as far as our main program goes, and although the results have not been checked, they do lend some encouragement." A week later Conant reports to General Groves that the Mark II should be shelved because of its reduced destructive capabilities and used only if other implosion methods failed. Vogel reasons that for the Mark II to be "put on the shelf," as Conant suggests it should be, it required first a successful proof firing. In his book *Images of America: Port Chicago* and in his provocative blog "Discussing Port Chicago," Dean McLeod makes charges similar to Vogel's.

In his book Vogel also questions the court-martial proceedings and propriety of the convictions. Captain William Parsons's brother-in-law was Captain J. S. "Jack" Crenshaw. Parsons had requested Crenshaw's appointment to the Navy court of inquiry. From his Los Alamos office Parsons corresponded frequently during the trial with Crenshaw. Vogel insists that "the proceedings and findings of the Court of Inquiry were corrupted by Captain Crenshaw who was derelict in duty as a member of the court by his failure to report in the court proceedings the known cause of the explosion, or failure to report to the court his reasons sufficient to believe that a specific cause of the explosion could be known by due diligence, or his failure to report to the court that testimony produced from his brother-in-law Captain Parsons would provide evidence relevant to determination of the cause of the explosion."

Vogel argues that because the court of inquiry was corrupted from the very beginning, the men tried and convicted in the formal mutiny court-martial proceedings were denied substantive due process. That being the case, Vogel insists that the Navy judge advocate vacate all the summary and formal court-martial determinations and convictions.

When Vogel wrote his book, he did not know that just days after the close of the mutiny trial, a San Francisco reporter discovered that Lieutenant Commander James Coakley was the brother-in-law of Lieutenant Ernest Delucchi. Had Vogel had access to this information, he surely would have challenged the probity of the trial, too.

Carl Matthews regained consciousness aboard a Navy hospital ship eight days after Lieutenant Leary was killed. Doctors told him that his ear had ruptured and that he was suffering from a bruised brain, and likely internal bleeding, too. Later Matthews would confess that he was an "emotional wreck," trembling and vomiting when startled by sudden noises and disturbed by his inability to remember the last days of the battle. Matthews spent the remainder of the war at the Quantico Marine Air Base. After the war he visited Lieutenant Leary's family, beginning a friendship that continues today. On that first trip he learned that the lieutenant's body never made it back from the cliff where he died. Matthews also visited the Nightingale farm in Skowhegan, Maine, and found everything—the house, the barn, and the giant maple tree—as his friend had described it. Mr. Nightingale thanked Matthews for coming and told him, "I have waited twenty years for this moment. Tell me about what happened to my son." When Matthews finished, Mr. Nightingale wiped the tears from his eyes. "I'm glad you came," he said. "Now I can die happy. I just could not die until I knew what had happened to my boy." Matthews participated in the filming of a Japanese public television documentary on the battle of Saipan. In 2004 he made his first trip back to Saipan for a ceremony commemorating the sixtieth anniversary of the battle. The following year he returned and served as one of the keynote speakers for the opening of the museum at American Memorial Park. On both trips he spent dozens of hours searching for Lieutenant Leary's remains. He was never able to identify the place where Wendell Nightingale was killed. The landing-day photo of Matthews, Nightingale, and Leary hangs in the Marine Museum at Quantico. Despite Lieutenant Leary's death, Richard Freeby was awarded the Silver Star for valor.

Robert Graf returned to Marine Camp Maui after participating in the invasion of Tinian. When he arrived at camp, standing before him was Dick Crerar. Crerar had been wounded during the West Loch explosion and was taken to a hospital in Oahu. In the chaos that followed the blast, his records were lost and everyone assumed that he had died. At Camp Maui, Graf again went through intensive field training. On February 19, 1945, at 9:02 a.m., as a member of the 23rd Marine Regiment, he was part of the first wave on Iwo Jima.

That first morning, Graf was wounded by an enemy shell, but he was not evacuated. On the morning of the second day, while helping to search the battlefield for wounded Marines, he discovered Major Fought's body. Just over two weeks later he was wounded again when an artillery shell landed near the company command post. The following day, back home in Ballston Spa, Graf's mother told the family that "Bobby" had been hurt. The previous night she had seen him in a dream "limping down the hall." Although Graf had lost a lot of blood, luckily for him the wound was not a serious one—he had taken a piece of shrapnel in the left buttock. Later he would write, "No missing limbs nor major damage but enough of a wound to leave this Hell Hole, this land of the Devil." On March 7, 1945, two black Marines carried him from an Iwo Jima field hospital to an amphibious vehicle and transported him and dozens of other wounded men to a hospital ship. Graf recuperated on Guam and then later at the U.S. Naval Hospital at Pearl Harbor. On April 29 he arrived back at Camp Maui to prepare for the land invasion of Japan. One day shy of three months after the Japanese surrender (November 14), Graf, Jimmy Haskell, and Andrew "Bill" Jurcsak were discharged. For many years after the war, they would sing the song that Haskell wrote while overseas:

> *History will tell about our journey across the sea*
> *How we stormed the bloody banks to take the enemy*
> *The foe was tough, but you know us, and on to victory,*
> *As we go marching on.*

> *Glory, Glory, what a hell of a way to die*
> *Glory, Glory, what a hell of a way to die*
> *Glory, Glory, what a hell of a way to die*
> *What a hell of a way to pass your life away.*

> *First we took the Marshall Isles and then we took Saipan*
> *Twenty thousand Nipponese lay bleeding in the sand.*
> *We rested for eleven days and then took Tinian,*
> *As we go marching on.*

*We sailed again out on the sea, to take that Iwo Isle*
*Volcanic ash and sulfur fumes poured down on us in style*
*At last our Flag was flying over Iwo's highest hill,*
*As we go marching on.*

On July 9, while on patrol, Frank Borta was nearly hit by a mortar. He blacked out and when he came to, aboard a hospital ship,
he thought he was paralyzed. For a number of days he could only
move his head enough to see that a Marine lying on one side of him
had a bullet in his belly, and on the other side, another Marine had a
severely fractured leg and only one arm. By the time the ship reached
the Marshall Islands, Borta was walking again. There he transferred
to a carrier that also served as a prison ship and was taking captured
Japanese soldiers to Hawaii. Aboard ship, Borta was plagued by
nightmares. In Pearl Harbor, Navy doctors interviewed him. When
they discovered that he was only seventeen, they told him that he had
done enough for his country and sent him to the Seattle Naval Hospital. One day while he was shining his shoes, he was summoned to
the administration building. There, standing in the room, was his father. "I wanted to make sure you still had your arms and legs," his
father said. That night, over beers, Frank told his father about Saipan.
"C'mon home, son," his father said. "You've done enough for your
country." Borta was home by early 1945. Later, during a successful
business career (international sales with Allied Van Lines), he would
visit Saipan numerous times. Like Matthews, he attended the sixtieth-
anniversary celebration.

On November 1, 1944, Edgar Huff joined the 5th Marine Depot
Company as a first sergeant. One month later he was bound for the island of Saipan, where he and his men were scheduled to train in combat tactics prior to the upcoming invasion of Okinawa. Instead, the
men were relegated to what Huff called "mule" work. They loaded
ships, burned latrines, blew up old and defective ammunition, and
cleaned up the island's Marine camps.

In March 1945, the 5th boarded a navy ship bound for Japan's Ryukyu Islands. The captain welcomed the men aboard and

announced the berthing arrangements: white officers would bunk in "officer country"; white NCOs and enlisted men would occupy decks two and three; all Negroes would be confined to the hold. On April 1, 1945, the 5th took part in a diversionary landing on Okinawa's southern beaches, where it was subjected to heavy fire. Two days later it was attached to the 1st Marine Division. For the duration of the battle, Huff and his men unloaded supplies and lugged them to frontline fighting troops and served as stretcher bearers and on burial crews. In late September 1945, the 5th was sent to China. In early 1946, after guarding coal cars in northeastern China, the 5th arrived back in San Diego. Days later, Huff took his men to Montford Point via train. Instead of riding in Pullman troop sleepers, the men were assigned to dusty, unheated cattle cars. On February 21, 1946, disgusted with the Marines' Jim Crow policies, Edgar Huff retired.

Urged by friends to reenlist, he signed on again in May 1946. Huff was made a master sergeant when President Truman signed Executive Order 9981, but like other Montford Point Marines he was ambivalent about the order. He resented the Marines' racist policies, but feared losing his identity as a black Marine. In the summer of 1951 he was sent to Korea. It was his first experience with an integrated company and the first time white Marines ever served under a black NCO. In Korea, Huff was transferred to a heavy weapons company, where he was the only black Marine in the unit and saw combat.

After the war, Huff became the first black sergeant major in Marine history. In 1955 he was transferred to French Morocco, Africa, U.S. Naval Base, Marine Barracks, Port Lyautey Naval Intelligence Center, where he guarded the King of Morocco. Returning to Camp Lejeune in 1957, he became the first black sergeant major of a Marine Corps regiment. In 1960, Huff was in charge of two busloads of Marine umpires traveling from Little Creek to Camp Lejeune when Jim Crow again raised its ugly head. The Marines stopped at a café to eat. Huff, who was in charge of the group, was not allowed to enter the restaurant. A white private had to buy him a sandwich.

Huff did two tours in Vietnam, where he was sergeant major of the largest combat force ever under Marine command, the III Marine, Amphibious Combat Force. In 1968, during the Tet Offensive, he won the Bronze Star for taking out an enemy machine gun and saving a group of white Marines. He was also awarded a Purple Heart and won the Combat "V" for saving a white Marine's life. In 1971 he did radio broadcasts over the Armed Forces Network and wrote articles about race relations. When he retired in September 1972, he helped to make a recruiting film for the Marines. That same year he was given the key to the city of Gadsden, Alabama.

Upon being discharged from the Navy, Sammie Boykin spent the rest of his life working for the city of Oakland. He remained dedicated to his country and proud of his service, but the events at Port Chicago disturbed him. Not until he attended his first summer ceremony commemorating the explosion did he begin to tell his family about his experiences at Port Chicago. Sammie Boykin passed away on October 25, 2009.

In early 1946, after being discharged, Percy Robinson went home to Chicago, got his college diploma, and took a job teaching electronics and mathematics at the Midway Television Institute in Chicago. During the summers, while loading and unloading freighters and barges at the Lake Michigan docks, he sometimes ran the winches. In the early 1950s, after a brief stint at RCA in Indianapolis, he moved to Los Angeles, where jobs were abundant. While going to night school at various colleges in the Los Angeles area, including USC and UCLA, he took a job with the Hughes Aircraft Company, where he worked his way up the ladder from test engineer to scientist. By the time he retired, thirty-five years later, he was in charge of one of the company's largest labs.

Although George Booth never did make it to Hampton University (as Lieutenant Delucchi promised), he, too, remained proud of his naval service. Owing partly to his experience at Port Chicago, Booth became an active member in the American Youth Democracy, which fought against discrimination and for workers' rights. Harry Truman's attorney general, however, thought otherwise and accused the organization of having Communist sympathies. Eventually Booth went to work for the city of Detroit, where he was one of only two blacks on the Water Board.

Despite what happened at Port Chicago, Joe Small remained proud of his service, though he rarely discussed the explosion or his role in the mutiny. He supported his family as a handyman who could do it all—carpentry, plumbing, and electrical. Everyone who knew him considered him to be a man of integrity and principle. He encouraged his children to be strong and independent thinkers. When one son became involved in the Black Panther movement, he said to him, "Son, there is no such thing as race." In 1958 a house fire took the lives of two of his children. Lillian, Small's wife, sustained burns over 90 percent of her body. Eventually two of Small's sons and one of his grandsons would serve in the Navy. Some of the Port Chicago fifty ended up changing their names and moving frequently in an effort to hide their past. Not Small. He found his peace in his family and in God.

Many of the loaders at Port Chicago had joined the Navy with hopes of serving their country as sailors bound for the South Pacific. In January 1946, Joe Small did finally do his tour, but it was under different circumstances than he had ever imagined. "We had no duties," he later recalled. "Nothing to do but make mess call, roam about the ship, and sleep. We rode and rode, just back and forth from one port to another. We never left the ship."

# REMEMBERING A WORLD WAR II
# TRAGEDY AT PORT CHICAGO

In March 2009, President Obama signed the
Omnibus Public Land Management Act that
created the Port Chicago Naval Magazine
National Memorial in Concord, California.
It is our country's 392nd national park and
commemorates the July 17, 1944, explosion,
in which 320 men died and almost 400 others
were injured.

# NOTES

## CHAPTER 1: "ANOTHER SUNDAY, ANOTHER PEARL HARBOR ATTACK"

West Loch is separated from Middle Loch by the Waipahu Peninsula.

The sailor's quote is from Robert Graf's memoirs.

When the Joint Chiefs of Staff finalized the date for Operation Forager, the invasion of the Marianas—Saipan, Tinian, and Guam—both the 2nd and 4th Marine Divisions began amphibious maneuvers at Maalaea Bay on Maui. In the latter part of April 1944, the Army's 27th Infantry Division did the same. By mid-May, the Marines returned to Maui to practice ship-to-shore movements. On May 17, in a dress rehearsal for the invasion, staged at Maalaea Bay, hundreds of amtracs ran up on the beaches, and 2nd and 4th Division Marine riflemen, working against the clock, assaulted pillboxes. Observers critiqued the operation, and afterward worked to fine-tune the landing plan. On May 19, during training off Kahoolawe Island, live naval gunfire and aircraft strafing were added to the exercises. During a four-day period, May 20–24, the Army's 27th Infantry Division held its own maneuvers on Oahu.

What Graf and Crerar may or may not have known was that because there were only six ammunition ships assigned to the entire Pacific, sixteen LSTs were forced to carry 740 rounds of five-inch, .38-caliber antiaircraft shells and the powder for them. Ten more LSTs carried 270 4.5-inch rockets, 6,000 rounds of 40-mm machine gun ammunition, and 15,000 rounds of 20-mm machine-gun ammunition.

According to an article titled "The Negro Problem in the Fourteenth Naval District," Hawaii was not a good place for black servicemen to be. The territory did not want them. Hawaii's delegate to Congress and its governor denounced their presence, and civic organizations passed resolutions of protest. The blacks were miserable, too. One wrote, "It is awful hard for one to concentrate all his effort toward the war when he has such a great battle to fight at home." Another wrote, "There are a great many southerners here that seem to think we Negroes have no place here or a right in the sun. They preach to the natives a nasty, poisonous doctrine that we must fight like hell to overcome. They tell the natives that we are ignorant, dumb, evil, rapers, and trouble makers. They have the native women to a point they are afraid to even speak to our Negro boys." Yet another black serviceman wrote, "Negroes are considered the lowest thing on this rock. . . . The white men have come here with tales of Negroes carrying dreadful diseases, being thieves, murderers and downright no good."

The black press published a three-part series called "Americans in Concentration Camps." The articles addressed the discrimination against American citizens of

Japanese ancestry. They also highlighted the lack of blacks in both the armed services and on defense projects and accused the U.S. government of drawing a deliberate color line.

Details of the West Loch disaster come from a variety of sources, including *The West Loch Story* by William Johnson, "The Navy's Hushed-up Tragedy at West Loch" from *Sea Classic* (November 2005) by A. Alan Oliver and Deloris Guttman at the African American Diversity Cultural Center Hawaii.

Rear Admiral Furlong was the commandant of the Pearl Harbor Navy Yard. Furlong had seen the first Japanese bombs hit Ford Island during the assault on Pearl Harbor.

The 29th Chemical Decontamination Company was most likely attached to Headquarters, Provisional Chemical Warfare Composite Battalion (a unit about which I found no additional information). Apparently this provisional composite battalion administered the 29th and other chemical units stationed in the area.

The original CINCPAC press release reported that Army casualties were eight dead, fifty-three missing, and nine injured. *The West Loch Story* by William Johnson, however, says that 163 men lost their lives and 396 were wounded in the disaster. Six LSTs and a handful of amtracs were destroyed. In *Saipan: Beginning of the End,* Major Carl Hoffman puts the number killed at 207: 112 from the 4th Division and ninety-five from the 2nd Division. Hoffman mentions nothing, however, about the majority of the deaths coming from the 29th Chemical Company.

Graf could not believe that his buddy Crerar did not know how to swim. Once a Marine could not even make it through boot camp without being able to swim, but late in the war the Marines were so desperate for men that they waived the requirement.

On Monday afternoon, May 22, Marine Corporal Robert Patrick Roberts, who had been at Tent City at Hickam Field with all the other Pacific replacements, when he heard a loud roar, figured he would go survey the damage for himself. What he saw was certainly worse than the *Honolulu Star Bulletin* described, and worse even than he could have imagined: the harbor covered in smoke, mangled pieces of steel, and Coast Guard boats still pulling dead bodies from the water. Later *Stars and Stripes* magazine would describe the explosion as a "minor incident."

The transient center, or Tent City, was built by the Seabees to house Marines staging through Pearl Harbor. Begun in October of 1943 by the 92nd Seabees, the camp was completed in four months. It was broken into two 5,000-man areas, each containing a complete system of utilities. Housing was provided in 1,250 tents erected over concrete floors, and eight 40-by-100-foot and fifty 20-by-48-foot Quonset huts.

Lieutenant Commander Joseph Hoyt was in charge of a flotilla of LSTs. Hoyt testified during the court of inquiry that the kind of load they were putting on the decks of the LSTs violated every safety precaution of the Navy. He pointed out that, if not for a bit of luck, every ship in the harbor could have exploded.

In December 1941, more than a year after President Roosevelt signed the controversial Selective Training and Service Act, every branch of service, especially the Navy, was still undermanned. Problems would continue throughout the war. In winter 1944 it took a threat from Navy Secretary Frank Knox to change President Roosevelt's mind about the need for more men. The Navy, he said, would have to "drastically curtail presently scheduled operations." Gradually the Navy expanded beyond the 3-million mark. By March 1944, however, the Selective Service was barely providing its quota, and the Bureau of Navy Personnel searched for ways and means to economize with those already in uniform. By July 1944, Admiral King would have to ask the president for an additional 390,000 men. Lack of numbers was a problem that would bedevil King until the end of the war. The U.S. Army that General Marshall took over in September 1939 stood nineteenth in the world with a total of 174,000 men—ahead of Bulgaria and behind Portugal.

## CHAPTER 2: BIG DREAMS

During his last few months of high school, Graf used the money he made as a stock clerk at a local five-and-dime store to go to the picture show and see every war movie he could—*Sergeant York, The Fighting 69th,* and *To the Shores of Tripoli.*

The Sans Soucie Hotel drew royalty and the wealthy from all across the world to the tiny town. Ballston Spa had inspired others, too. Stirred by the rolling hills and unbroken tracts of forest, James Fenimore Cooper used the area as the setting for *The Last of the Mohicans,* and Cooper wrote a portion of the book in the town's library.

Many upstate New Yorkers had fought in the 128th New York Volunteer Infantry—"Old Steady"—the regiment of Civil War fame.

## CHAPTER 3: LEAVING TEXAS

Camp Elliott was the site of a 26,000-acre base that the Marine Corps leased from the city of San Diego.

When Matthews and his fellow Marines finished a clip, men working the pits would check the paper targets. When one of them waved a large red flag back and forth, everyone knew what it signified. It was called "waving Maggie's drawers" and meant that a shooter had missed the target.

By the afternoon, Marines rushing back from liberty poured into camp. In a matter of hours, Matthews's B Company was just a few men short of full strength. Its mortar, machine gun, and rifle platoons were mobilized. Some platoons went to the San Diego docks to load ships, while others were sent out to patrol and defend Southern California's many small airstrips. Predictions were that Japan would follow up with an invasion of the mainland.

## CHAPTER 4: MOSQUITOES, MUD, AND MAYHEM

Admiral King regarded Samoa as the linchpin in the supply line between Hawaii and Australia, and fortified it with troops, aircraft, and war matériel. Many, including Lieutenant General Henry "Hap" Arnold, head of the Army Air Forces, disagreed with King about how to protect Samoa. Arnold considered the on-site defense unnecessary. In his opinion, heavy bombers would be able to protect Samoa and the line. King, however, insisted that some bases were too important to be lost.

King also believed that the ravenous Japanese navy had to be confronted. By early March 1942, Japan had roared through Hong Kong, Malaya, Guam, Rabaul and the Bismarcks, Singapore, Java, the Dutch East Indies, and Burma, and was not about to stop its territorial expansion. King's naval forces, however, were far inferior to Japan's. The Japanese had ten carriers, while the Americans had only three. The Japanese had twelve battleships, while all the American ones were either sunk, damaged, or unavailable. And Japan had twenty-five cruisers to the fifteen cruisers of the Pacific Fleet. There were similar disparities in destroyers and submarines. Nevertheless, King ordered piecemeal raids, flouting conventional naval strategy and scattering his carriers, and encouraging them to hit the enemy at every opportunity.

The Marines stationed on Samoa were aware that the two carriers (*Enterprise* and *Yorktown*) had left Samoa, and they felt isolated and vulnerable. They had all heard about the barbarity of the Japanese. On Rabaul, Japan's famed South Seas Detachment ran barges ashore and captured almost one thousand Australian soldiers. The Australians put up a heroic fight, but the Japanese forces overwhelmed them with sheer numbers. At Tol Plantation, the Japanese tied 160 Australian prisoners to coconut palms. While the remaining Aussies looked on, young Japanese trainees used the prisoners for bayonet practice.

When the 2nd Brigade arrived in Samoa, after two weeks at sea, it had an enormous task ahead of it. The brigade's orders were to finish what the previous defense battalion had started: a multi-island defense system code-named "Straw." This entailed constructing gun emplacements, bomb shelters, power plants, wharves, a hospital, warehouses, coastal and mountain roads, as well as clearing jungle, blasting coral for airstrips, stringing miles of barbed wire, filling in lagoons, installing secret ration storage shelters with enough supplies and medicine to keep eight hundred men alive for thirty days, caching ammunition and supplies along forest trails, laying mines, and stringing an anti-torpedo net across Pago Pago Harbor.

The Samoan Marines were better adapted to the climate and could negotiate the steep and slick mountain trails much better than the Americans. Without their help, the effort to stock the mountain shelters would have taken months longer.

For a Marine named Enzio Demage, a big-city guy from St. Louis, mail day provided the biggest laugh. The first delivery came after the Marines had been on Samoa for over three months. When the ship arrived, Matthews received one hundred letters from his mother, and copies of the local papers, the *Dawson Herald* and the *Hubbard City News*. Matthews read the papers and then, to be a good sport, he passed them on to Demage, who often kidded him about being a hick Texan. With all the guys gathered around, Demage read aloud from the the local news: "Little Johnny Spence brought an unusually large egg by the *Herald* office last week"; and "A cow, belonging to Cleave Johnson, was struck by the locomotive on the Cotton Belt railroad last Wednesday. The cow was badly injured and put out of its misery by a shot from the six-shooter carried by City Marshall McElroy." The Marines howled with laughter at the backwoods naïveté.

When Admiral Nimitz learned of the Japanese plan to invade Port Moresby—the U.S. Navy's Combat Intelligence Unit had broken the Japanese code just months earlier—he consulted with Admiral King and together they decided to send two U.S. Navy carrier task forces and a joint Australian-American cruiser force to oppose the Japanese offensive.

After Pearl Harbor, U.S. intelligence efforts focused on cracking JN-25 (the Japanese naval code). Leading the effort, code-named "Magic," was the U.S. Navy's Combat Intelligence Unit, called OP-20-G, which consisted of 738 naval personnel. The unit, housed in the basement of the 14th Naval District Administration at Pearl Harbor, was under the command of Commodore John Rochefort, who combined fluency in Japanese with single-minded dedication to the task. Using complex mathematical analysis, IBM punch-card tabulating machines, and a cipher machine, Friedman developed the ECM Mark III, the unit that was able to crack most of the code by January 1942. The blanket name given to any information gained by deciphering JN-25 was "Ultra," a word borrowed from British code-breaking efforts and stamped at the top of all deciphered messages.

On May 3 and 4, Japanese forces occupied Tulagi, in the southeastern Solomon Islands, though not without incident. Aircraft from the U.S. fleet carrier *Yorktown* surprised and sank several Japanese warships. The Japanese responded by sending its fleet carriers into the Coral Sea with the intention of annihilating the Allied naval forces. On May 7 and 8, the carrier forces from the two sides exchanged air strikes. The first day, the U.S. sank the Japanese light carrier *Shoho,* while the Japanese sank a U.S. destroyer and damaged a fleet oiler. On May 8, U.S. bombers hit the Japanese fleet carrier *Shokaku.* The Japanese retaliated, damaging two U.S. fleet carriers—the *Yorktown* and the *Lexington.* The end result, however, worked to the Allies' advantage. Because he had lost so many planes and the service of two carriers, Admiral Shigeyoshi Inoue called off the invasion of Port Moresby. What the Japanese had hoped to do by capturing Port Moresby was establish a base from which its bombers could pound the Allied supply line.

What the Japanese defeat did not do was save the men stationed on Samoa from the ravages of disease. Physicians stationed in Samoa soon learned that the island's steamy, bug-infested jungles were perfect incubators for a host of debilitating vector-borne diseases. By midsummer 1942, Carl Matthews had fallen victim to an undiagnosed illness that left him with oozing blisters all over his body, sapped his strength, and stripped him of nearly thirty pounds. The skin condition began innocently. The medical corpsman diagnosed it as a simple case of jungle rot, from which nearly every Marine stationed in Samoa suffered. When the lesions began to spread to his hands, and Matthews's feet swelled painfully, a concerned medical officer sent him by field ambulance to the regimental hospital. There a corpsman examined the oozing blisters and determined that Matthews had leprosy. The news left Matthews in a state of near panic. Growing up, he had read enough of the Bible to know that leprosy was one of the many scourges that the Israelites believed God had inflicted upon man in retribution for his sins. Bearing the mark of leprosy often meant a lifetime of pain and alienation.

When another physician dismissed the leprosy diagnosis, Matthews was enormously relieved. Still, however, his symptoms continued to stump the doctors. When his temperature climbed and his hands hurt too much for him to hold a fork, and he weighed in at less than 100 pounds, his physicians transferred him to the Samoan Hospital just north of Pago Pago. His condition worsened, and the head doctor decided that he needed to be sent back to the United States for treatment.

Three weeks later, Matthews was aboard the USS *Brazos,* bound for the United States. When the *Brazos* arrived at the dock in San Pedro, California, an ambulance waited to take Matthews to the lavish Lake Norconian Country Club, which had been turned into a naval hospital, near Riverside, California. There, amid the decidedly un-Marine-like amenities, he recuperated. James Roosevelt, son of the a president, was a patient in the officers' area.

The naval hospital sported a lake, mineral baths, two swimming pools, a billiard hall, a golf course, and a graceful dining room where staff members served sumptuous meals on fine china. To Matthews's delight, there was always fresh fruit and cold milk.

Movie stars often came to visit the patients, whom they treated like heroes.

Matthews met Kay Francis, Mary Beth Hughes, Randolph Scott, Claudette Colbert, and Red Skelton, and could not have been more starstruck. Claudette Colbert even kissed his forehead.

As Matthews recovered, he was invited to participate in a War Bond drive in Compton, California, where he rode in a red fire engine near the front of the parade, which was led by Rudy Vallee's Coast Guard band. Just behind Matthews, in an extravagantly decorated float, were the Sons of the Pioneers, a Western band that he had listened to while he was growing up in Texas. Before the parade kicked off, William "Hopalong Cassidy" Boyd, Matthews's boyhood idol, spurred his white horse alongside the fire engine and introduced himself.

The parade ended at Compton Stadium, where Matthews and the other servicemen were escorted to the main stage. The crowd applauded appreciatively. Boyd and Vallee spoke, Vallee sang "Lydia, the Tattooed Lady," and then people were urged to buy War Bonds and to have them signed by Matthews and the other military men. Matthews enjoyed the attention, scrawling his name and hometown on the bonds and posing for photographs with the buyers.

## CHAPTER 5: SEMPER FI

Graf had learned the basics of boot camp quickly: he moved his bowels in the morning, as ordered; he learned that the Marines did everything "double time"; he could take a shower, including soaping up and rinsing off, in under ninety seconds; he could recite his serial number quicker than his address; he could hit the deck running at 4:30 a.m.; scrub, or "holystone," the barracks floor until it was gleaming (to "holystone" the floor, troops threw sand onto it and then wet the sand with water; then they used cobblestones to rub the floor until it shone); rattle off the Marine Corps' eleven General Orders, Marine Corps history, its Core Values, and Code of Conduct, as well as he could recite the Lord's Prayer; and take apart and reassemble his '03 Springfield rifle as easily as he could slip on a pair of skivvies. The horrible lessons would come later.

After two weeks of practice landings, the 23rd returned to New River. There, Graf qualified for the first time with the Browning .30-caliber machine gun. He liked this medium machine gun, which spat out four hundred to six hundred Springfield .30-06 rounds a minute. But it was heavy, weighing over thirty pounds, and Graf did not envy the men who would one day be lugging it through the jungle. Graf also learned to blow up tanks. In battle they could sabotage tanks from spider holes by sticking a Molotov cocktail through the tank's exhaust slits or firing into its relatively unprotected underbelly. The bullets would bang around inside, killing or wounding its occupants.

In 1939, a colonel with the U.S. Army Corps of Engineers surveyed and mapped an area from Fort Monroe, Virginia, to Fort Sumter, South Carolina, paying special interest to the coastal areas. The map caught the interest of the War and Navy departments, which were searching for a new location for an amphibious training base. In the summer of 1940 a major and his pilot surveyed by air a huge swath of country from Norfolk, Virginia, to Corpus Christi, Texas, and pinpointed the fourteen miles of beach in Onslow County, North Carolina, which the colonel had discovered two years earlier. In February 1941 President Roosevelt authorized $1,500,000 to purchase a 174-square-mile tract for the Marine Corps. The area had been occupied by whites and African Americans since the Colonial era, and seven hundred families, mostly black, had to be relocated. Landowners were compensated, but many of the poor black sharecroppers who eked out a living on tiny plots of tobacco, peanuts, and sunflowers were not. The government moved them, along with their houses, cabins, farm buildings, and stores. The government also collected records on all the cemeteries and moved the remains to new ground outside the base. On April 5, 1941, Congress authorized $14,575,000 for the base's construction. The camp was officially activated on May 1, 1941, and the Marines used the rotting shacks, sagging tobacco barns, sheds, and privies that had been left behind as targets for artillery and mortar practice.

After returning from Cuba, the First Division filled out its regiments at Parris Island. In need of an operational staging area, it moved into New River in September 1941. New River was a camp only in name. The First Division's World War II historian called it "111,170 acres of water, coastal swamp, and plain, therefore inhabited largely by sand flies, ticks, chiggers, and snakes." A Marine veteran who had been in the Nicaraguan campaigns said that New River was worse than the jungle. Officers and men lived under canvas set up over wooden decks. But New River had everything the 1st Division needed: swamps, pine barrens, and miles of beach for amphibious landing training. In December 1942 the installation was named in honor of the 13th commandant of the Marine Corps, Lieutenant General John A. Lejeune.

In March 1943 the Marine Corps got another regiment, the 24th, which had just been organized on the West Coast. On May 1, a third regiment was added when the 24th was divided and half the men went on to form the 25th Marine regiment. The 4th Marine Division was formally activated on August 14, 1943.

Just a year before, no one would have dared to advertise a train full of Marines. After Pearl Harbor, sabotage was still a worry, and everyone knew that "loose lips sank ships."

### CHAPTER 6: ELEANOR ROOSEVELT'S NIGGERS

One of the South's most prominent papers, the Richmond, Virginia, *News Leader*, editorialized, "If Negro soldiers are to be drafted into the army or are to be accepted as volunteers, they must be treated as fellow-soldiers and not as vassals or as racial inferiors."

Letter from the fifteen black mess attendants on the *Philadelphia* is from the *Pittsburgh Courier,* October 5, 1940, page 4, and from Hayward Farrar's book, *The Baltimore Afro-American: 1892–1950.*

The quotes about the president and the "colored race" are from Secretary of War Stimson's diaries at Yale University. Stimson's thoughts on blacks and integration can be found in *On Active Service in Peace and War,* by Henry Stimson and McGeorge Bundy, and in Morris J. McGregor's *Integration of the Armed Forces.*

The quote from General George Marshall is from *The Papers of George Catlett Marshall,* vol. 2 (1981). For an accurate depiction of Marshall's feelings about the integration of the Army, see also Morris J. McGregor's *Integration of the Armed Forces.*

Robert Patterson's response to FDR is from George Flynn's *The Mess in Washington: Manpower Mobilization in World War II.*

The quote from the NAACP regarding blacks being denied democracy is from Christopher Moore's *Fighting for America: Black Soldiers—The Unsung Heroes of World War II.*

The *New York Daily News* carried full-page photos of the KKK and Southern sharecroppers. The caption read, "Should We Fight to Save the World . . . While These Things Continue at Home? Tell your president," the paper suggested, "that you want democracy to work properly at home before you fight for it abroad." Later that same year the *Pittsburgh Courier* published the results of a controversial opinion poll, showing that 90 percent of those questioned favored more aggressive demands for integration. Another 33 percent said it was more important to defeat racism at home than it was to bring Germany or Japan to their knees.

Presidential candidate Wendell Wilkie asked, "Are we always as alert to practice [democracy] here at home as we are to proclaim it abroad?"

Had Marshall truly wanted change, he had to look no further than the Merchant Marine model: total integration. Merchant Marines ate in integrated mess halls and bunked in integrated barracks, and black officers enjoyed the same privileges and responsibilities as their white counterparts.

Blacks had an impressive record in battle. In the war of 1812, General Andrew Jackson, the commander of U.S. forces on the Gulf Coast, raised an army of free black Louisiana volunteers. They fought bravely against British regulars, and Jackson commended them for their "courage and perseverance." After the war, however, the volunteers were not allowed to remain in the army. A War

Department memo insisted, "A Negro is deemed unfit to associate with the American soldier."

After Lincoln issued his Emancipation Proclamation, 180,000 black volunteers served in racially segregated combat units of the federal army known as the "United States Colored Troops." They displayed their courage at Port Hudson, Louisiana, on May 27, 1863, when they stormed the entrenched city and fought hand-to-hand with Confederate soldiers. One union officer wrote, "They were exposed to a terrible fire and were dreadfully slaughtered . . . all who witnessed their charges agree that their conduct was such as would do honor to any soldiers." By the end of the Civil War blacks made up 10 percent of the Union forces. Their death rate was proportionally much higher than that among white troops because they were often used as assault troops and given inferior medical care. Major General David Hunter wrote to Secretary of War William Stanton, "I find the colored regiments hardy, generous, temperate, strictly obedient, possessing remarkable aptitude for military training. . . . I am happy to announce to you that the prejudices of certain of our white soldiers against these indispensable allies are rapidly softening or fading out."

Union General Benjamin F. Butler, who was initially skeptical of black soldiers, wrote this commendation after the Battle of New Market in October 1864: "The colored soldiers by coolness, steadiness, determined courage and dash, have silenced every cavil of the doubters of their soldierly capacity." A decade later in a speech to Congress on the granting of civil rights to the Negro, Butler said that after that battle, "I swore to myself a solemn oath: 'May my right hand forget its cunning, and my tongue cleave to the roof of my mouth, if ever I fail to defend the rights of the men who have given their blood for me and my country this day and for their race forever.' And, God helping me, I will keep that oath."

Many blacks also became Indian fighters. General William Tecumseh Sherman, who was commanding general of the Army in 1877, was so impressed with their fighting skills that he recommended that the Army integrate its units just as the Navy had done.

In Cuba, black soldiers of the 10th Cavalry saved Teddy Roosevelt's Rough Riders. The 10th drew Spanish fire and then drove them into retreat. Shortly after the battle, Roosevelt complimented the black soldiers of the 9th and 10th cavalries for their bravery, saying that no Rough Rider would ever forget them. A white captain of the 10th Cavalry said, "I am perfectly satisfied that if they were called upon to march through the gates of Hades they would do so in the same jaunty manner in which they went up San Juan Hill." Newspapers across the country carried a poem called "The Charge of the Nigger Ninth." West Point Colonel James A. Moss, who also fought in Cuba, wrote later, "I do not hesitate to make the assertion that if properly trained and instructed, the Negro will make as good a soldier as the world has ever seen. . . . Anyone who says the Negro will not fight, does not of course, know what he is talking about."

When given the opportunity to perform more-challenging tasks, black units like the 345th Quartermasters made the 1,000-mile run from the Persian Gulf through Iran to the Russian border, transporting crucial war supplies to the Russians who were struggling to stop the German offensive. Blacks also served as engineers. Sixty percent of the men that hacked the rugged, 271-mile Ledo Road across India, Burma, and China were black. In 1942, three of the seven regiments building the "Pioneer Road" across Alaska and Canada were black. In early March 1943, Allied land-based bombers destroyed a Japanese convoy in the Bismarck Sea. The all-black 96th Engineer Battalion built the bases from which the American bombers took off and landed.

In 1936 Frank Knox was widely considered the best prospect within the Republican Party to run for president. At the Republican National Convention, however, Alf Landon had been announced as the nominee. On the drive home from the convention, Knox and his wife learned from a radio broadcast that Knox was the party's choice for vice president. Though he and Landon lost the election to Franklin D. Roosevelt, who carried every state but two, Knox gained admiration from the president and was named secretary of the Navy in 1940. In a bid for national unity, FDR also named another former Republican, Henry Stimson, secretary of war.

Walter White, secretary of the National Association for the Advancement of Colored People, was one sixty-fourth black. White's fair-skinned father died in excruciating pain when surgeons at the white wing of an Atlanta hospital, where he had been mistakenly taken for an emergency operation, refused to treat him.

The Selective Service and Training Act provided in its preamble that "(b) The Congress further declares that in a free society the obligations and privileges of military training and service should be shared generally in accordance with a fair and just system of selective compulsory military training and service." The third proviso of Section 3(a) gave practical application to this declared policy: "[A]ny person, regardless of race or color, between the ages of eighteen and forty-five, shall be afforded an opportunity to volunteer for induction into the land and naval forces of the United States for the training and service prescribed in subsection (b)." And the first proviso of Section 4(a) stated the obligation of the armed forces toward all men taken into service: "[I]n the selection and training of men under this Act, and in the interpretation and execution of the provisions of this Act, there shall be no discrimination against any person on account of race or color." A third position, however, gave the War Department final authority in deciding who would or would not be accepted into the military. Blacks volunteered for induction in record numbers, but many were turned away by the War Department and the new law provided them with no means of redress.

Just prior to draft registration day, President Roosevelt's press secretary, Stephen Early, announced a follow-up to the Selective Training and Service Act, a seven-point plan for the "fair and equitable utilization of blacks" in the military. As further evidence of Roosevelt's commitment to change, "Negroes will be drafted in proportion to their population ratio—about one to every eleven men; [t]hey will be used in every branch of service; Negro reserve officers will serve with outfits which already have Negro officers; [t]hey will be given a chance to earn reserve commissions when officers' schools are set up; [t]hey will be trained as pilots and aviation mechanics; Negro civilians will have an equal chance with whites for jobs at arsenals and army posts; Negro and white soldiers will not serve in the same regiments."

In an interview with correspondent Clark Lee, General Masaharu Homma boasted that Japan was prepared to sacrifice a generation of young men, if it came to war. Lee captured the general's haunting words in *Collier's* magazine. "We are prepared to lose ten million men in our war with America," Homma said. "How many are you prepared to lose?"

At the time Homma posed the question, the bigger uncertainty for the American military was, where would it get its men if war broke out? In December 1941, more than a year after President Roosevelt signed the controversial Selective Training and Service Act, every branch of service, especially the Navy, was still undermanned.

Another pressing question was whether or not young American men were ready to meet the trials of war. In the summer of 1941 the Army, in particular, was in disarray. Morale among soldiers was dangerously low. Men who had welcomed mobilization in 1940 and looked forward to their release in the fall of 1941 were forced to contend with the possibility that Congress, responding to President Roosevelt's request, would extend their period of service by eighteen months.

The Selective Training and Service Act, the piece of legislation with which President Roosevelt, on September 16, 1940, established the first peacetime draft in American history, was enormously controversial. The War Department, which had been studying conscription strategies for years, knew it would be. Some people considered it the act of a government betraying its fascist tendencies. On the Capitol grounds, protesters of the act burned in effigy the bill's champions. Six women, dressed as mourning widows, took up a silent vigil in the galleries of the Senate and then the House. The discussions in Congress regarding the bill turned tense. At one point in early September, not long before the vote, a fistfight broke out on the floor of the House.

In August 1941 the new bill's opponents (many Republicans and some Democrats) insisted that prolonging the service of soldiers represented a breach of contract; men had signed up with the belief that the act obligated them to serve for just one year. General Marshall lamented the language of the original bill, and the need for the extension, but insisted that "the battle worthiness of nearly every American division" was at stake. On August 12, 1941, the new bill came before the House of Representatives and passed by a single vote, when the speaker of the House abruptly shut down voting. Republicans fumed. House rules, they maintained, allowed those who wanted to change their vote time to approach the speaker before he announced the official tally.

Army camps across the country were already rife with discontent. The previous fall, after France had fallen and as the Luftwaffe bombed England, millions of citizen-soldiers had taken up the urgent call for national service. When a Gallup poll study, conducted among men ages sixteen to twenty-four, was published in the October 1940 issue of *Reader's Digest,* Selective Service officials took heart. "American youth," the article said, "is tough-fibered, loyal, and hopeful. The young people believe this is a good country, worth working and fighting for. They have faith in the future." Seventy-six percent of men surveyed did not object to one year of military service.

By the summer of 1941, however, the crisis had dimmed; because few people thought the United States was in imminent danger, soldiers no longer felt they had a purpose. They viewed their training as old-fashioned and inadequate. They also felt the sting of being ignored, and often avoided, by everyday citizens. Many felt that they were treated as "outcasts," "shunned" and neglected by the "nice girls." Servicemen across the country were looking forward to getting out and returning home to their families. As the debate over the new bill raged, *Life* magazine published a bombshell exposé on the mood of America's GIs. For the article, a *Life* reporter interviewed four hundred privates from five different regiments, from an unspecified division. Morale, the reporter concluded, had reached alarmingly low levels. "As far as the men can see," he wrote, "the Army has no goal. It does not know whether it is going to fight, or when or where." Writing in *Harper's* magazine, Mortimer Adler added his voice to the controversy. "Whether they go to war or not," he warned, "irreparable harm has been done to the young men of this generation." Adler implied that young men had become "cynical and immune to appeals of patriotism."

Debate in Congress over the unpopular bill fanned the flames of rebellion in Army camps across the country and soldiers talked openly of what they called "OHIO." They would stage a massive desertion, going "Over the Hill in October." Soldiers scrawled the code name OHIO on the inside of latrines, scratched it into sand paths, painted it on the hoods of trucks, on barracks walls, and on fieldpieces.

Deeply disturbed by the *Life* report, A. H. Sulzberger, publisher of the *New York Times,* asked the War Department and Brigadier General Alexander Surles, its director of the Bureau of Public Relations, if his paper could investigate the reliability of the report. To the amazement of some inside the military establishment, the War Department agreed to give the *New York Times* unfettered access to its army installations. In return Sulzberger pledged not to publish the paper's findings if he felt that they would not be in the nation's best interests.

Sulzberger assigned to the story Hilton H. Railey, a member of the *Times* staff, a field representative of the War and Navy departments during World War I, and a reserve officer in the Office of Naval Intelligence. Skeptical of the *Life* report, the patriotic Railey traveled 8,000 miles and interviewed thousands of officers and enlisted men. Working from Railey's notes, Sulzberger and Railey put together a confidential, two-hundred-page report titled "Morale in the U.S. Army." Railey's discoveries—low morale (resembling the morale of the country in general, and its lack of interest in the international situation), drunkenness, insubordination, fraternization between officers and enlisted men—alarmed the General Staff. Perhaps Railey's most disturbing observation, however, was that modern-day soldiers were a "different breed of cat" than World War I servicemen, and "bereft of national unity." He added that "little is sacred to these young men. . . . They do not feel like fighting for what they have because they don't *know* what they have." Railey continued, "The present breed is questioning everything from God Almighty to themselves."

Railey wrote, "Men of all branches . . . do not believe the U.S. is imperiled . . . it points . . . to their conviction that, 'This is England's war,' or is, at most, 'just another European brawl.' . . . The overwhelming majority believe that they are being dragged into a war which is none of their business . . . and distrust the president's relations with Mr. Churchill."

Sulzberger sent the report to Washington at the end of September 1941. In a memorandum to General Marshall concerning Railey's findings, Brigadier General L. J. McNair, who, as chief of staff of U.S. Army general headquarters, supervised the army training program, expressed his dismay. He wrote that the "revelations" were "astounding." After circulating the document to Army corps commanders, the War Department promptly classified it as secret. Sulzberger held up his end of the bargain and the pages of the *Times* never carried a whisper of what Railey had found.

While Railey focused on the American GI, and most especially on National Guard units, the implication of the report was far-reaching. It suggested that the military, in general, would be dealing with a less committed, less patriotic, softer, and more materialistic generation of young men. According to Railey, "We cannot whip Hitler with the force now in training."

The black community, in general, had turned against the president so much that some of his closest advisers feared that he had already lost the election. Later in the war, the leading black newspapers were very critical of FDR's administration, and the black press's intense coverage of racial abuses concerned FDR. The president feared that it was wearing away the black community's support for the war. FDR tried to persuade Walter White to muzzle the black press. White called a meeting of black publishers, including Carl Murphy of the *Baltimore Afro-American,* to warn the publishers about going too far in their criticisms. The FBI subjected black newspapers to intense scrutiny, and there had been talk about charging some black newspapers with sedition. In the January 1943 issue of *The*

*Atlantic Monthly,* Virginius Dabney, editor of the *Richmond Times Dispatch,* criticized the black press for "stirring up interracial hate."

After Steve Early suggested to newspaper and magazine reporters that the three civil rights leaders had approved the War Department's proposal, *The Crisis,* the official magazine of the NAACP, wrote that the Roosevelt administration had acted shamefully by not allowing "Negroes a fair chance in the armed forces." The statement was dated October 11 and read in full: "We are inexpressibly shocked that a president of the United States at a time of national peril should surrender so completely to enemies of Democracy who would destroy national unity by advocating segregation. Official approval by the Commander-in-Chief of the Army and Navy of such discrimination is a stab in the back of Democracy and a blow at the patriotism of twelve million Negro citizens." In the midst of the storm, Randolph wrote angrily to FDR: "I was shocked and amazed when I saw the newspaper reports that the Negro committee had sanctioned segregation of Negroes in the armed forces of our country because I am sure that the committee made it definitely clear that it was opposed to segregation of the armed forces of the nation." White chose another avenue and wrote to Mrs. Roosevelt that her husband's administration had regrettably forced his hand. White knew where the First Lady's interests and sympathies lay and knew that he could count on her to press her husband.

Black newspapers printed Randolph's call to march in big headlines so that all could see. Randolph raised money and rallied the black community: "Be not dismayed in these terrible times. You possess power, great power. The Negro stake in national defense is big. It consists of jobs, thousands of jobs. It consists of new industrial opportunities and hope. This is worth fighting for. . . . We call upon President Roosevelt . . . to follow in the footsteps of his noble and illustrious predecessor [Lincoln] and take the second decisive step to free America—an executive order to abolish discrimination in the work place. One thing is certain and that is if Negroes are going to get anything out of this National defense, we must fight for it and fight for it with gloves off."

According to NAACP leader Roy Wilkins, Randolph was a "tall courtly black man with Shakespearean diction and the stare of an eagle [who] had looked the patrician FDR in the eye—and made him back down."

General Holcomb's quotes are from *Blacks in the Marine Corps* by Henry Shaw and Ralph Donnelly and *The Right to Fight: African-American Marines in World War II* by Bernard Nalty.

## CHAPTER 7: THE RIGHT TO FIGHT

Hoping to stave off the entrance of blacks, every branch of service seized upon an Army War College report titled "The Use of Negro Manpower in War." The report was written by Major-General H. E. Ely. "In physical courage," the report concluded, "it must be admitted that the American Negro falls well back of the white man and possibly all other races." When a new War College report was issued more than a decade later, in 1936, it echoed the same sentiments, "As an individual the negro is docile, tractable, lighthearted, care free and good natured. If unjustly treated he is likely to become surly and stubborn. . . . He is careless, shiftless, irresponsible and secretive. He is unmoral, untruthful; and his sense of right and wrong is relatively inferior."

General Lewis Hershey, who presided over the Selective Service Board, loyally carried out the racist policies of the War Department. In direct violation of the Selective Service Act, which stipulated that there could be no "discrimination" in the selection and training of men, as long as a minority's numbers in the military did not exceed its percentage of the total population of the country, he established racial quotas. Ignoring the quotas, some state board directors sent men to induction stations by draft order number, regardless of race. This practice was especially common in the South, where state boards tried to send blacks to war in numbers exceeding established War Department allotments. These men were most often returned to Selective Service without a physical examination or were rejected for a host of contrived physical ailments. Hershey warned the defiant directors and local board members that those "who sent blacks to induction would be subject to suspension."

Blacks faced hurdles in the defense industry, too. They could work as janitors, but the better-paying positions as mechanics and aircraft workers were taken and reserved for whites. Echoing the resistance of the military establishment to using blacks, a belligerent Standard Steel spokesman told the Urban League, "We have not had a Negro working in 25 years and do not plan to start now." Vultee Air in California was equally emphatic: "It is not the policy of this company to employ workers other than those of the Caucasian race."

William Hastie, a black man, was an energetic advocate of integration and the person whom President Roosevelt chose to be the civilian aide to Secretary of War Henry Stimson. Regarding the military's stance on racial issues, Hastie said of Stimson, "Well, Mr. Stimson was concerned but he, in my judgment, had no feel for, no real perception of the problems of race in America, or their impact, or the relation of the military to them. He was a most honest and dedicated man, a patriot in the best and the highest sense of the word, but he was a man whose whole life in his practice of law, in his social contacts, his whole background, had isolated him from the areas, the problems, of which I was basically concerned. Mr. Stimson was entirely well meaning and I have no reason that he was in any way a prejudiced person. I always felt that he was basically uncomprehending as to the realities of the problems of race in the Army and in the American society generally. Secretary Patterson, a much younger man, was much more perceptive and I think did whatever he could, but, as I said, I think even more then than today, perhaps, or as much then as today, the civilian leadership in the War Department was a captive of the military."

Nevertheless, on July 2, 1941, Secretary of the Navy Frank Knox, who had gone on record saying that any service at sea other than cooking or serving food lay beyond the capabilities of nonwhites, created a committee to inquire into the "existing relationship between the United States Navy, United States Marine Corps and the Negro race" and to investigate whether the Navy should accept blacks for other duties. Its explicit purpose was to "investigate and report to SecNav the extent to which [sic] the enlisted personnel of the Navy and Marine Corps is representative of all United States Citizens, and in case there should be any evidence of discrimination because of race, creed, color or national origin, to suggest corrections."

As the Navy resisted the inclusion of blacks on a large scale, so, too, did the Army. William Hastie issued a biting report that left the Army stubbornly defending its policies. The essence of Hastie's paper was that the Army was doing an abysmal job of utilizing black troops. It began, "The traditional mores of the South have been widely accepted and adopted by the Army as the basis of policy and practice affecting the Negro soldier. . . . In tactical organization, in physical location, in human contacts, the Negro soldier is separated from the white soldier as completely as possible. . . . The isolation of Negro combat troops, the failure to make many of them parts of large combat teams, the refusal to mingle Negro officers—most of whom have had little opportunity to command and train soldiers in units with experienced officers of the Regular Army, all are retarding the training of Negro soldiers." He continued, "The newly enlisted Negro soldiers have been disproportionately concentrated in the Corps of Engineers, the Quartermaster Corps, and installations" where they perform "nonmilitary duties of unskilled and menial character" that were best left to "civilian employees. . . . Where there are both colored and white service detachments in the Overhead of a particular station, the most undesirable duties are assigned to the colored detachment."

William Hastie's papers are housed in the Harvard Law School Library. Hastie is also quoted at length in Morris MacGregor's exhaustive *Integration of the Armed Forces 1940–1965*. Marshall's reply to Hastie's proposal can also be found in MacGregor's book.

Secretray Knox's quote is from "The Negro in the United States Navy in World War II" (written by the Historical Section of the Bureau of Naval Personnel), which is a section of *The U.S. Navy in World War II*.

The Army's defense was that the concentration of blacks in labor units was justified by the proportionately large numbers of blacks in Class V, the lowest on the Army General Classification Test (AGCT). Hastie disputed this logic. "The evidence of field commanders," he wrote, "indicates that a high percentage of the men with little education or acquired skill at the time of their induction, can be used effectively in combat units. Many such men have basic intelligence and are eager to learn for the very reason that opportunity has been denied them in civilian life. And even for men of small intelligence there are many important jobs in Combat organizations."

Hastie added, "I sincerely believe that much of the difficulty being experienced in arousing the nation today is traceable to the fact that we have lost that passion for national ideals which a people must have if it is to work and sacrifice for its own survival. . . . Until the men in our Army and civilians at home believe in and work for democracy with similar fervor and determination, we will not be an effective nation in the face of a foreign foe. So long as we condone and appease un-American attitudes and practices within our own military and civilian life, we can never arouse ourselves to the exertion which the present emergency requires."

Hastie then went on to make a series of recommendations for the integration of black troops. Most were largely symbolic. The last point, however, in which he called for the Army to make a "beginning in the employment of soldiers without racial separation," served only to inspire the Army's intransigence. He submitted his recommendations to Robert Patterson, the assistant secretary of war, who in turn forwarded it to General Marshall with a note. Patterson asked, "Will you please give this your careful consideration and let me have your views on it? It will probably be best to have an oral discussion of these issues." In mid-November 1941, almost two months after Hastie presented his suggestions, Patterson reminded General Marshall that he hoped to discuss "at an early date Judge Hastie's memorandum of suggestions on Negro troops in the Army." Patterson had sent the memo to Marshall on October 6.

On December 1, 1941, Marshall finally addressed himself to the report. In a memorandum to Secretary of War Henry Stimson, he wrote, "A solution of many of the issues presented by Judge Hastie in his memorandum on 'The Integration of the Negro Soldier into the Army,' dated September 22, would be tantamount to solving a social problem that has perplexed the American people throughout the history of this nation. The Army cannot accomplish such a solution, and should not be charged with the undertaking. The settlement of vexing racial problems cannot be permitted to complicate the tremendous task of the War Department and thereby jeopardize discipline and morale.

"The problems presented with reference to utilizing negro personnel in the Army should be faced squarely. In doing so, the following facts must be recognized: first, that the War Department cannot ignore the social relationships between negroes and whites which has been established by the American people through custom and habit; second, that either through lack of educational opportunities or other causes the level of intelligence and occupational skill of the negro population is considerably below that of the white; third, that the Army will attain its maximum strength only if its personnel is properly placed in accordance with the capabilities of individuals; and fourth, that experiments within the Army in the solution of social problems are fraught with danger to efficiency, discipline, and morale."

Four days later, Marshall's Deputy Chief of Staff discussed the matter with Undersecretary Patterson, explaining that "[t]he immediate task of the Army is the efficient completion of our Defense Program. Nothing should be permitted to divert us from this task. Contrary to the bulk of the recommendations, every effort should be made by the War Department to maintain in the Army the social and racial conditions, which exist in civil life in order that the normal customs of the white and colored personnel now in the army may not be suddenly disrupted. The Army can, under no circumstances, adopt a policy, which is contrary to the dictates of a majority of the people. To do so would alienate the people from the Army and lower their morale at a time when their support of the Army and high morale are vital to our National needs."

Two days after Pearl Harbor, the NAACP wired Secretary Knox, asking whether, in light of the war effort, the Navy would accept colored recruits for other than the messman's branch. In the vacuum created by the committee's lack of a decision, the Bureau of the Navy issued a stock reply: there had been no change in policy and none was contemplated. Furious, the NAACP took its case to the president on December 17, 1941. The *Baltimore Afro-American,* which, prior to the war, had assured Roosevelt of the black community's support, lashed out, too. "Why not let the country go to the dogs and go about our business?" its editors asked in a stinging editorial.

Many of the conversations, and much of the correspondence, between FDR and Secretary Knox can be found in "The Negro in the United States Navy in World War II."

An editorial in the May 1942 issue of the magazine *Opportunity* blasted the Navy's policy of segregation. "They might have provided for the training of small units of white and Negro boys together as an experiment," the editorial read. "Vast experiments are being conducted with machines, why not experiment with men? But the Navy Department . . . chose rather to perpetuate and extend second-class status for citizens of color. Faced with a great opportunity to strengthen the forces of democracy, the Navy Department chose to affirm the charge that Japan is making against America to the brown people of Malaya, and the Philippines, India and the Dutch East Indies . . . that the so-called 'Four Freedoms' are for white men only."

FDR's comment about finding room for "colored enlistees" is from "The Negro in the United States Navy in World War II."

One biographer of Admiral King called his approach to blacks one of "benevolent ignorance." King was no racist. Rather, his opinion of blacks reflected the prejudices of his generation. He was largely ignorant of their condition, his attitudes informed by author Octavus Roy Cohen, who wrote stories for *The Saturday Evening Post.* Cohen said that he depicted Negroes as they were in the South, "the happiest people on the face of the globe." He loved Negro spirituals, sometimes told off-color ethnic jokes, and called black men "darkies" and Navy messmen "boys."

The use of African American manpower late in the war was a result of the massive attrition suffered in the winter of 1944 in Europe. As the infantry replacement pool evaporated in the ETO, radical steps were taken. In January 1945, General Eisenhower took the then-unprecedented step of allowing African American soldiers to volunteer as combat infantry replacements. The response was overwhelming. Soldiers accepted reductions in rank in exchange for the chance to fight. These men were assigned to hard-hit divisions, where they soon made an impression. Eager to prove critics of African American combat prowess wrong, these men made up for their lack of experience with reckless bravery. Most of the replacements continued to serve in effectively segregated units; most of the divisions, however, formed them into separate platoons or companies that were attached to white units.

A thorough description of the high-level discussions regarding the integration of the Navy can be found in "The Negro in the United States Navy in World War II."

## CHAPTER 8: THE FIRST

Many of the details for this chapter are taken from Lieutenant T. A. Larson's *History of the U.S. Naval Training Center, Great Lakes, Illinois, In World War II* and a thirty-five-page Naval Intelligence Service (Ninth Naval District) confidential memorandum regarding racial tension at the Naval Training Center, Great Lakes.

Though many doubted its validity, the Navy and Marine Corps used the Naval General Classification Test to discourage black enlistment. The exam was made up of of 150 multiple-choice questions, consisting of math, vocabulary, and basic logic, which emphasized spatial thinking. According to the Navy, the exam measured "usable intelligence" or "trainability." Scores were divided into five classes, with Class I scoring 130 or more and Class V scoring below 70. Once in the Navy, those who had scored poorly on the test had little prospect for technical training.

In his book *Hidden Heroism,* Robert Edgerton argues that the AGCT (the Army's version of the test) was used to prove that blacks were "innately stupid." What the Army wanted was black laborers to free whites for combat duty, and the AGCT, according to Edgerton, "provided the inferiority the Army was looking for."

Blacks scored on average lower than whites—sometimes significantly lower—which the War Department used as "proof" that blacks were less intelligent than whites and less able to perform military duties except labor. The Navy used the results of the tests to justify its policy of keeping blacks at shore installations, arguing that as a group they were less able to perform military duties other than labor.

The Committee on Selection and Classification of Military Personnel was created by the National Research Council at the request of the Adjutant General of the U.S. Army with responsibility for "development, construction, validation, and standardization of all personnel screening test and interview techniques for the Army."

Boykin and Cunningham were traveling north, but black servicemen traveling south of Washington, D.C., were moved from sleeping cars to segregated cars once they crossed what was known as the "black line."

The exact day of the Great Lakes announcement was June 6, 1942.

Details of the lieutenant's welcome speech are from Sammie Boykin.

Camp Robert Smalls was previously called Camp Morrow because it lay along Morrow Road. Robert Smalls was a pilot on a Confederate transport ship. In May 1862, Smalls ran the *Planter* out of Charleston Harbor and delivered it into the hands of a Union squadron. Smalls was honored for his heroism and was subsequently made a pilot in the Union Navy.

In September 1942, Armstrong established the "Remedial School," which was set up to teach the basics of reading, writing, and arithmetic to black recruits. One of the officers wrote, "The amount of time and effort required to train these recruits is admittedly much greater than is necessary for normal men. In view of the following considerations, it is exceedingly doubtful whether this expenditure is justified." According to reports, Negro regiments also had a very high percentage of non-swimmers—80 to 90 percent as compared with only 30 percent in white regiments and a "high rate of venereal disease found among men returning from leave."

Armstrong's officers complained that motivation was exactly what was missing among the black men. The recruits' priorities, the officers said, were the "improvement of the Negro race and complete equality," and not the war.

Some of the white training commanders at Great Lakes also questioned Armstrong's tactics, suggesting that he placed too much faith in recruits of limited ability, hurriedly promoted blacks of dubious achievement, made too many promises, and was soft on problem recruits, treating them with kid gloves for offenses that would have elicited courts-martial in white camps. Quietly they established their own, harsher system of justice, administering penalties "in a manner understandable to the Negro."

In July 1942, Armstrong set up what was called the "slacker squad" (also known as the Correction Squad) for recalcitrant recruits. Ignoring Armstrong's guidelines for disciplining problem recruits, training commanders took the punishment of slackers into their own hands. According to Lieutenant T. A. Larson, who wrote *History of the U.S. Naval Training Center Great Lakes, Illinois, in World War II* (Washington, DC: Office of Naval History, 1945), "Negro Training" meant "taking a recalcitrant recruit into a room where there were no witnesses and beating him." "The Negro in the United States Navy in World War II," from the Bureau of Naval Personnel, however, says of the "slacker squad" that "putting them in the brig would not cure ignorance, so instead they were put in a specially hard-worked and hard-drilled detail."

According to a Great Lakes Intelligence Report, only 5,549 blacks entered the Service Schools at Great Lakes between September 12, 1942, when the school was established, and July 18, 1944.

In September 1942, the presidents of the seventeen Negro Land Grant Colleges met in Chicago and went on record with the Negro press criticizing the Navy's failure to commission Negro officers.

In 1910 a host of cities throughout the South, following the example set by Baltimore's city council, ratified ordinances that allowed them to establish separate white and black neighborhoods. The trend spread north and west to St. Louis and Oklahoma City. When the Louisville city council tried to enact similar legislation, the NAACP filed a suit in federal court. One year later the Supreme Court struck down the segregation law, calling it unconstitutional. Proponents of the movement, however, fought back. Southern cities implemented methods that had proved successful in the North, achieving segregation through a mixture of intimidation, racially restrictive covenants (whereby a landowner would sign an agreement saying he would not permit a black to own or lease his property), discriminatory real estate practices, and zoning restrictions. In fact, the Federal Housing Authority's 1939 Underwriting Manual encouraged the practice, stating that "if a neighborhood is to retain stability, it is necessary that properties shall continue to be occupied by the same social and racial classes."

By the time Boykin walked through the gates of the U.S. Naval Training Center at Great Lakes, in Waukegan, Illinois, the perimeters of the modern black ghetto were firmly defined in Birmingham and other Southern cities as well as Northern cities like Chicago.

In March 1926 the front page of the *New York Herald* featured an exposé on Southern slavery. The stories reported that in fifty-one of Alabama's sixty-seven counties, nearly one thousand prisoners had been sold into slave mines and forced labor camps the previous year, generating $250,000 for local officials. In 1925 the state government earned $595,000 from the same practice. In excess of eight thousand men—nearly all black—worked on chain gangs in 116 Southern counties. By 1930 Georgia had more forced labor slaves than ever before.

Even in a large city like Mobile, blacks were forced to observe a 10:00 p.m.

curfew. A crime of indecency was the most serious charge. A black man could be accused of indecency for merely looking the wrong way at a white woman. A sheriff might turn a "criminal" or a fugitive over to an angry mob that would pour kerosene over him and set him afire. Those who survived lived in pain, their lips the color of charcoal, their hair, ears, and nose burned and shriveled to nothing. The jails were bad, but the camps to which sheriffs sent young black men raised misery to new heights. There, overseers routinely beat them. Those who avoided the whip and the club endured squalid living conditions and the threat of disease. Outbreaks of pneumonia, tuberculosis, and dysentery were common.

Blacks sought different things in the North. Inspired by flashy advertisements in newspapers like the *Chicago Defender* and the *Baltimore Afro-American,* they came by the thousands searching for economic opportunity and Henry Ford's five-dollar day. Some were lured by the promise of electric lights and indoor plumbing, while others left to escape oppression or to ensure that their children got a decent education. In the South, black schools got only ten cents of every dollar spent on public education, and were often nothing more than airy shacks with leaky roofs. They were plagued by a shortage of books, and taught by inferior, underpaid teachers. Even the brightest students went to school a quarter less than their white counterparts. Many Southern blacks received a poor reception in the Northern cities, where whites regarded them as uncouth, unclean, uneducated, and uninspired. Working-class immigrants especially resented their arrival.

They competed for jobs with immigrants, and industries often viewed blacks as a cheap source of labor. It did not take long for Northern cities to grow combustible. Angry whites, feeling their livelihoods (blacks competed for jobs, especially in the stockyards and meatpacking plants) and neighborhoods imperiled, beat, shot, and lynched blacks, and ransacked and burned their houses. In New York City; East Saint Louis, Illinois; Springfield, Illinois; and Chicago, rampaging bands of whites pulled blacks off trolley cars and dragged them off city sidewalks. In Chicago fifty-eight black homes were bombed between 1917 and 1921. In addition to using Southern blacks to man the factories of wartime industries, northern employers hired Southern blacks because of their utility as strikebreakers in labor disputes. In the 1920s, 877,000 blacks left their homes for the North. Many whites considered them a pestilence. One paper exclaimed, HALF A MILLION DARKIES BRING PERIL TO HEALTH.

The city of Chicago was the site of a violent riot during the summer of 1919. In July a heat wave settled over the city. Whites and blacks alike flooded the beaches of Lake Michigan, seeking relief. On July 27, at the 29th Street Beach, a black boy crossed into a "white" swimming area. Angry beachgoers battered him with stones, and the boy drowned. When a policeman investigating the incident refused to arrest any of the whites, and instead booked a black beachgoer for a minor offense, a group of blacks attacked him, hurling rocks at the whites who tried to rescue him.

Reports of the incident spread throughout Chicago. Blacks required little incitement.

The drowning of the boy and its aftermath released long-simmering racial resentments. For seven days, riots raged. White gangs talked of burning down the black ghetto and running its residents out of town. A mob of white men even threatened to ransack Provident Hospital. The first black-owned and -operated hospital in America, Provident was established in 1893 by Dr. Daniel Hale Williams, a black American surgeon, to provide blacks with medical services they were often denied. Police held off the mob, but violence broke out elsewhere, including the prosperous confines of Chicago's Loop district.

Much of the rioting, however, occurred in Chicago's Black Belt. Although six thousand National Guard troops and nearly three thousand police officers tried to protect the neighborhoods from white looters, arsonists, and thugs, many pushed their way in. Blacks were attacked in parks and on streetcars, too. But they were not just innocent victims. They fought back, attacking and stoning and stabbing white civilians.

By the night of July 30, the bloodiest of the battles had ended, though smaller skirmishes persisted for another four days. When, on August 3, police and national guardsmen gained control over the city, and Mayor "Big Bill" Thompson officially declared the riot over; the casualty count was grim. Twenty-three blacks and fifteen whites had died, more than five hundred people were injured, and more than one thousand families, mostly black, were left homeless.

Many Southern blacks came from the five-state region comprising Texas, Oklahoma, Arkansas, Louisiana, and Mississippi.

Langston Hughes described the spirituals and the blues as "pain swallowed in a smile."

The Jim Crow system of race relations was at its most powerful during the early years of the twentieth century. Some unscrupulous landowners did whatever it took to cheat their sharecroppers; somehow the ledger always indicated that they were in the red. Those who resisted would be reported to the local sheriff, who administered justice any way he saw fit. Some sheriffs threw sharecroppers into crude jails on specious charges. Sharecroppers formed unions in the 1930s, beginning in Tallapoosa County, Alabama, in 1931, and Arkansas in 1934. Membership in the Southern Tenant Farmers Union included both blacks and poor whites. As leadership strengthened, meetings became more successful and protest became more vigorous; landlords responded with a wave of terror.

The situation of landless farmers who challenged the system in the rural South as late as 1941 has been described by Arthur Draper and Ira Reid in

*Sharecroppers All.* They write, "He is at once a target subject of ridicule and vitriolic denunciation; he may even be waylaid by hooded or unhooded leaders of the community, some of whom may be public officials. If a white man persists in 'causing trouble,' the night riders may pay him a visit, or the officials may haul him into court; if he is a Negro, a mob may hunt him down."

The Mexican boll weevil devastated Louisiana's cotton crop in 1906, Mississippi's in 1913, and Alabama's in 1916.

The big fun for many black families was the annual revival, which often amounted to a week-long event of eating and socializing. Black families brought heaping bowls of turnip greens and black-eyed peas with ham hocks, sugar-cured ham and boiled ribs, fried chicken, squirrel, possum, raccoon and rabbit, biscuits and cornbread, and sweet potato pie.

## CHAPTER 9: PORT CHICAGO

Although the episode at the Fred Harvey Restaurant disturbed Boykin, nothing could diminish his faith or damage his morale more than an incident he experienced at Great Lakes in the fall of 1942. In mid-September, President Roosevelt and his wife left Washington, D.C., by train for a two-week, coast-to-coast inspection of Army camps, Navy yards, and factories. North of Chicago, the Roosevelts visited Great Lakes, the largest training center of its kind, home to Boykin's regiment of black naval recruits and nearly seventy thousand white trainees.

The Roosevelts spent nearly the entire day touring the base facilities in the company of the commandant. Then Eleanor insisted that they stop and see the separate Camp Robert Smalls, where the president's former black valet, George Fields, was in training. Boykin was on guard duty and was walking the perimeter of the base as the president's limousine passed. He could see the president and the first lady inside. Boykin had been an admirer of the president and was filled with pride when the car passed by his post. Later, when he learned that the Roosevelts had spent the day on the base and had paused at Robert Smalls long enough only—a few minutes perhaps—to watch a unit complete the obstacle course, he felt disappointed and let down by the president. Had he shown up earlier and visited with the trainees, he could have inspired not only the men at Camp Robert Smalls, but black servicemen across the country. He could have given them instant legitimacy. Instead, Boykin was forced to swallow his frustration as he often had before. One thing he had learned growing up in the Deep South was that a man, especially a black man, had a limited ability to affect a situation. That which he could not change, he simply had to accept. It was not resignation, but rather a strategy for making one's way in the world.

## CHAPTER 10: BOMBS FOR THE BLACK BOYS

Many details regarding the Port Chicago Naval Ammunition Depot and the town are drawn from Dean McLeod's *Port Chicago,* Ken Rand's *Port Chicago Isn't There Anymore,* and a document titled "War Time History of the U.S. Naval Magazine, Port Chicago, California (December 5, 1945)" from the Naval Weapons Station, Concord, CA, Communications Officer.

Some of the quotes are taken from my interviews and Tracey Panek's oral-history interviews with the Port Chicago survivors (Port Chicago Naval Magazine National Memorial in Concord, California).

Hawthorne, Nevada, was 120 miles southeast of Reno.

During World War I, Port Chicago was used as a shipyard, and the Shipping Board built steamers there.

Ironically, great Japanese oil tankers pulled up to the Associated Oil docks throughout the 1930s. There is evidence that the Japanese fleet that took part in the attack on Pearl Harbor got oil from ships that loaded at Association Oil in mid-1941, despite a national embargo.

Liberty buses at Port Chicago were not available until the fall of 1943.

The profile of Captain Goss is derived from his testimony during the mutiny trial.

In a letter dated 4/29/43, Captain Goss wrote the Bureau of Personnel via the Bureau of Ordnance concerning the "Manpower Shortage" at Port Chicago. "The principal trouble with these men, aside from the normal shiftless habits of Negroes, continues to be the attitude of fancied discrimination. This, as previously referred to on several occasions, is undoubtedly both originally inspired and continually fostered by sources outside the Navy. It appears to be the result of an organized drive by political pressure groups to secure and obtain greater advantages for colored people as a matter of privilege and without regard to prior demonstration of ability. As one example: it has been found that enlisted men from naval vessels loading at Port Chicago have been glad to use the bus transportation which the colored enlisted men scorn to use."

  (Captain Goss suggests that the term "nigger" was no more derogatory than "limey," "wop," or "kike.")

Details on the arrival and departure of ammunition ships, and the size and nature of their loads (projectiles, bombs, ammunition, etc.), are from Port Chicago's War Diaries.

Even FDR thought the Liberty ships were "dreadful looking objects." He called them "ugly ducklings." However, the Allies could not have won the war without them. Liberty ships would become the workhorses of the Pacific. They were durable, relatively cheap, and easy to build—on average, Kaiser Ship Yards was banging out a new 10,000-ton Liberty ship every six weeks—and capable of carrying 10,800 deadweight tons of cargo.

Details on propellants, fuzes, etc., are from a restricted Navy Personnel Manual (16194) on "Ammunition Handling"; a book on "Bombs and Fuzes" issued by the U.S. Navy Bomb Disposal School to graduates of a course in Bomb Disposal and/or Advanced Fuze and Explosive Ordnance; and a July 30, 1945, manual issued by the Naval Training School (Ammunition Handling) at the USNAD, Hingham, MA, on "Underwater Ordnance and Impulse Ammunition." The USNAD at Hingham also issued a number of other manuals: one on August 15, 1945, on "Navy Explosives"; one on August 1, 1945, on "Rocket Ammunition"; and one on "Gun Ammunition" issued on April 15, 1945. I also consulted an April 6, 1945, War Department manual on "Nonpersistent Gas Bombs: Handling, Shipping, and Storage."

According to Morris Soublet, Lieutenant White was one of the few officers who treated the black seamen like men and made a practice of never belittling them or calling them "boys"—at least to their faces. Nothing angered Soublet more than being called "boy." He confronted one white officer who consistently used racial slurs and made it clear that he was not going to tolerate it anymore. Whether or not he threatened physical violence, Soublet's reputation was such that the officer took him seriously.

The July 12, 1943, War Diary does not mention the officer's suicide.

## CHAPTER 11: LIKE A DOG ON A BONE

Details regarding Montford Point are from *Blacks in the Marine Corps* by Henry Shaw and Ralph Donnelly, and *The Right to Fight: African-American Marines in World War II* by Bernard Nalty.

Details of Edgar Huff's life are from my interviews with his son, Edgar Huff Jr.; from an unfinished manuscript about Huff's life called "Sweat and Tears"; from Perry Fisher's and Brooks Gray's *Blacks and Whites: Together Through Hell* (from the *U.S. Marines in World War II* series); from an oral-history transcript from the History and Museums Division of the U.S. Marine Corps; from a "Profiles in Courage" book by Lieutenant Colonel Jesse Johnson, titled *Roots of Two Black Marine Sergeants Major;* and from a collection of magazine and newspaper articles.

Seven hundred fifty thousand dollars was set aside to expand existing facilities and build new ones for the black camp at Montford Point.

Outnumbered members of the 1st Defense Battalion defended Wake Island when the Japanese invaded. The new battalion would be called the 51st Composite Defense Battalion.

Montford Point was separated from New River by the coffee-colored New River and twelve miles of scrub pine. Montford Point had once been used for combat training of Fleet Marine Force units.

Seventy-five percent of Montford Point's black Marines had been to college or were in college.

The code used by Edgar Huff Sr. was a code the Germans were never able to break.

At the Abraham Lincoln Monument in Springfield, Illinois, President Teddy Roosevelt addressed the service record of black Americans in Cuba. Roosevelt said, "Any man who is good enough to shed his blood for his country is good enough to be given a square deal afterward." Many southerners expressed outrage over the implications of Roosevelt's speech. Senator James Vardaman, a Mississippi politician and unabashed racist, called Roosevelt a "little, mean, coon-flavored miscegenationist." After a dinner reported by the press in which Roosevelt dined with Booker T. Washington, Vardaman again attacked the president, saying that the White House was "so saturated with the odor of the nigger that the rats have taken refuge in the stable."

    Senator Vardaman worried that "[u]niversal military service means that millions of Negroes . . . will be armed. I know of no greater menace to the South than this." Vardaman had little to worry about. Of the 400,000 African Americans who served in World War I, only 42,000 would serve as combat soldiers. The Marines refused all black recruits and the Navy enlisted only 1 percent of its manpower from African Americans. Ironically, during the Civil War, the Navy had been 25 percent black. But on March 16, 1878, the secretary of war prescribed a set of rules governing the enrollment of Marines: "No Negro, Mulatto or Indian to be enlisted. . . ."

After the Civil War, blacks placed their hopes in a spate of ambitious legislation, including the Thirteenth, Fourteenth, and Fifteenth Amendments and the Civil Rights Act of 1866 and 1875, which sought to grant them the rights of full-fledged citizens of the United States. In 1877, however, when the contested election between Republican Rutherford Hayes and Democrat Samuel Tilden ended in a compromise whereby Hayes was awarded the election in return for the Republican Party's promise to remove federal troops from the South, Reconstruction came to a screeching halt, and much of the South retreated behind a wall of xenophobia. The backlash against newly empowered blacks was considerable. Able, now, to operate without the threat of federally imposed cooperation, the Democratic Party wasted little time in reasserting white dominion over the former states of the Confederacy, and white supremacist groups, including the Ku Klux Klan, used a variety of tactics—both violent and nonviolent—to intimidate and control blacks.

For a brief time after the Civil War, it appeared that life for blacks in the South might change. Blacks acquired land, established businesses, registered to vote in large numbers, and even assumed positions in state governments. Private charities raised money for new schools and churches. With the withdrawal of federal troops, however, and the disappointment of the Supreme Court rulings, blacks saw many of the gains they had made in the aftermath of the Civil War undermined.

The Thirteenth Amendment, ratified in 1865, was the first of the great, transformational Reconstruction amendments. It extended the "blessings of liberty" to former black slaves and their descendants by abolishing slavery. The Fourteenth Amendment, the most contentious of the three (proposed in 1866 and ratified in 1868), expanded the definition of citizenship to include blacks and included three important articles that gave them rights in the court of law: the immunity clause, due process, and the equal protection clause. It also struck down the decision in *Dred Scott v. Sandford,* which attempted to deprive former slaves and their forebears of their constitutional rights. The Fifteenth, the last of the amendments, ratified in 1870, granted voting rights regardless of "race, color, or previous condition of servitude."

The Civil Rights Act abrogated the insidious Black Codes, which Southern states had passed to limit the freedom of ex-slaves. Laws differed in each state, but most compelled freed men to work for a white employer, prevented blacks from raising their own crops, restricted their travel—in some areas blacks needed permission from a white employer just to enter town—and subjected unemployed men to charges of vagrancy.

Included in the Civil Rights Act were also provisions to guarantee blacks the right to make contracts, to sue, to bear witness in court, and to own private property. President Andrew Johnson vetoed the bill, arguing that blacks were not qualified for United States citizenship and that the bill would "operate in favor of the colored and against the white race." Republicans, however, overrode his presidential veto in April 1866, and Congress passed the act. Nearly a decade later, Congress added the contentious Civil Rights Act of 1875 to the list of Reconstruction era laws. That act imposed criminal penalties against business owners who practiced racial discrimination. Many outraged southerners—and northerners, too—viewed the law as an infringement on their personal freedom of choice.

Alarmed blacks who believed that the Reconstruction amendments would provide them with legal refuge and recourse felt betrayed by a controversial 1883 Supreme Court decision. Responding to a number of black charges of discrimination—blacks were refused entrance to a hotel dining room in Topeka, Kansas, an opera in New York City, a San Francisco theater, and a passenger car on a train—the court concluded that the Civil Rights Act of 1875 was unconstitutional and that the 13th and 14th amendments did not authorize Congress to pass laws enforcing the amendments in the private sector. Kentuckian John Marshall Harlan was the lone voice of dissent.

Defending the ruling, Chief Justice Joseph Bradley explained that the Equal Protection Clause of the 14th Amendment had limits. Its focus was state-sponsored legislation, and state action of every kind "which impairs the privileges and immunities of citizens of the United States, or which injures them in life, liberty or property without due process of law, or which denies to any of them the equal protection of the laws." "Individual invasion of individual rights," he added, "is not the subject-matter of the [14th] Amendment." In the wake of the ruling, restaurants and hotels, even public drinking fountains, libraries, and parks, became off-limits to blacks. "Whites Only" and "Colored Only" signs became prominent throughout the South—and the North, too—rendering emancipation nothing more than an empty promise.

Nothing, though, struck a blow to the heart of black liberation like *Plessy v. Ferguson.* With its landmark ruling upholding segregation (Kentuckian Justice John Marshall Harlan was the lone dissenter), the Supreme Court gave the phrase "separate but equal" legal standing, initiating a wave of new legislation and business practices that allowed whites to further divide society along a color line. Blacks mounted challenges to the "separate but equal" standard, but those challenges proved fruitless. As long as whites observed the bare essentials of due process, they had the law on their side. A few years after the Supreme Court's decision in *Plessy v. Ferguson,* the *Birmingham Ledger* newspaper claimed disingenuously that "[t]he court of Alabama and schools of Alabama are open to Negroes and every door of opportunity can be entered and above all it is easier for a Negro to get rich here than anywhere else in the world." Though the claim was patently false, many white southerners comforted themselves in the belief that separate did not mean unequal, and that blacks, like whites, had access to good schools, justice, and the American dream. Martin Luther King scribbled a long note in the margins of his personal copy of Charles Silberman's *Crisis in Black and White.* "The South," he wrote, "deluded itself with the illusion that the Negro was happy in his place; the North deluded itself with the illusion that it had freed the Negro. The Emancipation Proclamation freed the slave, a legal entity, but it failed to free the Negro, a person."

By the time Woodrow Wilson, a Virginian, became president, many states had passed laws disenfranchising blacks. In fact, Jim Crow was so prevalent that W. E. B. Du Bois called the South "an armed camp for intimidating black folk." Wilson defended the principle of allowing Southern states to decide their racial issues free of Northern influence. In a move that civil rights groups and Republicans regarded as openly racist, Wilson permitted, and provided justification for, his cabinet members to segregate their offices of the federal government.

## CHAPTER 12: A WAR OF THEIR OWN

Eventually the Special Enlisted Staff (SES) at Montford Point made efforts to recruit Marines who were the children of immigrants and had grown up being called "wop," "dago," "Jew boy," and "kike."

Gilbert H. Johnson earned the nickname "Hashmark" because he wore on the sleeve of his Marine Corps uniform three of the diagonal stripes called hashmarks, indicating successful previous enlistments. Born in Mount Hebron, Alabama, in 1905, he joined the Army in 1923 and served two three-year hitches with a black regiment, the 25th Infantry. In 1933 he enlisted in the Naval Reserve as a mess attendant, serving on active duty in officers' messes at various installations in Texas. He entered the regular Navy in May 1941 and had become a steward second class by 1942, when he heard that the Marine Corps was recruiting African Americans. With infantry experience ranging from company clerk to mortar gunner and squad leader, Johnson felt he was ideally suited to become a Marine. As regulations required, he applied to the secretary of the Navy, via the commandant of the Marine Corps, for a discharge from the Navy in order to join the Marines. He received the necessary permission and reported to Montford Point on November 14, 1942, still wearing his steward's uniform. As he anticipated, he possessed vitally needed skills that resulted in his being chosen as an assistant drill instructor and later a drill instructor. He ended up supervising the very platoon in which he had started his training. Looking back on his days as a DI, Johnson conceded that he was something of an "ogre" on the drill field. "I was a stern instructor," he said, "but I was fair." He sought, with unswerving dedication, to produce "in a few weeks, and at most a few months, a type of Marine fully qualified in every respect to wear that much cherished Globe and Anchor." In January 1945 he became sergeant major of the Montford Point Camp.

Edgar Huff trained the 16th Platoon.

The infusion of men overwhelmed the system. It was a recipe for disaster unless Colonel Woods could get them trained and promptly assigned to a depot company or the stewards' branch. Montford Point was producing two depot companies per month, and by fall 1943, after the activation of the first ammunition company, it would organize one ammunition company per month. The 1st Depot Company left California in April 1943. Depot company members were equipped with rifles, carbines, and submachine guns.

Ammunition companies consisted of 251 men, spread out over four platoons. The 1st Marine Ammunition Company was formed on October 1, 1943. Between October 1943 and September 1944, a total of sixty-three combat support companies were created at Montford Point, including one ammunition company and two depot companies each month. The last of twelve ammunition

companies was activated on September 1, 1944. Men in the ammunition companies often served in battle and were armed with rifles and/or sidearms.

The addition of a second defense battalion (the 52nd) to absorb the new black
Marines did not solve the problem, either. No one seemed to want the 51st or the
52nd. The Marine general who headed up U.S. forces in Samoa (Samoan Area
Defense Force) explained why he was opposed to black Marines serving there.
According to him, when Samoa's light-skinned Polynesians, whom he considered
"primitively romantic," reproduced with whites, their offspring was "a very high
class half caste." Similarly, relations between Samoans and Chinese resulted in
"a very desirable type." The general insisted, however, that relations between
black Marines and Samoans would inevitably produce "a very undesirable citizen." The general encouraged the Marines to send the defense battalions to one
of the Melanesian islands, where the black American servicemen would not only
"cause no racial strain," but might actually "raise the level of physical and mental standards" among the black islanders. The general (Marine Major General
Charles Price) forwarded his recommendation to Marine Corps headquarters,
and two black depot companies that arrived in Samoa during October 1943 were
promptly sent elsewhere.

Edgar Huff and the rest of the drill instructors hurriedly put together a program
to train drill instructors. Pulling out the cream of the crop among the recruits,
they would send them to the school. After their crash course, they would take
over a platoon or two under the watchful eyes of senior instructors. The appren-
ticeship program worked well, and soon the drill instructors and their assistants
were taking the new recruits through an intense, eight-week training program.

The War Department used black men for jobs no one else wanted, at the same
time showcasing Negro sports stars to inspire black patriotism. Huff's favorite
fighter, Joe Louis, was a case in point. The military printed up posters of Louis in
uniform with a bayonet in his hands. The caption beneath the photo read, "We're
Going to Do Our Part." Later it sent Louis and Sugar Ray Robinson on a tour of
Army bases, where they participated in boxing exhibitions. The scheme, which
was dubbed the "world's greatest boxing show," was hatched by Truman Gib-
son, the new civilian aide on Negro affairs to the secretary of war. The trip would
provide a counterpoint to the country's racial unrest. If the quiet-spoken Louis
and the charismatic Robinson could not pick up black troop morale and foster
harmony between the races, no one could. Army photographers, attached to the
Signal Corps, followed the fighters everywhere.
     Their first stop was Fort Devens in the liberal state of Massachusetts, once
home to the 54th Massachusetts Volunteers, an all-black unit that had distinguished itself in the Civil War. In late 1943 another Negro outfit, the 366th Regiment, trained at Fort Devens. White and black soldiers alike attended the events.

For one, nearly seven thousand soldiers turned out, shouting and whistling their appreciation. The shows were great successes, and *Life* magazine, reporting on the event, summoned all the gravity it could muster, calling the black boxers' Fort Devens appearance "a quiet parable in racial good will." Louis and Robinson went on to visit Fort Meade in Maryland, Camp McCoy in Wisconsin, and a host of other Army installations. The two fighters enjoyed entertaining the troops, putting a good face on race relations in the military. But when they were out of earshot of the officers and the press, they heard the real stories of black soldiers who, often performing nothing but the jobs white soldiers did not want, the garbage details, felt that the Army had shortchanged them.

By late 1943 the War Department took the Louis-Robinson show to the South. Their first stop was Mississippi and then Fort Benning, Georgia. For Louis, long-forgotten memories came rushing back: his illiterate mother, only one generation removed from slavery, eking out a living in the Buckalew Mountains of eastern Alabama, where she raised a brood of children, moving from one tumbledown shack to the next. It was a South that made him uncomfortable. He wanted to be back in Harlem, strolling down 125th Street in the cool night air while jazz burst from the doors of the nightclubs. But Sergeant Joe Louis was doing his duty for his country, playing the part of the good soldier. It was a role that he believed in, until the traveling show arrived in Gadsden, Alabama, Edgar Huff's childhood home, and the goodwill that *Life* magazine had celebrated butted up against the reality of life in the South.

Camp Sibert was a U.S. Army chemical training base located just outside of Gadsden. Because it was already packed to capacity, Louis and Robinson were set up in a house off the base, and often they had to ride to and from Camp Sibert by public bus. Although they were famous boxers, they had to wait for the one Negro bus like the other black soldiers. The white line moved faster because there were two buses serving the white side.

One day, Louis, hoping to grab a seat on a public bus, grew impatient and decided that he would call a cab. The phone booth, however, sat in the whites-only section. Unaccustomed to being treated like an ordinary black man, Louis did not give it a second thought, and walked over to the phone booth. Louis made his call, and as he stepped from the phone booth, Robinson saw a white MP, holding a billy club, approach the champ. Like the black boy who had ventured into the "white" swimming area at Chicago's 29th Street Beach (the catalyst for the Chicago race riot), Louis had crossed the line separating white from black.

When the MP ordered Louis to get back to his area, Louis took offense. "I'm wearing a uniform like you," he objected. "What's my color got to do with it?"

When the MP placed his billy club against his midsection, Louis might have sent him crashing to the pavement, but the champ caught himself, just barely. "Don't touch me with that stick," he threatened.

Now everyone was riveted: the black heavyweight champion of the world facing off against a white MP in the state of Alabama. Not everyone knew who Louis was, but they all understood that he was more than a run-of-the-mill Negro soldier. When the MP raised his club, Robinson came to Louis's defense and sprang on the MP, wrapping his arms around his neck. More MPs came running. Black soldiers, recognizing Louis, grew angry and defiant. Then the MPs, realizing that the situation had the makings of a brawl or, worse yet, a race riot, stepped back, and instead of swinging their billy clubs and taking on the crowd, they called their lieutenant. By the time he arrived, the men had calmed down. Quietly he put Louis and Sugar Ray in a jeep and took them to the brig. By the time the two fighters reached the jail, however, Army officials at Camp Sibert, realizing that the War Department's goodwill tour was about to turn ugly, decided not to put the fighters behind bars.

Edgar Huff heard much of the news about his boxing hero, and fellow Alabaman, secondhand. It pained him to think that his people, brimming with a passion for their country and its ideals, were still being treated like outsiders. But he was not surprised. Perhaps Gadsden, the entire South, and the whole country was as narrow-minded and backward as ever. Maybe Eleanor Roosevelt had been right; maybe the United States was not "prepared for democracy." (The partial text of Eleanor Roosevelt's 1943 newspaper column read, "The domestic scene is anything but encouraging and one would like not to think about it, because it gives one the feeling that, as a whole, we are not really prepared for democracy.")

In his 1944 State of the Union address, FDR said, "If ever there was a time to subordinate individual or group selfishness to the national good, that time is now."

In January 1943, Paul McNutt, the head of the War Manpower Commission, wrote President Roosevelt that the military needed to induct blacks in proportion to their numbers in the general population—a goal of 10 percent. McNutt had already gone on record condemning the "color" barrier in the military and the defense industry as a "line against democracy." Prejudice, in his words, was "unpatriotic." But in pressing with President Roosevelt the issue of the underutilization of blacks—mid-1942 figures showed that blacks were available because their unemployment rates were three times higher than those for whites—he chose to appeal to the president's practical side. Not using blacks because of institutional intolerance was not only unjustifiable, it was a "waste" of manpower. Manpower reserves were being rapidly extinguished. If the military continued to resist accepting large numbers of blacks, it would be forced to take whites out of important jobs to meet draft quotas. He explained further that the percentage of blacks in the military was 5.9 percent, well below the 10-percent goal. McNutt proposed ending racial calls—the custom of taking white registrants rather than blacks who had earlier draft lottery numbers—a suggestion to which both the War Department and the Department of the Navy responded unfavorably, pointing out that bringing in large numbers of blacks required enormous planning.

Many accused McNutt of being a publicity hound and a bit of a grandstander (he also had a bad relationship with FDR), but others believed that he was genuinely opposed to discrimination. Whether McNutt was a bona fide proponent of black rights or an enthusiastic self-promoter who loved the stage and used controversial issues to propel himself front and center was a bone of contention for supporters and opponents alike. That said, he even took his case to the black press, praising the accomplishments of black soldiers and workers alike. In World War I, he had commanded two thousand black troops at Camp Jackson, South Carolina. While campaigning for the governorship of Indiana, he passionately denounced the KKK and the discriminatory poll tax. As governor he appointed blacks to influential state boards.

McNutt, however, persisted, taking another tack. On February 17, 1943, he wrote Secretary of War Henry Stimson, explaining that 300,000 blacks had been overlooked while draft boards were taking in white males, in direct violation of the Selective Service Act, which imposed a ban on racial discrimination. "The position," he wrote, "is not tenable." The Selective Service was drafting white married men with families and passing over single black men. McNutt, who had attended Harvard Law School, added that the practice possessed "grave implications should the issue be taken into the courts, especially by a white registrant. . . . The probability of action increases as the single white registrants disappear and husbands and fathers become the current white inductees, while Negro registrants who are physically fit remain uninducted." McNutt pressed Stimson to start accepting men regardless of color and according to their induction numbers. General Lewis Hershey, director of the Selective Service System, also wrote Stimson. "We feel impelled under the circumstances and under requirements of law that the selection of men . . . shall be made in an impartial manner . . . without regard to discrimination against any person on account of race or color." When Stimson replied to McNutt, he dismissed his concerns, writing that racial calls were not "discriminatory in any way." Despite his letter, General Lewis Hershey continued to do the military's bidding, filling racial calls as directed.

Late that same month, McNutt went directly to the president, who, though sympathetic to his argument, refused to overrule either Stimson or Secretary of the Navy Frank Knox. The president, however, encouraged Knox to review his ranks in an attempt to find places for blacks, including "shore duty of all kinds, together with the handling of many kinds of yard craft." The president further expressed his concern that if blacks were not used in proportion to their numbers in the population, it could produce both morale issues and serious legal issues for both whites and blacks. Meanwhile McNutt recommended that monthly quotas for blacks be increased from 2,700 per month to 7,350.

Many of the details about McNutt's efforts to push Secretary of War Stimson to integrate the armed services can be found in George Flynn's *The Mess in Washington: Manpower Mobilization in World War II.*

In February 1943 the Navy began taking all draft-age men via Selective Service. Estimating that more than 100,000 black draftees would enter the Navy by the end of the year if quotas were met, Frank Knox scrambled to formulate a plan to accommodate them, calling for the creation of twenty-four new "all-colored" construction battalions. Knox also authorized the establishment of "colored crews in the harbor craft and local defense force," "service companies at all ports of embarkation," an "increase in the number of colored cooks and bakers in the commissary branch for shore establishments within the United States, and finally "an increase in the percentage of colored personnel at section bases, ammunition depots, net depots and naval air stations on this continent." As before, Secretary Knox and the Navy failed to see blacks as more than a source of labor, giving priority to the Bureau of Ordnance requests for ammunition handlers at naval ammunition depots. Secretary Knox was as emphatic as ever that there would be no "mixing of crews" aboard ships. When black civil rights leaders called for the introduction of "all-Negro" units for transports, cargo and ammunition ships, fleet oilers, and other naval auxiliary vessels, where black petty officers would not be called upon to exercise authority over anyone other than "subordinates of their own race," Knox dismissed that notion, too. If the black community hoped that the Navy was on the cusp of change and that its men would be able to serve aboard combat ships, Knox's proposal fell far short of its expectations. The General Board (the advisory body of the U.S. Navy) had already weighed in on this issue, stating abstrusely that "[t]his prospect would involve an effort out of all proportion to the return in effective seagoing units which could be expected on the basis of the Navy's actual experience with vessels manned by crews of other than the white race." Because of its stance, the Navy was forced to curtail the training of blacks in seagoing positions.

## CHAPTER 13: A DESOLATE PLACE

Descriptions of Bronzeville's boundaries differ. According to Percy Robinson, its boundaries were 29th Street on the north, 63rd on the south, Cottage Grove on the east, and State Street on the west. As the population of Chicago exploded (44,130 in 1910 to 233,903 by 1930), the Black Belt expanded. In 1910 it was a narrow strip of land stretching from 18th Street to 39th Street, bounded by State Street on the east and the Rock Island Railroad tracks and LaSalle Street on the west.

Percy Robinson, like a lot of South Side blacks, never knew the name "Bronzeville." James J. Gentry, a theater editor for Anthony Overton, the publisher of the *Chicago Bee,* suggested that the paper use the word "Bronzeville" to identify the community, since it more accurately described the skin tone of most of its inhabitants.

Like his father, Percy Robinson was a fight fan. The hero of many South Side blacks was Jack Johnson, the heavyweight champion of the world. Johnson was a bold, in-your-face black man with a preference for white women, and whites' hatred for him was legendary.

Six years after retiring, James Jeffries, who had been a heavyweight champion, announced that he was returning to the ring to take back the heavyweight title "for the sole purpose of proving that a white man is better than a Negro." The matchup, with its racist overtones, was billed as "the Fight of the Century." On July 4, 1910, the hostile crowd booed Johnson, but nothing, it seemed, could shake the confidence of the grinning black fighter. He knocked Jeffries down twice, and might have done more damage had Jeffries's corner not thrown in the towel. The *Los Angeles Times* tried to discourage post-fight racial pride. "Do not point your nose too high," it said. "Do not swell your chest too much. Do not boast too loudly. . . . Your place in the world is just as it was." Some blacks encouraged Johnson to conduct himself in the "modest manner" of Booker T. Washington. Washington's secretary even wrote to Johnson asking him to follow Washington's example of "simplicity and humility of bearing." But blacks across the country wildly celebrated Johnson's victory, while angry white citizens and all-white police forces tried to stop them. Trouble ensued, with white-on-black and black-on-white clashes erupting in fifty U.S. cities in what were the first-ever nationwide race riots in the United States. In 1912, when Johnson was charged with violating the Mann Act—the trafficking of white women across state lines for immoral purposes—a pastor remarked that lynching "would be light punishment for his sins." Historian Jeffrey Sammons wrote that Johnson's rise "foreshadowed, and in some ways helped to create, the New Negro." Reverend Reverdy Ransom, founder of Chicago's Institutional Church and Social Settlement, said in a 1909 sermon, "What Jack Johnson seeks to do to Jeffries in the roped area will be more the ambition of Negroes in every domain of human endeavor."

Again, some details about Great Lakes are taken from Lieutenant T. A. Larson's *History of the U.S. Naval Training Center Great Lakes, Illinois, In World War I,* and a thirty-five-page Naval Intelligence Service (Ninth Naval District) confidential memorandum regarding racial tension at the Naval Training Center, Great Lakes.

By the middle of 1943 Great Lakes had changed its criteria for selecting the white officers who trained the black recruits. One officer explained that at Great Lakes, "We no longer follow the precept that southern officers exclusively should be selected for colored battalions. . . . We have learned to steer clear of the 'I'm from the South—I know how to handle 'em' variety."

Under Armstrong, Wednesday-night "happy hours" and talent shows became common occurrences. To bolster morale, he organized art and drama groups and entertainment departments. He encouraged recruits to perform, but also brought in professional entertainers. He established "Negro bands" and featured "Negro spirituals" during Sunday-evening Vesper hours. Promoting "Negro pride," he arranged exhibits celebrating black contributions to the arts, sciences, industry, education, and athletics. In May 1943 he presided over the dedication of a new school building with state-of-the-art classrooms and laboratories. He was also concerned with the recruits' free time. The regimental halls—the 18th Regiment at Robert Smalls, the 16th at Lawrence, and the 14th at Moffett—showed movies three nights a week with fifteen-minute sing-alongs preceding the showings. Finally Armstrong saw to it that each camp was outfitted with a recreational hall with table games, jukeboxes, and modern libraries.

For those, like Percy Robinson, who loved music, there was no place in the entire country that showcased talent like the three Great Lakes Navy Bands. The A Band, the best at Great Lakes, was the forty-five-piece Ship's Company Band at Camp Robert Smalls; the B Band, the next best, was the resident band at Camp Lawrence; and the C Band was out of Camp Moffett. According to Clark Terry and Jimmie Nottingham, two legendary trumpeters stationed at Great Lakes, and other instrumentalists who later went on to successful jazz and symphony careers after doing stints in the Navy, "There had never been so many good musicians at any one place, at any one time." FDR, a lover of jazz, was delighted. "The blacks have an abundance of musicians," he said, "and I want the Navy to have something in it besides messmen and stewards."

The Great Lakes Ship's Company Band was one of the most illustrious ever assembled. It included Terry and Nottingham in addition to Major Holly, Ernie Wilkins, Jimmy Wilkins, and Al Grey, as well as symphony orchestra performers Donald White, Thomas Bridge, and Charles Burrell. FDR's comment was the green light that Len "the Fox" Bowden, a St. Louis arranger, composer, and conductor who was second in charge of all the bands at Great Lakes, needed. With the president's enthusiasm and the support of the assistant chief of Naval Personnel, Bowden recruited the musicians he needed to build a top-notch band. Bowden was in charge of the Ninth Naval District, which extended from Colorado east to the Atlantic and from Tennessee north to Canada, and handpicked his other recruiters, who traveled to gigs from New Orleans to St. Louis to Kansas City to try to persuade black musicians, who suspected that the Navy was the exclusive preserve of white America, to join up. At Great Lakes, instead of being forced into roles as cooks and bakers, they could be rated as Musicians 1st or 2nd Class and could perfect their craft in the company of equally talented men.

Once Bowden and his team brought aboard the musicians—men like Mitchell "Booty" Wood went on to fame as a trombonist with Lionel Hampton, Duke Ellington, and Count Basie—they set out to prove to the world that their Great Lakes band was the best there was. What was obvious to everyone was that the Navy had recruited even better talent than one could find at Chicago's Club De

Lisa, the Rhumboogie, or the Three Deuces. In fact, until the Chicago Federation of Musicians complained, and Navy musicians were no longer allowed to take their instruments off base, the Great Lakes bands would sometimes gig in Bronzeville's clubs to the delight of audiences that knew groundbreaking music when they heard it.

What it meant for the musicians there was that during two- and three-hour jam sessions they were interpreting jazz in revolutionary ways and blowing wide the doors of music. Bowden was so proud that he formed a "Radio Band" made up of the best musicians from the three bands at Great Lakes. On a program known as the "Men O' War Radio Show," the Radio Band's music was broadcast throughout Chicago every Saturday night on the CBS network's area station—WBBM. A two-hundred-voice regimental choir, a vocal octet that included singers who had sung with the Hall Johnson Negro Choir, and a vocal quartet also performed.

For nightlife the Great Lakes recruits usually went into Chicago. Chicago had its race problems, but of all the northern cities, it was considered to be the most congenial to blacks, of which it had a large population—300,000-plus—over 10 percent of the city's total. Its mayor, Edward Kelly, who hailed from Bridgeport, an Irish enclave on Chicago's South Side, established a Committee on Race Relations and had a decent reputation with the city's black voters. What's more, on the South Side, black servicemen had over a sixty-block area in which to play. There, courtesy of the mayor's soft stand on gambling and prostitution, they could find anything they wanted. Service Center Number 3, at 49th and Wabash, had free sleeping quarters and nearly two hundred beds, which it assigned on a first-come, first-served basis. The YMCA on the 3700 block of South Wabash had another two hundred beds. For those searching out a more wholesome kind of fun, the South Side offered playing fields, swimming pools, beaches, and theaters, too. The various black organizations—the NAACP, the Urban League, the March on Washington, and the National Negro Congress—and their Chicago chapters saw to it that there was no shortage of recreational opportunities for the serviceman. For those intimidated by Chicago's reputation as Boykin had been, the local town of Waukegan, Illinois, had five separate black neighborhoods, enlightened black citizens who took their membership in the NAACP seriously, and a brand-new black USO. There was also Milwaukee, Wisconsin, north of the state line. The city's Sixth Ward was especially friendly to black servicemen, and on weekends drew large groups from Great Lakes. The Urban League was active in Milwaukee, as was the NAACP, which was run by activist attorney James Dorsey.

According to the War Diary, Lieutenant Delucchi arrived at Port Chicago on July 17, 1943.

Riots broke out across Detroit, fueled by rumors that whites had thrown a black woman and her baby off the Belle Isle Bridge. Enraged blacks stormed through a neighborhood breaking windows and looting stores, while white rioters approached from the opposite direction, burning cars and plundering businesses. City police and state troopers were soon overwhelmed—six were shot and another seventy-five injured—and began firing indiscriminately into the rebellious black crowds. A white doctor, entering a black neighborhood on a house call, was pulled from his car and beaten to death.

When the Detroit mayor and Michigan's governor begged the president to help, Roosevelt sent in federal troops. The troops restored peace two days later, but the NAACP, whom many accused of having instigated the violence, pointed out that three quarters of the people killed or injured or arrested were black. Four hundred fifty of the six hundred injured were black.

## CHAPTER 14: WHOM ARE WE FIGHTING THIS TIME?

Lieutenant Holman's arrival on September 29, 1943, is noted in the War Diary.

Lieutenant Holman would later testify that the black seamen "are not here because they want to be." Lieutenant Herbert Woodland would testify that Port Chicago got Great Lakes' "culls," the "lower class of Negro." He added, "The officers lacked training like myself. I'd never had any boot training; I never had any ship loading experience; I never had any ship rigging experience. . . ." Then he continued, "We have to push these boys sometimes too hard."

What frustrated Holman most was what he called the "superstitious" nature of the loaders, who did not object to handling mines or bombs—though they may have been uneasy around them—but had a paralyzing dread of projectiles. In training them, he practiced a kind of benign neglect; he teamed them with the few winchmen and ammunition handlers he felt he could trust.

The description of "selective discharge" is from Samuel Eliot Morison and from researchers at the Naval History and Heritage Command (Washington, D.C., Navy Yard).

In late November 1943, Captain Goss wrote to the commandant of the Twelfth Naval District regarding his inexperienced officers and "green" work crews.

On October 14, 1943, Inez White wrote to her husband's parents, "Bob is still working the midnight to 6 a.m. shift. They are putting a high tonnage on this shift. . . . When he comes home in the morning he's just about frozen and doesn't thaw out for several hours." Lieutenant White also scratched a few quick sentences. "Dear Folks," he said. "It's just about time to go to work and I don't feel like going. I am not sick but it is just too cold about 4 a.m."

Back home in Detroit, George Booth's buddies, whose draft numbers had not yet come up, were hanging out in Paradise Valley. Paradise Valley was the sexiest part of the sixty-square-block ghetto known as Black Bottom. The Valley was the place to be for a young black man looking for action in Detroit. Like Harlem and Bronzeville in Chicago, and the Fillmore in San Francisco, it had a vibrant nightlife with speakeasies, restaurants, brothels, and nightclubs such as the Paradise, the Tropicana, Club ElSino, Club Zombie, and Dee's and the Bird Cage, and was frequented by celebrities, civil rights leaders, jazzmen, athletes, politicians, petty crooks, and gangsters. The Paradise was the neighborhood's contribution to what was called the "Chitlin Circuit," a collection of theaters, including the Apollo in Harlem, the Uptown in Philadelphia, the Royal in Baltimore, the Howard in Washington, and the Regal in Chicago, that hosted the country's most prominent jazz musicians.

Black Bottom was named by early French farmers because of its fat, dark, fertile soil. Located on the city's lower east side, Black Bottom was the black community's answer to "deed restrictions" that prohibited blacks from renting or owning property in other parts of Detroit. Citizens who felt excluded from the city's power circles banded together. If the Ku Klux Klan could hold a rally outside Detroit's city hall, then they would build their own city hall and elect their own mayor. It was not an easy thing to do. Although the Michigan legislature outlawed slavery in 1837 (when Michigan became a state) and the state became a haven for escaped slaves, over one hundred years later, Detroit, which was founded by French slaveholders, was a pressure cooker of racial tension. Recruiters and labor agents combed the South enticing blacks (and whites, too) north of the Mason-Dixon Line with promises of high wages in Detroit's war factories. Detroit's black population doubled to 200,000 in the ten years between 1933 and 1943. Michigan Central Station was a whirlwind of activity as dozens of bewildered black families from the South's Cotton Belt arrived every day. The Detroit Urban League helped to team up the new arrivals with employers. The migrants, however, placed enormous strains on housing, transportation, and educational and recreational facilities. And many blacks found Northern bigotry, though less well publicized, every bit as vicious as what they had left behind. Some, determined not to endure the kind of treatment they had suffered before moving north, participated in a "bumping campaign." Newly empowered blacks walked into whites in public places, forcing them off sidewalks, or nudging them in elevators. Whites reacted angrily, the police adopted brutish tactics, and *Life* magazine called the situation in the city "dynamite."

Blind Blake, the influential blues guitarist, wrote a song called "Detroit Bound Blues," which included the lyrics "I'm goin' to Detroit, get myself a job / I'm goin' to Detroit, get myself a job / Tried to stay around here with the starvation mob / I'm goin' to get a job, up there in Mr. Ford's place / I'm goin' to get a job, up there in Mr. Ford's place / Stop these eatless days from starin' me in the face."

Paradise Valley teemed with an estimated 360 black businesses. Located principally along Hastings and Saint Antoine streets, these establishments encompassed hotels, barbershops, speakeasies, restaurants and bars, entertainment venues, banks, churches, drugstores, a newspaper—the *Michigan Chronicle*—bowling alleys, apartment buildings, service stations, taxicabs, a chapter of the Urban League, funeral parlors, smoke shops, business clubs, and a great deal more. It claimed heavyweight boxing champion Joe Louis, whose mother lived on McDougall Street, as its favorite son. Ella Fitzgerald, Benny Goodman, B.B. King, the Harlem Globetrotters, Langston Hughes, Louis Armstrong, Thurgood Marshall, Dr. Martin Luther King Jr., and Adam Clayton Powell all frequented Paradise Valley's elegant hotel, the Gotham, which was owned, managed, and staffed by African Americans.

For Booth, it was a source of pride that the city's Black Bottom neighborhood was home to Joe Louis and Sugar Ray Robinson. Although everyone knew that Louis lived in Chicago and Sugar Ray lived in Harlem, Booth claimed both fighters for the city. After Louis's family left Alabama, they moved to Detroit, and his mother still lived in Black Bottom. Sugar Ray, born Walker Smith Jr., had spent a good portion of his first decade in the city and had first tied on a pair of boxing gloves at Detroit's Brewster Recreation Center. So when Sugar Ray appeared on the September 1943 cover of *Ring* magazine, wearing his Army-issue uniform and saluting, Booth was beside himself with joy.

On their second day at Port Chicago, Delucchi ordered Booth and Crawford to report to the quarterdeck, his office. "What kind of work would you like to do?" he asked Booth. Booth was confused: Was the lieutenant asking what he wanted to do with his life? Booth answered that he liked to take pictures. Delucchi could have laughed in his face. Instead he said, "Well, you see, we don't have that around here." Then he asked Booth and Crawford if they would like to be carpenter strikers. The two looked at each other and shrugged. "What's a carpenter striker?" Booth asked. As Delucchi explained the duties, Booth thought, *Well, it sounds as good as any other job; I'll take it.*

The *Rainier* was bound for the Central Pacific—likely to support the invasion of Tarawa. When full, she would be carrying a tremendous load, including 111 cars of ammunition shipped from Mare Island, Hawthorne, and Puget Sound. The *Shasta* was filled largely with explosives. After unloading in the Hawaiian Islands, where her cargo would be loaded onto ships participating in Admiral Turner's invasion of the Gilberts, she would continue on to Brisbane, Australia, to aid MacArthur's push into Bougainville and his army's drive north up the coast of New Guinea. As for the *Alcoa Planter,* a portion of her load was also going straight to Turner.

The Navy made no bones about it; men had their needs. Port Chicago had a prophylactic station, which the guys could go to before and after liberty for either condoms or a penicillin shot.

The quote about the amount of cargo coming into and going out of Port Chicago reaching "astronomical figures" is from Captain Milton Smith Davis, port director.

Captain Goss's justification for not allowing Coast Guard observers was that the Navy and the Coast Guard operated differently and that conflicting orders confused the enlisted men. In a letter dated November 1, 1943, Goss wrote the Captain of the Port, San Francisco, a two-point memo. Point number two said, "Coast Guard details are not desired for merchant vessels loading at this Depot (Mare Island) or at the Naval Magazine, Port Chicago, unless specifically requested by the Commanding Officer." Of course, Goss was the CO. Goss had a copy of the memo sent to Keith R. Ferguson, Lieutenant Commander U.S. Naval Reserve Judge Advocate.

## CHAPTER 15: WAITING FOR WAR

Chappo Flats was part of the 123,000-acre Rancho Santa Margarita y Los Flores that President Roosevelt officially named Camp Pendleton in a September 1942 ceremony.

At night, while on maneuvers, the men sang around the fire. A song popular in the Old Corps was one of their favorites: "Over the sea, Let's go men / We're shovin' right off / We're shovin' right off again / Nobody knows where or when . . . / It may be Shanghai Farewell and good-bye Sally and Sue / Don't be blue / We'll just be gone for / Years and years and then . . ."

Graf and the rest of his company went through instruction on how to use the .50-caliber machine gun, .30-caliber light and heavy machine guns, 60- and 81-mm mortars, the 37-mm antitank gun, and the BAR (Browning Automatic Rifle).

## CHAPTER 16: BROKEN PROMISES

An incident at the St. Juliens Creek Annex at the Norfolk Naval Shipyard in Portsmouth, Virginia, should have convinced the Navy that it had to reform its racial policies. There, in May 1943, three hundred blacks, protesting discriminatory conditions, nearly rioted. A board of investigation criticized white officers for their "inept handling" of this and other racial altercations. The investigators reached the same conclusion that Lieutenant Commander Armstrong at Great Lakes had: it took special officers with special skills to handle black troops. Further investigation also cited the incident as yet more evidence that isolating groups of blacks from the general military population, instead of distributing them throughout the service, spelled trouble.

According to "The Negro in the United States Navy in World War II" (written by the Historical Section of the Bureau of Naval Personnel), which is a section of *The U.S. Navy in World War II,* memoranda circulated throughout the Bureau of Naval Personnel regarding the addition of blacks to fleet vessels. Echoing the civil rights leaders, the Bureau recommended that blacks serve aboard oilers and repair, coastal patrol, cargo, and transport ships, and also aboard LSTs, LCTs, and LCIs (the great expansion of the amphibious program provided opportunities for blacks), but the Navy dismissed the recommendation and perfunctorily created something akin to the "ordnance battalions," called "base companies." Under this plan the Navy would send black seamen to island bases in the South Seas with significant "colored" populations, where they would perform a variety of construction, maintenance, and ammunition-handling responsibilities. The rationale was similar to Marine Major General Charles Price's argument for sending the 51st Defense Battalion to Melanesia and not to Samoa. In Melanesia, so went his reasoning, black servicemen would "cause no racial strain."

Despite the concentration of blacks on the West Coast, in October 1943 the Bureau of Naval Personnel ordered naval districts across the country to transfer to Camp Shoemaker, California, monthly quotas of blacks from Naval Ammunition Depots (NADs). The plan was to send out one base company—two hundred men—each month. It also specified that the transfers from NADs to base companies were to be used as rewards for outstanding service.

Perhaps the biggest news of the new year to date (1944) was that Frank Knox, who originally dismissed the idea of having blacks serve as naval officers—he was convinced that they were happy being cooks, steward's mates, and mess attendants—bent to pressure from the NAACP, Eleanor Roosevelt, and Adlai Stevenson, then one of his assistants, and decided to allow sixteen men to become the first black American naval officers. At the time there were more than 100,000 black enlisted men in the Navy. In January the sixteen black candidates entered Great Lakes for segregated training. All sixteen survived the course, but only twelve were commissioned. In the last week of the course, three candidates were returned to the ranks, not because they had failed but because the Bureau of Naval Personnel had suddenly decided to limit the number of black officers in this first group to twelve. The twelve entered the U.S. Naval Reserve as line officers on March 17. A thirteenth man, the only candidate who lacked a college degree, was made a warrant officer because of his outstanding work in the course. Two of the twelve new ensigns were assigned to the faculty at Hampton training school, four others to yard and harbor craft duty, and the rest to training duty at Great Lakes. All carried the label "Deck Officers Limited—Only," a designation usually reserved for officers whose physical or educational deficiencies kept them from performing all the duties of a line officer. The Bureau of Naval Personnel never explained why the men were placed in this category, but it was clear that none of them lacked the physical requirements of a line officer and all had had business or professional careers in civilian life. Operating duplicate training facilities for officer candidates was costly, and the bureau decided shortly after the first group of black candidates was trained that future candidates of both races would be trained together. By early summer ten more Negroes, this time civilians with special professional qualifications, had been trained with whites and were commissioned as staff officers in the Medical, Dental, Chaplain, Civil Engineer, and Supply Corps. These twenty-two men were the first of some sixty Negroes to be commissioned during the war.

Inez White's letters were kindly donated to me by her brother-in-law, William White.

When determining how much ordnance Port Chicago could store, higher authorities in planning ammunition movements used the station's total barricade capacity without giving consideration to its respective capacity for high-explosive, projectile, and smokeless-powder cars.

By October 1943, the black "problem" in the Navy was so acute that the Navy staged the critical symposium. More than fifty officers attended, and openly discussed and criticized Navy policy. Organizers hoped that the conference could create a blueprint for the "treatment of Negro personnel" to which naval district commandants and base commanders could refer. Although the conference failed at this, its observations were considered instructive, and the notes from the conference were immediately circulated throughout the country.

Captain Clarence Hinkamp, who had served as captain of the USS *Texas* from May 1940 to August 1941, introduced the meeting. "It is realized," he said, "that there are many who have preconceived ideas regarding Negro personnel, whether we want them or whether we don't. But no matter what our choice in the matter may be, all we know is that we have them with us and we must follow the directives concerning them. Our prejudices must be subordinated to our traditional unfailing obedience to orders." Rear Admiral Fairfax Leary, commandant of the Fifth Naval District, then took the floor. "Gentlemen," he said, "we are faced with a problem—a very serious problem—in connection with our naval enlisted personnel and that is the introduction . . . of large numbers of Negro personnel . . . this is a fact . . . and it isn't a question whether anybody likes it or not. . . . The problem is growing and we have got to face it with all its complications . . . this is a situation we are faced with due to the manpower shortage. This is the reason why they are combing us out of present personnel and putting the other personnel in its place . . . from now on, where anybody wants an increase in complement, it is going to be Negro personnel."

A captain who had worked with black Seabees at Camp Peary in Newport News, Virginia, discussed the importance of blacks taking pride in their work and being given an opportunity to strive for rates. "It makes every colored man feel that he will receive that which he merits," the captain explained, "hence he will strive to go forward." The last attendee to speak was Lieutenant Commander Downes of the Hampton Institute. Captain Downes emphasized the importance of treating blacks as individuals, the obligation of officers to work hard to earn their respect, and the necessity of demonstration. Officers should not simply shout orders and expect blacks to execute them. "Negroes," he explained, "because of the lack of opportunity, do not have good verbal ability, that is they do not readily associate words and ideas."

Perhaps the symposium's most important finding was that discipline among black troops was often dependent on finding a respected black "Bossman" or "Head Man" who would help to keep the others in line.

## CHAPTER 17: ERNIE KING'S BELOVED OCEAN (THE STRATEGIC PICTURE)

Details for this chapter are drawn from Morison's *New Guinea and the Marianas*, Buell's *Master of Sea Power: A Biography of Admiral Ernest J. King*, Hoyt's *Nimitz and His Admirals: How They Won the War in the Pacific*, Larrabee's *Commander In Chief*, Willoughby and Chamberlain's *MacArthur, 1941–1951*, and Goodwin's *No Ordinary Time*.

Though Major "Pete" Ellis's plans were revised on numerous occasions, Ellis's predictions were basically correct. In his *Campaign in the Marianas*, Philip Crowl writes that Ellis predicted that the war with Japan would be "primarily naval in character . . . directed towards the isolation and exhaustion of Japan through control of her vital sea communications and through aggressive operations against her armed forces and her economic life." Ellis's plans also anticipated a "step-by-step process involving seizure and occupation of key Japanese islands in the Marshall and Caroline groups."

War Plan Orange had been "gamed" at the Naval War College for decades before World War II.

Pete Ellis, writing in 1921, hoped that Marines would become not just "skilled infantry men and jungle men," but "skilled water men" as well.

Originally Marrakech, which was home to British prime minister Winston Churchill's favorite hotel, the Mamounia, was to host the conference, but that city was deemed too dangerous. The Combined Chiefs settled on the Anfa Hotel, situated five miles outside of Casablanca on a ridge overlooking the ocean. The Anfa was shaded by stately palms, cooled by Atlantic breezes, and surrounded by comfortable villas with gardens of begonia and bougainvillea and orange groves. The picture could not have been more striking—the grand, ivory-white structure set against the red, sun-bleached soil.

Reminders of war were everywhere. General Dwight Eisenhower's troops, together with British General Bernard Montgomery's Eighth Army, were locked in battle on the blazing desert against Rommel's Afrika Korps. Axis agents swarmed the city. General George Patton's 3rd Battalion strung barbed wire around the compound, and guards roamed the grounds twenty-four hours a day. Troops were stationed on rooftops. Patton also positioned antiaircraft batteries throughout the area. Still he was uneasy, and eager for the negotiators to get on with their business; Patton knew that the safeguards could not be maintained indefinitely. Although some of the men attending the conference might have been alarmed by the heightened sense of security, King was unfazed. He, too, was obsessed with security. Besides, he had not come to Casablanca to wander the hotel grounds and admire the scenery. He was a man driven by a mission.

Although he had come to Casablanca with only one purpose, unlike his U.S. Army counterpart, the austere General George Marshall, King was not known for his temperance. A heavy drinker, he undoubtedly found the Muslim stricture against public consumption of alcohol bothersome. He was also an inveterate womanizer and a self-proclaimed "son of a bitch." One junior officer described him as "meaner than hell." King's admirers—which included President Roosevelt—appreciated his blunt honesty, loyalty, and unswerving determination. Even his detractors, who detested his self-assurance, admitted that he was a gifted leader with an energetic mind. Although he was fourth in his class at the Naval Academy, he was handsome and popular and widely recognized by students and the academy administration alike as the top cadet. Unlike MacArthur, he rarely got caught up in his own fame. Though he used a cigarette holder of carved ivory, he wore a drab gray uniform and distrusted the press and all undue publicity.

At Casablanca, King was convinced that most of his colleagues in the Hotel Anfa conference room did not understand Japan. The British, in particular, were so blinded by Hitler that they ignored the peril of Japanese aggression. King knew that despite the president's personal views, he could be swayed by Prime Minister Churchill. King was suspicious of the British tactic of isolating Roosevelt from the Joint Chiefs of Staff. Although he admired the prime minister's intellect, he realized that Churchill was not to be entirely trusted. To get what he wanted, Churchill was willing to use his powers of persuasion ruthlessly. King believed that he himself was the only one clear-headed and firm enough to defy the prime minister. In his book *Master of Sea Power,* Thomas Buell says that "King's biggest gripe was the President's double-talk." "Roosevelt was a little tricky," King later said, "and in some ways the truth was not always in him."

King irked the Brits. They found him tiresome, hot-tempered, and singularly absorbed with war against Japan. British General Alan Brooke, chief of the Imperial General Staff and the top military man in England, insisted that for King, "The European war was just a great nuisance that kept him from waging his Pacific war undisturbed." Brooke also believed until the very end that King sent matériel and ships to the Pacific to the detriment of the war against Germany.

Another British general said of King, "He was tough as nails and carried himself as stiffly as a poker. He was blunt and standoffish, almost to the point of rudeness." From the British delegation's perspective, Germany was clearly the more dangerous of the two enemies. Japan may have been bent on territorial expansion, but the German army was poised just twenty miles from the chalk cliffs of Dover across the narrowest part of the English Channel. The Luftwaffe had already demonstrated its ability to bomb British cities into rubble. What's more, Churchill desperately needed the USSR's support, and the only way to elicit that support was to show the Soviet leader, Joseph Stalin, that the Allies were wholly committed to defeating Germany. Nevertheless, King began diverting ships to the Pacific. "In the last analysis," King predicted, "Russia will do nine-tenths of the job of defeating Germany."

Convinced that the proper course was to invade Sardinia and Corsica in the Mediterranean, the Brits squashed General Marshall's plans to launch a cross-Channel invasion in 1943. They then made their priorities clear: a midsummer invasion of Sicily (for which King promised to deliver the necessary ships), strategic bombing raids against Germany, continued aid to Russia, and elimination of the German U-boat threat. They had come to Casablanca fully prepared to argue and support their cause—the Mediterranean offensive—and were receptive to little else. Marshall was upset that Roosevelt was moving away from cross-Channel invasion to the British view of a Mediterranean invasion. Deeply disappointed, Marshall suggested that if his men were not going to be used against Hitler, they should be used against Hirohito.

On January 30, 1943, King arrived back in Washington in time to witness the tail end of the city's worst-ever winter storm. Branches snapped under the weight of an inch of ice, and large trees fell across roadways. Wires and utility poles collapsed, cutting off electricity and telephone service. Nothing, though, could dampen King's spirits. He had made headway in Casablanca. Through sheer Scots doggedness, he had won a small but significant commitment from the intransigent Brits.

King's frequent trips to see Nimitz underscored his mistrust of the admiral. In King's mind, Nimitz sometimes took bad advice. "If only I could keep him tight on what he's supposed to do," King once said. "Somebody gets ahold of him and I have to straighten him out."

Several weeks after returning from California, King wrote a letter to Roosevelt from his dusty office on the third floor of the Navy Department building on Constitution Avenue. The Main Navy, as it was known, was an enormous, dreary building, which was never intended to be the Navy's home. In 1918 it was built as a temporary structure. Despite its size, war planners, officers, and a huge administrative staff packed its halls and dingy rooms. For the head of what was arguably the world's greatest navy, King's office was, for some, disturbingly nondescript. One colleague called it the "most disreputable" he had ever seen. King wrote from an unassuming flat-topped desk. Papers spilled out of his inbox, and

King often had to clear a space to write. The office, though, was his inner sanctum, and few, including Secretary of the Navy Frank Knox, summoned the courage to enter. King, however, descended each morning to the secretary's office on the second deck for an 0830 conference. It was King's outward and visible sign of subordination to civilian control of the Navy.

In August 1943, five months after Trident, the Combined Chiefs assembled again for the year's third major conference—Quadrant—held in Quebec. The meeting place was the Chateau Frontenac, a grand and graceful hotel overlooking the swirling currents of the mighty St. Lawrence River. Royal Canadian Mounted Police provided security, but in contrast to Casablanca, the mood was relaxed. The American contingent, in particular, was happy to escape the stifling heat of a Washington summer. When not in meetings, King strolled the boardwalk along the river. In the afternoon, many of the British and American participants took drives through the scenic countryside and visited historic sites and battlegrounds. During the off hours, comity reigned. One weekend all gathered aboard a steamer for a trip down the river. But in the conference rooms, the tone was boisterous and confrontational. The British had come to do battle with their old adversary, accusing King of disregarding the advice of British military planners and unilaterally developing plans for war against Japan.

Thomas Buell writes that "King's burning desire to become involved at Guadalcanal was a calculated risk. . . . King was undeservedly lucky when Rear Admiral Mikawa decided to retire from Guadalcanal after winning the Battle of the Savo Islands. The Japanese admiral could have destroyed every American transport at Guadalcanal, still filled with food, ammunition, and supplies for the Marines ashore. Had they been sunk, King's hopes for Guadalcanal would have been doomed."

According to Buell, King later said of MacArthur, "He could not understand that he was not to manage everything." General Marshall was also a strong advocate of a unified command. He wanted MacArthur in charge of the entire Pacific. Public sentiment was also on MacArthur's side. But King had no intention of letting the general assume power. He believed that MacArthur knew nothing about sea power. The Navy had been preparing for the showdown for over two decades, and he was not about to let a general dictate strategy. King considered it "heresy" for the Navy to subordinate to MacArthur and the Army. King believed that Marshall "Would do anything rather than disagree with MacArthur," who had been a prewar chief of staff of the Army, while Marshall was still a colonel.

For the grandiose MacArthur there was always only one route to Japan—his route, via the Philippines. In the autumn of 1942 the general had barreled headlong into the jungles of New Guinea, intent on making it back to the Philippines as quickly as possible. At Buna, his first battle on the island, the general pushed for an early victory and lost thousands of men from the 32nd Division to the Japanese and disease. To his credit, MacArthur learned from the bloodshed at

Buna, carefully picking future battles and outsmarting the Japanese. Yet MacArthur still resented his time on New Guinea's dimly lit stage, and yearned to return to the place he had fled in March 1942. For him it was a matter of personal redemption. MacArthur would have "blood on his soul" until he succeeded in liberating the Philippines.

Because the Pacific was an all-American venture, the Combined Chiefs of Staff devoted surprisingly little time to the details of that invasion.

The edict (contained in the Field Service Code, *Senjinkun*), which was issued by Hideki Tojo to soldiers going off to war, read, "In defense always retain the spirit of attack and always maintain the freedom of action; never give up a position but rather die."

In July 1934, Keisuke Okada was named prime minister. He was one of the moderate voices against the increasing strength of the militarists like Tojo, and became a target for extremist forces pushing for a more totalitarian Japan. He narrowly escaped assassination in February 1936.

## CHAPTER 18: BAPTISM BY FIRE

In August 1942, Congress approved the Tydings Amendment to the Selective Service Act, which permitted draft boards to defer agricultural workers "essential to the war effort." Discontent over agricultural deferments remained until the end of the war. General Lewis B. Hershey, director of the Selective Service System, wanted to draft all farmers and their sons whose agricultural production did not "substantially exceed" family consumption or add to the nation's food supply.

The amtrac was also called an LVT and an LCVP. Most Marines called them Alligators or amtracs. The first amtrac was a modified version of vehicles used by the inventor Donald Roebling to hunt in the Florida swamplands.

The First War Powers Act, approved just eleven days after the Japanese attack on Pearl Harbor, contained a broad range of executive freedoms for the prosecution of the war, including a provision for censorship. The day after it was passed, President Roosevelt signed Executive Order 8985, which established the Office of Censorship. Byron Price, the acting general manager of the Associated Press, was appointed as its director and remained in that office for the duration of the war. Price established a "Code of Wartime Practices" that forbade press subjects that contained information of possible value to the enemy. "Of possible value" was an ambiguous directive, but all the major news organizations and the 1,600 combat reporters and photographers voluntarily adopted the code, agreeing to police themselves. News about the war, however, also had to pass through the Office of War Information. The OWI coordinated the release of war news and worked to promote patriotism, restricting anything that it felt undermined the war effort.

Mrs. Graf had reason to be concerned. A photo in the September 20, 1943, issue of *Life* magazine reinforced her—and every other mother's—worst nightmare. Would her son die far from home on some godforsaken island in the middle of the Pacific? The photograph, shot by George Strock, showed American soldiers lying in the sand in New Guinea. The caption read, "Three dead Americans lie on the beach at Buna." In an adjacent full-page editorial, *Life*'s editors asked, "Why print this picture, anyway?" and then they explained their motivation. "Words," they said, "are never enough." The three dead soldiers were not named. *Life*'s editors implied that they would remain anonymous to honor the sacrifice made by American troops on battlefields across the globe.

The release of the photograph made history, sending shock waves across the country. For the first time in World War II, the U.S. public saw an image of dead American troops (other photos had appeared, but the bodies were always covered or in coffins). Many expressed outrage, accusing the press of "morbid sensationalism," and wondered how a high-profile magazine like *Life* had been allowed to publish the photo.

The truth was that *Life* published the photo with the full cooperation of the Roosevelt administration. In the past, Elmer Davis, a much-respected former CBS reporter and commentator who headed up the watchful Office of War Information, had appealed to the president to lift the edict against the publication of battlefield photographs, arguing that Americans "had a right to be truthfully informed" and suggesting that perhaps disturbing battlefield images would motivate the country to redouble its war effort. Persuaded by Davis, and convinced that Americans had grown complacent about the war, Roosevelt suspended the ban on images depicting U.S. casualties. After Roosevelt lifted the injunction, photos of dead soldiers appeared in the press regularly, though publishers often shadowed the victims' faces, name tags, and unit insignia.

In the 1930s the 1st Marine Brigade, based at Quantico, Virginia, staged landing exercises on Caribbean beaches. They also practiced amphibious assaults at Guantánamo Bay, Cuba, where they took to calling themselves "Raggedy-Ass Marines."

Quantico, Virginia, the training and strategic planning facility, disseminated the doctrine. General Alexander Vandegrift, the Marine Corps commandant, went so far as to say that the Marine Corps' greatest contribution to victory was "doctrinal," adding, "The basic amphibious doctrines which carried Allied troops over every beachhead of World War II had been largely shaped—often in the face of uninterested or doubting military orthodoxy—by U.S. Marines."

According to Gordon Rottman in *The U.S. Mechanized Infantryman in the First Gulf War,* in many ways the transformation of the Marines resembles the transformation of the Army after Vietnam. The end of the Vietnam War left the U.S. Army a spent force. Plagued by low morale, drug and race issues, and terrible public relations, the Army faced an uphill climb in the effort to rebuild itself. The story of this reconstruction is mirrored in the rise of the mechanized infantryman. Deciding that the key to future conflict lay in highly trained and mobile warriors who could be delivered quickly to battle, the army adopted the mechanized infantryman as its frontline troops. This new, all-volunteer force was given the best training and equipment that money could buy.

At the time of the Tarawa invasion, the U.S. Navy was the largest and most powerful in the world. Still, as late as August 1943, Nimitz considered the offensive far from a fait accompli. For months Admirals King and Spruance, General Holland Smith, and Admiral Kelly Turner, head of the Amphibious Task Force, debated the scope and targets of the invasion, with King arguing against the recommendations of Spruance, Smith, and Turner, and Nimitz in the middle, calmly assessing the evidence and his options. King advocated for an attack on Nauru in order to "broaden the front" and give the attack "suitable breadth." Using his endorsement of the two-front approach to the war in the Pacific, King adopted a two-axis approach to the Gilberts, and saw Nauru as the fulfillment of that vision. King also believed that an attack on Nauru would confuse and divide the Japanese air and naval forces defending the islands.

Aligned against him were Smith, Spruance, and Turner. Nauru, they said, was useless and too far (400 miles) from the main point of attack—the Tarawa atoll. Smith added that he did not have enough troops, or the transports to move them, to execute an attack hundreds of miles to the west. In a letter to Spruance, which the admiral then forwarded to Nimitz, who in turn passed it on to King, Smith and Turner made a case for Makin: it was in the same direction as the Marshalls, the next objective; it was large enough to accommodate an airfield; and, most important, it was closer to Tarawa, giving Spruance's fleet the ability to cover both assaults. By the end of the summer, Nimitz sided with Spruance, Turner, and Smith, and eventually King did, too, recommending to the Joint Chiefs of Staff that Nimitz be allowed to replace Nauru with the new target, Makin. Some planners wanted to jump the Gilberts and go directly into the Marshalls. Nimitz listened and finally settled on the southern route into the Central Pacific, taking the Gilberts first, as the ardent Spruance advised. Nimitz and King might have gone directly to the Marshalls, but Spruance, the strategist, argued for the Gilberts. The Gilberts, Spruance pointed out, were pivotal because they lay north and west of islands held by the Americans and south and east of the major bases held by the Japanese in the Marshalls and Carolines. He also argued that going straight into the Marshalls would be difficult, since the Americans knew little about them. The Japanese had held them since just after World War I. The Gilberts, on the other hand, were a British possession until 1941. If taken, the Gilberts would provide bases for reconnaissance of the Marshalls. Reconnaissance of the Marshalls needed to take place from a nearer base.

Although achieving consensus on Tarawa was not easy, the process reflected one of the strengths of Nimitz's team and of the admiral himself. Nimitz's down-home demeanor and his love of small-town axioms concealed both his intellect and ferocity. He had been able to assemble a tremendous collection of field commanders, in part because of his openness and his ability to keep his own prodigious ego at bay while managing the egos of others. As part of the planning process, he was willing to accept ideas that conflicted with his own, which inspired those around him to express their opinions freely.

Kwajalein perhaps contradicts the image of Nimitz as a master compromiser. Nimitz wanted to invade Kwajalein, and Spruance and Turner did not. Nimitz finally said to them, "Sitting behind desks in the United States are able officers who would give their right arms to be out here fighting the war. If you gentlemen cannot bring yourselves to carry out my orders, I can arrange an exchange of duty with stateside officers who can. Make up your minds. You have five minutes. Do you want to do it or not?"

Roosevelt knew Nimitz's strengths. In the early days of the war he told Frank Knox, "Tell Nimitz to get the hell out to Pearl and stay there till the war is won." The previous week Knox had flown to Pearl Harbor to assess the extent of the disaster, and he'd returned convinced that Admiral Husband Kimmel was not the man to be commander-in-chief in the Pacific. The following day he and Roosevelt decided that Nimitz would be their choice. At the time Nimitz was head of the Bureau of Navigation. Earlier that year, Roosevelt had offered him the second-highest-ranking post in the Navy, that of Commander-in-Chief, U.S. Fleet, but Nimitz asked to be excused, pleading that such an advance by a junior over so many officers his senior would generate ill will. Admiral Samuel Eliot Morison wrote of the choice of Nimitz, "No more fortunate appointment to this vital command could have been made."

Nimitz had an eye for talent and chose his field commanders well. For his senior commander he picked Admiral Raymond Spruance. Many considered Spruance the most intelligent, most thorough senior officer in the Navy. His fame extended back to the victory at Midway, in which he, after replacing Admiral "Bull" Halsey, performed superbly by boldly but carefully directing the carriers *Enterprise* and *Hornet* and the attacks on Yamamoto's fleet. After the battle Nimitz brought Spruance aboard as his chief of staff. At Nimitz's Pearl Harbor headquarters, the two admirals swam and took long walks together and grew close. Spruance admired his boss's intelligence, but more than anything else he respected what he called his "utter fearlessness." Spruance said of Nimitz, "He is one of the few people I know who never knew what it meant to be afraid of anything." Because he had a skin infection and was suffering from sheer exhaustion and was in no shape to fight a major battle, Halsey suggested that Spruance, an old cruiser commander, who had never before commanded a carrier, replace him. Nimitz took his advice and never regretted his decision. Captain Gilven Slonim,

USN, writing in the U.S. Naval Institute Proceedings, said of Midway that it was "the inception of the greatness of Admiral Raymond Spruance." King's flag secretary said, "I have never met a commander who did not prefer serving under the methodical Spruance. . . . My feeling was one of confidence when Spruance was there and one of concern when Halsey was there." Samuel Eliot Morison called him "one of the greatest fighting and thinking admirals in American naval history." Yet at Midway Spruance came under criticism for failing to engage Yamamoto after sinking four Imperial carriers. The Japanese fleet was still superior to the American fleet, and Spruance did not relish a night engagement. Spruance also knew that Nimitz preferred the competent to the flashy.

In mid-1943 Nimitz gave Spruance command of the newly created Central Pacific Force (which later became known as the Fifth Fleet in April 1944), the Navy's striking arm in the Central Pacific, and promoted him to the rank of three-star admiral. Spruance exercised his new authority by asking Nimitz to appoint two officers as his amphibious experts: the colorful Admiral Richmond Kelly "Terrible" Turner and the cantankerous, Alabama-born leatherneck General Holland "Howlin' Mad" Smith. Turner, whom Nimitz would name commander of the Joint Expeditionary Force, had a reputation for irascibility, much like King, but combined his short temper with a ferocious fighting spirit, an iron will, an unequaled attention to detail, and a keen and quick intelligence. After commanding amphibious forces for the landing on Guadalcanal and keeping those forces supplied, a Sisyphean task, Turner became widely regarded as a master tactician. The Japanese said Turner was like an "alligator—once he bites into something he will not let go."

In 1940 and 1941, Holland Smith taught new Marine units the art of amphibious warfare, but Spruance's first encounter with the general was while Smith was training the Army's 7th Division in San Diego for the invasion of the Aleutians. Like Turner, Smith drove himself and his troops hard. When it came time to choose a leader to direct the ground forces for the Central Pacific campaign, the mild-mannered Spruance knew that the combative general was his man. If Spruance initially feared the pairing of Turner and Smith, it would eventually prove to be one of his better decisions. One Marine officer said of them, "The two men struck sparks like flint against steel," adding that the partnership, "though stormy, spelled hell in bold red letters for the Japanese." One naval officer called Turner "the meanest man I ever saw, and the most competent naval officer I ever served with." Smith added, "Kelly Turner is aggressive, a mass of energy and a relentless task master. The punctilious exterior hides a terrific determination. He can be plain ornery." Smith, however, was critical of the Navy for what he called its "mental arteriosclerosis." An Army historian described Howlin' Mad Smith as "a bully, something of a sadist."

Tarawa was the first battle of the Central Pacific and the test of nearly two decades of joint Navy and Marine Corps planning. The force assigned to make

the frontal assault was Major General Julian Smith's 2nd Marines, half of them
hard-bitten veterans of Guadalcanal, the other half young men only recently out
of boot camp. Their target was the thirty-eight-island atoll's main port, Betio, a
291-acre scrap of coral, lying only feet above the surf line. But Betio, 1,000 miles
northeast of Guadalcanal and 2,400 miles west of Hawaii, was the most fiercely
defended beach in the world. The Japanese had constructed a four-foot barrier
wall of coconut logs and coral around the island. They had mined the beach and
laid down long strings of double-apron barbed wire. Tank traps protected their
command bunkers and firing positions, and nearly five hundred pillboxes were
reinforced with steel plates, concrete, and sand. A garrison of 4,800 men, many
of them first-rate naval troops, watched over the island behind quick-firing, eight-
inch, turret-mounted naval rifles called "Singapore Guns," heavy-caliber field
artillery guns and howitzers, including powerful 200-mm coastal defense guns,
heavy and light machine guns, 50-mm knee mortars, and tanks. Rear Admiral
Meichi Shibasaki told his troops that "a million Americans couldn't take Tarawa
in one hundred years." In early November, Admiral Koga learned of MacArthur's
invasion of Bougainville and decided that that was the major American thrust.
Then came the carrier strike on Nauru atoll, west of the Gilbert Islands. By the time
he realized that the Gilberts were the main target, it was too late. He sent troops
from Truk, but by the time they arrived in the Marshalls, the Gilberts were lost.

Major General Julian Smith knew he wouldn't have one million men, but he was
hoping to add the 6th Marines to his attack force. When Holland Smith and the
general in charge of the land invasion, informed him that they would be held
in reserve, Julian Smith realized that he would be trying to take an island for-
tress with only a two-to-one superiority in troops. Marine shock attack doctrine
clearly called for a three-to-one minimum.

The Navy unleashed a spectacular (3,000 tons of high explosives) but short-lived
bombardment on the morning of D-Day. One admiral boasted, "We do not intend to neutralize [the island], we do not intend to destroy it. Gentlemen, we
will obliterate it." But Admiral Chester Nimitz, commander-in-chief for Allied
air, land, and sea forces in the Pacific Ocean, hoping to get the Marines on shore
before the Japanese had time to regroup, limited the barrage to just three hours,
twenty minutes shorter than it was supposed to be, which meant that the enemy
had time to man their defenses while the Marines were still far from the point
of attack. (Note: A plan to drop 2,000-pound bombs as the coup de grâce never
materialized, and air support was canceled when it became clear that it could not
be done safely—the Marines crossing the seawall were so close to the defenders
that they would be hit by their own side's aerial bombardment. Reporter Robert
Sherrod wrote that despite the truncated barrage, everyone figured that most of
the Japanese "would be dead by the time we got to the island."

It was not to be. The first wave of 1,500 Marines went in on amtracs that crawled over the reef, plunged into the breaking waves, and chugged onto the beach. The rest, relying on faulty naval intelligence and obsolete tide charts (from 1841), came in on deeper-draft Higgins boats that slammed into the coral and stopped. Soon blood stained the surf red. Longtime residents had warned that the reef would be impassable. A pilot in a Navy patrol plane, looking down on the carnage, later admitted that he wanted to cry.

Holland Smith was already angry. Earlier he had been on Makin with General Ralph Smith and the slow-moving 27th Division, which was struggling on Butaritari Island, despite its being underdefended. After arriving on Betio, the primary disciple of the Marine doctrine of amphibious warfare became livid. Makin had been a fiasco, but Betio was a killing field. Naval bombardments (and minimal aerial bombardments) had failed to take out enemy blockhouses and pillboxes. Battleships and cruisers had pounded Betio, but they were not firing armor-piercing shells and most of their hits did little damage. That was left to his men—those Marines who were lucky enough to make it ashore alive. Ultimately Smith would liken Tarawa to Pickett's Charge at Gettysburg, and criticize the Joint Chiefs for authorizing the invasion instead of leaving Tarawa to "wither on the vine." Four thousand Marines assaulted the beach on D-Day. By midnight 1,500 of them were dead or badly wounded.

When Tarawa photos appeared in the press, and theaters across the country showed combat footage vetted by the Navy, angry editorials demanded a congressional investigation into the "fiasco." Shortly after being sworn in as the eighteenth Commandant of the Marine Corps, General Alexander Vandegrift said that Tarawa had "validated the principle of the amphibious assault." Grief-stricken mothers, however, reacted angrily, writing letters accusing Admiral Nimitz of sacrificing their sons for an inconsequential island many thousands of miles from Tokyo.

General MacArthur, choosing to forget that he had ordered his troops to attack Japanese bunkers head-on, Civil War style, at Buna on New Guinea's Papuan Peninsula, wrote the secretary of war, condemning the Navy for its "pride" and "ignorance." Still hoping that the Joint Chiefs would choose his New Guinea–Mindanao axis as the primary road to Tokyo, he called the Marine frontal attack at Tarawa "a tragic and unnecessary massacre of American lives" and an omen of the slaughter to come in the Central Pacific. MacArthur ended with a promise to Stimson: "If you give me central direction of the war in the Pacific, I will be in the Philippines in ten months."

Knowing that people back home were "not prepared psychologically to accept the cruel facts of war," Robert Sherrod penned an unflinching story titled "The Nature of the Enemy," which appeared in the July 1944 issue of *Time* magazine—though he wrote it shortly after Tarawa. Americans, he insisted, had to fortify themselves. Tarawa was a shocking portent, just the beginning of the savage Central Pacific campaign. Despite Americans' belief that the war would be short-lived, Sherrod wrote that every battle would be a fight to the death.

For the Japanese, Tarawa was a sacrificial conflict. Nearly four thousand men, imbued with a wartime myth that glorified *senshi*—literally "death in battle"—and forbade surrender, gave up their lives for a coral atoll that Japanese war planners had already decided to forfeit. Sherrod speculated that perhaps it was time to stop treating the Japanese as if they were capable of reason, and time to consider the option of their extermination. On Attu, in the Aleutian Islands, the first campaign he reported, hundreds of Japanese forces blew themselves up with hand grenades or impaled themselves on their bayonets. On Tarawa only seventeen Imperial Marines dared to risk dishonor by turning themselves over to the enemy. Others died fighting or in senseless charges. Marines also found countless Japanese lying in their foxholes with the backs of their heads blown off. To gain entry into the Yasukuni shrine, which venerated those slain in war, and to avoid capture, a Japanese soldier would remove his shoes, put the barrel of his rifle in his mouth, and pull the trigger with his toe. At the close of the battle for Tarawa, it seemed to Sherrod that Lieutenant General Masaharu Homma's prewar threat to correspondent Clark Lee amounted to more than casual defiance.

If, after Tarawa, Admiral Chester Nimitz wavered in his commitment to the Central Pacific and an amphibious doctrine that relied on initial striking power, speed, and high-risk "storm landings," he did not show it. On November 26 he flew from Pearl Harbor to Funafuti in the Ellice Islands and then on to the Gilberts. "Tarawa," he said, "knocked down the front door" to the Japanese defenses in the Central Pacific. He also asserted Tarawa's strategic importance: the captured airfield on the island of Betio would allow B-24 Liberators to conduct photoreconnaissance of the Marshall Islands.

In truth, Betio's strategic value was limited. Nimitz had squeezed in the attack between two Southwest Pacific Area efforts—the Marine invasion of Guadalcanal and MacArthur's February 1944 assault on the Admiralties—because he and his superior, Admiral Ernest King, understood the necessity of seizing the offensive, of keeping the Japanese guessing where the next battle would occur.

Over time, the shock and despair that much of the American public felt over the carnage at Tarawa faded away. But in December 1943, Tarawa was a public-relations disaster. The reality, however, was that future battles in the Central Pacific would more closely resemble Tarawa than Guadalcanal, a large island where Imperial forces were spread too thin to challenge the landing. After Tarawa, the objectives would likely be small, fiercely defended positions. Moreover, the land assaults on Guadalcanal had been supported by nearby service bases in the New Hebrides and New Caledonia Islands, whereas afterward the support would come from floating carrier forces and an armada of battleships providing ship-to-shore bombardment. It was an entirely new, largely untested mode of warfare. Smith hoped that the Marines' way of doing things would bring about quicker victories and reduce casualties, but the theory's only dress rehearsal had been Tarawa, which was a disaster despite Admiral Raymond Spruance's armada. It covered fifty square miles of ocean and included transports, nineteen carriers, twelve battleships, a flotilla of cruisers, destroyers, and minesweepers, 35,000 troops, and 6,000 vehicles. Nimitz had been made aware of the massive logistic "tail" the Central Pacific campaign would require while he was at the Naval War College in the 1920s. "The operations imposed upon BLUE [the United States]," he wrote in his senior thesis at the college, "will require a series of bases westward from Oahu, and will require the BLUE fleet to advance westward with an enormous train, in order to be prepared to seize and establish bases en route."

Operation maps showed that the Japanese had coastal defense guns, antiaircraft guns, machine-gun pits, pillboxes, circular German-style blockhouses, and antitank trenches. In addition to the Type 89 127-mm dual-purpose guns, the Japanese had four 37-mm guns, nineteen 13-mm dual-purpose guns, ten 20-mm antitank guns, numerous light machine guns, and infantry weapons.

Every Marine—though most of them had never been in battle—harbored a burning hatred of the Japanese. They had all heard the story of the Marine prisoners who were beheaded and mutilated by their Japanese captors on Wake Island. All, too, were familiar with the fate of the "Goettge patrol" on Guadalcanal. (Richard Frank writes that the fate of the patrol remained in the collective memory of the Corps.) In August 1942, twenty Marines responded to what appeared to be a Japanese attempt to surrender. It was a ruse and the enemy soldiers ambushed, then shot and bayoneted the Marines. The motto after that became "kill or be killed," and few Marines—or American combat men, in general—bothered to take prisoners. The Japanese fought like wild animals, so they were treated like wild animals. Many of the men who saw multiple battles in the Pacific would come to abhor the Japanese so much that the hate was like fear; they could taste it.

Bull Halsey said, "The only good Jap is a Jap who's been dead for six months." *Leatherneck,* the Marine monthly, ran a photo of Japanese corpses on Guadalcanal with a headline reading GOOD JAPS and a caption emphasizing that "GOOD JAPS are dead Japs." In *War Without Mercy,* John Dower suggests that American servicemen regarded the Japanese in the same way the Germans regarded the Russians—as *"untermenschen."*

Battle scenes on Roi-Namur are primarily drawn from the memoirs of Robert Graf, Colonel Albert Arsenault's memoirs, and interviews with (and writings of) Carl Matthews.

## CHAPTER 19: PARADISE

Details of Camp Maui are from Carl Matthews and dozens of other Marines who trained there.

The Army's Jungle Training Center was near Camp Maui.

Graf and More learned that the 2nd Battalion was being restructured and all heavy weapons companies, including Company H, of which they had been members for almost one and a half years, were being dismantled. The .30-caliber machine-gun platoons were attached to the companies they supported, while the .50-caliber machine-gun platoon and 81-mm mortar platoon were reassigned to Battalion. Each full-strength company would now have 247 men with three sections of light and three sections of heavy machine guns.

## CHAPTER 20: CAMP TARAWA

Details of Camp Tarawa are drawn from a variety of my interviews, including those with Frank Borta and Glenn Brem.

History of the "bastard battalion" (1st Battalion, 29th Marines) is from an account written by Lieutenant Colonel Tompkins and R. R. Keene's story in the June 1994 issue of *Leatherneck*.

Despite the excellence of Nimitz's team, Tarawa still was a bitter disappointment. Hoping to turn the disappointment of Tarawa into something positive, in early December Kelly Turner boarded a plane from the Gilberts to Pearl Harbor, where he met with Nimitz, who was just returning from the Ellice Islands. En route, Turner wrote an innocuously titled document called "Lessons Learned at Tarawa." It was hardly a bland after-action report, but rather a detailed denunciation of the invasion along with an impassioned analysis of what in the future it would take to avoid the mistakes of Tarawa. Turner's list was fourteen points long and covered everything from the need for longer and more thorough shelling, "greater angles of fire," to the significance of synchronizing bombardment with the movement of assault troops, to the speedy ship-to-shore movement of everything from heavy weapons to medicine to rations—but the first and most urgent item in his report dealt with the importance of obtaining amphibious tanks and LCI gunboats, especially amtracs capable of getting troops over the reefs and onto land. Turner estimated that in future operations each Marine division would need three hundred amtracs—preferably armored—and enough LSTs to transport them. At Tarawa, Holland Smith had demanded amtracs for the invasion. He received 125, too few to carry ashore the first three assault waves, but too many for the three LSTs to handle. Fifty tractors had no launching vehicles, and so were deck-loaded onto troop transports. Spruance also weighed in. "Flat trajectory fire support ammunition," he wrote, "proved ineffective against many shore targets. Greater angle of fall required."

## CHAPTER 21: ERNIE KING'S VICTORY

King's letter to Nimitz and Marshall is from *Master of Sea Power.* MacArthur's lobbying efforts are described by Larrabee in *Commander in Chief.*

Each Marine division was broken into three regiments, and each regiment was further divided into three battalions. In addition to three rifle units, a division would also include an artillery and howitzer regiment, an engineer regiment, tank and amphibious tractor battalions, an assault signal company, and a medical battalion.

New *Essex-* and *Independent*-class carriers as well as battleships, cruisers, and destroyers could sail at thirty knots.

Journalists referred to Truk as the "Gibraltar of the Pacific." After over two decades of isolation—the League of Nations had awarded the Caroline Islands to Japan after World War I—Mitscher knew almost nothing about Truk. The attack on Truk was the first large-scale, independent carrier strike ever attempted, dwarfing the Japanese ambush of Pearl Harbor.

All along, King's biggest problem was that few of his own colleagues, including Nimitz, saw the wisdom of capturing the Marianas. Like MacArthur, they believed that the target did not provide the kind of deep-water harbors the Navy needed. Also, because of the supremacy of the idea that the route to Japan went through the Philippines, Formosa, and China, they considered the Marianas an unnecessary diversion. They also believed that using Navy resources to capture a target so that the Army Air Force could conduct B-29 bombing raids on Japan was inimical to them. Vice Admiral Kinkaid, commander of the Seventh Fleet, bluntly summed up the feelings of many senior naval officers. "Any talk of the Marianas for a base," he said, "leaves me entirely cold." Fortunately for King, Lieutenant General "Hap" Arnold, head of the Army Air Forces, emerged as an enthusiastic partner. Arnold desperately desired a base for his new B-29 bombers and understood that the Marianas represented the fulfillment of that goal.

Now both King and MacArthur had their orders. After isolating Rabaul, MacArthur was to proceed westward along the northern coast of New Guinea, and then, on November 15, take Mindanao. King and Nimitz were to bypass Truk and seize the southern Marianas, isolate the Carolines, and then, on September 15, invade the Palaus, which would provide a base from which the Pacific Fleet could support MacArthur's November attack against Mindanao. Formosa would follow in February 1945. If Luzon was needed to support that attack, MacArthur would secure it first. Following the fall of Formosa, the China coast would be the next objective.

## CHAPTER 22: PRAISE THE LORD AND PASS THE AMMUNITION

Port Chicago's War Diary says that Captain Kinne showed up on April 27, 1944. Kinne's additional duties included Commanding Officer of the Enlisted Men's Barracks.

When James Forrestal became the new secretary of the Navy, following Frank Knox's death in late April, blacks got a leader sensitive to their plight and dedicated to providing equal treatment and opportunity for all men regardless of their color. Forrestal was a member of the National Urban League and a proponent of social equality, but he was no moral crusader. As undersecretary of the Navy and then secretary, he saw the issue of using blacks as full combat seamen as one of efficiency and simple fair play. While he accepted the argument of Admiral Randall Jacobs (head of the Bureau of Naval Personnel) that "you couldn't dump two hundred colored boys on a crew in battle," he also agreed with the Special Programs Unit of the Bureau of Personnel that large concentrations of blacks in shore duties lowered efficiency and morale. Just months before Forrestal became secretary, the Special Programs Unit published a groundbreaking pamphlet titled "Guide to the Command of Negro Naval Personnel," in which it argued that racial tension in the Navy was a serious problem that needed to be dealt with head-on. "The idea of compulsory racial segregation," it said, "is disliked by almost all Negroes, and literally hated by many. This antagonism is in part a result of the fact that as a principle it embodies a doctrine of racial inferiority. It is also a result of the lesson taught the Negro by experience that in spite of the legal formula of 'separate but equal' facilities, the facilities open to him under segregation are in fact usually inferior as to location or quality to those available to others."

The Special Programs Unit had to overcome much opposition within the bureau to get the pamphlet published in February 1944. Some thought the subject of racial tension was best ignored; others objected to the "sociological" content of the work, considering this approach outside the Navy's purview. The pamphlet stated further that "[t]he Navy accepts no theories of racial differences in inborn ability, but expects that every man wearing its uniform be trained and used in accordance with his maximum individual capacity determined on the basis of individual performance."

In his dispatch, after Secretary Knox's death, acting Secretary of the Navy James Forrestal praised the secretary, writing that he had "devoted himself unremittingly and without reserve to the best interests of the country and to the naval service." While Frank Knox had overseen an enormous growth in Navy personnel, he had done little for blacks. Forrestal, however, possessed the bureaucratic and political skills to achieve reforms.

Kinne's idea of posting daily tonnage totals was an idea inspired by the Navy's practice of putting up shooters' scores at the rifle range. Ambitious marksmen, striving for top honors, knew what they had to beat. While Kinne placed the chalkboard where everyone could see it, his main purpose was to remind the loading officers that they, in particular, were responsible for achieving tonnage targets. "It would be impossible," he believed, "to maintain a satisfactory loading rate with the type of enlisted personnel assigned to Port Chicago unless every officer in a supervisory capacity keeps continually in mind the necessity for getting this ammunition out."

The expansion envisioned by Captain Goss was approved by the commandant of the Twelfth Naval District in late 1943. Originally the idea was to construct twenty magazines in the tidal area. That idea, however, was dismissed in favor of the inland storage area option.

Percy Robinson even resorted to putting some seamen on report with the division's petty officer. The complaint would eventually reach Delucchi's desk. Robinson did not like going to "the man," especially Delucchi, but he just could not see any other way. Port Chicago's habitual loafers were put on what was called the "slacker squad."

This was the second of four explosions at the Hastings (Nebraska) Naval Ammunition Depot. The first happened in late January 1944 when a six-inch shell exploded. Three men from a Negro ordnance battalion were killed. On June 10, 1944, a civilian employee was decapitated when a detonator went off. The largest explosion occurred on September 15, 1944, when railroad cars exploded, leaving a crater 550 feet long, 220 feet wide, and fifty feet deep. Nine servicemen were killed and fifty-three were injured. There is still speculation that others were killed or injured, but the Navy has never released the complete records of the blast.

Captain Goss's memo about handling ordnance with greater care was dated May 8, 1944.

Port Chicago's seamen were asked to handle a wide variety of ordnance. The Caven's Point Army Depot in New Jersey handled more tonnage, but only worked with two types of ammunition. Consequently its men were able to load twenty tons per hour.

## CHAPTER 23: WHERE YOUNG MEN GO TO DIE

The two operations—Overlord and Forager—were the largest in the history of the world. Historians would regard June 1944 as the greatest month in military and naval history.

The comment regarding every soldier, sailor, aviator, and Marine, every piece of equipment, and the vast bulk of supplies for the Marianas invasion being American is from Samuel Eliot Morison.

For a complete explanation of the invasion plans, read Major Carl Hoffman's *Saipan: The Beginning of the End*.

Arrival dates differ. In *On to Westward*, Robert Sherrod says the troops arrived in Eniwetok not on June 6 but on June 8.

Some historians claim that a Japanese plane had spotted the task force. Spruance, however, always disputed the claim.

Japanese nationals living on Saipan brought over pianos for children studying the music of German composers. In Garapan, buildings lined the paved streets, among them a confectionary store, a store that sold Oriental dancing dolls, a shoe store, a market with fruit-flavored shaved ice, and two movie houses (Charan Kanoa also had one). Local martial arts, drama, and dance groups used the theater, and, depending upon the time of the year, residents enjoyed traditional Japanese performances. Men patronized the town's drinking houses, gambled on cockfights, and played Japanese board games like go and shogi. On the weekends families picnicked and listened to performances at the gazebo bandstand in Garapan. Children participated in social clubs and played *batu seremban* with stones from the beach, flew kites from the hills above Lake Susupe and along the beaches from Charan Kanoa north to Tanapag, played baseball, and swam in the beautiful blue-green waters inside the reef. The climate was hot, especially in summer, but tropical breezes and afternoon rain showers made the temperatures bearable.

For a fascinating account of the prewar crackdown on local culture and religion by Japanese administrators, read Sister Maria Angelica Salaberria's story "The War in the Pacific in Saipan."

When, during the Spanish-American War, the U.S. seized Spanish holdings in the Philippines as well as the island of Guam, the Spanish moved to sell their Micronesian holdings to Germany. Germany assumed control of the Marianas in 1899 and administered its Micronesian empire from the village of Garapan on Saipan. The Germans initiated a wide range of public-works projects—improved roads, clean water–delivery systems—and instituted compulsory education. They also tried to entice German farmers to the islands.

In the 1930s, Japan secretly began to fortify the Mariana Islands, building a major seaplane base at Tanapag Harbor in 1935, a naval airbase, called Aslito Field, and a variety of bombproof buildings, in violation of the League of Nations mandate. Although Japan claimed they were "civilian" projects, construction met much stricter military standards. During a six-year period between 1934 and 1940, the Japanese government spent 14 million yen to finance construction of questionable civilian projects in the Marianas.

In truth, Japan was solidifying its hold on Micronesia. In 1940, construction teams built bases at Kwajalein, Roi-Namur, Jaluit, Maleolap, and Wotje in the Marshalls, and early in 1941 the 4th Fleet dispatched the new 6th Base Force to defend them. These same crews erected long-range radio stations on Saipan and Kwajalein and a number of other islands to ensure uninterrupted communication between the South Seas and Tokyo. In 1941 Tokyo authorized the construction of fueling stations on Truk, Palau, Pohnpei, and the Marshalls to ensure the mobility of the far-ranging Japanese Fleet. Acknowledging the importance of Saipan as a transfer point for soldiers, a maintenance facility for aircraft, and a communications link with Japan's home islands, Tokyo sent engineers to Saipan to reinforce gun positions, and to build a fueling station there, as well as ammunition storage sheds, communications facilities and radio directional finders, troop barracks, torpedo storage sheds, and air-raid shelters.

Because the invasion happened months before the Japanese expected it (they thought they had until November, Nimitz's original date for the invasion), numerous batteries were not operational. Although many more guns never made it out of storage, Lieutenant General Hideyoshi Obata commanded considerable firepower. Obata had mistakenly assumed that the Americans would strike first in the western Carolines, and a few weeks before the invasion he left Saipan on an inspection tour. He made it back only as far as Guam and was stranded there during the battle.

Forty-two guns were discovered in storage at the Garapan naval depot at Tanapag. Three concrete revetments for Type 89 127-mm dual-purpose guns were built on Mount Nafutan near a radar emplacement. The guns never made it. American forces found three 120-mm dual-purpose guns lying on the ground at Laulau beach.

For a breakdown of Japan's plans for defending its Micronesian holdings, and General Obata's plans for holding Saipan, read D. Denfield's thorough *Japanese World War II Fortifications and Other Military Structures in the Central Pacific* and Gordon Rottman's *Saipan and Tinian 1944: Piercing the Japanese Empire*.

From the interior hills, Obata hoped his high-angle-firing howitzers, designed to pierce the thinly armored upper decks of the invasion vessels, might be able to drive off the American armada. It was a tactic that General Maresuke Nogi used successfully in the 1904 battle of Port Arthur during the Russo-Japanese War.

Admiral Kelly Turner told correspondent Robert Sherrod, "Yes, Saipan is going to be a tough one. But I think we have planned it well." Nevertheless, both he and Howlin' Mad Smith understood that it was going to be bloody and grim. "A week from today," Smith told Sherrod, "there will be a lot of dead Marines."

Mitscher made the decision to strike in the afternoon in order to vary the pattern. "Heretofore," he said, "all of our carrier attacks had been made in the early morning. It was believed that the enemy had become accustomed to this and would expect to continue this practice." Because the carriers had to head into the wind to launch their planes, Mitscher took his ships to the west side of Saipan.

Tokuzo Matsuyo, a noncommissioned tank officer, wrote in his diary: "13 June—At 0930, enemy naval gunfire began firing in addition to the aerial bombing, the enemy holds us in utter contempt." Another captured diary indicated that "[t]he greatest single factor in the Americans' success was naval gunfire."

On March 6, 1521, Magellan sighted the Marianas on his voyage westward. Based on chronicler Antonio Pigafetta's descriptions, Magellan may have sailed between Saipan and Tinian and landed on the latter. Later on, starving, scurvy-ridden Spanish traders used the islands as a rest stop on the long journey between Acapulco and Manila. In 1662, Luis de Sanvitores, a Jesuit, stopped briefly at Guam on his way to the Philippines. His glimpse of the islands led him to want to establish a mission there. Later he would establish the name "Marianas" for the islands in honor of Marie Ana of Austria, superseding the names "Ladrones" and "Islas de Latinas Velas." Discovery spelled doom for the native Chamorro population, which measured fifty thousand. After just a few years of Spanish occupation, the population had dropped to 3,500.

There's an alternate story regarding the naming of the Marianas. That story goes that in 1668 a small band of Jesuit priests established a mission on Guam, receiving essential support from Queen Mariana of Spain. In recognition of her support, they named the archipelago the Mariana Islands. It comprises fifteen islands that lie in a long, flat arc from Farallon de Pajaros in the north to Guam in the south, a distance of about 500 miles. The northern islands are a series of volcanic peaks rising abruptly from the sea. The southern group, which includes Guam, Rota, Aguijan, Tinian, and Saipan, is composed of coral limestone resting on a volcanic base. A fringing reef runs parallel to the shoreline and forms a narrow, protected lagoon for virtually the entire length of the western coast. By contrast, the eastern and northern coasts are ringed by high, rocky cliffs, which drop into the sea. Trade winds prevail during the dry season.

The details about Saipan's early history and pre–World War II history are derived largely from three books: Scott Russell's *Ancient Chamorro Culture and History of the Northern Mariana Islands,* Alexander Spoehr's *Saipan: The Ethnology of a War-Devastated Island,* and Francis Hezel's *From Conquest to Colonization.*

When the sergeant called for lights out, a number of men came to thank Matthews and the sailor. They said they felt calm and reassured, as if they had been to church.

## CHAPTER 24: THE TERRIBLE SHORE

Tokyo Rose's broadcast and names of songs she played are from R. R. Keene's article in the June 1994 issue of *Leatherneck* magazine and Reverend W. Charles Goe's *Is War Hell?*

The armored amphibians that brought the Marines to the beaches were from the 2nd Armored Amphibian Battalion and the Army's 708th Amphibian Tank Battalion. Aerial photographic coverage of Saipan was poor, and planners overestimated the amtracs' ability to negotiate the terrain.

The photo of Matthews, Leary, and Nightingale hitting the beach hangs in the Saipan Exhibit at the National Marine Corps Museum at Quantico, Virginia.

Details of the weather on invasion day are from the Archives and Special Collections at the Library of the Marine Corps.

Reverend Charles Goe provides us with a description of the invasion-morning prayers on some of the vessels, as well as the fears and the state of mind of the Marines.

Along the ridgeline above Lake Susupe and in the hills three miles east of Charan Kanoa, Lieutenant Colonel Nakashima's 3rd Independent Artillery Regiment had orders to pour artillery onto the beach. Observation posts contained large wall diagrams that marked registration, or firing, points on the reefs, the channels, the roads, and the beaches, and the 75-mm and 105-mm fieldpieces had excellent fields of fire.

General Schmidt opened up the 4th Division command post at 7:30 p.m. on D-Day.

Marines hated the head nets, which limited their vision and were so heavy that some complained they could not breathe.

Borta opted to use the M1, even though it was four pounds heavier than a .30-caliber carbine. The M1 also had superior muzzle velocity and hitting power.

Captain William Barr was later quoted in an article titled "Officers Pleased with Performance of Race Fighters" that appeared in the *Atlanta Daily World,* saying, "Mortar shells were still raining down as my boys unloaded ammunition, demolition material, and other supplies from the ammunition trucks. They set up 'security' to keep out snipers as they helped load casualties aboard boats to go to hospital ships. Rifle fire was thick as they rode guard on trucks carrying high-octane gasoline from the beach. A squad leader killed a Jap sniper that had crawled into a foxhole next to his. They stood waist deep in surf unloading boats as vital supplies of food and water were brought in . . . there were only a few scattered snipers on the beach. My boys accounted for several of these."

An article in the July 24, 1944, issue of *Time* magazine read, "Since June 1942, when the Marine Corps broke with 167-year tradition, and began recruiting Negroes, the marines, white and black, have carried on with none of the public race troubles that beset the vastly larger U.S. Army. Said one white Marine officer of this phenomenon: 'We take only the cream of the crop, and they are all so damn proud to be marines.' The Corps still has no Negro officers. But it has 16,000 strapping Negro enlisted men. Some of them have become hard-boiled drill instructors in the classic mold and some have reached the top enlisted grade—sergeant major. Most Negro marines are in service companies, but all marines are combat-minded."

*Time* correspondent Robert Sherrod wrote about the first black Marines to see action: "Negro marines, under fire for the first time, have rated a universal 4.0 on Saipan. Some landed with the assault waves. All in the four service companies have been under fire at one time or another during the battle. Some have been wounded, several of them have been killed in action. . . . Primarily they were used as ammunition carriers and beachhead unloading parties, but on Saipan some were used for combat. When Japanese counterattacked the 4th Marine Division near Charan Kanoa, twelve Negroes were thrown into the defense line. Their white officers said they accounted for about 15 Japs. One Negro jumped into a foxhole already occupied by a wounded white marine, who handed him a grenade. 'I don't know how to use this thing,' said the Negro. The wounded man showed him how. The Negro—named Jankins—threw the grenade, knocked out three Japs manning a machine gun. Said Lieutenant Joe Grimes, a white Texan: 'I watched those Negro boys carefully. They were under intense mortar and artillery fire as well as rifle and machine-gun fire. They all kept on advancing until the counterattack was stopped.'

"But Negro marines were at their best while performing their normal duties. Credited with being the workingest men on Saipan, they performed prodigious feats of labor both while under fire and after beachheads were well secured. Some unloaded boats for three days, with little or no sleep, working in water up to waist deep. Some in floating dump details were the first men to pile off their ship toward the beach. On an open transport, where a detachment of Negroes was left to load small boats, they volunteered to unload and tend the wounded who were brought back to the transport. They handled stretchers, washed the wounded and even wrote letters for them."

Marine Corps Commandant General Vandegrift was equally impressed. "The Negro Marines are no longer on trial," he said in the January 6, 1945, issue of the *Camp Lejeune Globe*. "They are Marines, period."

The 8th Marines who had been attacking eastward were ordered back from Lake Susupe to strengthen the 2nd Division's lines. The Marines backtracked reluctantly.

## CHAPTER 25: A LONG, BITTER STRUGGLE

The 4th Battalion of the 14th Marines set up along the coastal road about 350 yards inland from the beach. Amazingly, the battalion was ready to fire just over an hour after coming ashore.

Empty star-shell cases weighed thirty-five pounds. Because they often fell within American lines, they terrified the Marines. They also emitted a frightening "whir" that rattled the men almost as much as the Japanese artillery.

One Marine battalion commander praised the Army's 708th Tank Battalion, saying they took "more than their share of punishment" and "diverted enemy attention from the amphibious tractors carrying troops. . . . I shall always remember the excellent support given to my battalion by the Army LVT(A)s."

The 20th Depot Battalion's commanding officer, Captain William Adams, was quoted in the September 2, 1944, issue of the *Pittsburgh Courier,* in a story headlined NEGRO MARINES WIN BATTLE SPURS; DEFEATED JAPAN'S BEST ON SAIPAN.

PFC Leroy Seals of Brooklyn, New York, was wounded a few hours after the landing and died the next day.

The Japanese had hoped that the next U.S. objective would be against the Palaus or another site farther south, where the circumstances favored the Combined Fleet. Many thought that Mitscher's Task Force 58 attack on June 11 was a mere diversion. It was not until June 14 that Japan resigned itself to the inevitability of the attack on the Marianas. When it did so, it coordinated an aggressive approach, an effort that included the Combined Fleet and base air forces at Iwo Jima, Guam, Palau, Yap, and Wolei.

The 165th Infantry Regiment's problems began almost immediately. General Howlin' Mad Smith's decision to land the Army's 27th Division forced the 165th's commanding officer (Colonel Gerard Kelley) to land his men on the night of June 16, sacrificing order for speed. At 3:30 a.m. on June 17, elements of the regiment were scattered along three miles of sand from Red Beach south to Yellow Beach. With the majority of his men ashore, Kelley now faced an equally daunting task—assembling them in time for the morning advance.

The military government was hostile to the Catholic Church on Saipan. On one occasion the military governor said, "The Catholic Church must not be good, if Hitler is persecuting it so vigorously in Europe."

The 4th Division's artillery unit, the 14th Marines, landed on D-Day. The entire regiment was ashore by dark.

General Saito committed forty-four tanks and the Special Naval Landing Force to June 17's early-morning assault. Defense of the island was divided between the 31st Army, under Saito, and the Navy's Central Pacific Fleet and 5th Base Force, both of which were commanded by Admiral Chuichi Nagumo, who had directed the assault on Pearl Harbor. As the nominal head of the Saipan garrison, Saito's orders to Nagumo were simple: that he should personally direct the naval attack from the north, moving his troops down the coast road from Garapan in order to "annihilate the enemy's front line and advance towards Oreai [Charan Kanoa] Airfield." In the first seventy-five minutes of the battle, the 10th Marines fired eight hundred rounds. Perhaps resenting Saito's order, Admiral Nagumo never sent his troops into the battle. Major Carl Hoffman provides a detailed account of this battle.

## CHAPTER 26: A HEALTHY SPIRIT OF COMPETITION

Many of the details for this chapter are derived from Joe Small's unfinished account about his Port Chicago experience.

Japanese Americans were sent to internment camps, and any businesses they owned were sold or completely shut down and the spaces were leased out, usually to the new African American residents, who, because of racial covenants, were prevented from living in many other neighborhoods in the Bay Area.

White musicians also were fond of the Fillmore and often came to clubs to jam with African American musicians. The police, however, were not particularly happy about this form of integration, and staged many raids on black businesses. During the war years, the Fillmore's population was almost fifty thousand.

## CHAPTER 27: THE DEVIL'S BACKBONE

Admiral Frank "Jack" Fletcher had a valid operational reason to pull out of Guadalcanal. Because of the losses at Pearl Harbor, Midway, and the Coral Sea, the U.S. Navy was down to two carriers in the entire Pacific and couldn't afford to lose even one more.

The Japanese high command, anticipating a showdown, issued Imperial Headquarters Directive No. 373, ordering the navy and army to prepare for "decisive action" by the end of May.

Tojo was the minister of war from 1939 to 1944, and Osami Nagano was chief of the Navy General Staff from 1941 to 1944.

According to Morison, by mid-1944, Spruance possessed seven carriers to Japan's five, eight light carriers to its four, seven battleships to its five, sixty-nine destroyers to its twenty-eight, thirteen light cruisers to its two, and 956 planes to its 473. Japan had more heavy cruisers, eleven to eight.

Although Spruance was eager to engage the enemy, he was reluctant to expose his ground troops on Saipan to danger. Lending credence to his fears was a document that MacArthur sent him detailing Japanese carrier doctrine. Morison speculates that the document was Admiral Koga's Z Plan. Morison writes: "He is not to be blamed for assuming that the Japanese would divide their forces. But no reinforcements were coming south from Japan, and Ozawa had no intention of trying an end run. Defending himself Spruance later said, 'It would have been much more satisfactory if, instead of waiting in a covering position, I could have steamed westward in search of the Japanese fleet.'"

Japanese planes, which lacked armor and self-sealing fuel tanks, could attack from a distance of 300 miles and American planes, which were heavier, had a shorter range of 200 miles.

The reply of the chief of staff of the 43rd Division to Tojo is from Major Carl Hoffman's *Saipan: The Beginning of the End*.

General Ralph Smith's quote is from Hoffman.

Two days after taking the airfield, the Seabees began repairing it. By June 22, fighters were able to take off and land there.

In an article for the March 1999 issue of *World War II* magazine, John Wukovits offers a brief explanation of Operation A-Go and vivid details of the Battle of the Philippine Sea.

Statistics regarding Admiral Ozawa's losses vary from 383 lost to Samuel Eliot Morison's figure of 476, which includes land-based planes from Guam.

When Ozawa's flagship, the *Taiho*, exploded, only five hundred of the 2,150 crew members were saved.

When Mitscher said to his pilots, "Give 'em hell, boys," he added, "Wish I were with you."

Admiral Ozawa blamed the defeat not only on his own inadequacy, but also on the lack of skills of his untrained pilots. After consulting with the navy minister, Admiral Toyoda refused to accept Ozawa's resignation. Ozawa retained his command, and, according to Morison, was later bested by Admiral Halsey in the Battle of Cape Engano.

In the aftermath of the Battle of the Philippine Sea, many admirals expressed their dissatisfaction with Spruance's conduct. Admiral Jocko Clark claimed that "[i]t was the chance of a century missed." Mitscher wrote in his after-action report that "[t]he enemy escaped. He had been badly hurt by one aggressive carrier strike, at the one time he was within range. His fleet was not sunk." Admiral Montgomery wrote, "Results of the action were extremely disappointing to all hands." Then he added that it was "unfortunate" that Mitscher was "not permitted to take the offensive until too late to prevent the enemy's retirement." Morison makes an argument for Spruance. Mitscher, he points out, was "responsible only for Task Force 58," so "his absorbing passion was to destroy the Japanese carriers." Spruance, however, "had the overwhelming responsibility for Operation 'Forager'; for the Joint Expeditionary Force as well as the carriers; for the troops." Morison adds that his "objective was to secure the Marianas." On a more critical note, Morison writes that "a powerful striking force as mobile as the fast carriers should never be tied to the apron strings of an amphibious operation," and that "in view of the known strength of Ozawa's Mobile Fleet any possible 'end run' could have been dealt with adequately by the ships left to guard Saipan."

Eight years later, in a letter to Morison, Spruance wrote, "I think that going out after the Japanese and knocking their carriers out would have been much better and more satisfactory than waiting for them to attack us; but we were at the start of a very important and large amphibious operation and we could not afford to gamble and place it in jeopardy."

The Imperial Rescript was promulgated by the Emperor Meiji in 1882.

The "ghost" in the modern Japanese Army that allowed military strategists to forgo caution and field officers to push their troops beyond what was considered humanly possible was the samurai spirit. Around the ninth century, as feudalism evolved in Japan, samurai, or "those who serve," were a small, elite warrior class within the feudal system. Samurai emphasized the twin virtues of loyalty and self-sacrifice and evolved an ethic known as *bushido*, the "Way of the Warrior." In the first half of the twentieth century the Japanese military resurrected bushido, and distorted it as a way to transform Japan's entire male population into willing warriors. In fact, at the time, the whole of Japanese society was being systematically indoctrinated and militarized. Slogans were omnipresent: "One hundred million [people], one mind" *(ichoku isshin);* "Abolish desire until victory" *(hoshi-garimasen katsu made wa).* Dissent was aggressively suppressed. Unwavering dedication to the Emperor, to Japan, to a culture that considered itself morally superior to the bankrupt West, became the norm. In fact, by World War II, the average Japanese citizen had been instilled with a master-race mentality that was every bit as dangerous as its German counterpart.

## CHAPTER 28: VALLEY OF THE SHADOW OF DEATH

Von Clausewitz wrote the military treatise *Vom Kriege,* On War.

The annual rainfall in Saipan is 90–120 inches.

Details regarding the health of the men are from the Archives and Special Collections at the Library of the Marine Corps.

The word *malaria* comes from the Greek, meaning "unpleasant" or "odious." The *Aedes* mosquito also transmits yellow fever.

Japanese soldiers were sent off with comfort bags *(imonbukuro),* each one containing a hand towel *(tenugui)* and a loincloth *(fundoshi)* as well as a bar of soap, postcards, and a pencil with which they were encouraged to write in their diaries.

In *The GI War Against Japan,* Peter Schrijvers writes about how American servicemen, fueled by rage and revenge, adopted an increasingly savage attitude to their Japanese enemies. In *War Without Mercy,* John Dower explores similar developments in the psyche of American soldiers in the Pacific.

War in the Pacific, to quote E. B. Sledge, was fueled by a "brutish, primitive hatred." Perhaps nowhere was that more apparent than on Saipan. Veteran correspondent Ernie Pyle, who was transferred to the Mariana Islands from Northern Europe, observed this new attitude toward the enemy. "In Europe," he noted, "we felt our enemies, horrible and deadly as they were, were still people. But out here I've already gathered the feeling that the Japanese are looked upon as something inhuman and squirmy—like some people feel about cockroaches or mice." In *War Without Mercy,* John Dower cites a cartoon in *The American Legion Magazine* depicting monkeys in a zoo that had posted a sign reading, "Any similarity between us and the Japs is purely coincidental."

In one cave, Graf's Company E discovered dozens of women and children and a few adult men. Jimmy Haskell was in charge of taking them to the rear. Ever softhearted, he collected ration boxes and opened them up and passed candy out among the children, when he caught a man grabbing candy from a young girl. Haskell flew into a rage and smashed his rifle butt into the man's chest, sending him to the ground with a thud.

Even by the battle's second week, Japanese soldiers held on to hope that they could still defeat the Americans. One wrote in his diary on June 26, "This is the day the Westerners will be surprised."

The 106th Infantry regiment had been the 27th Division's reserve until June 20, when Holland Smith succeeded in convincing Admiral Turner that he needed it urgently.

The senior army official was Major General Sanderford Jarman, Saipan Garrison Force commander.

After the Marianas campaign, a board of Army officers inquiring into the dismissal of Ralph Smith asked Colonel Ayres, the 106th's commanding officer, what would have happened had he pressed the attack through Death Valley. "My candid opinion," Ayres answered, "is that the regiment would have disappeared."

That evening Robert Sherrod saw Holland Smith at his headquarters, describing the general as "nervous" and "remorseful." In an attempt to explain his actions, Holland Smith said, "Ralph Smith is my friend, but, good God, I've got a duty to my country. I've lost seven thousand Marines. Can I afford . . . to let my Marines die in vain? I know I'm sticking my neck out—the National Guard will chop it off—but my conscience is clear. I did my duty."

Disappointed with the progress of the Army's 165th Regiment at Makin during the assault of the Gilberts, Smith asserted that "any marine division" would have taken the island in one day, whereas the Army took three. He bemoaned the regiment's "lack of offensive spirit," but added that it was less a fault of the men than of the leadership—specifically the 27th Division commander, General Ralph Smith. Of his army counterpart, Howlin' Mad Smith said, "Had Ralph Smith been a Marine I would have relieved him of his command on the spot." The quote about relieving Smith is from *Coral and Brass*. This was the source of the enmity between Lieutenant General Richardson, Army commander in the Central Pacific, and Holland Smith. Richardson resented the way Smith stormed ashore and berated Ralph Smith.

Gordon Turner's Princeton University paper "Dual Conflict: A Study of Saipan" notes that many of the problems between the Marines and the Army originated from fundamental tactical differences and poor lines of communication. He notes that Army regiments often received Howlin' Mad Smith's orders for 7:00 a.m. attacks between midnight and 5:00 a.m., leaving them little time in which to prepare for the day's advance.

A thorough discussion of the conflict can also be found in Harry Gailey's *Howlin' Mad vs. the Army: Conflict in Command, Saipan 1944*.

## CHAPTER 29: TAPOTCHAU'S HEIGHTS

In *On to Westward*, Robert Sherrod quotes a staff officer on the problems of taking Mount Tapotchau: "We can't sit back and expect artillery and naval gunfire to blast 'em out of those caves."

Quote about Japanese tactics from Sherrod.

Quote about holding Tapotchau from Hoffman.

Japanese phrases—*Kosan se yo!* ("Surrender!") and *Detekoi!* ("Come out!")—are from a May 26, 1944, D-2 Section handout titled "Useful Japanese Words and Phrases for Frontline Troops."

Details about General Saito's various command posts are provided by the interrogation of Major Yoshida.

In *Hirohito and the Making of Modern Japan*, Herbert Bix writes that in Tokyo, Hirohito's chief aide, General Hasunuma, and the Board of Field Marshals and Fleet Admirals delivered a sobering report to the Emperor. Saipan, they said, was already lost. An angry Hirohito insisted they put those words in writing, and abruptly left the room.

On June 27, Holland Smith trudged up a narrow path to a shrine near the top of Mount Tapotchau. A Marine historian wrote that the "entire island lay stretched visibly before him, like a huge aerial photograph."

In his June 1994 article for *Leatherneck* magazine, "The Orphan Battalion That Took Mount Tapotchau," R. R. Keene offers excellent details regarding the 1st Battalion, 29th Marines' assault of the Japanese position on top of Mount Tapotchau.

## CHAPTER 30: *GYOKUSAI*

The Americans had a hard time at Nafutan Point despite having antiaircraft guns, mortars, and tanks at their disposal. The forces at Nafutan Point were from the Army's 105th Infantry's 2nd Battalion. Howlin' Mad Smith could have used his 3rd Division Marines, which were part of his Southern Attack Force, but he was saving that division for the invasion of Guam.

Smith was still displeased with the progress of the Army. He had turned over command of the 27th Division to Major General Sanderford Jarman with the hope that the energetic general could get his troops moving. A day later Jarman relieved Colonel Ayres, commanding officer of the 106th's 2nd Battalion, and that same night he sent a message to the entire 27th Division: "This division is advancing against a determined enemy that must be destroyed. . . . I know I can depend on every member of the 27th to get into this fight with everything he has. Good hunting to every man."

Even with the delays during the Battle of the Philippine Sea, and a variety of logistical problems caused by Saipan's shoals and reefs, the lack of channels, and near-constant shelling, the black shore parties managed to do the near impossible. The explosion at West Loch complicated their task. To avoid delaying Operation Forager, white Marines from the 4th Division, like Robert Graf, hurriedly put supplies aboard LSTs often without regard for order, observing much less rigorous combat loading procedures. On Saipan, this caused more than a few headaches for the black shore parties. But this difficulty they handled, too, and now that their regular duties were largely done, many of them looked forward to the opportunity to be combat soldiers.

Just a week into the battle, the evacuation of the wounded reached a crisis point. On June 23 the hospital ships *Relief* and *Samaritan*, filled to capacity, left for Guadalcanal. Painted pure white with a red cross superimposed over a green stripe that ran around the ship, the *Relief* and *Samaritan* followed the route taken by a number of transports. The hospital ship *Solace* had already made a round-trip to Guadalcanal. With the lengthening and widening of the runway at Aslito Field, air evacuation from the island began on June 25. By the end of the operation, 860 casualties were taken to the Marshall Islands by air. During the early stage of air evacuation, planes were not supplied with medical attendants. Consequently, casualties died en route. Upon being taken on a ship, the wounded were classified based on the seriousness of their injuries and given red casualty tags that indicated who should be attended to first.

Details on the condition of the Japanese soldiers are from Hoffman, Sherrod, and G-2 report No. 21, "Re: Interrogation of Commander Jiro Saito of the 5th Base Force." The translation was done by Lieutenant Colonel T. R. Yancey. In his diary, Saito wrote, "In everyone's mind he is thinking that before he dies he would like to have a bellyful of water, but there is none to be had."

General Saito made the decision to move his command post after surviving a fierce 8th Marines mortar barrage. The post was located one mile to the north of a line that stretched from the Tanapag Hill 221–Hill 112 area to the east coast.

Today Muchot Point is known as Micro Beach. It's located inside the American Memorial Park between the boat marina (Smiling Cove and the downtown Garapan area right next to the Hyatt). It was the site of the first Carolinian settlement on Saipan in the 1815 diaspora of Satawalese homesteaders led by Chief Aghurubw. He is buried on Managaha Island, which is still called Ghalaghaal Island by the Carolinian population in Tanapag. The Carolinan name of that village was Arabwal (named after the green beach vine that still grows there).

Lieutenant Chaffin would win the Navy Cross for his leadership and heroism. The bad news for the men of the 29th was that they had lost Lieutenant Colonel Tompkins, who was wounded by a shell fragment. When General Edson, CO of the 2nd Division, came up to check on Tompkins, the colonel said, "Hey, Red, this battalion has had it. They should be relieved—they're burned out." Frank Borta overheard Tompkins say this to General Edson.

Liberator bombers started using the runway in August, and by mid-October B-29s began using it. This was the nightmare scenario that Hirohito so feared—planes with the capability of reaching Japan's home islands.

Dead animals and bloated human corpses lay among the ruins of Garapan.

In early July, after weeks of contending with the island's roughest terrain, the 8th Marines received a much-needed rest and the unit was moved into a bivouac rest area one mile inland from Red Beach 3, north of the Lake Susupe swamps.

Colonel Louis Jones, commanding officer of the 23rd Marines, pulled the 2nd Battalion out of reserve. Its job was to hold the American position against Japanese counterattacks.

The quote about the "hateful, bearded face of the enemy" is from a captured diary. Diary writing had a long history in Japan, especially field diaries, *jinchu nikki/nisshi*. According to Aaron Moore's "Essential Ingredients of Truth: Soldiers' Diaries in the Asia Pacific War," the diary was considered the "mirror of truth" *(makoto no kagami)* and also one's last testament *(igonsho)*. Japanese soldiers often used their diaries for self-mobilization.

Notes on the *gyokusai* are from Haruko Taya Cook and Theodore F. Cook's article "A Lost War in Living Memory: Japan's Second World War."

Apparently General Saito was suffering from shrapnel wounds received in the bombing. Details from "The Last Days of Lieutenant General Saito."

Details regarding the act of seppuku differ from historian to historian. These details are taken from Harold Goldberg's *D-Day in the Pacific* and Victor Brooks's *Hell Is Upon Us*.

"The Last Days of Lieutenant General Saito" is a captured Japanese officer's personal account that was translated by Lieutenant Colonel T. R. Yancey. This document describes General Saito's physical and emotional condition and his various command posts. It also provides a description of Saito's death and the preparations for the *gyokusai*. This document is included in the appendix to Major Carl Hoffman's *Saipan: The Beginning of the End*. Yancey also produced translations of many of the prisoner interrogations, including that of Major Kiyoshi Yoshida, an intelligence officer of the 43rd Division. Yoshida's confessions confirmed many of the American assumptions about the course of the battle: that the invasion had taken Saipan's defenders by surprise; that naval gunfire had devastated many enemy positions; that the loss of Mount Tapotchau was a turning point in the battle; and that the Japanese radio and telephone communication during the battle was poor.

Robert Sherrod, Harold Goldberg, Gordon Rottman, and Francis O'Brien *(Battling for Saipan)* provide vivid details of the *gyokusai*.

## CHAPTER 31: RED FLAGS

The *Bryan* had arrived at the Port Chicago Naval Ammunition Depot on July 13.

According to Lieutenant Terstenson, there was not a winchman who knew how to "pick up a load and check the swing of it [the load]."

According to Port Chicago's regulations, Lieutenant Terstenson could have, or perhaps should have, halted all loading at the No. 4 hold. Port Chicago regulations said, "Any member of this detail is authorized to stop any loading or handling operation . . . which he deems unsafe . . . until such time [as] can be determined by the Loading Safety Officer, and if need be, referred to the officer-in-charge for a decision."

In the past, Lieutenant Commander Holman had shut down a hold when a handle broke off a winch. That was a serious problem, since the handle was the operating lever for the throttle, the steam control. But a valve or brake problem was a different story. Holman was unconcerned about the brake problem on the No. 1 winch. "If a winch is working properly," he said, "you don't need brakes." Later he testified that if the steam failed, the compression would lower the load slowly. What he apparently did not consider was how some of Port Chicago's inexperienced winchmen, of whom he, too, had a low opinion, would react to the loss of steam.

Lieutenant Terstenson wanted to use a forklift with a pallet on which to place the bombs, or, at the very least, to use a thrum mat to cushion their fall. He also objected to the hoisting of Mk-47s in steel nets because of the inevitable shifting and clanging. He proposed standing the bombs on end on a tray surrounded by a guard board. That way, he argued, if the worst should happen and a lug become unhooked, the bombs would not fall to the deck or into the hold.

Captains Kinne and Goss had made it clear that "the handling and stowage of ammunition would be subject to the approval of the loading officer." Had none of the loading officers talked with the seamen about handling Torpex-filled bombs, or was that another depot rule that would go unenforced? What was missing from Port Chicago was a uniformity of procedure. Everyone seemed to have different expectations and preferences. Tobin liked using nets for bombs, and Holman preferred slings; Cordiner insisted on using thrum mats, while Ringquist thought they were unnecessary. Some officers liked electric mules for breaking open railroad cars, while others felt that men using sledgehammers and pinch bars could do it better. There were lieutenants who punished negligence and inefficiency, and some who looked the other way.

Terstenson testified that the ship's gear was the responsibility of the division officers. Prior to coming to Port Chicago on January 15, 1944, Lieutenant Terstenson was Pier Superintendent for the Army Transport Service at San Francisco.

Captain Goss wrote, "All bombs look alike to individuals of limited intelligence."

The Navy Bureau of Personnel was not of much help, either. It did not issue a comprehensive "ammunition handling" manual until 1945, meaning that no standard practice for handling high explosives, much less 40-mm cartridges, even existed. The Port Chicago Naval Ammunition Depot had to rely on what officers considered the Coast Guard's "impractical" regulations and an incomplete document called the "U.S. Naval Magazine, Port Chicago, California, Manual of Loading and Dock Procedure." Lieutenant Woodland would later testify that those documents were seldom consulted. "They were kept on file," he said, "but the officers were not notified that such material was available." Lieutenant Tobin, for instance, had never seen the Coast Guard regulations, while Lieutenant Commander Ringquist did not know that a Port Chicago manual even existed. According to the testimony of some of the officers, a Coast Guard manual was kept down at the pier for officers to refer to. Captains Goss and Kinne were negligent for not insisting that all new officers read the manual.

### CHAPTER 32: ISLAND OF THE DEAD

Regarding the 27th Division's efforts to repulse the charging Japanese soldiers, Army historian Edmund Love wrote, "For the next four hours this group of men put up one of the great defensive fights in American history." Lieutenant Colonel William O'Brien (from Troy, New York), commander of the 1st Battalion, 105th Regiment, was awarded the Medal of Honor posthumously for his heroism. Edmund Love writes a riveting account of his heroism. Eventually, however, onrushing Japanese soldiers overwhelmed O'Brien.

The 1st and 2nd Battalions of the 105th Infantry Regiment killed an estimated 2,295 Japanese. Its Headquarters Company killed at least 650. In the area where the 1st and 2nd Battalions of the 106th Infantry and the 3rd Battalion of the 105th Infantry fought, burial crews discovered 1,366 dead Japanese, raising the total to 4,311. The assumption among the 27th Division was that most of them had perished during the *gyokusai*. The Americans, too, suffered heavy casualties. Out of the 1,100 men who made up the 1st and 2nd Battalions, four hundred died and another five hundred suffered wounds sustained in the battle.

In "A Lost War in Living Memory," Haruko Taya Cook suggests that exaggerations of how many civilians killed themselves on Saipan became part of the Allied propaganda to justify dropping the atomic bombs. The myth, she writes, was that "[b]ehind the soldiers are the people of Japan as a whole, themselves united in the cause of their Emperor . . . 'One Hundred Million Bullets of Fire.'" Cook writes further that "[m]ore than any other event during the course of the war, with the exception of the atomic bombs themselves, the notion—engendered by propagandists—that the overwhelming majority of the Japanese civilian population of Saipan, largely women and children, willingly took their lives rather than submit to the Americans, shaped the memory of the final year of the Pacific War. . . . Was not any force, any action, any act, no matter how criminal it might appear under normal circumstances, justified if it meant the annihilation of such thinking? Was it not essential to stop treating the Japanese as rational beings, and proceed with the extermination of all, if necessary? Rather than being cleared up, the myths around Saipan have multiplied. . . . It is vital when considering the consequences of such thinking that we recall that most of the one million Japanese civilian casualties in the war . . . occurred in the last twelve months of the conflict. Between July 1944 and August 1945, as Japan's leaders sought to protect themselves and the institutions they claimed to serve, the people of Japan were in fact sacrificed under a national slogan that was eventually refined into 'One Hundred Million Die Together,' a natural extension of the illusory image of Saipan. Death became a tool useful for the survival of the Imperial System itself at the end of the Lost War." In other words, according to Cook, this wartime myth was "coordinated, calculated, mobilized and subsidized" by government fiat.

Some historians say thousands leaped. Cook maintains that the figure was in the hundreds.

James Fahey's lurid account of watching bodies float by is from his *Pacific War Diary*.

Regarding the quote "Hell is upon us," in *Goodbye, Darkness,* William Manchester says that Hirohito said this. Donald Miller, in *D-Day in the Pacific,* says that these were the words of one of Hirohito's military advisers. Brooks, in *Hell Is Upon Us,* says it was Vice-Admiral Shigryoshi Miwa who said this. Miwa predicted that the loss of Saipan paved the way for the withering bombing campaign on the home islands.

Admiral King was right when he said, "The Marianas are the key of the situation because of their location on the Japanese line of communications between the home islands and the empire." Robert Sherrod called Saipan "Japan's Pearl Harbor," while noting that in fact "Saipan is a thousand miles closer to Japan's coast than Pearl Harbor is to America's."

## CHAPTER 33: HOT CARGO

Ordnance tonnage figures are 522 tons of M66 bombs, 247 tons of M65 1,000-pounders, and 283 tons of 500-pound M64s.

With Liberty and Victory ships, the practice was to load the heaviest cargo in the lower holds so that the ship's center of gravity was well below the water line. In rough seas this helped to stabilize the vessels.

By 7:00 p.m. the *E. A. Bryan* was carrying a total of 4,379 tons of ammunition and explosives, including 328 tons of antiaircraft projectiles and another 320 tons of igniter charges in the lower portion of her No. 1 hold; and, in her No. 2 hold, 54 tons of Mk-47 Torpex-loaded aerial depth bombs and 1,052 tons of 500-, 1,000-, and 2,000-pound bombs.

In the *Bryan*'s No. 3 hold, the seamen had already loaded 1,049 tons of M65s. The No. 4 hold held 475 tons of 500-pound bombs (M64) and another 315 tons of 325-pound depth bombs (Mk-54) filled with Torpex. The No. 5 hold contained 166 tons of antiaircraft projectiles, 360 tons of 40-mm cartridges, and another 260 tons of projectiles for a three-inch, .50-caliber naval gun.

Exact tonnage figures for the *Bryan* vary. Port Chicago's seamen were able to load between 800 and 1,100 tons every twenty-four hours.

Regarding the markings on the bombs, prior to 1941 the Army and Navy had separate manufacture and designs for all bombs, and each service had distinctive nomenclature to indicate a particular piece of ordnance. The Navy nomenclature was prefixed by the word "Mark," abbreviated as "Mk." The Army used much the same method until 1925, when it changed its nomenclature to avoid confusion with the Navy. All Army items since then have been named M (for model), followed by an Arabic numeral. In 1941 a joint committee for standardization of ordnance known as the Army-Navy Standardization Board was created. Since then bomb production has been approved by the Standardization Board for joint issue to Army and Navy forces. Designs accepted by this Board are designated by the prefix "AN" (Army-Navy) followed by the Army or Navy name of the design. Thus, an Army bomb approved for joint production would be named AN-M and a Navy bomb would be named AN-Mk. Bomb sections of Army-Navy manuals usually consisted of four parts: U.S. Army "modified mark" series bombs; U.S. Army "M" series bombs; U.S. Navy "Mk" series bombs; and U.S. Army-Navy "AN" series bombs.

The *Quinault* docked at Port Chicago at 6:00 p.m. that evening. There was a shortage of eight-inch lines to keep the ship snug against the pier. The ship wanted to pull away from the dock. By 9:00 p.m., however, because of changing tides, the *Quinault* was resting against the dock.

Ringquist saw that the men were having trouble rigging the *Quinault* due to what he called her "non-standard equipment." He also noticed that a number of the cargo whips, which ran through heel and head blocks to the winches, were on backwards. He instructed the division's walking bosses to have them corrected. Other than a pile of oily rags and some lubricating oil in drums, which he ordered to be taken off the ship, everything seemed to be in order.

Robert Allen says that loading on the *Quinault* was supposed to begin at midnight. Lieutenant Commander Holman, however, testified that it was supposed to begin at 2300 hours on July 17.

Captain Kinne believed that Port Chicago was an altogether safer place. He had sent some of his officers to loading school, others to observe loading operations at military and commercial ports across the country, and still others, like Lieutenant Woodland, to Great Lakes for a class run by Navy psychologists in "handling Negro personnel." As for the black seamen, he was convinced that the large new recreational facility would bolster morale. He was also certain that the shorter shifts (divisions were working eight-hour shifts with one hour for lunch) and a regular liberty schedule (the seamen got one twenty-four-hour liberty pass every eight days) were helping to improve working conditions.

There's a discrepancy among the various documents regarding the number of cars on the pier. The Los Alamos diagram shows sixteen, but among the Port Chicago explosion records at Los Alamos there is a document that identifies only ten cars. On page 640 of the Court of Inquiry, Lieutenant Commander Holman testifies that "[i]t was not the practice to have more cars on the pier than was necessary, because of the limited space." Defense, however, questioned him about what he meant by "more than was necessary." It became clear that "more than was necessary" was very subjective. Loading interruptions were discouraged. The "accumulation of explosives" was a common practice at ammunition depots across the country, and was standard operating procedure at Port Chicago.

A 1,000-pound armor-piercing bomb filled with TNT was called an M33. Opposite the Bryan's No. 2 hold were two cars carrying another 108 tons of 350-pound Mk-47 bombs.

Shipping bombs with fuzes was considered dangerous. If a bomb was dropped, the fuze could ignite the smaller bombs in the cluster. There were two main types of fuzes: the ignition fuze and the detonating fuze. The first one contained an initiating explosive and a magazine of black powder. The action of the initiator ignited the black powder and that, in turn, either ignited the explosive filler (black powder or a mixture of black powder and TNT) or initiated the action of an auxiliary detonating fuze, which induced the detonation of a high-explosive filler. The detonating fuze contained an initiating explosive and a booster. Once detonated, the booster detonated the projectile filler.

Although the Port Chicago Navy Court of Inquiry mentions M7 or Mk-7 incendiary bombs, the extensive and "confidential" U.S. Navy Bomb Disposal School book (United States Bombs and Fuzes), dated June 1, 1944, does not mention these bombs. Peter Vogel says there was no World War II–era incendiary cluster bomb with that name. In Chapter 10 of his book *The Last Wave from Port Chicago,* Peter Vogel speculates that the M7 was actually the 500-pound M17, a cluster of 110 four-pound M50 magnesium incendiary bombs, or the 220-pound M19, a cluster of thirty-six six-pound jellied oil M69 bombs.

On June 14, 1944, Captain Kinne posted his new safety regulations.

Lieutenant Woodland considered the 3rd Division the best when it came to "all around handling of ammunition, carefulness, knowledge of stowing and all." His winch drivers, petty officers, carpenters' mates, and junior officers were "topnotch."

On July 17, Lieutenant Woodland was on liberty. While he rested at his home in Walnut Creek, he knew that White and Blackman understood what was expected of them. Lieutenant White wrote in a letter to his parents on July 17, just after returning from Lake Tahoe, that Lieutenant Woodland had fallen ten feet into the hold of a ship and broken his arm. White was just back from Lake Tahoe after a week's holiday with his wife, Inez.

Lieutenant Vernon Shaner, the 6th Division's head officer, did not think highly of his men. Lieutenant Shaner, expressing dismay about the men assigned to him by Lieutenant Commander Holman, said to Lieutenant John Kelly that the 6th Division "got all the rogues in the country."

During the rigging of the ship and loading, officers were supposed to remain down at the pier. Woodland was critical of other division heads who returned to the barracks or allowed their junior officers to do the same.

Woodland gave White and Blackman specific instructions. He knew that prior to loading, the lieutenants would assemble the men and "explain explicitly" how they wanted the ordnance handled, especially the large bombs, the M7s with the fuzes, primers, detonators, and anything packed with Torpex. Woodland cautioned the officers to be aware of the "hundreds of little problems." Don't worry about the tonnage, he told them; "the tonnage will come." Apparently the division had shaped up since the mutiny that Inez White referred to.

Captain Kinne wrote his officers in May commending them for their "excellent work in loading the USS *Rainier.*" Lieutenant Woodland, in turn, praised Captain Kinne for his efforts to make Port Chicago a better place.

Navy and Army depots across the country employed contract stevedores, but perhaps owing to Captain Goss's distrust of them, Port Chicago and Mare Island did not.

During his testimony, Lieutenant Tobin said, "I think that anybody that is around this ammunition has a feeling of concern. . . . I personally believed that this ammunition would explode and I felt that there was a high probability." Lieutenant Michael Hart, who was in charge of Division 5, a general working division that the men called the "Suicide Squad," later testified that the men were "inadequate for the hazardous job."

Lieutenant Tobin said that Captain Goss's visits to the pier were very rare. However, he did see him there on May 5 to inspect the new pier shortly after it had been widened.

During the trial, Captain Kinne said, "I would very seriously object to having a Coast Guard officer sent to police any activity over which I have command or over which I was in charge."

## CHAPTER 34: END OF THE WORLD

Disaster-relief organizations were at the depot and in town by early morning on July 18.

Percy Robinson was transferred to the Mare Island Naval Hospital with lacerations to the forehead.

The towns of Pittsburg, Concord, Walnut Creek, and Martinez also suffered damage. Windows were broken in San Mateo County, more than twenty miles across the bay. Reverberations from the explosion were felt seventy miles east in Stockton, California. Shell casings were found miles from the depot.

According to the July War Diary, the fire occurred in Barricade B-206. Peter Vogel says there were only 140 cars in the revetment area.

Details of the wave hitting the lighthouse are from Peter Vogel. By the time the wave hit, it had lost much of its power.

One hundred nine people in the town of Port Chicago suffered injuries, mostly lacerations from flying glass. Eye injuries were common. Many also suffered damage to their eyes from looking at the intense flash of light. Miraculously, no one was killed. Most of Port Chicago's businesses and 90 percent of its homes suffered damage. The Red Cross brought in 80,000 board feet of lumber for repairs.

After weeks of hunting, search parties eventually discovered only fifty-one bodies that could be identified. Only a few identifiable pieces of the *Bryan* were ever found.

According to Peter Vogel, the crater underneath the *Bryan* was oval-shaped and 600 feet from point to point, and 300 feet across. The Port Chicago and Halifax explosions were considered to be of the same order of magnitude.

Captain William Parsons wrote a report on the explosion called "Memorandum on Port Chicago Disaster, Preliminary Data, 24 July 1944." It can be found in Box 671, World War II Command File, Operational Archives Branch, Naval Historical Center, Washington, D.C.

## CHAPTER 35: DOWN THE BARREL OF A GUN

After the explosion, Morris Rich was transferred to five or six ships, which reinforced his belief that he had been "shanghaied."

On July 19, the *San Francisco Chronicle* opened with the headline BLAST DEATH TOLL NOW 377; 1,000 INJURED! The second paragraph of the story began, "Destruction of the huge Army arsenal at Benicia, only seven miles from the scene of the Port Chicago catastrophe, was averted by miraculous chance. The blast according to military officials caused damages there (at the Benicia Army arsenal) estimated at $150,000 to the arsenal facilities and injured six persons."

The cleanup at Port Chicago included transferring ammunition from damaged boxcars to certified cars. This was done by the black enlisted men. According to the War Diary, Navy Seabees and 42nd Construction Battalion also assisted.

During his testimony, Lieutenant Tobin insisted that he had given every man a direct order to return to work, claiming that he had said, "I am going to give each one of you an order to 'turn to' for the purpose of carrying out your regularly assigned duty of loading ships . . . there is no reason to fear the ammunition which we are going to handle here as much as you might fear some of the ammunition we handled at Port Chicago. We will handle no depth charges or bombs. . . . I want each of you to consider carefully the consequences of refusal to obey orders because all of you who refuse will be charged with refusal to obey the lawful order of a superior officer." Tobin then walked up to each man and said, "I am ordering you to turn to for the purpose of loading ships. If you obey that order, step to the rear, if you refuse to obey that order, give your name to Lieutenant Clement."

Details regarding Captain Goss's report to Admiral Wright are from Leonard Guttridge.

Mississippi Representative John Rankin petitioned to reduce the maximum compensation for the families of the victims to $3,000. Some said that his rejection of the $5,000 grant was racially motivated.

The Bureau of Ordnance thought that if it abandoned its "policy of operating the station with 100 percent colored enlisted personnel," it could achieve 100,000 tons per month with "no difficulties."

In his book *Mutiny: A History of Naval Insurrection,* Leonard Guttridge writes, "The mental stresses accumulated during life-and-death crises can work their harm later as a kind of insidious aftermath, a post-action proneness to even the smallest grievance. And the absence of some restorative, ideally in the form of home furlough if not complete release from active service, becomes a grievance of itself, with the appropriate potential for mutiny."

Regarding the "don't work" petition, Joe Small told author Robert Allen, "I knew—I guess mostly from instinct—that anything in writing is more damaging to you than a verbal conversation. And when you put your name on a list, then you become a supporting part of whatever that list stands for. And there's very little chance of your changing your mind even if you wanted to."

Details on Admiral Wright's speech are from Leonard Guttridge's article "Port Chicago Mutiny," from *Readings in American Naval History,* fifth edition.

Wright's exact quote is from *Revolutionary Worker* no. 1092 and from my interview with George Booth. What the admiral did not say was that he alone had the power neither to decide whether the men had committed mutiny nor to have them put before a firing squad. They would need to go before summary courts-martial, whereupon two thirds of the members would need to agree that the punishment warranted death. The president of the United States would also have to agree.

The coercion of statements would become an issue during the mutiny trial. Seaman Second Class Martin Bordenaze said, "I knew the statement Lieutenant Briggs took down was wrong, but I signed it because I thought I had to." This quote is from an article in the October 10, 1944, edition of the *San Francisco Chronicle,* "Three on Trial for Mutiny Tell of Fear." Lieutenant Patrick Gilmore Jr. admitted that he did not take detailed notes concerning the defendant's version of the affair, but wrote them later as nearly as possible in the charged individual's own words. Details regarding Gilmore's admission are from the *Chronicle* of October 19, 1944. According to various testimonies in the trial transcript, the interrogating officers said the Navy would "go lighter and easier" on them if they made statements.

Women made up 13 percent of the shipbuilding industry in 1943, the peak year of ship construction in the United States. That number was 18 percent by the end of 1944. Most women were recruited as a result of the U.S. government's famous

"Rosie the Riveter" campaign. Women started as clerks or as canteen and cleaning workers, but many became welders. By the middle of 1943, black workers made up 10 percent of Marinship's workforce.

Acetylene gas explosions and fires were fairly common occurrences despite the rigid safety practice codes, though few people actually died. Later, however, many of the people whose job it was to insulate the ships' pipes and parts of the ships' engines with asbestos suffered and died from asbestosis and cancers related to exposure.

## CHAPTER 36: PROVING MUTINY

Most of the details of the trial are taken from the trial transcript provided by the Naval History and Heritage Command.

After the war, Coakley would hold Earl Warren's position as district attorney and would establish a reputation for his dogged prosecution of anti–Vietnam War activists and Black Panthers.

On September 14, 1944, newspapers from San Francisco to New York were chock-full of war news from the front. The *San Francisco Chronicle* ran an article with the headline 5,000 PLANES DROP 10,000 TONS ON REICH. The *New York Times* led with three headlines: AMERICANS OUTSIDE AACHEN, WIN A REICH TOWN; THIRD ARMY FORGES AHEAD ON MOSELLE FRONT; PHILIPPINES AIR BATTLE COSTS FOE 200 PLANES. Another headline proclaimed, TRIUMPH IN FRANCE VICTORY OF SUPPLY. "This is our kind of war now," the article said. "With a supply line stretching more than 500 miles from the Normandy beaches to the German frontier, all the skills peculiar to peacetime America are being called into play to keep the soldiers at the front supplied with gasoline, bullets and food. . . . It is the steady flow of war materials to the front that has enabled our army to move forward faster than the Germans or the Russians."

Not long into the process, Lieutenant Veltmann's lawyers discovered that two of the so-called mutineers were seamen who, because of physical limitations that made them unfit for loading, had been made cooks. When asked if they would be willing to load ammunition, the two had answered "no."

William Winthrop's quote is from Guttridge.

In *Mutiny: A History of Naval Insurrection,* Leonard Guttridge explores the various definitions of mutiny and how they had been applied in naval history. The Uniform Code of Military Justice with its Manual for Courts Martial became effective on May 31, 1951. It established that preconceived intent applied to only a one-man mutiny. In its other form, "collective insubordination," no intent was required. *Winthrop*'s necessity of conspiracy was abandoned. Nevertheless, the Navy continued to resist using the mutiny charge, preferring, instead, to use phrases such as "combat refusal," "strike," "work stoppage," "demonstration of grievance."

On September 16, 1944, the *New York Times* reported on another explosion at the Naval Ordnance Depot in Hastings, Nebraska. The headline read, HASTINGS NAVY DEPOT BLAST KILLS 3 SAILORS; 56 INJURED AND A MAIN BUILDING WRECKED. The article continued, "Two victims were Negro sailors and the third a Coast Guardsman. . . . The explosion tore a crater in the ground 550 feet long and twenty-five feet deep. The blast was heard at McCook, 125 miles away, and at Jamestown, Kan[sas], 100 miles distant."

Near the end of the trial, another officer confessed that he had edited many of the statements of the seamen, adding words and sentences that he thought would help Judge Advocate Coakley, and extracting others.

Lieutenant Commander Coakley was incensed by Alphonso McPherson's charge. Later he lashed out at Lieutenant Veltmann for coaching the witness. Coakley then tried to tag McPherson as a liar and a coward. The lieutenant claimed that McPherson had made up the shooting charge just as he had lied about being in too much pain to load ammunition. McPherson maintained that he had suffered internal injuries in the explosion. Coakley accused McPherson of being someone who "was always complaining about one kind of ailment or another." Two days later he was vindicated when he was rushed to the hospital with a double hernia.

Details of McPherson's testimony are in the October 5, 1944, edition of the *San Francisco Chronicle*.

On October 5, Lieutenant Coakley began the day by issuing a "categorical denial" that he had ever told any of the Port Chicago men that they would be shot if they refused to load ammunition. The *San Francisco Chronicle* reported Coakley's denial in its October 6 issue in an article headlined THE MUTINY TRIAL: COAKLEY DENIES MAKING THREATS.

## CHAPTER 37: PUTTING THE NAVY ON TRIAL

The NAACP had pressured Secretary Forrestal to allow Thurgood Marshall to sit in on the court-martial.

Marshall had already won a case in a Maryland county demanding equal pay for black teachers. The state, realizing that fighting the equal-pay issue on a county-by-county basis would be expensive, passed a law setting a single standard for black and white teachers.

The one Supreme Court case, which Marshall argued with William Hastie, dealt with the constitutionality of Texas's all-white primary elections. In April 1944, the Court ruled that white primaries were unconstitutional. If Texas allowed political parties to limit their nominees and voters to whites, the Court said, "It endorses, adopts and enforces the discrimination against Negroes."

The NAACP was fielding hundreds of letters from black soldiers complaining about their second-class status. Marshall wondered why the military, like the South, expended so much effort keeping rights from blacks. Surely it would be easier to integrate.

During the trial, Joseph James, head of the NAACP's San Francisco branch, commented on the case, emphasizing the sacrifices that blacks had made for the war effort. "Negroes as a group," he said, "have been faithful to their country . . . and have received very little in return."

Elmer Boyer, Lieutenant Ernest Delucchi's chief petty officer, buttressed Marshall's argument. Boyer was the one whom Delucchi had asked to write down the names of the men who would not work. He testified, however, that at no point had he heard the lieutenant give the seamen an order to load. A Navy psychiatrist also bolstered the general defense claim that the men were seriously traumatized by the explosion. That memory—both physical and emotional—caused them to rebel against the idea of ever working with ammunition again.

Some of the details regarding Thurgood Marshall are from Juan Williams's excellent book *Thurgood Marshall: American Revolutionary*.

The absurdity of trying to operate two equal navies, one black and one white, had been obvious during the war. Only total integration of the general service could serve justice and efficiency, a conclusion the civil rights advocates had long since reached. With the enlistment of the Chief of Naval Personnel in the cause, the move to an integrated general service was assured. The equal treatment and opportunity for Negroes in the Navy, however, remained an elusive goal.

## CHAPTER 38: PUNISHING THE SEAMEN

Walter McDonald of the San Diego NAACP urged the Navy to go easy on the "mutineers."

## CHAPTER 39: THE SINS OF A NATION

W. E. B. Du Bois edited the NAACP's magazine *The Crisis* for twenty-five years.

FDR's memo to Eleanor said simply, "for your information." Eleanor Roosevelt's letter to Secretary Forrestal was dated April 5, 1945.

The editorial from the November 2, 1944, edition of the *San Francisco Chronicle* was reprinted in the December 2, 1944, edition of the *Pittsburgh Courier* with the headline CALIFORNIA DAILY DISAPPROVES SENTENCES OF 50 NEGRO SEAMEN. It pointed out that forty-four out of fifty of the mutineers had perfect conduct ratings of 4.0.

Instead of handing out severe punishments to Percy Robinson and the other 207 men, the Navy had chosen to treat them with compassion, sentencing them to ninety days' hard labor (of which they had already served seventy one days) and fining each of them half a year's pay. A seaman first class made sixty-four dollars a month, and a seaman second class made fifty-four dollars a month.

The *Chronicle*'s story on "Nimitz's Secret Weapon" quoted Captain Edward Pare, a staff member for the Service Squadron for the Pacific Fleet. Pare boasted that the Saipan invasion alone had demanded more fuel (and more of everything else) than the entire Pacific Fleet had used in 1943.

In an article dated October 21, 1944, the *Chicago Defender*'s John Robert Badger called the mutiny trial a "hot potato." The title of the article was PORT CHICAGO MUTINY TRIAL OF 50 BECOMING HOT POTATO FOR NAVY.

On August 15, 1945, Emperor Hirohito announced Japan's surrender. The announcement was a recorded radio address.

The following month the Navy acted, reducing all the mutineers' sentences by one year. William Fechteler, the assistant chief of Naval Personnel, wrote the letter, confirming the reduction, to Secretary Forrestal on September 8, 1945.


## EPILOGUE

In the period between July 9 and the evacuation of the 27th Division on October 4, the army killed nearly two thousand more enemy soldiers who were hiding in various places across the island.

Herbert Bix *(Hirohito and the Making of Modern Japan)* and Harold Goldberg *(D-Day in the Pacific)* say the date was July 18, Japanese time, which would be July 17, U.S. time.

In his book *The Port Chicago Mutiny,* Robert Allen asserts that the blast was "on the same order of magnitude as the atomic bomb that would be dropped on Hiroshima just over a year later."

In *New Guinea and the Marianas,* Samuel Eliot Morison describes in detail what the word "colossal" means: during Operation Forager, the Fleet alone used 6,378 rounds of fourteen- and sixteen-inch shells; 19,230 rounds of six- and eight-inch shells; and 140,000 rounds of five-inch shells. According to Morison, "The fighting lasted so long and naval gunfire was in such demand by ground forces" that ammunition ships could barely keep up. The captured diary of a Japanese soldier on Saipan underscores Morison's argument. "The greatest single factor in the American's success," the diary read, "was naval gunfire."

A Marine document confirms Morison's conclusion. It reads, "Certainly the four major artillery units performed a vital function at Saipan. There were 291,459 rounds fired during the operation. This figure cannot tell the whole story; time and time again the 75's, 105's, and 155's brought timely, effective fire on the enemy points of resistance."

After the disturbance in Detroit, the Jackson, Mississippi, *Daily News* blamed Eleanor Roosevelt. "It is blood upon your hands, Mrs. Roosevelt," the paper intoned. "You have been . . . proclaiming and practicing social equality. . . . In Detroit, a city noted for the growing impudence and insolence of its Negro population, an attempt was made to put preachments into practice."

Thurgood Marshall saw the mutiny charge and sentence as a "frame-up" and accused the Navy of charging the men "solely because of their race and color." Civil rights leaders had been warning about it for years; black servicemen historically received inordinately severe sentences for acts of insubordination.

Black numbers aboard ships were limited to 10 percent of the crew, and on August 9, 1944, King informed the commanding officers of twenty-five large fleet auxiliaries that Negroes would be assigned to in the near future.

Forrestal was convinced that in order to succeed, racial reform must first be accepted by the men already in uniform; integration, if quietly and gradually put into effect, would soon demonstrate its efficiency and make the change acceptable to all members of the service. In August 1945 the Navy had some 165,000 Negroes, almost 5.5 percent of its total strength. Sixty-four of them, including six women, were commissioned officers, and black sailors were being trained in almost all naval ratings and were serving throughout the fleet, on planes and in submarines, working and living with whites.

Lester Granger reported that Forrestal said to King, "I'm not satisfied with the situation here. I don't think that our Navy Negro personnel are getting a square break. I want to do something about it, but I can't do anything about it unless the officers are behind me. I want your help. What do you say?" Admiral King sat for a moment and looked out the window and then said reflectively, "You know, we say that we are a democracy and a democracy ought to have a democratic Navy. I don't think you can do it, but if you want to try, I'm behind you all the way."

The executive order allowed Truman to bypass Congress. Otherwise, representatives of the "Solid South," all white Democrats, would likely have stonewalled legislation.

An August headline in the *Chicago Defender* jubilantly proclaimed, MR. TRUMAN MAKES HISTORY. The *Pittsburgh Courier*, however, questioned the president's sincerity. It was politically expedient for him to affect an ostensibly vigorous civil rights stance while keeping his language vague. A. Philip Randolph responded to the order by canceling his call for a boycott of the draft.

Responding to Congressman Miller, the Navy said that there was "nothing unfair or unjust in the final outcome of any of the Port Chicago courts-martial."

The B-29 was a marvel. The United States government, which began development on it shortly after Pearl Harbor, invested more in it than it did in the Manhattan Project. It was money well spent. The B-29 carried the biggest bomb load of any plane ever built—four tons more than the B-17—and had a range of 3,800 miles. It could fly more than sixteen hours nonstop. Its compartments were pressurized so that even at 40,000 feet, crews could fly without oxygen masks or heated flying suits. Initially the plane was plagued with mechanical problems. Engines overheated, the planes caught fire, and pilots and crews were killed. Hap Arnold wanted the best bomber pilot sent back from the ETO to make the B-29 operational. That man was Paul Tibbets, "Mr. B-29."

The Japanese ridiculed the "precision bombing" as "blind bombing." In Nagoya, the Mitsubishi Aircraft Engine Works was the target. The rest of Ciardi's quote is "That meant women and old people, children."

Napalm was developed by Standard Oil and Du Pont.

The March 9, 1945, bomber attack on Tokyo would have killed more than 100,000 people, had 1.5 million not already evacuated the city.

By March 1945, the ethical line that the mass killing of civilians represented had already been crossed. In late July 1943, the British Royal Air Force launched a succession of night raids against Hamburg, Germany, killing 45,000 people and leaving 400,000 homeless. In ten days the RAF killed more civilians than Great Britain lost to German bombs during the entire war. In Dresden, Germany, the

RAF and the American 8th Air Force launched four bombing raids that ignited a firestorm that engulfed a portion of the city, killing 40,000 civilians, most of them refugees fleeing the Soviet Red Army.

Japan's fourth-largest city, the imperial capital of Kyoto, was spared.

The uranium core, along with the plutonium core for the second bomb, nick-named "Fat Man," arrived on Tinian shortly after "Little Boy" was brought ashore. Named after Churchill, it was bigger and more powerful than "Little Boy."

# BIBLIOGRAPHY

## SAIPAN

### Books

Alexander, Joseph H. *Storm Landing: Epic Amphibious Battles in the Central Pacific.* Annapolis: Naval Institute Press, 1997.

———. *Utmost Savagery. The Three Days of Tarawa.* New York: Ivy Books, 1995.

———. "World War II: Fifty Years Ago: Amphibious Blitzkrieg at Tinian." *Leatherneck,* August 1994.

Ambrose, Stephen, and Brian Villa. "Racism, the Atomic Bomb, and the Transformation of Japanese-American Relations." In *The Pacific War Revisited,* edited by Gunter Bischof and Robert I. Dupont. Baton Rouge: Louisiana State University Press, 1997.

Bartlett, Tom. "One Step at a Time." *Leatherneck,* November 1965.

Beltoe, James, and William Beltoe. *Titans of the Seas: The Development and Operations of American Carrier Task Force During World War II.* New York: Harper and Row, 1975.

Bernstein, Barton J. "The Perils and Politics of Surrender: Ending the War with Japan and Avoiding the Third Atomic Bomb." *Pacific Historical Review* 46, no. 1 (1977), 1–27.

Berry, Henry. *Semper Fi-Mac: Living Memories of the U.S. Marines.* New York: Arbor House, 1982.

Bix, Herbert. *Hirohito and the Making of Modern Japan.* New York: HarperCollins, 2000.

Brcak, Nancy, and John R. Pavia. "Racism in Japanese and U.S. Wartime Propaganda." *The Historian* 56, no. 4 (1994), 671–84.

Brooks, Victor. *Hell Is Upon Us: D-Day in the Pacific, Saipan to Guam, June–August 1944.* Cambridge, MA: Da Capo Press, 2005.

Browne, Courtney. *Tojo: The Last Banzai.* New York: Holt, Rinehart and Winston, 1967.

Buell, Thomas B. *The Quiet Warrior: A Biography of Admiral Raymond A. Spruance.* Boston: Little Brown, 1974.

———. *Master of Sea Power: A Biography of Fleet Admiral Ernest J. King.* Boston: Little Brown, 1980.

Cabrera, Genevieve S. "Historic and Cultural Sites of the CNMI: The National Register Sites." CNMI Division of Historic Preservation, 2005.

Cameron, Craig M. *American Samurai: Myth, Imagination, and the Conduct of Battle in the First Marine Division, 1941–1951.* New York: Cambridge University Press, 1994.

Cant, Gilbert. *The Great Pacific Victory.* New York: John Day, 1946.

Chapin, Captain John C. *Breaching the Marianas: The Battle for Saipan.* Washington, DC: History and Museums Division, Headquarters, U.S. Marine Corps, 1994.

———. *Breaking the Outer Ring: Marine Landings in the Marshall Islands.* Marines in World War II Commemorative Series. Washington, DC: History and Museums Division, Headquarters, U.S. Marine Corps, 1994.

———. *The 4th Marine Division in World War II.* Washington, DC: History and Museums Division, Headquarters, U.S. Marine Corps, 1974 (reprint of 1945 edition).

———. "Night Operation" (poem). History and Museums Division, Headquarters, U.S. Marine Corps.

———. "Proud to Claim the Title" (poem). Archives and Special Collections, Library of the Marine Corps, Quantico, VA.

Chappell, John D. *Before the Bomb: How America Approached the End of the Pacific War.* Lexington: University Press of Kentucky, 1997.

Ciardi, John. *Saipan: The War Diary of John Ciardi.* Fayetteville: University of Arkansas Press, 1988.

Cole, Bernard D. "Struggle for the Marianas." *Joint Force Quarterly* 7 (Spring 1995), 86–93.

Condon-Rall, Mary Ellen, and Albert E. Cowdrey. *The Medical Department: Medical Services in the War against Japan. United States Army in World War II: The Technical Services.* Washington, DC: Center of Military History, United States Army, 1998.

Cook, Haruko Taya, and Theodore Cook. "A Lost War in Living Memory: Japan's Second World War." *European Review,* October 2003 (vol. II, no. 4), 573–93.

Cook, Haruko Taya, and Theodore Cook. *Japan at War: An Oral History.* New York: New Press, 1992.

Cook, Haruko Taya. "The Myth of the Saipan Suicides." *Military History Quarterly* 7, Spring 1995.

Cooper, Norman V. A. *A Fighting General: The Biography of General Holland M. "Howlin' Mad" Smith.* Quantico, VA: Marine Corps Association, 1987.

Craven, Wesley, and James Cate. *The Army Air Forces in World War II.* Chicago: University of Chicago Press, 1948.

Croizat, Victor J. *Across the Reef: The Amphibious Tracked Vehicle at War.* Quantico, VA: Marine Corps Association, 1989.

Crowl, Philip A. *Campaign in the Marianas: The War in the Pacific.* Washington, DC: Center of Military History, U.S. Army, 1993.

Currin, William. "Saipan Remembered." *Leatherneck,* June 1984.

Daniels, Gordon. "Before Hiroshima: The Bombing of Japan, 1944–45." *History Today* 32 (January 1982): 14–18.

Davis, Kenneth. *FDR: The War President, 1940–1943.* New York: Random House, 2000.

Denfeld, D. Colt. *Japanese World War II Fortifications and Other Military Structures in the Central Pacific.* Saipan: Commonwealth of the Northern Mariana Islands, Division of Historic Preservation, 2002.

————. *Hold the Marianas: The Japanese Defense of the Mariana Islands.* Shippensburg, PA: White Mane Publishing, 1997.

Denfeld, D. Colt, and Scott Russell. "Home of the Superfort: An Historical and Archeological Survey of Isely Field." Micronesian Archeological Survey, Report No. 21, 1984.

Dower, John. *War Without Mercy: Race and Power in the Pacific War.* New York: Pantheon, 1986.

Doyle, William. *Inside the Oval Office: The White House Tapes from FDR to Clinton.* New York: Kodansha America, 1999.

Drea, Edward J. *In the Service of the Emperor: Essays on the Imperial Japanese Army.* Lincoln: University of Nebraska Press, 1998.

Dull, Paul S. *A Battle History of the Imperial Japanese Navy (1941–1945).* Annapolis: Naval Institute Press, 1978.

Dyer, George Carroll. *The Amphibians Came to Conquer: The Story of Admiral Richmond Kelly Turner.* 2 vols. Washington, DC: Department of the Navy, 1972.

Eichelberger, Robert L. *Our Jungle Road to Tokyo.* New York: Viking Press, 1950.

Ellis, Major Earl H. *Advanced Base Operations in Micronesia.* Washington, DC: Department of the Navy, Headquarters, U.S. Marine Corps, 1921.

Everett, Robert E., Sr. *World War II: Battle of Saipan.* Self-published, 1996.

Fahey, James J. *Pacific War Diary, 1942–1945.* Westport, CT: Greenwood Press, 1974.

Feifer, George. *Tennozan: The Battle of Okinawa and the Atomic Bomb.* New York: Ticknor & Fields, 1992.

Forrestal, E. P. *Admiral Raymond Spruance, U.S.N.: A Study in Command.* Washington, DC: Department of the Navy, 1968.

Frank, Benis M., and Henry I. Shaw Jr. *Victory and Occupation: Vol. V of the History of U.S. Marines Corps Operations in World War II.* Washington, DC: Historical Branch, U.S. Marine Corps, 1968.

Frank, Richard B. *Downfall: The End of the Imperial Japanese Empire.* New York: Random House, 1999.

Freidel, Frank. *Franklin Roosevelt: A Rendezvous with Destiny.* Boston: Little Brown, 1990.

Fussell, Paul. *Wartime: Understanding and Behavior in the Second World War.* New York: Oxford University Press, 1989.

Galbadon, Guy. *Saipan: Suicide Island.* Saipan: self-published, 1990.

Gailey, Harry A. *Howlin' Mad vs. the Army: Conflict in Command, Saipan 1944.* Novato, CA: Presidio, 1986.

———. *The War in the Pacific: From Pearl Harbor to Tokyo Bay.* Novato, CA: Presidio, 1995.

Goe, Lieutenant W. Charles, Chaplain USNR. *Is War Hell?* Self-published, 1947.

Goldberg, Harold J. *D-Day in the Pacific: The Battle of Saipan.* Bloomington and Indianapolis: Indiana University Press, 2007.

Goodwin, Doris Kearns. *No Ordinary Time: Franklin and Eleanor Roosevelt: The Home Front in World War II.* New York: Simon & Schuster, 1994.

Graf, Robert. *Easy Company: My Life in the United States Marine Corps during World War II.* Self-published, 1986.

Harries, Meirion, and Susie Harries. *Soldiers of the Sun: The Rise and Fall of the Imperial Japanese Army.* New York: Random House, 1991.

Hayes, Grace. *The History of the Joint Chiefs of Staff in World War II: The War Against Japan.* Annapolis: Naval Institute Press, 1982.

Head, Major Samuel J. "Supporting Arms in Amphibious Operations, Past and Present." CSC 1991, Globalsecurity.org.

Hearn, Chester G. *Carriers in Combat: The Air War at Sea.* Mechanicsburg, PA: Stackpole Books, 2005.

Hezel, Francis X., S.J., *From Conquest to Colonization.* Saipan: Division of Historic Preservation, 1989.

Hoffman, Carl W. *Saipan: The Beginning of the End.* Nashville, TN: Battery, 1950.

Hopkins, George E. "Bombing and the American Conscience during World War II." *The Historian* 28, no. 3 (1966), 451–73.

Hough, Frank O. *The Island War: The United States Marine Corps in the Pacific.* Philadelphia: Lippincott, 1947.

Hoyt, Edwin P. *To the Marianas: War in the Central Pacific, 1944.* New York: Van Nostrand Reinhold, 1980.

———. *Japan's War: The Great Pacific Conflict.* New York: Da Capo, 1986.

———. *How They Won the War in the Pacific: Nimitz and His Admirals.* New York: Lyons, 2000.

Hudson, Jack, and Kay Hudson. *American Samoa in World War II.* American Samoa Government, Department of Parks and Recreation, 1994.

Hurt, R. Douglas. *The Great Plains During World War II.* Lincoln, NE: University of Nebraska, 2010.

Huston, John W. "The Impact of Strategic Bombing in the Pacific." *The Journal of the American–East Asian Relations* 4, no. 2 (1995), 169–79.

Inui, Genjirou. *My Guadalcanal.* Self-published.

Iriye, Akira. *Power and Culture: The Japanese American War, 1941–1945.* Cambridge, MA: Harvard University Press, 1981.

Isley, James, and Philip Crowl. *The U.S. Marines and Amphibious War.* Princeton: Princeton University Press, 1951.

James, Doris Clayton. *The Years of MacArthur, 1941–1945.* Boston: Houghton Mifflin, 1975.

Johnson, William L. C. *The West Loch Story.* Seatle: Westloch Publications, 1986.

Johnston, Richard W. *Follow Me! The Story of the Second Marine Division in World War II.* Nashville, TN: Battery, 1987.

Jones, Don. *Oba: The Last Samurai.* Novato, CA: Presidio, 1986.

Kahn, E.J., Jr. *The Stragglers.* New York: Random House, 1962.

Kahn, Sy M. *Between Tedium and Terror: A Soldier's World War II Diary, 1943–45.* Urbana and Chicago: University of Illinois Press, 1993.

Keegan, John. *The Face of Battle.* New York: Penguin, 1976.

Keen, Sam. *Faces of the Enemy: Reflections of the Hostile Imagination.* San Francisco: Harper and Row, 1986.

Keene, R. R. "The Orphan Battalion That Took Mount Tapotchau." *Leatherneck,* June 1994, 20–23.

Kennett, Lee. *G.I.: The American Soldier in World War II.* New York: Scribner, 1987.

King, Ernest J. *U.S. Navy at War, 1941–1945: Official Reports to the Secretary of the Navy.* Washington, DC: United States Navy Department, 1946.

Ladd, Dean. *Faithful Warriors: The Second Marine Division.* Spokane, WA: Ladd Communications, 1994.

Lane, John E. *This Here Is "G" Company.* New York: Brightlights Publications, 1997.

Larrabee, Eric. *Commander in Chief: Franklin Delano Roosevelt: His Lieutenants and Their War.* New York: Touchstone, 1987.

Laurie, Clayton D. "The Ultimate Dilemma of Psychological Warfare in the Pacific: Enemies Who Don't Surrender, and GIs Who Don't Take Prisoners." *War and Society* 14, no. 1 (1996), 99–120.

Lockwood, Charles, and Hans Christian Adamson. *Battles of the Philippine Sea.* New York: Thomas Crowell, 1967.

Love, Edmund G. *The 27th Infantry Division in World War II.* Nashville, TN: Battery, 2001.

MacArthur, Douglas. *Reminiscences.* New York: McGraw-Hill, 1984.

Manchester, William. *American Caesar: Douglas MacArthur 1880–1964.* Boston: Little Brown, 1978.

———. *Goodbye, Darkness: A Memoir of the Pacific War.* New York: Little Brown, 1979.

Mason, John T., Jr., ed. *The Pacific War Remembered: An Oral History Collection.* Annapolis: Naval Institute Press, 1986.

Matthews, Carl. *The Feather Merchant.* Self-published.

McGee, William, and Sandra McGee. *Pacific Express: The Critical Role of Military Logistics in World War II.* Vol. 3 of *Amphibious Operations in the Pacific in WWII.* Tiburon, CA: BMC Publications, 2009.

Moore, Aaron William. "Essential Ingredients of Truth: Soldiers' Diaries in the Asia Pacific War." *Japan Focus,* August 27, 2007.

Morison, Samuel Eliot. *History of United States Naval Operations in World War II*. Boston: Little Brown, 1947–62.

———. *New Guinea and the Marianas, March 1944–August 1944*. Vol. 8 of *History of United States Naval Operations in World War II*. Boston: Little Brown, 1951.

———. *Aleutians, Gilberts and Marshalls*, Vol. 7 of *History of United States Naval Operations in World War II*. Boston: Little Brown, 1953.

Nichols, David, ed. *Ernie's War: The Best of Ernie Pyle's World War II Dispatches*. New York: Simon & Schuster, 1987.

O'Brien, Francis A. *Battling for Saipan*. New York: Ballantine, 2003.

Oliver, A. Alan. "The Navy's Hushed-up Tragedy at West Loch." *Sea Classic*, November 2005.

Petty, Bruce M. *Saipan: Oral Histories of the Pacific War*. Jefferson, NC: McFarland, 2002.

Potter, E. B. *Nimitz*. Baltimore: Naval Institute Press, 1976.

Poyer, Lin, Suzanne Falgout, and Lawrence Carucci. *The Typhoon of War: Micronesian Experiences of the Pacific War*. Honolulu: University of Hawaii Press, 2001.

Proehl, Carl W. *The Fourth Marine Division in World War II*. Nashville, TN: Battery, 1988.

Reister, Frank A., ed. *Medical Statistics in World War II*. Washington, DC: Office of the Surgeon General, Department of the Army, 1975.

*Reporting World War II: American Journalism 1938–1946*. New York: Library of America, 1995.

Richardson, Herb. "A Baby Cried." *Leatherneck*, November 1979.

Rottman, Gordon L. *Saipan and Tinian 1944: Piercing the Japanese Empire*. Oxford, UK: Osprey Publishing, 2004.

———. *The Marshall Islands 1944: Operation Flintlock, the Capture of Kwajalein and Eniwetok*. Oxford, UK: Osprey Publishing, 2004.

———. *US Marine Corps, 1941–1945*. Oxford, UK: Osprey Publishing, 1995.

———. *US Mechanized Infantryman in the First Gulf War*, Oxford, UK: Osprey Publishing, 2009.

Roush, Roy William. *Open Fire!* Apache Junction, AZ: Front Line Press, 2003.

Russell, Scott, *Operation Forager: The Battle for Saipan*. Commemoration of the 50th Anniversary, Saipan: Division of Historic Preservation, June 1994.

———. *Tiempon I Manmofo'na: Ancient Chamorro Culture and History of the Northern Mariana Islands*. Saipan: Division of Historic Preservation, 1998.

Salaberria, Sister Maria Angelica. "Time of Agony: The War in the Pacific in Saipan." Micronesian Area Research Center, University of Guam, 1994.

Schrijvers, Peter. *The GI War against Japan: American Soldiers in Asia and the Pacific During World War II*. New York: New York University Press, 2002.

Segel, Thomas D., USMC (retired). "Guy Galbadon—Do You Remember?" *Leatherneck*, August 2010.

*Semper Fidelis: The U.S. Marines in the Pacific, 1942–1945*, edited by Patrick O'Sheel and Gene Cook. New York: William Sloane Associates, 1947.

Sharpe, George. *Brothers Beyond Blood: A Battalion Surgeon in the South Pacific*. Austin, TX: Diamond Books, 1989.

Shaw, Henry. *History of Marine Corps Operations in World War II*. Washington, DC: U.S. Marine Corps, 1950.

Shaw, Henry I., Jr., Bernard C. Nalty, and Edwin T. Turnbladh. *Central Pacific Drive: History of the U.S. Marine Corps Operations in World War II*. Washington, DC: Historical Branch, G-3 Division, Headquarters, U.S. Marine Corps, 1966.

Sherrod, Robert. *On to Westward: War in the Central Pacific*. New York: Duell, Sloan and Pearce, 1945.

———. *Tarawa: The Story of a Battle*. New York: Duell, Sloan and Pearce, 1944.

———. "The Nature of the Enemy." *Time*, August 7, 1944.

Smith, Holland. *Coral and Brass*. New York: Scribner, 1950.

Smith, Stanley E., ed. *The United States Marine Corps in World War II*. New York: Random House, 1969.

Spector, Ronald. *Eagle Against the Sun: The American War with Japan*. New York: Random House, 1985.

Spoehr, Alexander. *Saipan: The Ethnology of a War-Devastated Island*. Chicago: Chicago Natural History Museum, 1954.

Steinberg, Rafael. *Island Fighting*. New York: Time Life Education, 1977.

Stewart, William. *Saipan in Flames*. Self-published, 1993.

Stewart, William. *Ghost Fleet of the Truk Lagoon*. Missoula, MT: Pictorial Histories Publishing Co.

Taylor, Theodore. *The Magnificent Mitscher*. New York: Norton, 1954.

Toland, John. *The Rising Sun. The Decline and Fall of the Japanese Empire, 1936–1945*. New York: Random House, 1970.

Tierney, Emiko Ohnuki. *Kamikaze Diaries: Reflections of Japanese Student Soldiers*. Chicago: University of Chicago Press, 2006.

Torok, Tibor. *Stepping Stones Across the Pacific: A Collection of Short Stories from the Pacific War*. New York: Vantage, 1999.

Turner, Gordon B. "Dual Conflict: A Study of Saipan." Master's degree thesis, Princeton University, April 15, 1948.

Van der Vat, Dan. *The Pacific Campaign: The U.S. Japanese Naval War, 1941–1945*. New York: Simon & Schuster, 1991.

Weigley, Russell F. *The American Way of War: A History of United States Military Strategy and Policy*. New York: Macmillan, 1973.

Wheeler, Richard. *A Special Valor: The U.S. Marines and the Pacific War*. Annapolis: Naval Institute Press, 2006.

Willard, Chaplain W. Wyeth. *The Leathernecks Come Through*. Grand Rapids, MI: Fleming H. Revell Co., 1944.

Willoughby, General Charles A., and John Chamberlain. *MacArthur, 1941–1951*. New York: McGraw-Hill, 1954.

Winters, Harold A. *Battling the Elements: Weather and Terrain in the Conduct of War*. Baltimore, MD: Johns Hopkins University Press, 1998.


## Letters and Papers

Arsenault, Colonel Albert. "My Life and Early Times." Quantico, VA: Archives and Special Collections, Library of the Marine Corps, 1964.

Craig, Frank S., Jr., 1918–1945. Quantico, VA: Archives and Special Collections, Library of the Marine Corps.

Craven, Captain John Harold, Chaplain Corps, United States Navy (retired). Quantico, VA: Archives and Special Collections, Library of the Marine Corps, 1980.

Fukuzo, Obara, "Gekisen." Translated by Edward J. Rasmussen. Carlisle, PA: United States Military History Institute, 1976.

George, Robert L. *Too Young to Vote*. Madison WI: Wisconsin Veterans Museum, 2001.

Hampton, Major Everett "Bud." Personal papers.

Johnson, Bernard F. "A Member of Co. C, 1st Battalion, 29th Marines." From Frank Borta's private collection.

Luebke, Emilie E. *Five Feet to the Gates of Hell: Corporal Mark E. Deterik, WWII Marine*. Brillion, WI: Zander Press, Inc. 2006.

Moore, David, Cdr. USN. "The Battle of Saipan: The Final Curtain." 2002.

Nakajima, Chikataka, Commander. "Interrogation Nav 34, October 21, 1945, United States Strategic Bombing Survey Interrogation of Japanese Officials [OPNAV-P-03-100].

Norkofski, Warren L., 27th Infantry Division. Wisconsin Veterans Museum, 2005.

Operations Report, 4th Marine Division. Quantico, VA: Archives and Special Collections, Library of the Marine Corps.

Orsock, John. "Memories of the Invasion of Saipan," from Frank Borta's private collection, 1994.

Praniewicz, Albert A., 4th Marine Division, 25th Marines. Wisconsin Veterans Museum, 2005.

Railey, Hilton Howell. Wisconsin Veterans Museum, 1941.

Stewart, William. Collection of Diary Excerpts from Japanese Soldiers.

Sullivan, William D., 4th Marine Division. Wisconsin Veterans Museum, 2000.

Swindle, Don. "Memories—F Company, 2nd Battalion, 23rd Regiment, 4th Marine Division."

"The Last Days of Lieutenant General Saito." Captured account, July 14, 1944, translated by Lt. Colonel T. R. Yancey. Quantico, VA: Archives and Special Collections, Library of the Marine Corps.

"Useful Japanese Words and Phrases for Frontline Troops." D-2 Section, Camp Pendleton, Oceanside, CA.

Wantanabe, Lieutenant. Quantico, VA: Archives and Special Collections, Library of the Marine Corps, 1942.

Weber, Roman J., 27th Infantry Division. Wisconsin Veterans Museum, 2005.

## Oral Histories

Bohstedt, James H., 4th Marine Division, 4th Signal Company. Wisconsin Veterans Museum, 1995.

Chipman, Clayton, 4th Marine Division, 4th Signal Company. Wisconsin Veterans Museum, 1995.

Hirsbrunner, Paul A., 4th Marine Division. Wisconsin Veterans Museum, 1996.

Library of Congress, Veterans History Project. Interviews with hundreds of veterans who served on Saipan.

Scovill, Roger P., 2nd Marine Division, 10th Marine Regiment. Wisconsin Veterans Museum, 1997.

Tompkins, Dorothy C. Kramschuster, U.S. Army Nurse Corps. Wisconsin Veterans Museum, 2004.

Van Ells, Paul A., 4th Marine Division, 4th Tank Battalion. Wisconsin Veterans Museum, 1994.

Wallack, Robert. Quantico, VA: Archives and Special Collections, Library of the Marine Corps.

## PORT CHICAGO

### Books and Articles

Adero, Malaika, ed. *Up South: Stories, Studies and Letters of This Century's African American Migrations.* New York: New Press, 1993.

*African Americans and WW II.* Washington, DC: Association for the Study of Afro American Life and History, 1994.

Akers, Regina T. "A Very Special Tribute." *Pull Together* 33 (Fall/Winter 1994).

———. "The Port Chicago Mutiny, 1944." In *Naval Mutinies of the Twentieth Century, an International Perspective,* edited by Christopher Bell and Bruce Elleman. Portland, OR: Frank Cass Publishers, 2003, 193–211.

Allen, Robert L. *The Port Chicago Mutiny: The Story of the Largest Mass Mutiny Trial in U.S. Naval History.* New York: Warner Books, 1989.

Altoff, Gerard T. *Amongst My Best Men: African Americans and the War of 1812.* Put-in-Bay, OH: Perry Group, 1996.

"Ammunition Handling." NAVPERS 16194 (Restricted).

Anderson, Jervis. *A. Philip Randolph: A Biographical Portrait.* New York: Harcourt Brace, 1973.

Aptheker, Herbert. "The Negro in the Union Navy." *Journal of Negro History* 32 (April 1947).

*Articles for the Government of the United States Navy (Rocks and Shoals).* Washington, DC: Department of the Navy, Navy Historical Center, Washington Navy Yard, 1930.

Astor, Gerald. *The Right to Fight: A History of African Americans in the Military.* Cambridge, MA: Da Capo Press, 1998.

Bailey, Beth, and David Farber. *The First Strange Place: Race and Sex in World War II Hawaii.* Baltimore, MD: Johns Hopkins Press, 1992.

Bailey, Beth, and David Farber. "The 'Double-V' campaign in World War II Hawaii, African Americans, racial identity, and federal power." *Journal of Social History,* Summer 1993.

Bak, Richard. *Louis: The Great Black Hope.* Dallas, TX: Taylor Publishing Co., 1996.

Baldwin, Davarian L. *Chicago's New Negroes: Modernity, the Great Migration, and Black Urban Life.* Chapel Hill: University of North Carolina Press, 2007.

Barbeau, Arthur E., and Florette Henri. *The Unknown Soldiers: Black American Troops in World War I.* Philadelphia: Temple University Press, 1974.

Barlow, William. *Looking Up at Down: The Emergence of Blues Culture.* Philadelphia: Temple University Press, 1989.

Bartlett, Tom. "Sgt. Maj. Edgar R. Huff: Paving the Way." *Leatherneck,* February 1990.

Bland, Randall W. *Private Pressure on Public Law: The Legal Career of Justice Thurgood Marshall.* Port Washington, NY: Kennikat Press, 1973.

*Bluejackets' Manual United States Navy.* Annapolis: United States Naval Institute, 1917.

Bottomley, Gillian. *From Another Place: Migration and the Politics of Culture.* Cambridge, UK: Cambridge University Press, 1992.

Buchanan, A. Russell. *Black Americans in World War II.* Santa Barbara, CA: Regina Books, 1972.

Bullock, Penelope L. *The Afro-American Periodical Press, 1838–1909.* Baton Rouge: Louisiana State University Press, 1998.

Canyon, Steve, and Laurel Canyon. "!They Called It Mutiny! The Port Chicago Explosion." *Sea Classics,* October 2006.

Chalk, Ocania. *Pioneers of Black Sport: The Early Days of the Black Professional Athlete in Baseball, Basketball, Boxing and Football.* New York: Dodd, Mead, 1975.

*Chicago Defender.* Articles regarding the mutiny trial, September 16–November 25, 1944.

Cocklin, Robert F. "Report on the Negro Soldier." *Infantry Journal* 59 (December 1946): 15–17.

Cooper, Anna Julia. *Voices from the South.* New York: Oxford University Press, 1988.

Correrro, Jennifer. "World War II's First Black Marines Trained at Montford (North Carolina)." *Air Force Times* 57, no. 42 (February 24, 1997).

Crew, Spencer. *Field to Factory: Afro-American Migration 1915–1940.* Washington, DC: Smithsonian Institution Press, 1987.

Culp, Ronald K. *The First Black United States Marines: The Men of Montford Point, 1942–1946.* Jefferson, NC: McFarland and Co., 2007.

Dalfiume, Richard M. *Desegregation of the U.S. Armed Forces: Fighting on Two Fronts, 1939–1953.* Columbia: University of Missouri Press, 1969.

Davis, John W. "The Negro in the United States Navy, Marine Corps and Coast Guard." *Journal of Negro Education* 12 (July 1943).

Department of the Navy Bureau of Yards and Docks. *Building the Navy's Bases in World War II: History of the Bureau of Yards and Docks and the Civil Engineer Corps, 1940–1946.* Washington, DC: United States Printing Office, 1946.

"Doris Miller: First U.S. Hero of World War II." *Ebony* 25 (December 1969).

Edgerton, Robert B. *Hidden Heroism: Black Soldiers in America's Wars.* Boulder, CO: Westview Press, 2001.

Elphick, Peter. *Liberty: The Ships That Won the War.* London: Chatham Publishing, 2006.

Fahey, James C. *The Ships and Aircraft of the United States Fleet.* Santa Rosa, CA: Arm & Armour Press, 1981.

Farr, Finnis. *Black Champion: The Life and Times of Jack Johnson.* London: Macmillan, 1964.

Farrar, Hayward. *The Baltimore Afro-American: 1892–1950.* Santa Barbara, CA: Greenwood Press, 1998.

Fisher, Perry E., and Brooks E. Gray. *Blacks and Whites Together Through Hell: U.S. Marines in World War II.* Turlock, CA: Millsmont Publishing, 1993.

Flynn, George Q. "Selective Service and American Blacks During World War II." *Journal of Negro History* 69 (Winter 1984): 14–25.

Flynn, George. *The Mess in Washington: Manpower Mobilization in World War II.* Santa Barbara, CA: Greenwood Press, 1979.

Floyd, Samuel. "An Oral History: The Great Lakes Experience." *The Black Perspective in Music* 11, no. 1 (Spring 1983).

Foner, Jack D. *Blacks and the Military in American History.* New York: Praeger, 1974.

Frederickson, George. *The Black Image in the White Mind: The Debate on Afro-American Character and Destiny, 1817–1940*. New York: Harper and Row, 1971.

Gibbs, C. R. "Blacks in the Union Navy." *All Hands* 695 (December 1974).

*Great Lakes Bulletin*, August 15, 1942; February 5, March 10, March 31, June 2, 1944.

Green, Robert E. *Black Defenders of America 1775–1973*. Chicago, IL: Johnson Publishing Company, 1974.

Greene, Lorenzo J. "The Negro in the Armed Forces of the United States, 1619–1783." *Negro History Bulletin*, March 1951, 123.

Grossman, James R. *Land of Hope: Chicago, Black Southerners and the Great Migration*. Chicago: University of Chicago Press, 1989.

Guttridge, Leonard F. *Mutiny: A History of Naval Insurrection*. Annapolis, MD: Naval Institute Press, 1992.

———. "Port Chicago Mutiny," *Readings in American Naval History*, 5th edition.

Hamann, Jack. *On American Soil: How Justice Became a Casualty of World War II*. Seattle: University of Washington Press, 2007.

Haygood, Wil. *Sweet Thunder: The Life and Times of Sugar Ray Robinson*. New York: Knopf, 2009.

Hope, Richard O. *Racial Strife in the U.S. Military: Toward the Elimination of Discrimination*. New York: Praeger, 1979.

Hutchinson, Earl Ofari. "Explosion at Port Chicago." *American Legacy*, Fall 1999, 59–68.

Johnson, Jesse L. *Roots of Two Black Marine Sergeants Major*. Perth, Australia: Ebony Publishing, Inc., 1978.

Keen, Sam. *Faces of the Enemy: Reflections of the Hostile Imagination*. San Francisco: Harper and Row, 1986.

Kelly, Mary Pat. *Proudly We Served: The Men of the USS Mason*. Annapolis: Naval Institute Press, 1995.

Killens, John O. *And Then We Heard the Thunder*. New York: Knopf, 1963.

Kinston, Warren, and Rachel Rosser. "Disaster: Effects on mental and physical state." *Journal of Psychosomatic Research* 18, no. 6 (December 1974), 437–56.

Kirby, Jack Temple. *Rural Worlds Lost: The American South, 1920–1960*. Baton Rouge: Louisiana State University Press, 1987.

Lee, Ulysses G. *The Employment of Negro Troops: The United States Army in World War II*. Washington, DC: Center of Military History, U.S. Army, 1966.

Lemann, Nicholas. *The Promised Land: The Great Black Migration and How It Changed America*. New York: Vintage Books, 1992.

Lilly, J. Robert. "Military Executions During WWII: The Case of David Cobb." *American Journal of Criminal Justice* 20, no. 1 (1995).

Lindstrom, Lamont, and Geoffrey M. White. *Island Encounters: Black and White*

*Memories of the Pacific War.* Washington, DC: Smithsonian Institution Press, 1990.

Litwack, Leon F. *Been in the Storm So Long: The Aftermath of Slavery.* New York: Vintage Books, 1979.

———. *Trouble in Mind: Black Southerners in the Age of Jim Crow.* New York: Knopf, 1998.

MacGregor, Morris J., Jr. *Defense Studies: Integration of the Armed Forces 1940–1965.* Washington, DC: U.S. Army Center for Military History, 1981.

MacGregor, Morris J., Jr., and Bernard C. Nalty. *Blacks in the United States Armed Forces, Basic Documents,* vol. 6. Wilmington, DE: Scholarly Resources, 1977.

Marks, Carole. *Farewell, We're Good and Gone: The Great Black Migration.* Bloomington: Indiana University Press, 1989.

McGuire, Phillip. *He, Too, Spoke for Democracy: Judge Hastie, World War II, and the Black Soldier.* New York: Greenwood Press, 1988.

McGuire, Phillip. "Desegregation of the Armed Forces: Black Leadership, Protest and World War II." *The Journal of Negro History* 68, no. 2 (Spring 1983), 147–58.

McGuire, Phillip, ed. *Taps for a Jim Crow Army: Letters from Black Soldiers in World War II.* Santa Barbara, CA: ABC-CLIO, Inc., 1983.

McLeod, Dean L. *Images of America: Bay Point.* Charleston, SC: Arcadia Publishing, 2005.

———. *Images of America: Port Chicago.* Charleston, SC: Arcadia Publishing, 2007.

McPhatter, Thomas H., Cpt. CHC USNR (Ret.). *Caught in the Middle: The Dichotomy of an African American Man: A Historical Autobiography of Leadership.* San Diego, CA: Audacity Books, 1993.

McPherson, James M. *The Negro's Civil War: How American Negroes Felt and Acted During the War for the Union.* Urbana and Chicago: University of Illinois Press, 1982.

Martin, Harvey V. "A Mushroom Cloud: What Really Happened at Port Chicago in 1944, a Nuclear Explosion?" *Napa Sentinel,* 1990.

Medford, Edna Greene, and Michael Frazier. "'Keep 'Em Rolling': African American Participation in the Red Ball Express." *Negro History Bulletin,* December 1993.

Meuller, William R. "The Negro in the Navy." *Social Forces,* October 1945, 110–15.

Miller, Richard E. *The Messman Chronicles: African Americans in the U.S. Navy, 1932–1943.* Annapolis: Naval Institute Press, 2004.

Modell, John. "World War II in the Lives of Black Americans: Some Findings and an Interpretation." *Journal of American History* 76 (December 1989), 838–48.

Moore, Christopher. *Fighting for America: Black Soldiers: The Unsung Heroes of World War II*. New York: Presidio Press, 2005.

Moore, H. E. "Toward a Theory of Disaster." *American Sociological Review* 21, no. 6 (December 1956).

Motely, Mary Penwick. *The Invisible Soldier: The Experience of the Black Soldier: World War II*. Detroit: Wayne State University Press, 1975.

Murray, Florence, ed. *The Negro Handbook 1946–1947*. New York: Current Books, 1947.

Nalty, Bernard C. *Strength for the Fight: A History of Black Americans in the Military*. New York: Free Press, 1986.

———. *The Right to Fight: African-American Marines in World War II*. Washington, DC: History and Museums Division, Headquarters, U.S. Marine Corps, 1995.

"Navy Charter on Race Relations and Equal Opportunity." *All Hands* 651 (April 1971), 46.

Nelson, Dennis D. *The Integration of the Negro into the U.S. Navy*. New York: Farrar, Straus and Young, 1951.

"Nonpersistent Gas Bombs: Handling, Shipping, and Storage." War Department Technical Bulletin, April 6, 1945. Washington, DC: U.S. War Department.

Osur, Alan M. *Blacks in the Army Air Forces During World War II: The Problem of Race Relations*. Washington, DC: Office of Air Force History, 1977.

Parks, Robert J. "The Development of Segregation in U.S. Army Hospitals, 1940–1942." *Military Affairs* 37 (December 1973), 145–50.

Packard, Jerrold M. *American Nightmare: History of Jim Crow*. New York: St. Martin's Press, 2003.

Pearson, Robert E. *No Share of Glory*. Pacific Palisades, CA: Challenge Inc., 1964.

*Pittsburgh Courier*. Articles regarding the mutiny trial, July 29, 1944–December 2, 1944.

*Proceedings—United States Naval Institute*. Vol. 38. Annapolis: U.S. Naval Institute, The Lord Baltimore Press, 1912.

Quarles, Benjamin A. *The Negro in the Making of America*. 3d edition. New York: Collier, 1996.

———. *The Negro in the Civil War*. Boston, MA: Little Brown, 1953.

Rand, Ken. *Port Chicago Isn't There Anymore But We Still Call It Home*. West Jordan, UT: Media Man! Productions, 2008.

Reddick, L. D. "The Negro in the United States Navy During World War II." *Journal of Negro History* 32, no. 2 (April 1947), 201–19.

———. "The Relative Status of the Negro in the American Armed Forces." *Journal of Negro Education* 22, no. 3 (Summer 1953).

Rowan, Carl. "The Navy's Search for Blacks." *Washington Star*, October 16, 1970.

Rowland, Buford, and William Boyd. *U.S. Navy Bureau of Ordnance in World War II.* Washington, DC: Government Printing Office, 1953.

Sandburg, Carl. *The Chicago Race Riots, July 1919.* New York: Harcourt, Brace and Howe, 1919.

Sandler, Stanley. "Homefront Battlefront: Military Racial Disturbances in the Zone of the Interior, 1941–1945." *War & Society* 11 (October 1993), 101–15.

Saunders, Kay, and Helen Taylor. "The Reception of Black American Servicemen in Australia During World War II: The Resilience of 'White Australia.'" *Journal of Black Studies* 25 (January 1995).

*San Francisco Chronicle.* Articles regarding the mutiny trial, July 19–October 23, 1944.

*San Francisco Examiner.* Articles regarding the mutiny trial, September 15– November 11, 1944.

Schneider, James G. "Negroes Will Be Tested! FDR." *Naval History* 7, no. 1 (Spring 1993).

Schneller, Robert J., Jr. *Breaking the Color Barrier: The U.S. Naval Academy's First Black Midshipmen and the Struggle for Racial Equality.* New York: New York University Press, 2005.

Seligson, Tom. "Isn't It Time to Right the Wrong." Parade.com, February 26, 2005.

Shaw, Henry I., Jr., and Ralph W. Donnelly. *Blacks in the Marine Corps.* Washington, DC: History and Museums Division, Headquarters, U.S. Marine Corps, 1988.

Sherwood, John Darrell. *Black Sailor, White Navy: Racial Unrest in the Fleet During the Vietnam War Era.* New York: New York University Press, 2007.

Shibutani, Tamotsu. *The Derelicts of Company K: A Sociological Study of Demoralization.* Berkeley: University of California Press, 1978.

Silberman, Charles E. *Crisis in Black and White.* New York: Random House, 1966.

Silvera, John D. *The Negro in World War II.* New York: Arno, 1969.

Smith, Larry. *The Few and the Proud: Marine Corps Drill Instructors in Their Own Words.* New York: Norton, 2006.

Smith, Graham. *When Jim Crow Met John Bull: Black American Soldiers in World War II Britain.* New York: St. Martin's Press, 1988.

Sterling, Dorothy. *Captain of the Planter: The Story of Robert Smalls.* New York: Doubleday, 1958.

Stillwell, Paul, ed. *The Golden Thirteen: Recollections of the First Black Naval Officers.* Annapolis: Naval Institute Press, 1993.

Sutherland, Jonathan D. *African Americans at War: An Encyclopedia.* Santa Barbara, CA: ABC-CLIO, Inc., 2004.

Taylor, Porcher L., Jr. *Damn the Alligators: Full Speed Ahead: The Autobiography of Porcher L. Taylor, Jr., Ph.D., Colonel U.S. Army (retired),* self-published, 2004.

Terkel, Studs. *The Good War: An Oral History of World War Two*. New York: Pantheon, 1984.

Terry, Wallace. *Bloods: An Oral History of the Vietnam War by Black Veterans*. New York: Ballantine, 1984.

"The Port Chicago Mutiny." *Revolutionary Worker* no. 1092, February 25, 2001.

Theill, Coral Anika. "World War II Montford Point Marines: Honoring and Preserving Their Legacy." *Leatherneck,* January 2011.

*This Is Our War: Selected Stories of Six War Correspondents Who Were Sent Overseas by Afro-American Newspapers*. Baltimore: The Afro-American Company, 1945.

*Uniform Code of Military Justice*.

"United States Bombs and Fuzes." U.S. Navy (Confidential), June 1, 1944.

"United States Navy Explosives." Instructional Pamphlet 1 (Confidential). Hingham, MA: Naval Training School (Ammunition Handling), United States Naval Ammunition Depot, August 15, 1945.

"United States Navy Gun Ammunition." Instructional Pamphlet 2 (Confidential). Hingham, MA: Naval Training School (Ammunition Handling), USNAD, April 15, 1945.

"United States Navy Gun Ammunition." Instructional Pamphlet 2 (Confidential). Hingham, MA: Naval Training School (Ammunition Handling), USNAD, April 15, 1945.

"United States Navy Rocket Ammunition." Instructional Pamphlet 4 (Confidential). Hingham, MA: Naval Training School (Ammunition Handling), USNAD, August 1, 1945.

"United States Navy Underwater Ordnance and Impulse Ammunition." Instructional Pamphlet 4 (Confidential). Hingham, MA: Naval Training School (Ammunition Handling), USNAD, July 30, 1945.

U.S. Army Service Forces. "Leadership and the Negro Soldier." Army Service Manual, Washington, DC, 1944.

U.S. Army War College, History Section. "The Colored Soldier in the United States Army." Report, 1942.

U.S. Navy, Bureau of Yards and Docks. *Building the Navy's Bases in World War II: History of the Bureau of Yards and Docks and the Civil Engineer Corps, 1940–1946*. Vol. 1. Washington, DC: U.S. Government Printing Office, 1947.

Valle, James. *Rocks and Shoals: Naval Discipline in the Age of Fighting Sail*. Annapolis: Naval Institute Press, 1980.

Veronico, Nicholas A. *Images of America: World War II Shipyards by the Bay*. Charleston, SC: Arcadia Publishing, 2007.

Vogel, Peter. *The Last Wave from Port Chicago, 2001–2009*, self-published on the Web.

Ware, Gilbert. *William Hastie.* New York: Oxford University Press, 1984.

Wesley, Charles H. "World War II: Reaching Toward Desegregation." *National Guard* 43 (February 1989), 30–33.

White, George, Jr. "African Americans, World War II." In vol. 3 of *Americans at War,* edited by John Resch. Detroit: Macmillan Reference USA, 2005.

Williams, Juan. *Thurgood Marshall: American Revolutionary.* New York: Times Books, 1998.

Wilson, Ruth Danenhower. *Jim Crow Joins Up.* New York: Clark, 1945.

Wolfenstein, Martha. *Disaster: A Psychological Essay.* Glencoe, IL: Free Press, 1957.

Wollenberg, Charles. "Black vs. Navy Blue: The Mare Island Mutiny Court Martial." *California History* 58, no. 1 (Spring 1979).

Woodford, Frank B. and Arthur M. *All Our Yesterdays: A Brief History of Detroit.* Detroit: Wayne State University Press, 1969.

Wynn, Neil. *The Afro-American and the Second World War.* New York: Holmes and Meier, 1976.

## Documents, Letters, and Papers

"Abstract of Report of Explosion, No. 1." Washington, DC: Joint Army Navy Ammunition Storage Board, October 12, 1944.

Booth, George. Personal papers.

Boykin, Sammie. "Reflecting" (on my years in the U.S. Navy). Personal papers.

"Conference with Regard to Negro Personnel." Headquarters Fifth Naval District, Naval Operating Base, Norfolk, Virginia, October 26, 1943.

"Disaster, 17 July 1944." Attachment to War Diary, Naval Magazine, Port Chicago, CA.

"Executive Summary of the Petition for Pardon for Seaman Second Class Freddie Meeks, United States Navy." Courtesy of G. Brian Busey, Morrison & Foerster, LLP, Washington, D.C.

General Correspondence, Twelfth Naval Distict, 1942–1945.

General Correspondence Files, 1944–47, Secretary of the Navy James V. Forrestal. Washington, DC: National Archives.

General Correspondence Files, 1944, Eleanor and Franklin Roosevelt. Hyde Park, NY: Franklin D. Roosevelt Library.

General Office Files, 1940–55, National Association for the Advancement of Colored People. Washington, DC: Manuscript Division, U.S. Library of Congress.

General Office Files, 1943–45, NAACP Legal Defense and Educational Fund, New York.

Historical Reports of Naval Ammunition Depot, Concord, Naval Ammunition

Depot, Mare Island. Washington, DC: Department of the Navy, Office of the Chief of Naval Operations.

"History of the U.S. Naval Training Center, Great Lakes, IL, in WWII, 'Negro Training.'" Washington (DC) Navy Yard: Bureau of Naval Personnel Library.

Huff, Edgar R., Jr. Personal papers.

Larson, Lieutenant T. A. "History of the U.S. Naval Training Center Great Lakes, Illinois, in World War II." Prepared for the Office of Naval History, Navy Department, December 28, 1945.

Letters from Inez White to Lieutenant Raymond Robert White's parents. William White, personal papers.

"Marking of Overseas Shipments: Alphabetical List of Places, Alphabetical List of Shipping Designators." Navy Department, Office of the Chief of Naval Operations, February 6, 1943.

Naval Intelligence Service, Ninth Naval District, Great Lakes, IL, confidential memorandum, July 20, 1944. "Racial tension in Ninth Naval District—Study of." Great Lakes, IL, Naval Training Center.

Orders and Memoranda of Captain N. H. Goss, Commanding Officer, Naval Ammunition Depot, Mare Island, CA.

Orders and Memoranda of Captain M. T. Kinne, Officer in Charge, U.S. Naval Magazine, Port Chicago, CA, June 14, 1944.

Parsons, William S. "Memorandum on Port Chicago Disaster, Preliminary Data, July 24, 1944." Washington, DC: World War II Command File, Operational Archives Branch, Naval Historical Center.

Reddick, L. D. "The Negro in the United States Navy in World War II." Historical Section, Bureau of Naval Personnel.

"Regulations Governing Transportation of Military Explosives on Board Vessels During Present Emergency." Washington, DC: U.S. Coast Guard, October 1, 1943.

Rendleman, Lt. Richard J. Letters and first chapter of novel, from Richard J. Rendleman Jr.

Robinson, Percy, Jr. Personal papers.

"Safety Orders Explosives." M. T. Kinne, Captain USNR, Officer in Charge, U.S. Naval Magazine, Port Chicago, CA, June 14, 1944.

Small, Joseph R. Personal papers.

"The Negro Problem in the Fourteenth Naval District." Washington, DC: U.S. Navy Yard, September 3, 1943.

Tracy Panek's interviews with Port Chicago explosion survivors for the Port Chicago Naval Magazine National Memorial, National Park Service.

Trial Transcript, General Court-Martial, "Case of Julius J. Allen, Seaman Second Class, U.S. Naval Reserve, et al.," September 14–October 24, 1944. Washington, DC: Navy Judge Advocate General's Office.

Tuggle, Carl, Personal Papers.

Twelfth Naval District, "Record of Proceedings of a Court of Inquiry Convened at the U.S. Naval Magazine, Port Chicago, California, July 21, 1944." U.S. Navy Judge Advocate General's Office, Washington, DC. Also at National Archives and Records Administration, Pacific Sierra Region, San Bruno, CA.

U.S. Navy Bureau of Ordnance, "War Time History of U.S. Naval Magazine, Port Chicago, California." In *Bureau of Ordnance, Selected Ammunition Depots*, Library, Washington (DC) Navy Yard.

U.S. Navy, Press and Radio Release. "Commanding Officer Praises Negro Personnel Who Served at Port Chicago After Explosion Monday Night, July 20, 1944." Washington, DC: World War II Command File, Operational Archives Branch, Naval Historical Center.

U.S. Naval Magazine Port Chicago, California. "Station Order 10-45." 17 February 1945. *Selected Ammunition Depots, Volume 2*. Washington, DC: World War II Administrative History, Navy Department Library, Naval Historical Center.

U.S. Navy Twelfth Naval District, Records of Proceedings of a Court of Inquiry (Finding of Facts, Opinion and Recommendations). Convened at the U.S. Naval Magazine, Port Chicago, California, July 21). 1944. San Bruno, CA: U.S. National Archives, Pacific Sierra Region.

War Diaries, Twelfth Naval District, December 1942–November 1944. San Bruno, CA: National Archives' Federal Record Center.

War Time History of the U.S. Naval Magazine, Port Chicago, California, December 5, 1945, in *Selected Depots Vol. 2*. World War II Administrative History #127-B, Navy Historical Center, Washington, DC.

## Oral Histories

Edgar R. Huff. Washington, DC: History and Museums Division, Headquarters, U.S. Marine Corps, 1975.

Hall, Obie. Quantico, VA: Archives and Special Collections, Library of the Marine Corps.

Little, Robert D. Quantico, VA: Archives and Special Collections, Library of the Marine Corps.

Montford Point Marine Interviews (the nation's first African American Marines).

# ACKNOWLEDGMENTS

This book is a work of nonfiction based on information contained in war diaries, reminiscences, trial transcripts, letters, scrapbooks, memoirs, self-published books, oral histories, and stories related to me by veterans and their surviving family members and friends. While every attempt has been made to faithfully reconstruct historical events, some of the scenes and dialogue, though based on reliable documentation, are necessarily approximations of what actually happened.

I do not pretend to have written the complete history of the Port Chicago disaster or the battle for Saipan. Because of the book's large historical scope, I've focused on a small number of men whose stories are representative of the whole. Consequently there are countless sailors, Marines, and soldiers who are missing from these pages. It is my hope, however, that I have described an experience that all Port Chicago's sailors, Montford Point Marines, and veterans of the Saipan campaign will recognize.

Without the official Marine narrative *Saipan: The Beginning of the End*, written by Major Carl Hoffman, I would have been left with nothing more than a collection of individual perspectives on the war. Major Hoffman's book enriches my story. Anyone interested in studying the battle more closely would benefit enormously from his outstanding work of history.

My descriptions of Saipan's topography are based on World War II–era photographs, interviews with veterans and island residents, and personal observations. In 2009 I made a monthlong trip to Saipan. Although the island has, of course, changed since the war, there are enough limestone cliffs, hidden caves, tangled ravines, patches of thick jungle, long beaches, and small farms left to give one a picture of what the island's landscape looked like in 1944.

The story of the Port Chicago explosion and the subsequent mutiny trial would have been impossible to write without Professor Robert Allen's groundbreaking *The Port Chicago Mutiny*. I am indebted to Professor Allen for his prior research, which I have used in constructing my story, and for his general magnanimity. I would also like to thank the Naval History and Heritage Command for making the extensive mutiny trial transcripts available to me. My sincere thanks, too, to the Navy Judge Advocate General's Corps. The task of interpreting and making sense of the events of the mutiny trial would have been difficult without their assistance.

Every book is a collaboration, and I owe an enormous debt of gratitude to a long list of people: From the 29th "Bastard" Battalion the good-natured Frank Borta for his cooperation and patience in fielding my endless questions. Thanks, too, to Frances Borta for her graciousness and hospitality. To Glenn Brem, who survived not one but three of the Pacific's savage battles, and to Robert Patrick Roberts, a storyteller in the great Southern tradition; from the 2nd Battalion of the 23rd Marines, the charismatic Carl Matthews for his dedication to this project. A talented writer, Carl will be self-publishing his World War II memoirs under the title *The Feather Merchant*. Thanks also to Don Swindle for his commitment to preserving the history of the battle, to Jack Campbell, Richard Freeby, Orville Matte, and the countless and kind men of the 2nd Battalion 23rd Marines who offered their memories. Thanks also to Major Everett "Bud" Hampton, Frank Kappel, Raymond Heise, Walt Biernacki, Richard Elliott, Joe Heafy, Arden Menge, Dale Cook of the 4th Marine Division Association, David Brown of the 2nd Marine Division Association, and Wayne VanDerVoort.

A huge and hearty thank-you to the ever-amiable Edgar Huff, Jr., who granted me access to his collection of documents relating to his father's storied career. I hope that one day a feature filmmaker adapts his father's wonderful story to the big screen. Thanks, too, to Joe Geeter, Finney Greggs and the Montford Point Marine Association and Museum for granting me access to its oral history collection.

Thanks to Richard Hengsterman, who made Robert Graf's extensive memoirs available to me; to Joanne Mould; Alisa Whitley of the Library of the Marine Corps; and Rob Taglianetti and Sue Dillon of the Marine Corps History Division. A very special thanks to the Marine Corps History Division's chief historian, Chuck Melson, for his clearheaded assessment of the book's accuracy.

I owe a debt of gratitude to Russell Horton and Ann Hamon of Wisconsin Veterans Museum. The museum—and its talented staff—has been a wonderful resource for me on this book and my previous one, *The Ghost Mountain Boys*. Thanks, also, to Alexa Potter at the Library of Congress Veterans History Project, the Naval History and Heritage Command, and Patty Everett of *Leatherneck* magazine.

My appreciation is not confined to the United States. I owe much to Bruce Bateman, marketing manager for the Marianas Visitors Authority and amateur historian, who read an early version of this book and scrutinized it for its accuracy. I'd also like to thank Sam McPhetres, a professor at the Northern Marianas College, Scott Russell, executive director of the Northern Mariana Islands Council for the Humanities, Robert Hunter at the Northern Mariana Islands Museum, and William Stewart for granting me access to his collection of translated Japanese diaries.

For the Port Chicago story, I must give abundant thanks to the spirited Percy Robinson for his razor-sharp memory, and to Sammie Boykin for his dignity and quiet resolve. Sadly, Mr. Boykin passed away before I finished this book. Many thanks, also, to the warm-hearted George Booth, who submitted to many hours of interviews, to Carl Tuggle for his insights, to Robert Edwards, Irwin Lowery, Morris Rich, to the gracious and now-deceased Lillian Small, who gave me access to her husband's entire Port Chicago collection. Some of the scenes with Joe Small are taken from Small's unfinished book about his Port Chicago experience. To Lester Small, Joe Small's son, for his reflections on his father's character. and to Reverend Diana McDaniel and Spencer Sikes Jr., who made my initial introductions to the Port Chicago men possible.

I particularly wish to thank Mark Wertheimer and Barbara Posner at the Naval History and Heritage Command, Brian Busey of Morrison & Forrester, who petitioned then-President Clinton for the pardon of Freddie Meeks, William White, Richard Rendleman, historians

John Keibel and Dean McLeod, the indefatigable Betty Reid Soskin, Porcher Taylor, John Coster Mullen, Jim "Dr. Dynamite" Dann, Deloris Guttman at the African American Diversity Cultural Center in Hawaii, Robert Glass and Rose Mary Kennedy at the National Archives San Francisco, and my diligent researcher, Kathleen O'Connor, for her unflagging efforts in helping me get at the meat, and truth, of this story. This book would not exist if not for her energy and commitment.

I am indebted to a number of archives, museums, and oral history projects, which aided me immeasurably. Thanks to the National Archives (and Nathaniel Patch), the Port Chicago Naval Magazine and National Memorial, the National Park Service, the Great Lakes Naval Museum, the National Association for Black Veterans, and again, to the Montford Point Marine Association.

I can't forget my editor, the talented Sean Desmond, for his wisdom, patience, and encouragement, and David McCormick, my agent, for his enthusiasm for this story, his counsel, and his friendship. Thanks to my very good pal Jon Clark for always keeping an eye on my family and the homestead when I'm on the road, to my close friend Dan Brennan, upon whom I inflicted half-baked explanations of the book's narrative arc, to my brother in misery, inspiration, and libation, writer Stephen Coss, and to my wife, who managed to offer sharp criticisms of early versions of this book while still keeping our love alive.

A world of thanks to my writer friends Logan Ward and Tom Doherty for their generosity of spirit and keen-eyed reads, which made this book so much better. Thanks also to my buddy writer Dean King, who, despite his busy schedule, has always lent a helping hand. Thanks to my newfound friend Hugh Lynch, professor emeritus at the Naval War College, who went beyond the call of duty by taking time away from his own book to catch my mistakes and to offer his thoughtful insights. Whatever inaccuracies remain are mine. My indebtedness extends, also, to Peter Vogel for his close read of my rough draft and for his intelligence and judgment. Thanks, also, to my brother-in-law, Sean O'Conor, who has read all three of my books in their early stages, and whose input I value greatly. I cannot overlook John Caldwell, whose willingness to share his knowledge of ordnance (as well as his books and manuals on handling ammunition) was a great help to me. John was a junior-grade lieutenant at the Naval Ammunition Handling School at the Hingham, Massachusetts, depot when Port Chicago blew. Men from the class in front of his were sent to California to replace the officers killed in the explosion.

An ocean of thanks to the indispensable Burns Ellison—novelist, astute editor, researcher, and best of buddies. Burns has been with me on all three of my books, pushing and challenging me to bring my characters—and my story—to life and to use language precisely and sparingly. I hope that someday a publisher recognizes the brilliance of his novel *White-Out,* and I will have a chance to reciprocate.

Finally, I would like to offer a heartfelt and love-filled thanks to my family: my wife, Elizabeth, our three spirited daughters, Aidan, Rachel, and Willa, my mother and father, and the rest of the Campbell clan, and my close friends, for reminding me every day of my blessings.

# INDEX

484 Index

WITHDRAWN

U.S.S.R.

Sea of
Okhotsk

MONGOLIA    MANCHURIA

Vladivostok

Mukden

SINKIANG    Peking    Sea of    JAPAN
                       Japan
                              Tokyo
CHINA    Tsingtao

TIBET    Shanghai    Nagasaki
      Chungking    Hankow    East
                       China
         Chengtu    Sea    Okinawa
INDIA    Kunming    Amoy
            Swatow    Iwo Jima
         Canton    MARIANA
BURMA    HONG KONG    ISLANDS
      South    Saipan
   SIAM    China Sea    Luzon    Guam
Rangoon  (THAILAND)    Manila    CAROLINE ISLANDS
Bay of
Bengal    Truk

30.00                              6/13/1?

Indian O    New
            Guinea    Coral
                       Sea

**LONGWOOD PUBLIC LIBRARY**
800 Middle Country Road
Middle Island, NY 11953
(631) 924-6400
mylpl.net

**LIBRARY HOURS**

The Pa

0

| | |
|---|---|
| Monday-Friday | 9:30 a.m. - 9:00 p.m. |
| Saturday | 9:30 a.m. - 5:00 p.m. |
| Sunday (Sept-June) | 1:00 p.m. - 5:00 p.m. |

Sydney